AF361278

FRUIT OF THE ORCHARD:
READING CATHERINE OF SIENA IN
LATE MEDIEVAL AND EARLY MODERN ENGLAND

JENNIFER N. BROWN

Fruit of the Orchard: Reading Catherine of Siena in Late Medieval and Early Modern England

UNIVERSITY OF TORONTO PRESS
Toronto Buffalo London

ISBN 978-1-4875-0407-6

Library and Archives Canada Cataloguing in Publication

Brown, Jennifer N. (Jennifer Nancy), author
Fruit of the orchard : reading Catherine of Siena in late medieval and
early modern England / Jennifer N. Brown.

Includes bibliographical references and index.
ISBN 978-1-4875-0407-6 (cloth)

1. Catherine of Siena, Saint, 1347–1380 – Manuscripts.   2. Devotional
literature, English (Middle) – History and criticism.   3. Transmission of
texts – England – History.   4. Literacy – England – History.   5. Books
and reading – England – History.   6. Christian women saints – Italy –
Biography.   7. England – Religious life and customs.   I. Title.

BX4700.C4B76 2019   282.092   C2018-903123-9

University of Toronto Press acknowledges the financial assistance to its
publishing program of the Canada Council for the Arts and the Ontario Arts
Council, an agency of the Government of Ontario.

Dedicated to my father, Francis Cabell Brown Jr (1936–2014). I miss you every day.

And to Dante, Best Dog of All Dogs (2004–2017), who sat by my side for every word.

Contents

Acknowledgments

My first notes on this book date to 2008, so I have nearly ten years of acknowledgments that have accumulated as I have conceived, researched, written, and revised it. The Saturday Medieval Group has seen every portion of this book in every stage, and there is not enough gratitude for the help of Valerie Allen, Glenn Burger, Matthew Goldie, Steven Kruger, Michael Sargent, Sylvia Tomasch, and, most recently, David Lavinsky. Valerie went above the call of duty by reading the book in its entirety before I sent it out, as has Matthew who has read, reread, and reread the introduction to help me work out the kinks. The friendship and conviviality of this group and its members have been at the heart of my intellectual life for over a decade, and I do not think I would know how to write without them. This book is largely fuelled on good coffee, bagels, and lox!

Many colleagues have listened to or read parts of this book, giving me needed advice and direction. Nicole Rice has long been a sounding board for my work, and the first seeds of this book were edited by her for a collection. She really helped me shape the book that was to come and has been an invaluable reader and friend. Julie Orlemanski read and helped me formulate my book proposal when I needed another set of eyes. Kevin Alban drove me all over Devon in search of Catherine's rood screens, and although the drive was harrowing, the company was wonderful. Jennifer Borland buoyed me through many a Kalamazoo and what seemed like an endless process from proposing the book to getting it completed. Roberta Magnani and Sonja Drimmer both tracked down manuscripts for me in British libraries and sent me images when I could not be there myself, demonstrating yet again the true generosity of time and effort I repeatedly find among medievalists. Sarah Salih and Michelle Sauer walked all over Siena with me to track down Catherine's landmarks (and her head). Others who heard, read, or responded to conference papers and articles are many, demonstrating the real collegiality at the heart of medieval studies. These include (and I know I am forgetting people): Jessica Barr, Susannah Chewning, Clare Copeland, Alison Frazier, Vincent Gillespie, Cathy Grisé, Bob Hasenfratz, Ian Johnson, Ryan Perry, Catherine Innes-Parker, Liz Herbert McAvoy, Laura Saetveit Miles, Janine Peterson, Denis Renevey, Sara Ritchey, Jill Stevenson, David Wallace, Nancy Bradley Warren, Diane Watt, Jocelyn Wogan-Browne, and Naoe Yoshikawa. Thank you, too, to Suzanne Rancourt whose cheerful encouragement has been most welcome, and the staff at University of Toronto Press who made copy editing and other tasks seem easy. Many, many thanks to the anonymous peer reviewers who challenged me and made the book immeasurably better with their insights, questions, and suggestions. I think it goes without saying, but I will say it, any faults and errors are entirely my own.

I have been fortunate to have such wonderful office mates through this process and the members of the Department of English and World Literatures at Marymount Manhattan College are no doubt nearly as happy as I am to see this book through. Special thanks to Cecilia Feilla, Martha Sledge, and Magdalena Mączyńska who have had to hear about Catherine of Siena for a long time! The MMC librarians deserve thanks for tracking down obscure editions and hard to find texts for interlibrary loans, as do the helpful librarians at New York University, the British Library, Cambridge University, and Oxford University. I am especially grateful to have been awarded a year's leave from the college in 2013–14, when the vast majority of the book was initially drafted. During that year, I also had the support of the Wertheim Room at the New York Public Library, a haven for writers from all over the city and in all stages of work. It was a wonderful place to read and write about Catherine.

My friends were genuinely interested in my work (or were excellent at feigning so), and I have shared many a meal and drink where I was allowed to talk through the book and my obstacles. Special thanks to the Brooklyn Babies group, especially Sara Malakoff and Leslie Stone. Jessica Toonkel and Caroline Tiger continue to support my every endeavour and will be the first to cheer me on. I also must acknowledge the hard work and support of our babysitter, Korean Martin, who takes such good care of my kiddos, which allows me to do what I love knowing that they are adored and in her capable hands.

Finally, my family continues to be my centre. Both of my parents very proudly sat in the front row when I presented some of my work at the New York Public Library in January 2014; I am so happy that my father heard the work and expressed his pride. My mother has always supported my work and has spent lots of time with the kids while I typed away in another room. I won the lottery with my husband, Jeff Nemanick, who is my biggest cheerleader and has taken every small step (a finished chapter, a sent out proposal) and every big one (a contract!) as a sign that we should open a good bottle of wine. Who am I to say no to that? Finally, to Nate and Bee, who have only known Mama to be working on her book, and who I know will be endlessly disappointed in its lack of pictures, but whose hugs, smiles, and laughter are the best parts of my day.

1. Catherine of Siena on a fifteenth-century rood screen at Holy Trinity Church in Torbryan, U.K. The Churches Conservation Trust.

2. Catherine of Siena (?) in a rood screen at Horsham St Faith's Church, U.K. Photo courtesy of Matthew Champion.

3. Catherine receiving her revelation, from *The Orcherd of Syon*. Printed by Wynkyn de Worde (1519), fol. 2. © The British Library Board.

4. Catherine with her nuns, from *The Orcherd of Syon*. Printed by Wynkyn de Worde (1519), fol. 4. © The British Library Board.

FRUIT OF THE ORCHARD

Finding Catherine of Siena in Late Medieval and Early Modern England

Searching for Catherine in England

The fourteenth-century mystic Catherine of Siena (1347–80) at first seems an elusive figure in late medieval and early modern England. Looking to find the fifteenth-century rood screen image of Catherine in the small church of Torbryan, Devon, can take hours, even from nearby towns.[1] The traveller must drive through many narrow roads and lanes, twisting her way up and down the rises, until the church appears at the top of a steep hill. The image does not disappoint upon arrival. One of just a few surviving English rood screens with an image of Catherine, it shows her in all her splendour: crowned with thorns and brilliantly coloured. With her heart clasped in her right hand, alluding to an exchange of hearts she makes with God, her left hand is raised in a greeting that resembles a benediction. In contrast with some of the other female saints depicted on the screen whose downcast eyes signal their modesty, Catherine's gaze looks out at the viewer directly, reminding her of the powerful, political visionary the painting represents. The texts about Catherine, too, seem both dispersed and hidden throughout late medieval England. Among vernacular women's visionary texts, she appears to be eclipsed by the other major lay Continental mystic of the time, Bridget of Sweden, her counterpart in desiring that Pope Gregory XI abandon Avignon for Rome. Bridget's texts were more widespread than Catherine's, with parts of her *Revelations* surviving in several manuscripts and excerpted in various medieval devotional treatises, sermons, and miscellanies.[2] Bridget's name was also more known due to the Bridgettine Order's prominent monastic house in England, Syon Abbey.[3] But when one does find Catherine, she is there in full – brilliant, complex, and brightly lit against a background of late medieval and early modern devotional culture. This Continental visionary woman has a textual tradition that was firmly incorporated into the devotional practice of medieval England. By examining her texts, we can explore the tensions and contradictions in English medieval devotional culture, as well as see how questions of authorship, authority, gender, reception, and practice are intertwined – and discover how these strands are picked apart during the religious unrest of the Reformation.

This book examines the late medieval and early modern English texts by and about Catherine, and the contexts of their circulation, in order to trace how devotional reading was practised and was changing through a period of increased literacy, the rise of the printing press, and religious turmoil. At times representing an orthodox world view, and at others a more subversive heterodox one, Catherine's multiplicities are made apparent in the Reformation when both Catholics and Protestants use Catherine's words and legacy to serve their own purposes.

The generic category of medieval and early modern "English devotional literature" is vast and convoluted, encompassing subgenres as varied as hagiographies, texts of religious instruction, meditations, lyrics, prayers, and sermons (among others). Temporally, too, these genres underwent vast changes as they moved through the Middle Ages, affected by heresies at home and abroad, by trends in religious devotion, by changing political ties, and by papal edicts. In the years with which I am most concerned in this book, from 1380 (the year of Catherine's death) to 1610 (the year of a recusant publication of her *vita*), England's devotional literary landscape expanded and changed dramatically, encompassing as it did a growing literate audience, the rise of the printing press with William Caxton and Wynkyn de Worde, the appearance of the heretical ideas of John Wyclif and the lollards, and the ideological battles of the Reformation. The genre of devotional literature is porous and malleable, and texts by and about Catherine of Siena stand at its centre, touching on hagiographic, meditative, didactic, and visionary literature.

At first glance, Catherine's light presence in England contrasts with her fuller one in Continental Europe. The Italian saint has a literary tradition that spread quickly and afar. Within only a few years after her death, texts by and about Catherine were found throughout and far outside of Italy, including *vitae*, her letters, and her own book, *Il Dialogo*.[4] However, by the mid-fifteenth century, some of that literary tradition was established in England, and it left a considerable mark on the history of insular vernacular devotional manuscripts and early printed books. The English dissemination of Catherine's tradition is all the more notable because of the relative paucity of women's mystical activity in late medieval England. Indeed, a fervour which had swept much of the Continent, especially England's close neighbours in France and the Low Countries, was largely absent from English culture. The two standout examples of women's mystical piety in England – the late medieval visionaries Julian of Norwich and Margery Kempe – have been at the centre of many studies in the past two decades, often discussed as templates for women's spirituality generally in late medieval England, even though most evidence seems to point to these cases as isolated and unusual.

By all accounts, Catherine of Siena herself was an exceptional figure. She was known as a visionary, a prophet, a rebel, a politician, a peacemaker, and an author. Born in 1347, the twenty-fifth of twenty-six children, Catherine received a vision from Christ as a young child that led her to vow her virginity to him and turn towards an ascetic life. Her visions include a mystical marriage to Christ and the reception of the stigmata. Catherine had a political life as well. Intent on moving the papacy back to Rome, Catherine ingratiated herself into the Church hierarchy and wrote to and ultimately visited Pope Gregory XI (c. 1329–1378) for that cause. By 1377, when the papacy did indeed return to Rome, Catherine began to dictate her *Dialogo*, detailing her visions and understanding of the divine. Shortly after her death in 1380, her confessor Raymond of Capua wrote her *vita*. Because of her active life and multiplicity of identities, many religious orders counted her among their own – in England we see her associated with and claimed by the Dominicans, the Augustinians, the Carthusians, and the Bridgettines – and her texts appealed across other reading populations. Catherine's *vita*, dictations, and *Il Dialogo* survive in every possible form: in highly expensive illuminated manuscripts meant for monastic and aristocratic use, excerpted and often unattributed in miscellanies owned by both laity and preachers, in early printed books with ties to wealthy convents and royal homes, and – soon after the Reformation – by recusant Catholics abroad.

Catherine serves as an important representative of English piety, integrated as she is into the devotional landscape of the time and read in varied contexts. By looking at the manuscripts and printed books regarding Catherine of Siena in England, we can comprehend the array of their readers across centuries. Described in broad strokes,

Continental models contrasts with English models, which tend to be much more ascetic in descriptions of women's piety. Catherine's visionary and political attributes press on the boundaries of what was acceptable for women in Europe at the time, but especially in England, which did not have as much of a culture of visionary women's writing as in Italy, France, Germany, and the Low Countries.[5] This contrast between English models and Continental ones is represented, for example, in the fact that an English Cardinal, Adam Easton, formally examines (and exonerates) Bridget of Sweden's *Revelations* for heresy. Despite scepticism like this, Catherine is unexpectedly everywhere in the devotional fabric of medieval and early modern English piety in drastically different contexts and for varied audiences. In addition, the way in which authors, scribes, and compilers adapt Catherine is a revealing lens for understanding English devotional culture with all of its contradictions and tensions of orthodoxy, subversion, and heresy. By looking at the Catherine texts, who read them and how, we can map the landscape of late medieval and early modern English vernacular devotion.

The title of this book, *Fruit of the Orchard*, comes from the given English title of Catherine of Siena's *Dialogo*, *The Orcherd of Syon*. When examined in context, her *Orcherd* offers a particularly telling example of English devotional reading practices. This early fifteenth-century translation, made deliberately for the nuns at Syon Abbey just outside of London, suggests specific methods of reading, telling the readers that the book is an orchard of spiritual comfort, with both sweet fruit and bitter herbs that need to be taken in order to receive the pious counsel therein:

> Þis book of reuelaciouns as for ʒoure goostly comfort to ʒou I clepe it a fruytful orchard ... In þis orcherd, whanne ʒe wolen be conforted, ʒe mowe walke and se boþe fruyt and herbis. And albeit þat sum fruyt or herbis seeme to summe scharpe, hard, or bitter, ʒit to purgynge of þe soule þei ben ful speeful and profitable, whanne þei ben discreetly take and resceyued by counceil.[6]

This lyrical opening gives way to an extensive prologue about how to read, what to read, and in what ways that reading should be tasted and digested. *The Orcherd*'s original text, *Il Dialogo*, has multiple, overlapping lives as a visionary dictation from Catherine to her confessor and scribes, a translated text, a manuscript in Syon Abbey's library, and later a book printed by Wynkyn de Worde; it is at once public and private, spoken and written, monastic and lay, gendered and universal, subversive and orthodox. As such, *The Orcherd*, along with the other texts by and about Catherine of Siena, together provide original insights into late medieval and early modern England reading appetites and practices, and the changes these undergo over time.

Recent studies have painted a picture of reading audiences and expectations in medieval England, but none carries out a longitudinal study on a concrete set of texts as this project does, showing how a reading program was altered and adapted for various religious audiences. Some studies of late medieval readers – male and female, lay and religious – have argued that the lines between these two groups are not as distinct as previously thought.[7] Scholars on both sides of the medieval and early modern divide have advocated for blurring boundaries of periodization and examining more closely trans-Reformation cultural shifts and continuities.[8] There has also been some excellent work on Catherine in the past decade, both about the woman herself and her textual legacy. Suzanne Noffke's publication of Catherine's *Dialogo* and letters in translation have encouraged further studies of Catherine herself, and books by Thomas Luongo, Jane Tylus, Grazia Mangano Ragazzi, and the recent collections of essays *A Companion to Catherine of Siena* and *Catherine of Siena: The Creation of a Cult* have contributed to a fuller picture of Catherine, her writing, her activities, and her milieu.[9] These works have all advanced the understanding of who Catherine and her followers were and how her public and private personae intersected. Few of these texts, however, look at England as most of Catherine's textual (and personal) tradition comes from Italy and its neighbouring countries. Rebecca Krug's *Reading Families: Women's Literate Practice in Late Medieval England* maps out various women readers and their texts, including those surrounding *The Orcherd of Syon*, while Nancy Bradley Warren's *The Embodied Word: Female Spiritualities, Contested Orthodoxies, and English Religious Cultures, 1350–1700* examines Catherine in the context of the English tradition, looking especially at how her textual legacy interacts with, and responds to, other women's spiritual texts and writers of the time (most specifically, Julian of Norwich and the writings of Bridget of Sweden). I build on both Krug's and Warren's work but focus directly on Catherine and the English vernacular works concerning her: Stephen Maconi's letter supporting her canonization, the frequently copied "The Cleannesse of Sowle," *The Orcherd of Syon*, her hagiographical *Legenda major*, and her print tradition through the early seventeenth century. I am giving what Sara Poor has called a "vertical view" of one author and her textual voice, tradition, and authority.[10]

I am not attempting here to provide a historical reading of Catherine herself or trying to map out the actual path a text may have taken through the Continent to find its way to being translated or printed in late medieval and early modern England, although I will address the larger context of dissemination. This book is not a survey of Catherine's English cult or tradition. I hope to show that despite the uncertainties surrounding the circulation and dissemination of Catherine's English texts, it is obvious that they took on meanings and audiences in a way that no individual or authority fully controlled. We can thereby see more clearly how devotional culture spread and developed in a complex pattern woven by priests, translators, scribes, readers, and printers. I intend to show how the texts about Catherine may serve as a test case for medieval devotional reading generally, and, in its specifics, lay reading, monastic reading, and women's reading. The late medieval and early modern eras represent times of upheaval in reading practices, redefining the boundaries of public and private. Texts which seem private – letters from confessors to penitents for example – introduce many of the Catherine texts in the anthologies and miscellanies, showing how they have moved into a public sphere. Likewise, a book used for private meditation but owned communally – such as *The Orcherd of Syon* – travels from its convent context to the printed page, which was both public in its commercialism but privately owned and read by lay and religious readers alike. In addition, I am looking at a set of texts that fall under the revelatory theology that Kathryn Kerby-Fulton examines in *Books Under Suspicion*, texts that are "sources of theological freedom and of theological danger," ones that can be both celebrated and condemned depending on where they are found and who is reading them.[11] In that book, Kerby-Fulton remarks on the "diversity of medieval intellectual and spiritual experience," and that in many ways the time was one of "*failed* censorship" in the face of Archbishop Arundel's *Constitutions*, which attempted to curtail religious texts in the vernacular.[12] Here, I examine those tensions and diversities within one set of texts. Catherine of Siena is a particularly rich subject for a close inquiry because the texts about her are as diverse as the woman herself: revelatory, meditational, instructive, and hagiographical.

The specific focus of this book is on Middle English texts because the devotional texts most read and listened to by women religious and lay readers were in the vernacular. In addition, as Eliana Corbari has pointed out in her study of late medieval sermon literature in Italy, vernacular texts show the kind of theological education that is happening outside of the monasteries and universities and is a way of reading how high theological concerns are being translated to the laity. These texts fall under the broad umbrella of "vernacular theology," that Corbari notes was "a tradition that existed in parallel to the better known scholastic and monastic theologies of the Middle Ages, and was particularly opened to and influenced by women. Medieval monastic, scholastic, and vernacular theology formed a triadic relationship."[13] Additionally, the Middle English Catherine tradition is broad. In addition to the several works attributed to Catherine by name in England, many texts circulated anonymously, thereby extending her influence without it being recognized as hers; works attested to her are dramatically recontextualized to appeal to a wide network of disparate audiences.

This book examines provenance, production, distribution, as well as intended and actual reception of these texts. My findings are that Catherine's texts form a node of dense connection among other devotional texts, and that she functions as a critical point of juncture between individuals and communities. As Catherine is translated and removed from her original context and rearticulated in an English one, she becomes representative of various strands of English piety despite her Continental origins. Further, as I will explore in chapter 2, Catherine herself has incorporated into, and reflected back, a kind of English piety through the influence of an English adviser. Ultimately, her texts are so dramatically recontextualized in the different redactions that each single "work" is itself a network of texts; we might even say that there are as many versions of each work as there are redactions of it.

Catherine, Her Manuscripts, and Their Transmissions

Unlike many visionary women of the medieval period, Catherine is quite well documented. Her relatively full record is largely due to the highly literate network in which she participated and the nature of her political life, moving among men whose correspondence was important and has been preserved. Although most of the major events of Catherine's mystical and visionary life happened before her political career and textual record began, they are documented through Raymond of Capua's *Legenda major* and are attested to in other sources. Born in 1347, she received a vision from Christ in 1353 and shortly afterward vowed her virginity to him. Her sister's death in 1362 was a turning point for Catherine, and she moved away from the married life her parents wanted for her and towards an ascetic life of devotion. Around 1368 Catherine's mystical marriage to Christ took place, an important moment in her *vita* and one that is often depicted in artistic representations, although the marriage does not figure largely in surviving English texts or images about Catherine.[14] Only one year later, she joined the Dominican *mantellatae* in Siena, a "third order" composed of lay women who were primarily dedicated to caring for the sick and other works of charity. The *mantellatae* flourished under Dominican guidance after Catherine's death, largely due to the visibility and *exemplum* she brought to its existence.[15] This in-between state between lay and religious granted the *mantellatae* some ecclesiastical privileges while allowing them a freedom of movement and oversight that membership in an order would prohibit.[16]

Catherine's textual tradition really began in the year 1370. This was the year that Gregory XI became Pope and it coincided with the inception of Catherine's letter-writing career. There remain extant nearly four hundred of Catherine's (complete and incomplete) letters, the earliest dated to around 1370 and the last close to her death a decade later. Noffke notes the breadth of Catherine's correspondence, writing that the letters "are addressed to persons as diverse as popes and prisoners, queens and prostitutes, to intimate friends and relatives and to persons Catherine had never met face to face."[17] Catherine's actual "literacy" is disputed – both contemporary sources and modern ones debate her ability to read and to write, but whether the pen was held in her hand or another's, Catherine's epistolary output was significant.[18] We know that her letters were dictated, and although she used a variety of scribes, a coherence of style, repeated phrases, and syntax suggests that Catherine composed the letters herself and that her scribes faithfully wrote her words. Her letters are one of the most astonishing textual legacies for any medieval woman and attest to her broad social networks, political connections, and learning.[19] The collection of advisers, scribes, followers, and confessors came to be known as Catherine's *famiglia*. Significantly, some of Catherine's early scribes were women, although they are eventually supplanted by male authorities who take over the bulk of her writing.[20] This may serve as a metaphor for what happens to Catherine's own writings as they are reshaped and translated in order to be widely and palatably disseminated, frequently stripped of seemingly unorthodox or more controversial elements.

In addition to her letters, several other sources attest to Catherine and her works. The first of these is an anonymous account of Catherine written by an author who met her in Florence in 1374 when she was there for a meeting of the Dominican General Chapter. It in some ways corresponds with Raymond of Capua's later account of Catherine's life – although there are a few differences – and the (potentially lay) author seems to have had notes or correspondence from Catherine's first confessor, Tomaso della Fonte.[21] Also in that year, Raymond became Catherine's confessor. Shortly after, she received the stigmata, visible only to her; as with her mystical marriage, this iconographical depiction of Catherine common in Italy is absent from surviving English images and most English descriptions of Catherine.[22] In 1376 Catherine, with much of her *famiglia*, travelled to Avignon to meet the pope. This period is well accounted for in Catherine's own letters, and, as we shall see, in her follower Stephen Maconi's letter concerning Catherine as part of *Il Processo Castellano*, a collection of documents put together by her follower Tommaso d'Antonio of Siena (known as Thomas Caffarini) to promote and defend Catherine's cult.[23] Many of Catherine's scribes also wrote down the prayers that she recited in moments of ecstasy. A collection of twenty-six of them circulated under the title *Le Orazioni*.[24] These survive in both Italian and in Latin, but do not seem to have much dissemination outside of Italy (although two of the manuscripts are now housed in Vienna and Munich).

Around 1377, Catherine began the composition of her visionary text *Il Dialogo*, which she dictated in her native Sienese to her followers.[25] Catherine's *Dialogo*, given the title because it is structured as a dialogue between Catherine and God, took her nearly a year to dictate to her scribes, and it is considered her major accomplishment and one of the great works of medieval mysticism. In her letters, Catherine referred to it as "my book," recognizing its coherence and length as well as the importance it held for her. Noffke posits that the style of the book "betrays not only … 'ecstatic dictation' but also a great deal of painstaking and sometimes awkward expanding of passages written earlier. There is every reason to believe that Catherine herself did this editing."[26] Catherine's book was translated into Latin no fewer than three separate times by her followers – Stephen Maconi, Raymond of Capua, and Cristofano di Gano Guidini – indicating a strong desire to disseminate her words well beyond Siena.[27] The medieval evidence, though, shows that it likely did not spread as far as was hoped. Catherine's cult in other countries was far more dependent on the transmission of her *vita* by Raymond of Capua, and, as noted by Catherine Mooney, Pius II's bull of canonization "failed to mention either her ability to write, miraculous or human, or her letters and

Libro."[28] The return of the Avignon papacy to Rome in 1377, for which Catherine was largely credited, was followed in 1378 by the Great Schism with Urban VI's ascent to the papal throne (and the Antipope Clement VII's election in opposition). Catherine died in 1380 without having seen the resolution of the political events towards which she had laboured.[29]

Raymond of Capua's *Legenda major* is the most important witness to Catherine's life, and it was imitated and shortened by Thomas Caffarini in his *Legenda minor,* followed by his more original *Libellus de Supplemento,* which expands on Raymond's work.[30] Caffarini was intent on Catherine's canonization and promoted her cult more thoroughly throughout Italy and beyond. He saw it as a part of the work of promoting the Dominican order, and these dual desires (promoting Catherine and the order) are evident in his additions to the corpus of Catherine texts. Where Raymond focused on the spiritual qualities of Catherine and her life, Caffarini does not shy away from the miraculous or the gruesome. Raymond had been scrupulous in writing only about what he had seen or events to which credible witnesses had attested, but Caffarini recognized the value of the fantastic in promoting a saint and through his two texts highlighted all that was extraordinary about Catherine. As Daniel Bornstein explains, "Tommaso's emphasis was on Catherine's more striking deeds and dramatic miracles: gripping episodes that preachers would elaborate into sermons that would inspire the amazed wonderment of their hearers. As a result, the Catherine that emerges from Tommaso's writings is even more astonishing and inimitable than the saint portrayed by Raymond."[31] However, Caffarini's texts were apparently localized to Tuscany and its environs (although he is responsible for the dissemination of some of the other texts regarding Catherine that, like Raymond's life, spread well beyond what are today's Italian borders).[32]

The particular practice of lay piety that Catherine represented was not otherwise available to English women in the late medieval or early modern period. There was no notably active third order, as with the Dominican *mantellatae* of which Catherine was part, and there were no beguines, the semi-religious women's communities that were widespread throughout the Low Countries and France. The English visionary Margery Kempe's account of her own public battles demonstrates that the hybrid social and religious interactions that Catherine also represented were met with suspicion in England. The anchoress is probably the closest representative in England to the lay but religiously devoted life represented by the third order and the beguines. Even in Italy, where lay piety had a flourishing moment in the fourteenth century, Catherine was an anomaly.[33] Despite many measures, letters, and testimonies taken shortly after her death, and the translation of her head and other relics to the Dominican church in Siena in 1384 (where they remain and are visited to this day), Catherine's canonization was not secured until 1461, a date roughly contemporary with most surviving English manuscripts concerning Catherine. However, many of the extant English texts predate her canonization by a few decades, which is a testament to her popularity and her importance there even without an official papal recognition.[34] Catherine's canonization was a fraught and lengthy process, begun by Raymond of Capua in 1395 after the completion of his *Legenda major*, continued by her followers – most notably Thomas Caffarini – and ultimately completed by Pius II. The Catherine that is finally canonized is stripped of much of her mystical and political framework (there is no mention of her stigmata, for example), which indicates some of the issues concerning her cult and canonization.[35] Caffarini's translation and dissemination effort results in a German translation of her *vita*, known as the *Geistliche Rosengarten*, which had a notable medieval circulation. A French translation of her *vita* survives in a few manuscripts, but appears to be unrelated to Caffarini's efforts.[36]

The English tradition, however, is markedly different from the continental evidence. Very few of the texts which make up the whole of Catherine's tradition spread to England during the late medieval or early modern era; in fact, there are no signs that Caffarini's texts, Catherine's letters, or her prayers were ever copied in any English manuscripts.[37] But what may seem at first glance to be a small remnant of a great body of work, upon closer examination displays a rich interplay of Catherine's texts with English society.[38] What does survive in the English vernacular will be treated in full throughout this book, with manuscripts and books listed in the tables in appendix B. The earliest English manuscripts concerning Catherine date from the mid- to late fifteenth century, very shortly after or contemporary with her canonization: one copy of Stephen Maconi's letter regarding Catherine, three copies of *Il Dialogo* in translation (known as *The Orcherd of Syon*), one excerpt from *The Orcherd*, eight copies (although some of these differ markedly from one another) of a testimony of Catherine's known in Latin as the *Documento Spirituale* and in English as "The Cleannesse of Sowle" (some copies differing markedly from one another), and three excerpts of Catherine's *Legenda major*.[39] Later, Wynkyn de Worde printed both a full translation of Raymond of Capua's *Legenda major, The Lyf* of Catherine (1492, 1500), as well as *The Orcherd of Syon* (1519). Henry Pepwell published selections of *The Lyf* in 1521, and John Fenn put forth a new translation of the *Legenda major* in 1609.[40]

The likely source, as we shall see, for the transmission of some of these texts is Catherine's follower and scribe, Stephen Maconi. Maconi, who had become Prior General of the Carthusian order, made it part of his mission to disseminate texts about Catherine throughout the community. Jeffrey Hamburger and Gabriela Signori note that "Maconi is said to have presented copies [of texts by and about Catherine] to great rulers, such as the kings of England and Hungary, the duke of Austria, and others. Further copies were sent by him to Ghent, Prague, Trier, Prussia, and Rome."[41] Because the Carthusians were invested generally in the translation and dissemination of religious works, there was an efficient pipeline of texts from the Continent (mostly the Low Countries) to England.[42] Given the prominence of the Carthusian Charterhouse of Sheen, and the closely connected Bridgettine house, Syon Abbey, the Carthusian order appears a likely route for several of her texts. The Bridgettines also had connections of their own, and the Bridgettine brothers in England evidently may have borrowed and copied manuscripts from the Florentine house known as "Paradiso" during a trip to Rome in order to petition the pope to overturn a ban on double monasteries. Another likely source for the transmission of these texts to England is William Flete, an English Augustinian canon and early follower of Catherine with ties to the Augustinian house in Cambridge. The excerpt known as "The Cleannesse of Sowle" comes from Flete and probably reached England through his transmission.[43] A booklist from the Augustinian Priory at Thurgarton lists a (now lost) Catherine text, and it is possible that this may have been the Latin basis for the Stephen Maconi letter to be eventually housed in the Carthusian Charterhouse of Beauvale.[44] We can only speculate as to how these texts actually arrive in England, however, because the pathway is not clear for any of the extant manuscripts.

These records represent a fluid tradition over a long period of time. Any study of medieval manuscripts is admitting a certain level of conjecture – very few texts have a provenance secure enough to know by whose hand it was penned, what versions are authorial, and which readers saw it. Even more speculative is the question as to what readers gleaned from that text. Jacques Le Goff speaks to the difficulties that are layered upon this when discussing an actual historical person, in his case Saint Louis:

> This task demanded first of all the positing of a problem, the search for and criticism of sources, the treatment of the subject within a time period long enough to capture the dialectic of continuity and change, a style of writing capable of highlighting the attempt to explain, an awareness of the current stakes in dealing with the question to be treated. In other words, the task also required an awareness of the distance that separates us from the question to be dealt with.[45]

There are many layers here to the texts I am surveying and analysing – they are grounded in the historical life of Catherine, but, by the time they are in the translated English forms I am examining, they are divorced from that reality and have taken on metaphorical, theological, and political implications that they may not have intended. In addition, many of them have been translated from their Italian and Latin contexts into not only the English vernacular but into an English devotional climate that has different boundaries and constraints, influenced by location, time, and civic pressures.

Evidence of Catherine's Cult in England

Evidence of pious activity – bequests, inscriptions, illuminations, rood screens – maps out both a private and public landscape of devotion to Catherine of Siena throughout England and, indeed, extending even to Scotland. From the south in Devon up through to the north in Edinburgh, there are vestiges of interest in her intercession and her cult. While this book focuses on the textual remains of Catherine's cult and the literary interest in her, the artistic and public elements demonstrate a broader presence in English culture than simply that of the literate or religious. The more private ones, such as an image in a Book of Hours or a dinner recitation of Catherine's *Lyf* for a noblewoman, show the personal connection to Catherine individually held by some members of medieval English society. What would have been only the purview of religious or aristocratic women in the beginning of the fifteenth century may have found its way into merchant families by the end of it, and certainly the audience for Catherine texts changes dramatically by the sixteenth and seventeenth centuries.[46] For several devoted followers,

Catherine represents a model of orthodoxy and devout piety, despite her simultaneous reputation as an intercessor in Church affairs.

Cecily of Neville, the mother of Kings Edward IV and Richard III, gives us a clue as to one of the ways in which Catherine was read and received in late medieval England. Cecily had every reason to style herself as a pious and devout woman after the death of Richard III, who had been removed from the throne in a rebellion by Henry Tudor and who was widely vilified. Sometime after Richard's death in 1485, but before Cecily's death a decade later, an ordinance was printed that explained her schedule and devout activities.[47] The ordinance describes Cecily's daily life, specifying the devotional texts she heard at dinner each night:

> Me semeth yt is requisyte to understand the order of her owne person, concerninge God and the worlde. She useth to arise at seven of the clocke, and hath readye her Chapleyne to saye with her mattins of the daye, and mattins of our lady; and she is fully readye she hath a lowe masse in her chamber, and after masse she takethe somethinge to recreate nature; and soe goeth to the Chappell hearinge the devine service, and two lowe masses; from thence to dynner; during the tyme whereof she hath a lecture of holy matter, either Hilton of contemplative and active life, Bonaventure[,] de infancia, Salvatories legenda aurea, St. Maude, St. Katheryn of Sonys, or the Revelacions of St. Bridget.[48]

Cecily's daily schedule is by every measure extremely pious. Her day starts with devotion, is punctuated by prayer, and finishes with recitations of holy works. These named works are significant. They provide a survey of many of the most popular devotional texts of the late fifteenth century: Walter Hilton's treatise on the mixed life, Nicholas Love's *Mirror of the Blessed Life of Jesus Christ* (here described as "Bonaventure"), the *Golden Legend,* and the texts of the three women visionaries: Mechthild of Hackeborn, Bridget of Sweden, and Catherine of Siena. Many of these books recur in her will where her granddaughter Bridget, a nun at the Dominican Priory of Dartford, received the *Legenda Aurea*, the visions of Mechthild, and the book of Catherine of Siena (the will specifies the "life" of Catherine, indicating that the "book" is most likely a translation of the *Legenda major* and not that of the *Dialogo*). Another granddaughter, Anne de la Pole, who was then prioress of the Bridgettine Syon Abbey, received Cecily's copy of Bridget's *Revelations*. Both women received three named books, altogether a kind of mini-library of late medieval devotion: "I geve to my doughter Brigitte the boke of *Legenda Aurea* in velem, a boke of the life of Saint Kateryn of Sene, a boke of Saint Matilde ... Also I geve to my doughter Anne, priores of Sion, a boke of Bonaventure and Hilton in the same in Englishe, and a boke of the Revelacions of Saint Burgitte."[49] Both in the description of her daily devotions and in the inheritances outlined in her will, Cecily is presenting an image here. Devotion to Catherine of Siena, among this display of an especially literary pious devotion, displays an essential part of that construction.[50]

Cecily's ordinance and will provide a sense of how devotional books were used and transmitted in late medieval England, at least among the aristocracy. Her evening reading is an extension of the devotion of her day, but it is also separate, as the texts selected are not Books of Hours or prayers. Coinciding with her dinner, spiritual food complements her earthly nourishment. The subsequent movement after Cecily's death of the texts from a lay household into the convent shows how freely books travelled between readers, especially women readers, and how precious books truly were. The ordinance also provides a hint as to how Catherine of Siena was understood in late medieval England. Clearly, she is known; this is not some obscure saint who needs more exposition by the writers of the ordinance, and she is listed with Bridget, who we will see is far better known in England yet frequently coupled with Catherine. That the last three books mentioned in the ordinance are those of visionary women (Mechthild, Bridget, and Catherine) and two from visionary lay women, demonstrates how orthodox these texts could be considered and how fully they were integrated into the spiritual and devotional landscape of the time. However, the textual reception of these women and the practice of mystical or visionary activities seem distinct. The former has a place in medieval England, the latter less so. As we shall see, translators and compilers of Catherine's work endeavour to highlight the devotional elements of the mystical experience while simultaneously discouraging its practice.

Catherine subtly appears at times elsewhere throughout Britain. In 1517, a Dominican convent was dedicated to Catherine in Edinburgh, Scotland, although it was shortly thereafter dissolved during the Reformation.[51] In a probably related Dominican manuscript, Edinburgh, MS 30, Catherine is included in the calendar.[52] A beautifully illuminated fourteenth-century book of hours, Cambridge, Fitzwilliam Museum MS 48, known as the Carew-Poyntz Hours, has an undated image of Catherine prostrate before an altar. She is painted over a drawing of another subject, suggesting a later devotion to her which supplants the earlier image of another saint; this rewriting possibly coincided with Catherine's canonization which no doubt brought more attention to her.[53] The early provenance of the manuscript is unknown, but it was eventually owned by Elizabeth Poyntz (married to the wealthy courtier and landowner John Poyntz) at the end of the fifteenth century. All of these are just small evidentiary pieces of Catherine's cult and indications of what survived the destruction of the Reformation, hinting at a wider reach in England, but also pointedly precise and found where we may expect her: among the Dominicans and among aristocratic women.

There are also some broader signs of Catherine's influence. The four rood screen images of Catherine that survive suggest a public devotion to her. The rood screens that divided church chancels from naves were frequently painted with images of saints or biblical scenes. Most English rood screens were painted over or destroyed during and after the Reformation, so what remains today hardly represents what may have previously existed, but the fact that these images of Catherine survive indicates that there were probably more. As David Griffith has noted, the iconography of screens like these provide "a useful measure of changes in reading and devotional practices and offers one way of mapping lay contact with mystical texts" because they are relatively easy to repaint and replace, unlike a stained glass window or church carving.[54] In addition to the screen in Torbryan, the description of which I began this introduction, there remain two other Devon images of Catherine: at medieval churches in East Portlemouth[55] and Wolborough.[56] At a church in Horsham St Faith, Norfolk, a screen commissioned by William Wulcy and his wife had what is now a badly defaced image of Catherine of Siena next to a relatively untouched one of Bridget of Sweden, holy women that Eamon Duffy calls "highly unusual choices" of saints to include.[57] Duffy and Denise Despres both suggest that the image may have come from a Wynkyn de Worde print of Catherine included in both his *Lyf* of Catherine and in *The Orcherd of Syon*, and indeed the images are strikingly similar.[58] In these images, Catherine is holding a book, crowned by thorns, holding a heart. Her stigmata are absent. In the Dominican Dartford Priory, the altar retable dating from the early fifteenth century has an image that is likely, although not clearly, Catherine of Siena.[59] A West Sussex church in Cocking has a late fifteenth-century bell inscribed with Catherine's name, and in 2007 the now-Anglican Church was christened "the Church of St. Catherine of Siena" as a result of this inscription.[60] Catherine is at once both nowhere and everywhere.

Vernacular Piety, Gendering Readers, and Catherine of Siena

The anonymous Middle English translator of Raymond of Capua's *Legenda major* writes in his introduction to the text that Catherine resides between the private inspiration she receives from God and how she conveys this inspiration to the men around her, suggesting that Catherine represents a confluence of the immediate, the oral, the public, and the private. The second part of the *vita*, he says, covers the subject of "the conuersacion of this holy mayde and vyrgyn wyth men, and how the yeftes the whiche she had receyued of our lorde pryuely enclosed wythin her-self, were openly shewed to the worlde: And firste how our lord bad her that she sholde be conuersaunt amonge men."[61] She receives the words of God, privately, "enclosed within herself," but then learns how to transfer that to the men around her through her words and actions. "Conuersacion" here means manner of living, devoting oneself to Christian ideals, but by the end of the sixteenth century the word had become what we understand now, denoting dialogue and the exchange of speech. Catherine must convey a manner of living, and this becomes her articulated legacy, as we have seen in how she is appropriated by Cecily Neville as an instructive text during her mealtimes.[62]

Catherine of Siena, like her contemporary and frequent textual partner, Bridget of Sweden, remained hard to define and categorize in late medieval England. Her indeterminacy makes her easy to appropriate, offering a variety of texts and ideas for her readers. The kind of piety Catherine practised in Italy, as a member of a Dominican "third order," was not available to English laity who sought the discipline and devotion of the religious life without formal structure of hierarchy or living. Her third order status and celebrity afforded her a freedom of movement and mind that a formal structure may not have permitted. She represented in her *vita* an in-betweenness that was barely represented in England, either in reality or textually. She also represented a mystic and a visionary woman, a figure and textual authority that flourished on the Continent but is seen in a more muted form in medieval England. There were so few models for English women of this kind of mysticism, and very little evidence that the visionary piety encouraged among nuns in the Low Countries and Germany was ever part of the devotional landscape of English nunneries, so Catherine's decidedly visionary literature stands out. Catherine additionally represented a kind of public and political piety also very much discouraged for women in practice, both in England and on the Continent.

Her lay status provided a framework in which the kind of activism she practised was possible. However, Bridget's role as mother offered her a sanctioned social role that was more familiar to her devotees, and the eventual order in her name gave her a place within the Church that was also easier to identify and, in some ways, control. Syon Abbey's prominence in medieval England, as we will see, provided Bridget and her texts with a clear place in society that Catherine did not have. Even so, Bridget repeatedly needed English supporters of her revelations and her rule, and these defences implicitly defend Catherine as well even as they draw attention to the fact that there is something in contention.[63] Catherine, like Bridget, resides in the nexus of vernacularity, heterodoxy, and visionary women that roused suspicion.

Catherine of Siena's texts also reside between the oral and the written, Latin and the vernacular, the public and the private in a way not frequently seen in one discrete set of English texts. Because her texts were in the vernacular, they also dwell between the literate and the illiterate; literacy often meant a Latinate literacy and many devotional texts had an oral life through sermons. It is useful to think of the circulation of texts about Catherine in England as part of what Brian Stock has called a "textual community," that has essentially a two-tiered system: "A small inner core of literates, semi-literates, and non-literates followed the interpretation of the text itself. But the literates within the heretical or reform group could also preach outside it to nonliterates whose only bond with the founders was by word of mouth. Yet, these nonliterates had already begun to participate in literate culture, although indirectly."[64] In this way, for every documented reader or owner of a manuscript, there is an implicit community of "readers" who are receiving the information aurally or who have read the text in other ways. Likewise, there is a community of producers that help create the final artefact of the manuscript. As Margaret Connolly and Raluca Radulescu have noted, the book is created by authors, scribes, compilers, and book producers who, with readers, "were agents in broader cultural, political, and social processes of change, whether knowingly or not."[65] Part of my project is to tease out the implications of these intersections both in their creation and over time. For example, translators and compilers may have chosen women as the intended recipient of texts such as *The Orcherd of Syon*, but the manuscript provenance and textual use clearly signal a wider audience. As with many writings directed at women religious readers and lay readers of both genders, several of the surviving codices and even the printed books surrounding Catherine are preceded by letters addressing these imagined readers. For example, the translator of *The Orcherd* speaks directly to the sisters he imagines are reading the book: "And now, sustren, I ceese of þis prologue," and the translator of the text consistently changes the masculine Latin *lector* (reader) to "maydens." Wynkyn de Worde's *Lyf* of Catherine begins "Audi filie et vide. Here Doughter & see," and John Fenn's recusant translation of Catherine's *Legenda major* starts with an address to an unnamed "Madam." One miscellany containing Catherine's "The Cleannesse of Sowle," British Library, MS Royal 18.A.X., has an address right before selections from William Flete's *Remedies against Temptations* that begins: "Dere sistere I haue in partie understonde by thyn writyng of diuerse temptaciouns & taryinges that thou hast suffered and ʒit suffrist." The extant English manuscripts I study here include words dictated by Catherine, spoken in rapture and in full knowledge of them, as well as words written by various followers – William Flete, Stephen Maconi, and Raymond of Capua. The texts are written and disseminated by Catherine's male followers, and although they gender their readers as female, these men are, of course, Catherine's first audience. While these manuscripts and books therefore had documented male readership (both religious and lay), actual readers must, to an extent, embody the addressed reader as the woman or women. Just as reading in the late Middle Ages is moving between something done aloud and silently, something done collectively and alone, these texts demonstrate both male and female reading practices.[66]

Catherine had some direct connections to England that are worth noting. The most important is her association with the Augustinian friar William Flete, a Cambridge graduate who lived near Siena and advised Catherine. Flete has been largely overlooked as an important influence on Catherine's spirituality and for influencing the dissemination of her texts and her cult in medieval England. She also wrote letters to the English mercenary Sir John Hawkwood, known to Pope Gregory XI, as well as to Jean Froissart and Niccolò Machiavelli. Catherine addressed Hawkwood repeatedly, exhorting him to join the Crusades on the behalf of the pope – which he did. Later, Richard II appointed him as ambassador to the Roman Court. A few scholars have also suggested that Catherine's hagiographer, Raymond of Capua, was in contact with William Bakthorpe, a powerful Dominican and prior of Lynn, as part of his campaign to spread Catherine's cult abroad.[67] If this is true, it is likely that Margery Kempe, who knew

Bakthorpe, would have heard Catherine's *vita* at least in part. Certainly, it is unlikely that Kempe could have travelled to Rome without hearing about Catherine, given her popularity in Italy.

But more than these direct connections, Catherine's texts illustrate many intersecting strands of late medieval devotion that are different from other Continental traditions in medieval England. This book is also not just about Catherine in England, but Catherine in English. How and why did Catherine get translated into the vernacular? And how does this process of transmission and translation make new meaning for its readers? In England, all the surviving excerpts of Catherine's texts are in English, not Latin (in which complete copies of Catherine's work survive).[68] Although two lengthy complete texts of Catherine's circulate (the translations of her *Legenda major* and her *Il Dialogo*), the vast majority of her extant texts survive in miscellanies and other compilations. The excerpts in the miscellanies appear alongside other circulating religious texts, indicating that there was most likely a fair number of Catherine's texts in English that have not survived. The vernacular allows for a lay and female religious readership, and the evidence shows that the excerpts are remarkably mobile – found in virtually every context of extant manuscript with every possible literate audience – but often land in the hands of a female religious or lay audience. Very frequently, Catherine's writings are coupled with male authorities who serve to validate and temper her. As Liz Herbert McAvoy has recently written, the embedding of women's visionary works, like Catherine's, "into the writings of an emerging 'canon' of male-authored devotional writings belies the misleading notion of separate, distinct, devotional literary traditions for men and women during the period."[69] Catherine is tightly woven into the full fabric of medieval devotional culture, especially in this edited and arranged format.

This book also seeks to find what happens to the Latin texts when they are rearticulated for a vernacular audience in their translation. We can turn to Margery Kempe here as an interesting "test case," a late medieval hearer/reader of contemporary devotional texts, particularly mystical ones. Barry Windeatt notes that "Kempe's facility in absorbing and applying recent contemplative literature from home and abroad is symptomatic of fifteenth-century confidence in re-reading the English contemplative classics, often in radically edited selections, rearrangements, and compilations which represent forms of critical interpretation through recontextualization."[70] By looking at this process of editing, rearranging, and compiling the Catherine texts, we can further understand how medieval English devotional culture is partly constructed. In addition to this scribal, translated, and written transmission, this book also examines Catherine herself and how her words are transmitted and preserved, and how they capture the sense of oral mystical dictation, the medium in which they were initially conveyed. Karma Lochrie writes that in the process of a mystic and visionary's spoken text being written down by a male amanuensis, "the fundamental orality of mystical texts is subsumed under this literary/exegetical model of textual production."[71] Lochrie notes that the mystical text becomes freed from generic conventions, and in fact defies them – it is part body, part utterance, part collaboration, and it gives language to the unspeakable. *The Orcherd of Syon*, "The Cleannesse of Sowle," and some parts of *The Lyf* originate in Catherine's utterances, and they resurface in England as oral texts that were read as part of the nuns' devotions at Syon Abbey or read aloud to Cecily of Neville during her dinner. Her *Dialogo*, certainly, was conceived by Catherine as a book that *she* was dictating and writing, not a compilation of her revelations conceived by her confessor. In this way, the orality of Catherine's texts survives its translations and disseminations, and it possesses an immediacy that is tangible. Catherine's texts strongly resist the kind of interpretation a male scribe may impose on his female charge's words, but that imposition is nevertheless there in some form. The medieval compiler or reader still tries to put them into recognizable schematics through form, juxtaposition, or editorial choices. The contrast between the "voice" of *The Orcherd*, dictated by Catherine, and that of *The Lyf*, constructed by Raymond of Capua, is notable for the stark difference between what had been delivered orally and what was written. Her voluminous letters, with multiple scribes responsible, also attest to a control over her literary production that may not have been the same for other women visionaries.

These fissures between the oral and the written, the female voice and the male scribe, likewise reveal the fractures between scholastic theology and popular lay devotion. In 1436, contemporary with many of the Catherine manuscripts examined in this book, a council is convened in Basel to determine the orthodoxy of Bridget of Sweden's revelations, demonstrating that any debate as to the validity and importance of women's visions had been far from settled. A certain English bishop, known only as Reginald, wrote a defence of Bridget for that council. The defence, surviving in one Insular manuscript, reads more broadly as a justification for popular lay devotion surrounding affective piety and the sensual comprehension of Christ.[72] This, Alexander Russell notes, serves to champion "elements of popular devotion which had aroused the scorn of Wyclif and the unease of many scholastic theologians."[73] Catherine's texts, like Bridget's, inhabited the in-between spaces of lay piety and scholasticism in England. However, unlike Bridget, Catherine does not so obviously carry the weight of formal defences and constant surveillance, allowing her texts more malleability for compilers and readers.

Chapter Descriptions

I have structured each chapter of this book around one aspect or element of Catherine's English textual tradition. Each chapter highlights a different way in which meaning is made through the process of transmission, editing, and translation. To this end, I am not only engaging in textual analysis, but also looking at the physical objects of manuscripts and books, especially at how rubrics, prefaces, and provenance further inform how Catherine of Siena was integrated into English devotional culture and was likewise emblematic of its divisions, contradictions, and tensions. Each manuscript raises a separate question of authorship and authority. Each represents a text that was mediated several times among Catherine's lived experience or words, her scribes and confessors, the English translators and compilers, and the contexts within which readers eventually held those texts. The tension between what is sanctioned and what is subversive pulls at the heart of these contradictions and interpretations. This is in large part due to the fact that there are hagiographic texts about Catherine and visionary texts by her. The former, written by religious men, place Catherine within the Church hierarchy and adhere to hagiographic conventions that confine her within an orthodox schematic. The latter, however, can fall into the suspicions that accompany all visionary texts that purport to be directly from God. Nicholas Watson has described the English male mystic Richard Rolle as similarly "potentially uncontrollable," because he is "in a position to lay powerful claims to an authority which lies outside and above ecclesiastical institutions, even to deny the authority which inheres in those institutions."[74] Catherine represents both a heterodoxy and an orthodoxy, the features of which are highlighted or sublimated through the process of transmission and interpretation throughout the later Middle Ages and come to a conclusion in the Reformation where both Protestants and Catholics point to Catherine's writings as examples that prove their theologies.

The first chapter of this book, "Compiling Catherine: The Visionary Woman, Stephen Maconi, and the Carthusian Audience," looks at how manuscripts about Catherine were disseminated and translated and who their intended audience was in theory if not in practice. This chapter examines the history and reception of women's visionary texts in medieval England and situates Catherine both within and outside of that tradition. The touchstone for this chapter is a letter written by Stephen Maconi, the Prior General of the Carthusian order who had been one of Catherine's scribes and devoted followers. Written as a defence of Catherine, whose legacy and canonization were very much in dispute after her death because many saw the pope's return to Rome and the subsequent Church schism as precipitated by Catherine's visions, the letter focuses on a personal account of Maconi's travels to the papacy at Avignon and the Catherine he knew and witnessed there. Surviving in a sole manuscript that contains the only English hagiographic accounts of the Low Countries mystics Marie of Oignies, Christina *mirabilis,* and Elizabeth of Spalbeek, the text finds a place in a book featuring a kind of mystical women's spirituality with a limited textual tradition and seemingly rare practise in medieval England. By looking closely at the Maconi letter and the collection in which it travelled, I delineate the difference between the reception of mystical texts and the practice of mysticism – a tension that will run through all subsequent texts concerning Catherine – and the ways in which intended audiences and actual ones could alter understanding.

In the second chapter, "William Flete, English Spirituality, and Catherine of Siena," I argue that Catherine somewhat articulates an "English spirituality" that she in part learns from her adviser William Flete. Flete, an English Augustinian friar, left his home for a more austere life in Siena where he met and counselled Catherine. His *Remedies against Temptations,* a treatise advising its readers how to overcome and atone for everyday sins, survives in several English manuscripts and is frequently compiled with Catherine's "The Cleannesse of Sowle." Flete's influence on Catherine should not be underestimated; he became an important spiritual authority for her own devotional understanding, and we can see his words echoing in hers. In this way, what appears to be less common in the English devotional landscape – a visionary woman's writing – is actually embodying something more orthodox. In researching this book, I discovered that "The Cleannesse of Sowle," one of her major texts which had previously been identified as an excerpt from *Il Dialogo,* is in fact a translation of Flete's *Documento Spirituale* concerning Catherine, a record of an ecstatic vision that he witnessed.

This passage, detailing a dialogue Catherine has with God about maintaining purity, is one of the earliest representatives of Catherine's own theological reasoning, predating all of her letters and *Il Dialogo*. The fact that "The Cleannesse" survives in so many venues in England suggests that Flete sent it back to his Augustinian brethren, seeing Catherine as a corrective to the problems in English spiritual practice that he had already recognized and addressed. Much of the knowledge about Catherine and the creation of her cult in England may be largely due to his efforts. This chapter underscores some of what is English about Catherine's theology and the ways in which it lines up with other late medieval accounts of temptation and penance.

Chapter 3, "Catherine Excerpted: Reading the Miscellany," demonstrates the ways in which Catherine's texts were abbreviated in various tracts to accommodate different strands of late medieval English spirituality so that she was presented in turn as pedantic, methodological, visionary, and mystical. I look at the "miscellaneous Catherine," in particular the dissemination of "The Cleannesse of Sowle," which survives in several manuscripts, and which describes God's lessons to Catherine on maintaining spiritual and corporeal purity. These manuscripts represent many aspects of English devotional literacy: highly illuminated private texts, small preachers' handbooks, monastic compilations, and even a "lollard" manuscript. Two additional excerpts (one from Catherine's *Legenda major* and another from her *Il Dialogo*) describe how readers may discern whether the source of a vision is demonic or divine. These excerpts together, more than the complete versions of Catherine's texts, demonstrate the ways in which different compilers shaped Catherine into the kind of textual authority that they needed for the purposes of their anthologies and readerships. Who Catherine is and the purpose she serves is not inherent in the text itself but rather in the editorial choices of the compiler. Indeed, this chapter demonstrates that in excerpted form Catherine is often removed entirely and replaced with an anonymous "sely soule" (a holy soul), a stand in for any reader; this makes her more ubiquitous, yet erases her name and presence from the text.

Catherine's real and imagined connection to Bridget of Sweden is explored in chapter 4, "*The Orcherd of Syon*: How to Read in the Convent," which also examines how *The Orcherd* was translated to appeal to the Bridgettine nuns of Syon Abbey. Prepared originally for the sisters there, and surviving in three extant manuscripts and two publications from Wynkyn de Worde's press, *The Orcherd of Syon*, the Middle English translation of Catherine's dictated visionary tome *Il*

Dialogo, is a text that diverges from the standard English reading for women in that it embraces both a literary life (complete with directions as to how to read carefully and thoroughly) and a visionary one. I discuss Syon Abbey as a centre of devotional book production in the later Middle Ages, and how the printing of *The Orcherd* is an essential first step in what would become an important part of the abbey's identity of providing devotional material for the laity. *The Orcherd* most clearly delineates the difference between reading about revelations and its practice; indeed, the translation is set up to encourage the former while discouraging the latter. Ultimately, this chapter explores how a text clearly meant not only for a nunnery, but a very specific one, translates to lay readers outside of the cloister, and how that interplay between transmitters and recipients of Catherine's works alters the meaning of *The Orcherd*.

In chapter 5, "Catherine in Print: Lay Audiences and Reading Hagiography," I argue that Catherine's printed texts are inextricable from a larger pattern of growing private lay devotional reading in England. *The Lyf of Katherin of Senis*, the English translation of Raymond of Capua's *Legenda major*, is likely the first book printed by Wynkyn de Worde after he takes over William Caxton's press in 1492. He will become known for printing devotional books, and he begins that reputation with *The Lyf*. Raymond's text largely strips Catherine of the more controversial elements of her actual life, such as her stigmata, and closely follows the conventions of other hagiographic texts. I look closely at de Worde's audience and the act of private lay reading, as well as the role *The Lyf* plays in building a devotional audience for de Worde. Henry Pepwell, one of de Worde's printing rivals, published a collection of mystical texts in 1521 that included several excerpts from *The Lyf*. This volume demands examination as it also contains selections from Margery Kempe's *Book*, drawing a connection between the two women, at least in its compiler's and readers' minds. A copy of this book owned by the British Library shows selective defacement by its owners during the Reformation, providing clues as to how Catherine was read and understood during that tumultuous time. Wynkn de Worde and Pepwell together give *The Lyf* the most prevalent late medieval and early modern presence of Catherine. By the time of the Reformation, all references to Catherine are grounded in *The Lyf*, not in any of her revelatory or visionary texts.

My concluding chapter, "Reforming Reading: Catherine of Siena in an Age of Reform," discusses the early modern incarnations of Catherine and her texts, following Pepwell's 1521 devotional anthology. Here, we see the many tensions and opposing elements of Catherine's corpus and legacy teased out and used for various purposes by Catholics and Protestants alike. Elizabeth Barton, the "Holy Maid of Kent" who was arrested and executed for her prophecies regarding Henry VIII and Anne Boleyn, is publicly sanctioned for her use of Catherine as a model visionary and prophet. John Fenn, an English Roman Catholic priest living in exile in Belgium, translates Raymond of Capua's *Legenda major* in 1609 for a convent of recusant nuns, holding Catherine as a model of orthodox female resilience in the face of hardship. Here, Catherine, who was known for bringing the Avignon papacy back to Rome, is used to encourage England back to its own rightful Church. Nearly simultaneously, John Foxe's Protestant treatise *Acts and Monuments* claims Catherine for its own cause, both criticizing the belief in her revelations while also suggesting she predicted the Reformation and saw it as a collective good. Delineating the conflicts at large in English Christianity, these Reformation-era examples expose the two opposing Catherines: the model of orthodoxy, and the dangerous example of false reformation.

By tracing these textual remnants of Catherine through late medieval and into early modern England, I hope to present a sense of how texts and textual traditions may stem from Catherine and then be used and adapted by various writers, compilers, and readers, depending on their individual agendas and needs. Because so many of Catherine's texts are directed at the gendered reader, there is a suggested interplay between the male scribe or translator and the imagined female reader, but in reality there exists a more complex tapestry of lay, religious, male, female, Catholic, and Protestant readers. Despite an impulse to categorize texts and their readers as "orthodox," "lollard," "women," and "monks," I show here that the evidence of Catherine of Siena's texts and readers presents an alternative taxonomy, one that blurs the oral and the written, the public and the private, and the subversive and the orthodox. The text and the woman are made and remade to serve the reader, the time, and the place, revealing how translators, editors, and readers work together to create meaning and adapt the text to their devotional moment and context.

Chapter One

Compiling Catherine: The Visionary Woman, Stephen Maconi, and the Carthusian Audience

Carthusians, Audience, and Compiling Catherine[1]

For a translated text, there are three layers of authority that need to be considered: the original text, its translator, and – for any miscellany or anthology – the compiler. The compiler of the Bodleian Library, MS Douce 114 (hereafter, Douce 114), examined in this chapter, gets at some of the essential textual questions that arise when we look at Catherine of Siena in medieval England. This manuscript represents a hybridity. Its provenance is monastic, yet it seems to have been translated and assembled for laity. The text would offer very different, but equally substantial, lessons depending on its reader. By translating the text, or copying an already translated text, the scribe knows that the audience is most likely going beyond the learned monastic one. There is a new audience that, inscribed by the process of vernacularization, needs to be addressed by the translator or compiler: Who are these new readers going to be and why should this text be made available to them? The compiler recognizes that the audience could include lettered and religious men, but may also include the laity and those whose theological comprehension is possibly less astute. Some authors, such as the anonymous translator of *The Orcherd of Syon*, are very specific in answering these questions, but most, like the compiler of the anthology examined in this chapter, are more oblique. In the structure of his compilation and in a *coda*, the compiler attempts to negotiate the various levels of readers his text may encounter and guide them in their comprehension of the whole.

Throughout this chapter, I am using Stephen Maconi's letter about Catherine found in Douce 114 to situate her within several important contexts.[2] First, I examine how she is placed among other Continental visionary women and their reception in England, with particular focus on how these women's texts were disseminated and to whom. This chapter looks especially at the Carthusian context in which many revelatory texts circulated, Douce 114 included, which complicates questions of audience as the order was cloistered and did not administer to women readers (the natural recipients of many of these texts). Finally, Maconi's letter highlights one of the central discrepancies within Catherine's tradition: she is always controversial and yet one of the most famous, approved saints of her day. His letter is written in the face of that controversy, and it carries through to the translated codex as well. How that controversy is digested depends largely on who is reading, and this chapter engages how the reception of an unintended audience may inflect our reading of the text.

While the path and provenance of several of the extant medieval and early modern texts regarding Catherine are unknown, it is certain that Douce 114 was owned by the Carthusian Charterhouse of Beauvale in Nottingham. This is not surprising; many of the devotional texts we have from England's late medieval period were either copied by or owned by the Carthusian order, and the texts concerning Catherine are no exception.[3] Surviving library catalogues from Carthusian houses attest to great interest in women visionaries, with Bridget of Sweden, Mechthild of Hackeborn, and Catherine of Siena all well accounted for, and indeed the only complete copies of Margery Kempe's *Book* and the short text of Julian of Norwich's *Revelations* were Carthusian in origin.[4] The dissemination of Carthusian texts is largely due to a conscious and international effort on the part of the order to make texts available throughout its houses across Europe, and it was probably at the urging of one of Catherine of Siena's important followers, the Carthusian Stephen Maconi. Jeremy Catto notes:

While Carthusians by no means had a monopoly over the distribution of texts, they had distinct advantages: the creation of a spiritual library in both Latin and vernacular languages from texts which might have originally been written in French, Italian, Dutch, German, or English was a task prefigured by the instruction of an early prior, Guigo II, to copy and circulate devotional texts. The systematic translation of texts, however, seems to have marked a new project in which Carthusians in many parts of Europe needed to cooperate. Though no direct evidence of any plan survives in the archives of the Order, it is likely that much of the original impetus came from Stephen Maconi, Prior of the Order from 1398 to 1410, who had been an early associate of Catherine of Siena and was instrumental in the Latin translation and circulation of her letters and *Dialogo* throughout the Order. Significantly, these were not written by a Carthusian; texts by both Carthusians and outsiders were adopted, translated and diffused without distinction.[5]

The Carthusian Charterhouse of Sheen was closely connected to its neighbour, the Bridgettine Syon Abbey whose nuns were the intended recipients of *The Orcherd of Syon*, and it seems possible that a manuscript of *Il Dialogo* would have arrived in England via Maconi's hands. However, the version of *Il Dialogo* which served as a basis for *The Orcherd of Syon* was copied from Cristofano Guidini's translation of Catherine's book, not Maconi's own translation, which offers the possibility of another form of transmission – perhaps through Bridgettine channels rather than Carthusian ones.[6] The least known of the English Catherine texts almost certainly did arrive through Maconi – a letter written by Stephen himself in support of Catherine's canonization, penned in the face of its opposition and written as part of a collection of testimonies and letters spanning half a decade which supported Catherine's sainthood, known as *Il Processo Castellano*.[7] Regardless of transmission, the Middle English translation in Douce 114 clearly had a connection to the Carthusian monks who read and copied it at Beauvale Charterhouse.[8]

The texts in the Douce 114 anthology are deeply rooted in Continental mysticism and affective piety, containing, in addition to the letter concerning Catherine, the Middle English lives of Elizabeth of Spalbeek, Christina *mirabilis*, and Marie of Oignies, as well as a translation of the thirteenth-century German mystic Henry Suso's *Horologium Sapientiae*.[9] Two different hands appear in the codex, with the majority of the Suso written by the second hand, and the women's lives and end of the manuscript written by the first.[10] Stephen's letter follows the three beguine lives, making a neat unit of four.[11] The collection as a whole, Barry Windeatt notes, "is strikingly at variance with the much-repeated modern orthodoxy that medieval English spiritual advisers – sanely countering the unsettling influence of Rolle, not to mention excitable continentals – discouraged interest in extraordinary asceticism and contemplative exceptionalism."[12] The Carthusians were definitely interested in what Kathryn Kerby-Fulton calls "left-wing orthodoxy," books that do not fall along an orthodox/heterodox binary, but – like Marguerite Porete's *Mirror of Simple Souls* – depend on readers to parse meaning and properly receive the text.[13] These countervailing clerical trends may account for the fact that many of the Carthusian texts like Douce 114 or Margery Kempe's *Book* do not survive outside of that monastic context.[14] The collection shows, as with Catherine texts in general, how it at once may stand as both representative and unique. However, as we shall see, there is a deliberate program and design to this manuscript unlike the miscellanies and other compilations we will examine in chapter 3.

Stephen Maconi's letter is, of all the Catherine texts, the one most clearly linked to the Carthusians in both its content and its codicology. The Charterhouse at Sheen was the home of the only surviving English copy of Stephen's letter in Latin; the letter survives in Oxford, Magdalen College, MS 141, from the second quarter of the fifteenth century, roughly contemporary with Douce 114. Magdalen College 141 belonged to John Dygon, a recluse at Sheen from 1435 to 1449, and it contains several devotional texts, including a Latin version of Walter Hilton's *Scale of Perfection*, Book I. However, while the Carthusians may appear to be the source for this Middle English text, it seems that Stephen's letter, and possibly *The Orcherd of Syon*, originated in or were shared with the Augustinians at Thurgarton Priory. The priory, home to Walter Hilton, also once owned what was most likely a Latin version of Stephen's letter, "littere quedam de vita sancte Katerine de Senys."[15] This one followed the lives of Elizabeth, Christina, and Marie in the same order as found in Douce 114, so was likely the basis for the Douce 114 translation.[16] The same booklist also attests to a copy of Catherine's *Dialogo*, "reuelaciones sancte Katerine de Senys in j volumine ligato."[17]

The Carthusians interest in women's visionary writing helped both protect the individual texts, as well as integrate the women's texts into devotional anthologies and thus the devotional culture of the period. Their interest conversely had the effect of sequestering some of the texts as a whole, but the presentation allowed for a more subtle integration into the devotional fabric defined by anthologies and miscellanies. Liz Herbert McAvoy has recently shown how women's visionary works like those of Mechthild of Hackeborn's writings, which moved through the Hanseatic League into England, remain "vital for our full understanding of the way in which female spirituality imbricated the wider male-authored canon, both devotional and secular, in the fifteenth century and beyond."[18] Just at the texts by Catherine can straddle a line between heterodox and orthodox, largely dependent on context and provenance, so, too, do they move between a sense of scarcity and ubiquity. The total number of vernacular medieval manuscripts containing texts concerning Catherine are relatively few, but her prominence in and the completeness of many of these manuscripts demonstrate a larger presence in the devotional culture of medieval England than may be surmised merely by looking at the number of surviving manuscripts. The Douce 114 manuscript is now the only extant version of Stephen's letter in English, but its place in a vernacular devotional anthology speaks to a wider readership than this indicates.

Although the copy's provenance was Beauvale Chaterhouse, Douce 114 was not originally translated for cloistered monks. The explicit that follows the four women's lives, but precedes the Suso text, is written by the self-described compiler of the codex, or at least of the first part therein. The contents of the explicit point to an audience different from a monastic one, naming both male and female laity as part of its intended reach. This is especially interesting because the Carthusian order did not include pastoral care as part of its mission; indeed, the order was structured as a community of recluses more than a traditional monastic order, and stressed silent prayer and meditation. Clearly, the translation's final home in the Beauvale Charterhouse was not its intended destination. However, the explicit serves as a good example of how Catherine texts are potentially translated, adapted, and changed in medieval England to suit different readers and is worth examining in full. The explicit reads:

A shorte Apologetik of this Englisshe compyloure: Seynt James the Apostil seith that whoso synneth not in tunge, hee is a parfite man. Wherfore the turner of this Englysshe that is not but simply undirstandynge as here the soth preueth, [preyeth] lowely and mekely alle men and wymmen that in happe redith or herith this Englyshe that they be not ouer capcyous ne curyous in ful many clauses and variauns of stile and alle so vnsuynge of Englyshe as vmwhile Sotheren, otherewhile Northen; but the cause why nedith not to be tolde. And specially he besecheth lettird men and clerkes, if they endeyne to see thes bokes, that they wol be fauorabil and, beinge reders or herers of this Englysche, forgif hym alle defautes that he hath made in compilynge thereof rather arettynge his lewdnesse to symple ignorauns and obedyens thanne to pryde or presumpcyone. For wite alle men that he – the which drewe this Englysche so as is oute of Latyne – knowynge his owne simpilnesse and vnkonynge, durst not haue presumed to take siche a labour on hand but if his souereyn hadde bidden hym whome he

> myghte not ageyne seye ... Whoso redith this, preye[s] for the writer that
> god gif hym a good ende and if hit profit, hele of body. Amen.[19]

The word "compyloure" could mean both author and chronicler in Middle English, and there are at least two layers at work here. The writer was a translator, as he further names himself in the text as the "turner of this Englysshe" and the person who "drewe this Englysche so as is oute of Latyne";[20] however, scribal errors throughout the text, and other evidence here in the prologue, also indicate that it is a copy from another manuscript, not the original translation. So there is likely an original translation, but also a "compiler" in a more traditional sense who has put together a text for an intended readership.[21] Indeed, this compiler seems particularly worried about the reaction of the "lettird men and clerkes," prefacing his comments to them with "specially," who may read the book and take note of his errors ("alle his defautes"). In another sign that the compiler is not the translator, he notes his awareness of "variauns of stile" and "vnsuynge," or discord, among the English that combines southern and northern dialects.[22] This self-consciousness about style and dialect demonstrates an awareness of how a translated text is a disruption of the text, but also that it creates a new narrative where word choice and style matter. The manuscript also presents an anthology, an intentionally composed collection, rather than a miscellany of a more random nature.[23]

The vernacularity of the text coupled with its association with female visionaries, an occasionally fraught category, together may make the manuscript somewhat volatile as a whole. Some anxiety about the process of translation into the vernacular is also reflected here. This does not reflect in the explicit itself, but there is certainly some caution following Archbishop Arundel's 1409 "Lambeth Constitutions" that attempted to quash the lollard heresy by regulating vernacular devotional texts and their circulation.[24] Nicholas Watson argues that the campaign against lollardy had the additional effect of ultimately silencing the composition of original "vernacular theology" that had nothing to do with lollardy but that may have been treated with suspicion. While Watson points out there was certainly "some gap between principle and practice," that is, that even texts in direct violation of Arundel's decree would continue to be written, copied, and disseminated, he argues that the major theologically innovative vernacular texts were written before the Lambeth Constitutions take effect, or well after.[25] But translations were a primary concern for Arundel, and some evidence demonstrates a real awareness on the part of translators of its implications. For example, the "Memorandum of Approbation" preceding Nicholas Love's *Mirror of the Blessed Life of Jesus Christ*, a version of the *Meditationes vitae Christi*, explicitly states that the text was presented to Archbishop Arundel for approval (which it received).[26] To what extent composition, translation, and dissemination of vernacular devotional texts was affected by the Lambeth Constitutions has been the subject of much scholarly debate, but certainly there is increased awareness on the parts of translators and disseminators of vernacular religious texts that their words are open to some scrutiny.[27] The anxiety of vernacularity may have been outsized in comparison to the actual threat of heretical charges, but Michael Sargent notes that there is a "potential threat [that] has its own affective existence."[28] The post-Arundel environment apparently does not hamper the translation of the text, but it may partially account for the slim evidence of any circulation of it outside of the charterhouse. It is in the coupling of the vernacularity and the visionary texts that the manuscript had at least a valence of suspicion surrounding it. It is no coincidence, for example, that the Cardinal Adam Easton first speaks against the Wycliffites (and perhaps informs the papacy about the growing English heretical movement) and is later appointed to assess Bridget of Sweden's orthodoxy; while he condemns the first and defends the latter, they are both held up to scrutiny.[29]

However, the explicit also ends with a traditional humility topos – the compiler notes that he was an unworthy and untalented translator who was only doing the bidding of his "soueryn," and should not be blamed for the errors inherent in the text. Although this portion appears to be directed at the "lettird men and clerkes," the rest of the explicit implicates a lay audience with the "men and wymmen" who are its potential readers and listeners. The address does not seem to assume they are its primary readers, though, almost as if they would be accidental. This discrepancy between the address and the text's place in Beauvale means it is possible, even likely, that a near identical version did circulate outside of the monastery and to lay readers. This manuscript shows just how many audiences, real and imagined, a medieval text might have had. Despite the seeming isolation of a manuscript that is a unique witness, we can here speculate some broader network than indicated. The explicit's gesture towards a more expansive audience may help us envision another model of circulation that does not necessarily depend on the evidence of manuscript survival. Even one additional copy outside of the cloister may have had a multitude of readers, through a kind of shared existence in the model discovered to have been the case with the so-called Common Profit books, where books were commissioned and shared among a discrete group of London laity, or have been part of a kind of lending library for poorer clergy.[30] In this model, we cannot solely judge a text's popularity or reach on the number of manuscripts, and, conversely, may see its presence in a devotional anthology as proof of a kind of prominence in a shared text.

Douce 114, Women's Visionary Literature, and the English Audience

Stephen's letter at first appears to be out of place in the manuscript to which it belongs. The codex begins with the translation of three *vitae* of beguines of the Liège diocese that share similar themes and were written in the same time and place (and that evidence demonstrates circulated together elsewhere).[31] The lives of Elizabeth of Spalbeek, Christina *mirabilis*, and Marie of Oignies are overtly mystical, contemplative texts that describe extraordinary powers of vision, prophecy, and miraculous behaviours of three thirteenth-century women from the Low Countries. Then there is Stephen's letter – written nearly one hundred years later (much more contemporary to the manuscript's first audience) – different geographically, and lacking many of the mystical qualities in the first three lives. The Suso piece, which concludes the codex, takes up approximately a third of the manuscript. But the letter's position in the manuscript and its translation into Middle English were clearly intentional. It serves both as *coda* for the grouping of women's lives and as the centre of the manuscript itself. All taken together, the texts reveal different registers of response to women's visions in the English context.

Douce 114 is an important artefact because it represents some of the relatively scarce evidence of a genre that really flourished on the Continent, that of mystical and visionary women's texts, in medieval England. Here, I am not simply using "visionary" and "mystic" interchangeably, but these are categories that frequently intersect. The visionary does "see" things; she is sent visions from God that illuminate or predict. Frequently, she understands herself or others comprehend her as a conduit, a receptacle for God's word. The mystic suggests a kind of contact with the godhead or Christ, and an affective and deeply felt emotional attachment to the divine. If there is a clear division between the two terms, I would argue that the mystic has some control over her relationship to the divine and it is directed outward, while the visionary has no control and the vision is directed inward.[32] All four women in Douce 114 (Elizabeth of Spalbeek, Christina *mirabilis*, Marie of Oignies, and Catherine of Siena) satisfy both definitions. Although English devotional texts lightly embraced a philosophy of affective piety for their women readers, the texts most espoused and disseminated did not encourage a practice attributed to either visionary or mystical literature: an unmediated relationship with God. Affective piety, conversely, focused on the human Christ and meditative texts that brought the reader closer to understanding that humanity (or the humanity of the Virgin Mary), and this tradition remains strong in England from the high Middle Ages (with, for example, the twelfth-century Ailred of Rievaulx's texts) through to the Reformation. The tradition of affective piety was similarly strong on the Continent, but there it rose concurrently and significantly overlapped with a tradition of visionary women. In the twelfth century the abbess Hildegard of Bingen had what was essentially the first in a series of documented visions and prophecies by Continental holy women that culminates with the power and controversy of Teresa of Avila centuries later.

With this proliferation of women's visionary activities came a proliferation of accompanying texts – records, *vitae*, prophecies. And while some women are charged with heresy and treated with suspicion, for example the fourteenth-century Marguerite Porete, whose *Mirror of Simple Souls* led to her execution in 1310, many of the women are celebrated as local saints and their texts widely copied and disseminated. What was treading on potentially dangerous heterodox ground in the fourteenth century developed a broader reading audience by the sixteenth century, so these fifteenth-century texts represent a reading practice in flux.[33] André Vauchez has argued that the mystic is embraced when her words and access to the divine help the cause of the powerful men who champion her, but when their role is completed, they are expected to "return to the ranks and leave the positions of leadership to the learned."[34] The official story of the saint, the *vita* or accounts, may follow this trajectory, while continued local veneration or the dissemination of more disruptive texts demonstrate some resistance to this development. This tension accounts for some of the gaps in the zeal of the original authors and hagiographers and the treatment or editing these same texts may have received from a later reader.

Porete's execution, however, was fortunately an anomaly, but still illustrates the continued tension both inside and outside the Church as to how believed and supported mystics and visionaries should be.[35] This was not necessarily gendered, although women mystics were more open to criticism and distrust. For example, the fourteenth-century Dominican mystic Meister Eckhart was roundly condemned by Pope John XXII (although after Eckhart's death). Why some visionaries are supported and some are condemned is not immediately evident; what is heresy in one may be heralded as spirituality in another. Location, gender, and institutional support all contribute to what constitute accepted mystical or visionary texts, and, as Vauchez suggests, how they support and advance influential male champions around them has a lot to do with their celebration or condemnation. These tensions surround not only the mystic herself, but the texts she produces or that are produced about her. While Porete is executed, her book continues to live on both as a heretical text and an orthodox one. We can read it as a good test case as to English treatment of women's mystical works, as it survives in Middle English translation (although unattributed to Porete, and thus assumed to be of male authorship by its scribe and annotator). Despite its survival, Michael Sargent has argued that "whether we like it or not, medieval ecclesiastical authorities were very nearly successful in annihilating Marguerite Porete's work" and that we are lucky that any evidence of it has survived.[36] He suggests that the book probably had no readers other than the Carthusians.[37] Kathryn Kerby-Fulton, who believes that the *Mirror* did reach lay audiences, writes that the glosses provided by an early reader and that continue to travel with the text betray an anxiety about its content and how it is read.[38] As with Douce 114, the Middle English *Mirror* may have been initially prepared for a wider circulation, but, met with some concerns or suspicions about the text in the hands of unprepared readers, it was kept inside a monastic context.

Middle English devotional literature was filled with accounts of visions – especially in hagiographic or meditative accounts – but the narratives of nearly contemporary visionary women was largely lacking.[39] There were some English texts that would qualify as "mystical," the writings of Richard Rolle, for example, but these, too, do not have that generic mix of hagiographic and visionary that give the personal and more immediate sense conveyed in the lives of Marie of Oignies or Christina *mirabilis*.[40] These women from the Low Countries are bringing with them and their manuscripts the spirit of the *Devotio Moderna*, a religious reform movement to return to ascetic and contemplative religious ideals; this movement was never condemned as heretical, but had much in common with the Wycliffite philosophies in England, which had been. The English reader was understandably careful with reading texts that represented this philosophical outlook. Accordingly, Kerby-Fulton outlines the various responses to texts that are not fully orthodox in medieval England: "We have, next to official censorship itself, suspicion, and in the middle, grudging tolerance, followed by tacit tolerance, then, even further along, enthusiastic tolerance, and finally, 'intolerable tolerance.' When someone's tolerance becomes intolerable to someone else, the spectrum can become a cycle."[41] The "official censorship" of the illegal translation of some theological and biblical texts as outlined in the Lambeth Constitutions may not be the primary practice (and, indeed, Kerby-Fulton is responding to Nicholas Watson's thesis here), but there remains a larger spectrum of responses to texts that do not align fully with an orthodox agenda. The texts about Catherine can fall along at nearly every point on this scale, but juxtaposed to the beguine women in Douce 114 would certainly have qualified that group for "grudging tolerance" if not outright "suspicion."

Access to this type of women's visionary literature, of course, encouraged the practice of visions themselves, so the texts that clearly had some circulation – those by or about Mechthild of Hackeborn, Bridget of Sweden, and Catherine – are often accompanied with reading directions or glosses that encourage the example of the text but discourage its practice. The most notable practising women visionaries in England, of course, are Julian of Norwich and Margery Kempe. The latter is very clear that she had heard read to her the life of Marie of Oignies and Bridget of Sweden, both women whom she took as models. It is in this context that the survival of Douce 114 with its visionary women is so important. The level of "suspicion," though, depends on the audience – there are two groups of readers, and a monastic reader's access to the texts is not nearly as fraught as a layperson's. The former reader presumably has the proper theological form in mind through which to read the visionary; the latter is far more open to misinterpretation through this unmediated access to the texts. The fact that Douce 114 is a Carthusian manuscript with an implied laity in its translation and intent allows us to read the text in these two ways. We know through library holdings and other manuscripts that the Carthusians read and seriously interacted with these visionary texts, unencumbered by a sense of subversion and protected by their maleness and monastic identity. For example, one Witham manuscript, also containing a copy of Suso's *Horologium,* has marginal citations referring to both Catherine of Siena and Mechthild of Hackeborn as analogues, demonstrating how these texts melded and intersected for the monastic reader.[42]

Stephen's letter, then, has a purpose in following the three notably different beguine lives, and in encouraging an intersectional reading practice. Barry Windeatt reads into the group of four, particularly with Catherine's placement as last, as an endorsement of a kind of mystical contemplation encouraged among the Carthusian readers. He writes:

> The letter about the much more contemporary figure of Catherine of Siena even describes her preaching "ful quykke and speful sermons" to two popes and assorted cardinals … If this seems a world away from the clumsy clerical suspicion of Kempe's discourse as preaching, it demonstrates – along with the larger interest in an intense para-mystical spirituality of the beguines – just how adventurously receptive and risk-taking might be some knowledgeable English Carthusian students of contemplative life. Concluding the collection with a letter about the modern Catherine of Siena, with its authenticity from personal acquaintance, serves to update how the three beguine lives are also presented as if from intimate knowledge and brings all these remarkable holy women's accomplishment into the present as a dynamic possibility and example for "alle men and wymmen þat in happe rediþ or heriþ þis englyshe" and hence for a readership beyond the translator's circle and control.[43]

The effect of ending with Catherine does, as Windeatt suggests, "update" how the beguine lives may be read and, in effect, lived by the reader. Eschewing the ecstatic and physical devotion of Christina (whose mortifications involved throwing herself into an oven and freezing waters), Elizabeth (a stigmatic who re-enacted the Passion on a daily basis), and Marie (who cut out and hid chunks of her flesh), Catherine is presented as an almost sedate alternative whose meditative prayer-trances numb her to external pain and activity. For the Carthusian readers of Catherine's life who are personally and professionally connected to its author, the text reinforces a one-degree of connection to the saint and her "realness" – a quality perhaps absent from the three previous lives and even from the *Horologium* of Henry Suso, who had died in 1366, around three-quarters of a century prior to the manuscript's creation.

Catherine's mystical qualities, obvious in other accounts of her life and her own writings, are notably absent from Maconi's letter. His construction of Catherine is written in response to suspicions about her holiness, a kind of *probatio* responding to the criticisms her legacy faced after her death. The stripping of her visionary elements here serves not only to cement her position as an important saint but also to validate the other women in the collection. Her juxtaposition to the more exuberant mysticism of the beguines marks her as being along the same lines, but the letter itself shows a more subdued piety. More importantly to the Carthusian readers of Douce 114, though, is Stephen Maconi's authorization of the woman and the text that are both essential elements for understanding how it might have been read within and outside the monastic context. As Prior General of the Carthusian's *Grande Chartreuse* during the schism, he carries an especially weighty authority for his monastic readers.

Adapting Catherine for the Cloister

The Carthusians who read Stephen Maconi's letter within Douce 114 would have had an additional reason for doing so as the manuscript draws an explicit connection between the saint and the order. The letter would have offered a spiritual balm that may have appealed most directly to novice or young monks still adjusting to the monastic life, giving them a maternal figure in a life that was devoid of one. To understand what the Carthusians may have seen in Stephen's letter concerning Catherine (besides his own Carthusian affiliations), especially with the more prestigious and official Raymond of Capua *Legenda major* in circulation, one must first look at Stephen's relationship to Catherine. He very clearly saw himself as Catherine's son, a fact that comes through strongly in Maconi's narrative and in Catherine's own letters; a sentiment that Catherine reinforced among her followers, the *famiglia* who called her "mama." Maconi joined Catherine on her journey to Avignon in July of 1376, and one of the first letters we have from this time is Catherine's to Maconi's mother, Giovanna di Corrado Maconi, who apparently had written to Catherine complaining about the absence of her son. Catherine reminds Giovanna that God's servants must leave their families in order to serve him, and then she writes: "I want you, I beg you for the love of the slain Lamb, to use this knowledge to assuage the grief and heartache you have felt because of Stephen's departure. Be glad! Be happy! For this will surely make his soul and yours grow in grace."[44]

Later, in November, upon their return to Italy, Catherine again writes to his mother, scolding her for loving her children over God and reminding her that Maconi needs to leave his family in order to serve the divine will. She closes with this passage:

> Be patient, and don't be disturbed that I've kept Stefano so long, for I've taken good care of him. I've become one with you in love and affection, and so I've taken what belongs to you as if it were my own! I trust you haven't minded too much. I want to do all I can for you and for him, even to the point of death. You, his mother, gave birth to him once; now I want to give birth to him and to you and to your whole family in tears and in sweat, by my constant prayers and desire for your salvation.[45]

That Catherine saw Maconi as a kind of son is obvious by these letters; she fashions her image as a replacement for Giovanna both metaphorically and literally ("I've become one with you in love and affection"), even claiming the right to "give birth" to him again. She positions herself as a kind of universal mother, empowered by her special relationship to God, which offers salvation both to Maconi and to Giovanna.

Maconi's letter, written retrospectively when he was the head of the *Grande Chartreuse*, was written to a Dominican priest in Venice and was originally part of a much fuller and more official document. Catherine's canonization was a long and fraught process, complicated by the papal schism, the view of women visionaries, the difficulty of getting Bridget of Sweden canonized, and the various and sometimes competing strategies of Catherine's supporters.[46] Catherine's follower and the author of several texts concerning Catherine, Thomas Caffarini, had started the wheels in motion for her canonization soon after her death in 1380 and in earnest in 1398 in Venice, where he was based after he had founded there and become director of a convent of Venetian *mantellatae* (the Dominican third order to which Catherine belonged). But Caffarini and Catherine's other supporters were facing considerable obstacles in the attempt to canonize Catherine, led by theologians such as Jean Gerson who explicitly blamed Catherine (and Bridget of Sweden) for encouraging the pope's move to Rome, which precipitated the schism. When Caffarini moved some of Catherine's relics to Venice and began celebrating Catherine as a saint in fact, it prompted seven prominent petitioners to demand a full investigation of her veracity and possible sainthood in order to bring calm and closure to what was an increasingly unsettling debate, formally petitioning the bishop of Castello.[47] The enquiry known as *Il Processo Castellano*, so named because it was at the behest of Bishop Francesco Bembo of Castello, was to determine whether local activities dedicated to Catherine and the veneration of her relics could continue without an official papal recognition of sainthood. The letters collected for this purpose, Maconi's among them, were eventually used to secure Catherine's canonization in 1461.[48] Much of this context is redacted from the Middle English version presented in Douce 114. In Italian codices that contain the letters and documents of *Il Processo Castellano* in full, and in which Maconi's letter is the third of twenty-six testimonies, his text is preceded with an introductory paragraph, explaining that he heeded the call to respond and explain the virtues of Catherine. He alludes to Matthew 5:15 that, just as men do not put a candle under a bushel, Maconi is putting his light on a candlestick to illuminate the world.[49] The final paragraph, too, is missing from the translated text. In this, several witnesses to Maconi's letter sign their names and credentials, validating the words he had written.[50] Otherwise, however, the translator is mostly faithful to the Latin, omitting little and staying true to the spirit and meaning of his words.

Although much of Maconi's letter focuses on Catherine's virtue and some of her miracles (and is also, as he is aware, meant to be presenting "in open forme, trewe informacyone of the dedys, maners, vertues, and doctrines of famos holynesse of the virgyn blyssed Kateryn of Senys"), the letter is also touchingly personal and gives insight into how Maconi responded to Catherine's maternal attentions and the separation from his family.[51] He recollects joining Catherine's travelling group to Avignon, where she petitioned Gregory XI for the papacy's return to Rome, and recounts a private conversation he had with Catherine just prior to that time where she predicts he will leave his life behind to join her group of followers:

> Forsooth, a litil while after, the forseyde holy virgyn seyde to me in priuite, "wite thou ful wele, beloued sone, that the most desyre that thou has shal be sone fulfilled." I perceyued that and was sumwhat astonyed, for I coude not fynde what I wolde haue in the worlde, but rather I forsoke alle worldly godes. Therfore I seyde: "O ful dere modir, I prey yow what is the moste desyre that I haue?" "Seke thou," quod she, "in thy herte." And I answeryd to hir: "Soothly most byloued moder, I can fynde no gretter desyre in me than to be contynuelly nere yow." And sodenly she answeryd, "and that shal be." Forsothe, I coude not vndirstonde the maner how it myghte so be, honestly or vantagely, for vnlikly condycyone of either state. Hee, soothly, to whome nothinge is impossibil, thurgh a

meruelous maner, ordeyned hir to go to a certeyne place to oure lorde Gregore, Pope Elleuenth. And so, thof I vnworthy, was accepte felowe of so holy a company, litille settynge by and leuynge my fader and my moder, brether, sister, and alle my cosyns, countynge myselfe blessyd for the virgyns presens.[52]

Maconi's account is remarkably reflective of Catherine's own letter to Giovanna, his mother, about his need to leave parents and family, but it also establishes Catherine as his new "mother" and shows him entering an alternative familial structure in the fellowship of the Avignon group. To the English medieval reader, particularly the monastic one, this letter underscores the replacement of a biological family with a spiritual one. In addition, Stephen's letter alludes to Matthew 19:29: "And every one that hath left house, or brethren, or sisters, or father, or mother, or wife, or children, or lands for my name's sake, shall receive an hundredfold, and shall possess life everlasting," likening Catherine to Christ for whom her followers leave their families. While Maconi's mother insisted that he did not need to leave the world in order to serve God, his call to serve Catherine and ultimately the Carthusians overrides his own mother's wishes. The fact that the letter is in English may have appealed to lay brothers or novices with little or no Latin, but it would have been read by a broad audience of Carthusians, who number among their texts several in the vernacular.[53] The letter has a twofold purpose: to give a spiritual mother figure to men whose real mothers may be absent, and to reinforce the notion of a new spiritual family that replaces the earthly one. Thus Catherine becomes an amalgam of Mary, Christ, mother, and father to Maconi and – by extension – to his readers.

Although the Catherine that is presented here is one that is lightly prophetic and visionary (she knows Maconi's desires even though he cannot articulate them himself; she seems to know in advance that they will be travelling to see the pope in Avignon), this is not the focus of the passage nor of his recollection of Catherine. For him, the real astonishment is in his own recognition that he wants nothing other than to be near Catherine, "I ... was sumwhat astonyed, for I coude not fynde what I wolde haue in the worlde, but rather I forsoke alle worldly godes." Telling her, "Soothly most byloued moder, I can fynde no gretter desyre in me than to be contynuelly nere yow." For Maconi, Catherine's real gift is in allowing him to have his own self-knowledge of the life he wants to lead. For the monastic reader, this is an affirmation of a calling or desire to live an ascetic and pious life, as the Carthusians had the reputation of being one of the strictest orders, devoted as it was to an eremitical ideal and contemplation.

Maconi follows this memory of joining Catherine's group with her deathbed demand that he join the Carthusian order, despite the fact that nearly all of her companions, and Catherine herself, were affiliated with the Dominicans. This point is not inconsequential; the Dominicans were also most prominent in spreading texts concerning Catherine and her cult, but Stephen's dual role as Catherine supporter and Carthusian is part of the power and authority of his testimony:

> Soothly, while she labored in hir laste ende, she ordeyned with summe men what they shulde do after hir passynge. Afterward, turnynge hir visage to me, she seyde (and strecchyng forth hir fyngyr): "Forsothe, I bydde the on Goddes byhalue and in vertue of obedyens that on alle maner wyse, thou go to the Charteus ordyr.[54] He hath called and chosen the" … And as she byhighte with mouthe that worde, so she felled fully in dede … For whanne she badde me of obedyens of God that I schulde go to the Charteus ordyr, I desyred not to entir that ordyr or any other. But sithen she was gon to God siche desyre was kyndelyd in my herte to do that biddynge, that if alle the worlde wolde haue agayne seyde me, I myghte no wise haue graunted. As experiens techyd in the whiche ordyr, how mykel and what she hath wroghte and yit wirketh with hir sone, thof vnprofitabil and vnworthy; hit is not this tyme to telle.[55]

Again, there are several points of interest here to the Carthusian audience. First, of course, is Catherine's nearly final request that one of her favourite confidants and followers should enter the order. He did not obey his real mother, Giovanna, in her desire for him to stay home, but here he responds to his spiritual mother's request to enter a Carthusian charterhouse. Further, he writes that he had no desire "to enter that order or any other," a sentiment surely shared by many young men upon entering the monastic life, but he responds to the call of both Catherine and God after her death. The translator replaces the more poetic Latin phrase describing Catherine's death as a movement "ad ethereas mansiones," or to "ethereal mansions," simply with "she was gon to God," but otherwise remains true to the text.

This "spiritual mother," albeit textual, may be a necessary feminine presence in what is a delineated male space. Maconi's letter serves as a mirror for these young men and also guides them to a mother figure, Catherine, to mentor them as he was mentored. He later tells us that this letter is written when he is sixty years old – in 1411 – thirty-one years after Catherine's death, a testament to the kind of power Catherine continued to have over his life. Maconi concludes this section by ascribing nearly all of his spiritual fervour to Catherine (third only to God and the Virgin Mary), and reminding his readers of not only her importance in his life but also his in hers. In this way, he validates what he is saying about Catherine and simultaneously authorizes himself through Catherine's approval:

> Neuertheles, this dare I seye: that after God and the blessed Virgyn Mary, I trowe … more bounden to the holy virgyne Kateryn than to eny creature of the worlde. And if oght of gode were in me, I rette alle to hir aftir God. Hit may be perceyued by scripture that I haue hadde summe yeeres more thanne many other men ful homely conuersacyone of hir in writynge lettirs and hir priuetis and parte of hir boke – the which I wrote after hir owne maydenly mouthe. For abouen my deseruynge, she loued me ful affectuosly with moderly charyte so that many of hir sones bare hit heuy and hadde a maner of envye.[56]

Maconi highlights his intimacy with Catherine, reminding the Dominican recipient of his letter of what he no doubt already knew: that Maconi served as Catherine's amanuensis for her *Dialogo*. In addition, if there is any doubt that he was special to Catherine, he dispels it with his last comment here that many of her other "sons" bore his favouritism badly and were envious of his connection to Catherine. In this way, the choice of the Carthusian order becomes special. It is the chosen destination for Catherine's chosen follower. The spiritual mother of Catherine is here coupled with the Virgin Mary, invoking two "mother figures" for men who have no shortage of father figures in God, Jesus, the pope, and all the hierarchy of their order from the prior downward.

Carthusian readers may have been the unexpected recipients of the translated text represented in Douce 114, but in some sense they were an even more appropriate audience than either lay men, women, or the original dignitaries addressed in Maconi's petition. The testimony offered both spiritual and personal guidance to the Carthusian brothers, and its vernacularity perhaps made it seem even more familiar, more individual to these readers. The power of Catherine and the significance of Maconi's letter are attested to in the speed with which it is disseminated, translated, and copied. Douce 114 is dated between 1425 and 1450, only decades after Stephen penned his text and a mere decade before Catherine's canonization. If the dating on the earliest side is correct, this would be the earliest English text we have concerning Catherine, as most are dated mid- to late fifteenth century. The manuscript's transmission is clearly linked to Maconi's important position in the Carthusian order and his agenda for transmitting texts, but also helps situate how English women's visionary texts were read in a monastic context.

Converting the Doubters and Making a Saint

Stephen Maconi's letter is intended to support the bid for Catherine's contested canonization, and part of his agenda aims to assure his readers that Catherine's powers were authentic and divinely inspired. While the letter reaches England nearly simultaneously with Catherine's eventual canonization, it is written when such an outcome was far from a sure thing, and the tone of the letter – the defence – would have helped authorize women's visionary texts generally and Catherine's more mystical literature specifically. The letter was not a routine hagiographic recounting of a saint's miraculous abilities, but rather the justification of that sainthood as part of the Bishop of Castello's inquiry. As noted earlier, *Il Processo Castellano* lasted from 1411 to 1416, so Maconi's letter is one of the first entries into what would become its corpus, dated at 1411.[57] This bid was unsuccessful and Catherine was not canonized until much later, but it is this "quarelle made at Venese in the byshopes palys anens the halowynge of the feste or commemoracyone of the same virgyn" that has prompted Maconi's testimony.[58] He recognizes that it is a "quarelle" (*querele* in Latin, which can also mean "grievance") in which he is participating, and he is offering evidence to be used within that debate.[59] The factuality of his account is actually important to his readers, and he knows it. His writing represents the process of making Catherine into Saint Catherine. George Ferzoco notes that a feature of the testimonies given at *Il Processo Castellano* indicates "a primary concern of Catherine's promoters may have been that someone might attach her teaching, especially regarding two fraught issues: the legitimacy of the pope and his rightful place in Rome; and the holy woman's ecstasies."[60] In this way, Stephen's letter fits in with works that were being disseminated through England. Kerby-Fulton has suggested that works that emphasized *probatio* and *discretio spirituum* (a genre we will look at more closely in chapter 3) flourished as a process of eliminating ambiguity as to "where the theology implied in a vision deviated from biblical or established church doctrine," and while not a formal *probatio*, Maconi's letter has many of its elements.[61] This has the dual purpose of addressing his original audience's concerns about Catherine as saint and the later English audience's anxieties surrounding women's visionary texts.

Maconi spends a little time on Catherine's miraculous abilities, powers that her hagiographer Raymond of Capua had largely ignored.[62] For example, he is careful to explain what happened during her moments of ravishment where she would become transfixed, stiff, and unmoving:

> Sothly, if she were compellyd sumtyme to her doynges of the world or vnprofitabil woordes to soule hele, she was sodeynly rauyshed in swogh of hir body, abode there withouten any felynge as beynge in prayer. In that maner ilke a daye she was raueshed, as wee sawe oure selfe. I seye not a hundreth or a thousande sythes, but mykel more oftener. Hir membres abode stille, alle starke and vnmouabil, so that the bones firste myghte a bristen, than hir membris myghte be bowed.[63]

Rather than focus too specifically on recounting many of the miraculous activities in Catherine's life, thus making her worthy of reverence and sainthood, Maconi instead repetitively references the notions of witness and amazement, validation at the forefront of his missive. Catherine's ravishment, which causes such stiffness in body that her bones seem literally about to break, was seen by "oure self," and not merely once, not even "a hundreth or a thousande sythes," but even more frequently. Catherine's miraculous state is, in fact, her normal state of being.

Although much of his insistence on veracity, as we shall see, invokes male clerical witness of the miracles and holy moments he describes, Maconi recounts one moment that would have been conversely resonant to the doubting woman lay reader. While in Avignon, he writes that the pope's sister and her daughter-in-law attended mass with Catherine. While the sister was devout, the daughter-in-law was vain and doubtful of Catherine, who had entered a trance during the service. This doubting daughter-in-law decided to test the veracity of her transcendence:

> Sothly sche [the daughter-in-law], that wrecche as I trowe, thoghte that the virgyn feyned. Therfore, after masse; sche shewed of deuocyone to putte hir face vndir the fete and pricked hir fulle sharply with a nedil in the fete

many tymes.[64] But she stode stille vnmoued, for so hadde she stonden thof she hadde cut of the fete. And after alle were gone, and the virgyne come ageyne to hir bodily wittes, hir fote bygan to ake sore so that she myghte vnnethes walke. Thanne wymen that were with hir in cumpany loked where the ake was and they sawe deed blode[65] of prickynge and vndirstode openly the malyce and vnbileue of hir, that wrecche.[66]

This scene seemingly takes place in a predominantly male space (in Avignon at the papal court, during a mass), yet Maconi has framed this entire account by the women involved. This is no small thing, as many of Catherine's followers were male, and certainly that made up the pre-dominance of travellers along with her to Avignon. But in this moment the actors are not the pope, nor Catherine's confessors, nor even Stephen himself. Instead, in addition to Catherine, we have the pope's sister, the sister's daughter-in-law, and the women who "were with [Catherine] in cumpany." There are other ways in which this moment is gendered femi-nine – the wielded weapon is a needle. Maconi uses this moment to illus-trate the veracity of Catherine's meditative and transcended state. Her body was on earth, but without feeling, because her soul was soaring in prayer. Sarah Macmillan has suggested that the compiler of Douce 114 moves from the bodily mortification of the beguines towards a philoso-phy of asceticism with Catherine; Suso closes the collection, contrast-ing Catherine's demonstration of "love rather than bodily mortification" with Suso's complete transcendence of the body.[67] Yet, here, we see a Catherine that has unwittingly subjected herself to bodily mortification because of her deep meditative state. Rather than an *exemplum*, where the reader should follow Catherine's example, this incident warns against being the "wrecche" of the daughter-in-law. Although she accuses Catherine of "feigning," she is the one who "shewed of deuocyone" in a moment of deception. Although Maconi is writing what seems to be a letter to only one man, he understands that the letter will have a broader public audience and agenda. He also seems to intuit a female audience as the potential doubters. Surely, for a member of the Church hierarchy, he would do better with recounting the papacy's and various bishops' endorsement of Catherine and her miracles (which he does as well, but not in such a specific anecdote), but this story and its elements are about the common woman, her doubt, and how Catherine counters it.

Maconi acknowledges that he could have chosen from several exam-ples to convince his reader of Catherine's authenticity, so it is telling that this is the one he opted to recount. He concludes the description of the episode, explaining that the true miracle of her ravishment were the moments where she would literally levitate off the ground in her state of prayer: "Anens the whiche raueshid a state of hir or grete meruel is not to be lafte, but to be thoghte on with a dewe worship. For namely whan hir soule trauelyd hitselfe feruently in prayer with summe hye thinges and harde, and bisyed hit to ascende with grete strengthe, hit reryd vppe the heuynesse of the body from the erthe."[68] Notably, the Latin is clearer here about what actually happens to Catherine, noting, "gravedinem etiam corporis a terra sublevabat," the weight of her body is raised up from the earth. The Middle English "reren," used here, while having the meaning of to raise up, also has a more common understanding of sitting up or to be raised up in a passive sense.[69] This miraculous activity is not out of place in the collection of women's hagiographies in Douce 114. Catherine's textual neighbour Christina *mirabilis*, for example, earns her epithet by flying to the rafter of a Church at her own funeral (from which she resurrects). The activity is out of place, however, in the English textual remnants of Catherine's life. Most of the miraculous activities of Catherine's life and post-mortem are recorded in sources that are never translated (such as other testimonies in *Il Processo Castellano* and Caffarini's *Libellus de supplemento*).

Maconi ends his letter with a *coda*, swearing again to the veracity of his account. Here, he invokes the safety of his own soul in the truth of his words, pointing to the witnesses and the purpose of the letter. In contrast with the earlier testimony of the women surrounding Catherine, the witnesses he calls on at the end of the letter are implied to be the monks he shepherds at the *Grande Chartreuse*, all male authorities. He begins by swearing to his truthful words:

> Also god forbede fro the clennes of my consciens that I wolde wityngely and ageyne conscyens modil any othere thinge amonge any maner wordes of myne than the sympil sooth. For I woot that the mouthe that lyeth slees the soule, ne gode nedes to haue oure lesynges, ne sum yuel dedis are not to be done that therof shulde come gode. Therfore ful certeyn be yee that I haue seyde the selfe sothe tellyng that atte is writen aboue and affermynge the treuthe for the whiche not oonly I prefir othe after your askynge and offer me redy to swere vndir any fourme that is expedyent.[70]

The phrasing is interesting here, noting that there may be suspicion among his readers of mendacity in order to insure Catherine's sainthood. He assures his readers that lying would put his own soul in peril and, more importantly, that even if the end was Catherine's canonization (the "gode" he is hopeful for), it neither justifies the means of "lesynges" nor "yuel dedis."

Further confirming the truth of his statement, Maconi ends with an invocation of not only witnesses, but notaries and the application of his seal, to validate the text.[71] He ends with hyperbole to banish his doubters – that he would put his hands in the fire in order to confirm the truth of his words. Here, the translator has condensed several identifications of named witnesses and testimonies to the truth of Maconi's words, and instead reformulated the ending to be in Maconi's own voice swearing to that fact:

> But that more is as I so seye, for siche a sothe to be confermed and to the worshyp and edifcacyon comforte and hele of myne euen cristen, I am redy to putte my handes in the fyre, as he wel wote to whome no thinge is hydde – to the whiche is louvynge worshep and ioye with outen ende amen. Writen in the hous byfore seyde the xx vj daye of October, in the yeere of oure lorde MC[C]CCXI vndir the open hande of two notaryes in presens of many witnesses and with appensyone of oure gret couente seel to the testymone of trewthe and atte I shulde fulfille youre askynge.[72]

Such insistence on validity proved to be necessary, however, as Catherine's canonization was so contested after the schism and the blame so intense that both she and Bridget bore for its aftermath. Opposed and dismissed by major theologians such as Jean Gerson and other detractors as a woman led by false visions and great imagination, Catherine needed the support of powerful men like Stephen Maconi and her confessor, the Master General of the Dominicans, Raymond of Capua, in order to get the canonization she ultimately did (and well after their deaths).[73] With both Carthusian and Dominican support, some major orders were behind Catherine's sainthood and ultimately won the battle for her legacy. While the English manuscript is removed from this political turmoil, the insistence on validity takes on a new valence when considered against a backdrop of suspicion of women's visionary and affective powers. For the readers of Douce 114, Maconi's repeated emphasis on witness serves to validate the manuscript's contents as a whole.

A Political Catherine, Douce 114, and English Readers

In addition to emphasizing the validity of his account, Stephen Maconi strives against a perception of Catherine as too political, too mobile, too outspoken. Her association with the Dominican *mantellatae* strengthened this impression on the Continent, although it may have not held any strong association for the English readers who had no English equivalent.[74] However, Stephen simultaneously frames his discussion of Catherine at a centrally political event in her life, the trip to Avignon to convince Pope Gregory XI to return to Rome. He manages this balance by discussing Catherine's piety on the trip, not her purpose, and insisting on her overall devotional purity. The tension between the pious Catherine and the political one reflects many of the contradictions for which Catherine stands, and lays bare the more obvious tensions surrounding the authenticity of her visions, prominently questioned by some contemporary theologians. The way that Maconi's letter negotiates the balance of the former tension illustrates the way a reader may understand the latter.

Maconi draws on his position and age to insist on Catherine's holiness, while employing carefully chosen vocabulary to depict her as a passive recipient of her gifts and abilities, not acting upon her own authority or agency:

> Neuertheless, I consideryd bisily with grete diligens, wordes, maners, dedys of hir in alle thinges, lesse and more. And for my wille is to conclude mykel in a litil on my conscience byfore God and alle Holy Chirche, I bere hir trewly this witnesse: that thof I wote myselfe a synner, neuertheles, I haue hadde sexty yeere gon and more knowleche of many and ful famose seruants of God and euere sawe or herde of mykelle here byfore any Goddes seruaunte that hath ben in ilke a vertue in so ful, parfyte, and hye degre. Wherfore as worthy was, she was countyd of alle men an ymage of alle vertues and moste brighte myrrour of Goddes god men.[75]

The Catherine that Maconi presents here is a servant of God, whose most important attribute is virtue; she is perfect in it, a bright mirror, above other "ful famose seruants of God," that the readers may have known. This passage also challenges Catherine's gender, particularly in its translation. The Latin "servorum Dei" (servants of God) is translated here as "Goddes god men." Of course, someone's "man" can be his "servant," but the change is intentional. The goodness she is reflecting is here gendered male in a way that it is not in the original. Her reflected goodness is literally a *virtue*, from the Latin *vir*, meaning man. The fact that she is a "servant," an "image" (or *simulacrum*), and a "mirror" removes Catherine's subjectivity entirely – she is not the actor, but the acted upon – and truly frames her as a vessel of goodness and piety. Not a subject in herself, Catherine is a reflection of the real (and only) subject, God. Her political agency and visionary activities are not at the forefront.

Drawing attention to Catherine's use and reliance on confession, Maconi underscores what would not have been lost on its later English audience where confession was emphasized in the face of any perceived Wycliffite challenges to the sacrament. Here, Catherine's miracle entails knowing a supplicant's sins and convincing him that confession is the only remedy:

> Wherefore for so grete fruyte of soulles that she didde in siche maters, Pope Gregore elleuenth gracyously graunted to hir to haue contynuelly with hir three confessorous, with ful grete auctorite. Neuertheless, sumtyme come hir summe synners so harde bounden of the fende that they withstode hir on all wyse and seyde, "Soothly, lady, if yee seyde to me that I shulde go to Rome or to Seynte James, I would fulfille hit withouten fayle. But of this poynte of confessyone, I praye yow, spare me, for I maye not." Atte last, whan she myghte not ouercome hym noon other maner, she seyde to hym in priuite: "If I telle the cause wherfore thou wilte not be confessed, wilte thou be confessed after." Than hee, as astonyed and ouercomen, byhighte to do so. And she seyde thanne: "Ful dere brother, we maye othere while bihidde from mennes yen, but neuuere fro the sighte of god. Therfore, siche a synne that thou didist in siche tyme and siche place is that where thurgh the fende so confoundys thy thoghte siche a manere that hee latis the not be confessyd." And he, seyng hymselfe so taken, felle downe ful lowely at hire feet with mykel wepynge, askynge forgifnes and forthwith was confessed.[76]

Here, Catherine privileges confession, a sacrament, above other practised forms of penance (such as pilgrimage to either Rome or Compostela), and posits it as the ultimate form of defence against a wily devil lying in wait for the souls of men. She also lays out a kind of circular logic for the sinner (and, by extension, for the reader) that God already knows our sin, so the confession is not a surprise to him, but a conscience cleansing of the soul. It takes Catherine's miraculous understanding of the sin to convince the sinner to repent, demonstrating to Maconi's readers Catherine's close relationship to God (she knows the man's sins) and her profound effect on the people (she convinces them to confess).

However, Maconi cannot fully avoid the political and social Catherine – it is, after all, who she was – and that Catherine is likewise described in his letter. Although the letter is following on the heels of descriptions of extremely overt visionary and mystical women, it de-emphasizes Catherine's visionary abilities and focuses more on her devotion and actions in Avignon. Following the three beguine narratives that precede it, the letter in effect closes the sequence with the least subversive of the three. Catherine's text here is used as a kind of validation of women's visionary experience without itself being particularly visionary. It emphasizes her power and communication with important men, and her ability to impress them. In one episode, three advisers of the pope, including an archbishop, go to confront Catherine and prove that she is unworthy to speak to him. The status of the men is not incidental; indeed, Maconi recounts that the pope's doctor tells him that "if the comynge of hem three were layde in o balauns and the comynge of alle that are in the courte of Rome were layde in another, the comynge of tho three wolde weye mykel heuyer."[77] This impressive description is not lost on the reader of Douce 114 who placed a carat in the margin of the manuscript (one of very few notes of marginalia in the entire codex). The men who come to question Catherine are not charging her visionary experience, although they bring it up, but are most concerned at her audacity in speaking to the pope about political matters; her purpose there, to convince the papacy to return to Rome from Avignon, is never explicitly mentioned, only hinted at. They say to her: "We haue mykel meruel sethen thou arte a vile litil womman that thou takith vpon the to speke of so grete a mater with oure lorde the Pope."[78] Catherine's status as a "vile little woman" is contrasted to the "great matter" of which she speaks. Gender, and the fact that women should not be politically engaged, is clearly the qualifier that is upsetting the bishops most here, not her visions.

Unsatisfied, the men test her, clearly suspicious of both her abilities and her intelligence, shaming her confessor who cannot answer the logical questions they pose, while Catherine (just moments before described by the questioners as a "vile woman") does so deftly. She teaches without preaching, demonstrating her theological and intellectual superiority to the pope's advisers, but maintaining humility. She is questioned about her ravishment and her lifestyle, and is also asked about how she can tell good spirits from bad, a question she answers in her own writings in the form of *discretio spirituum* both in her *Dialogo* and through Raymond of Capua in her *vita*.[79] The presence of that question here demonstrates just how fully it was on the mind of her detractors and those suspicious of her visionary claims. Catherine maintains both her piety and her political aims, being both "meke" and "enlumyned" for her testers:

> They put to hir ful grete questyons and many namely of hir abstraccyons and raueshynge and maner of most singulerly liuyng. And sythen the apostil seith that the aungel of the fende transfiguris hym into an aungel of lighte, how she wote or noon whether she be deceyued of the deuel. And many other they seyde and purposed to her. And in effecte the disputacyone lasted to the nyghte. Otherewhile Maister John [her confessor] wolde haue answeryd for hir, and thof he were maister in dyuynite, neuertheles they were so myghty that in a fewe wordes they confoundid hym and seyde "yee aghte to be ashamed to sey siche wordes in oure presens. Late hir answere, for she answers vs mykel better than yee" … Atte laste they wente alle hir weye booth edifyed and comfortyd, tellynge oure lorde the Pope that they neuere fonde soule so meke nor so enlumyned.[80]

The bishops' conclusion is abrupt, but in the end the bishops are not only convinced of Catherine's holiness and devotion, but they themselves have been "edifyed" in the process. Catherine has passed their test. The only woman of the four in Douce 114 who was canonized and the only one whose power and cult extended far beyond her local area, Catherine is presented as a teacher and theologian, not as a visionary. She faces considerable opposition, embodied in the archbishop and his companions who are surrounding the pope, but she bests even her confessor in the discussion and they leave convinced of her enlightenment – not her divine powers.

The triple audience of the manuscript (the intended readers of *Il Processo Castellano*, the lay audience of men and women, and the Carthusians of Beauvale Charterhouse) have the spectre of Catherine's heterodoxy raised and acquitted within the context of Stephen's text. Each audience has a new challenge in terms of Catherine. The first audience at *Il Processo Castellano* questions and must be convinced of her sanctity. The second of vernacular lay readers must read her in terms of the visionary women to which she is juxtaposed, where her political activities soften their extreme asceticism, and their asceticism counters her politics. Finally, the Carthusians read her visions as tempered by her edifying theological outlook, examined and ratified by the bishops and the pope. What works for the original readers continues to work for later ones even though the context and cultural anxieties have shifted.

Douce 114 and Catherine Texts in England

Stephen Maconi's letter and Douce 114 both represent many of the aspects of all the texts concerning Catherine of Siena in late medieval and early modern England. Some of the English interest may have been due less to her role in moving the papacy back to Rome and more to her role in moving it out of France. The earliest extant English manuscripts are from the first quarter of the fifteenth century, following very closely on Henry V's successes in Harfleur and Agincourt, turning points in England's favour during the Hundred Years' War. However, the bulk of the surviving manuscripts concerning Catherine are from the mid-1450s and later, after England had lost France, a loss that began with another famous visionary woman, Joan of Arc, and her victory in Orleans in 1428–9 and that ended fairly decisively in 1453 with the battle of Castillon. A late fifteenth-century English reader may very well harbour significant anti-French sentiment, and the fact that Catherine is credited with convincing Pope Gregory XI to move the Church from France back to Rome may have helped disseminate her text. Just a generation earlier, Richard II had strongly supported Urban as pope and Rome as the papal seat for various political and religious reasons, not least because of anti-French sentiment.[81] For this reason, a text so closely concerned with Catherine's mission in Avignon, such as Maconi's letter, may have found an audience outside of the cloister.

Maconi's letter is ultimately disseminated and translated because of invested male interest in Catherine and the spread of her cult. This will be the case with William Flete's "The Cleannesse of Sowle" and Raymond of Capua's *The Lyf of Saint Katherin of Senis*, as well. Maconi's translated letter appears to have had both monastic and lay readers in intent (if not in practice), as have nearly all of the extant English Catherine texts. And, although it in itself is a complete work about Catherine, like *The Lyf* and the *The Orcherd of Syon*, it is one that has been anthologized and put in a compilation that is meant to be part of a broader devotional context. This process of compilation will be part of the presentation and distribution of all copies of "The Cleannesse of Sowle" as well as some excerpts from *The Lyf* and *The Orcherd of Syon*. As the earliest of Catherine's texts, transmitted and translated only a few decades after Catherine's death, it establishes an early English interest in the saint and serves as a paradigm for all the texts to follow.

It is appropriate to begin with Maconi's letter, too, as he himself is probably a gateway by which so many of the Catherine texts reached England. By the end of the fifteenth century, Catherine and her texts will be fully part of the corpus of English devotional literature, and although she will never reach the heights that Bridget of Sweden does in England, she will become one of the only visionary women to have any kind of real presence there. As these texts are copied, disseminated, translated, and printed, Catherine will not be some far-off Italian saint to her readers, but an English one who mirrors the contemporary devotional ethos. Her temporal proximity to her readers, so much more so than most of the other saints whose hagiographies were popular throughout England, makes her a compelling model of a visionary, a politician, and a pious ascetic, all at once. But as with Maconi's letter, each new and unanticipated audience must contend with and make meaning from all of the tensions and contradictions that the multifaceted Catherine brings with her into the text.

Chapter Two

William Flete, English Spirituality, and Catherine of Siena[1]

William Flete: Mentoring Catherine

A young scholar, well on his way to earning an advanced degree at Cambridge University, became disillusioned with the academic life, disgusted by the cut-throat attitudes of his seniors, and called into question his very vocation as a man of letters and of God. He took a year off just before finishing his doctorate of theology and chose to reflect and write about his convictions instead. It was 1357, and it was during this time that William Flete (d. c. 1390), an Austin Friar, wrote his *Remedies against Temptations* (*De remediis contra temptaciones*), decided to commit himself to the hermetical life, and soon after departed to the strict Augustinian monastery known as Lecceto near Siena, Italy.[2] While she was only ten years old at the time and would far eclipse him in the annals of history, it was here that Flete first met Catherine of Sienna. It was here, too, that Catherine's English story actually began.

Flete, also known as "William of England" or sometimes the "Bachelor of Lecceto" (for his scholarly credentials), remains largely absent from accounts of Catherine's life and is omitted completely in any analyses of her English textual afterlife. Robert Fawtier, a historiographer and Catherine scholar of the early twentieth century, notes that much of his life is obscure, not least because the many texts concerning Catherine mention him only in passing.[3] Although Benedict Hackett rehabilitated Flete to his importance in Catherine's life through several articles and a book, scholars who work on Catherine persist in overlooking his influence on her life. Various sources put Flete's and Catherine's first face-to-face meeting anywhere from 1368 to 1374, but it is clear that they had correspondence early in Catherine's theological formation and that he advised her spiritually before she met her more well-known adviser and confessor, Raymond of Capua (who would later write her *Legenda major*).[4] The earliest extant letter from Catherine to William is dated from 1375, but its familiar and intimate tone indicate a long-standing relationship.[5] Either way, Flete plays a role in the earliest accounts of Catherine's life and activities. The anonymous *Miracoli* of Catherine of Siena, the only lengthy contemporary account of Catherine's life (most were written shortly after her death), describes the Catherine the unnamed author came to know in 1374, during a visit to Florence:

> In Lecceto, only four miles away from Siena, is a place for the hermits of Saint Augustine. An English friar called the Bachelor of Lecceto has lived there for more than twelve years. He is a venerable man of great wisdom, sanctity, and solitude. He often lives in the wilderness where he has found caves in remote and harsh areas. He carries books with him so that he avoids conversations with people. He goes to church and then returns to his place. He is a man of mature counsel; he is a friend of God, and a man of great exemplarity. He avoids speaking unless the situation makes words necessary. He has never seen Catherine, or she him, but they are connected by the Holy Spirit and speak of each other with great devotion and respect.[6]

The *Miracoli* is remarkable in that it is not hagiography, but a contemporary account of Catherine as she ministered and travelled (it is not even clear if the author is religious or lay). The fact that Flete is so clearly identified at this point demonstrates what a large role he played in her life early on. Flete himself would have been unknown to the Florentine *Miracoli* author, so the hearsay description is most likely Catherine's. This bookish, thoughtful, quiet hermit is Catherine's most concrete connection to England. That he is also described as full of great counsel and an example to Catherine further indicate the influence he has on her own spiritual development and growth. Hackett has demonstrated that the detail in this account – that Flete and Catherine had never seen each other – is certainly false. He notes that "Bartolomeo Dominici ... Catherine's second confessor at the Dominican priory in Camporeggio, Siena, testified under oath at the process of her canonization that she had been visiting Flete at Lecceto by 25 January 1368."[7]

Catherine's relationship with William Flete would last until her death, and he serves the purpose of both adviser and confessor to her not only as a young woman finding her spiritual way but, later, as a public figure who commands audiences with the pope. On her death-bed, Catherine will bequeath the care of her vast network of followers, her *famiglia*, to Flete, attesting to her admiration and respect for him (despite an earlier public falling out). Hackett argues that Catherine really owes much of her spiritual understanding to her relationship with Flete. He writes that Catherine's theology and Flete's influence are represented in her letters:

> These letters by no means contain the whole of Catherine's doctrine, but they do show that during this period her fundamental teaching on self-knowledge and knowledge of God was firmly established. The two-fold doctrine forms the core of what is, in all probability, the first letter ever dictated by Catherine. The recipients were ... the community of Santa Marta convent in Siena, which was under the spiritual direction of the friars of Lecceto. Catherine's understanding of the self-knowledge and knowledge of God is pure Augustinianism, and this dominant feature of her letter is further illustrated by her description of sin as "quella cosa che non è," a definition which Augustine was the first to formulate.[8]

More than simply absorbing some of the doctrines of Augustinian theological beliefs, however, Catherine instead absorbs the world view Flete held and wrote about prior to ever leaving England for the Tuscan landscape. The early Catherine shaped by her conversations with this English friar recurs throughout her life and writing.

In this chapter, I would like to suggest that one part of the "Englishness" of Catherine of Siena is due to the fact that rather than solely representing a foreign Continental spirituality, Catherine mirrors an already familiar English devotion in part by channelling back to England the thoughts, ideas, and philosophies of William Flete. Indeed, Flete's influence on late medieval spirituality has been much overlooked, but his influence is enormous. The *Remedies* is integrated in to many manuscripts and theological treatises, and should be considered one of the defining texts of late fourteenth- and early fifteenth-century devotion. The tenets, scope, and influence of Flete's *Remedies* are integral to late medieval spiritual understanding, and the ideas, philosophies, and even the vocabulary of Flete is reflected and brought forth in the English texts concerning Catherine, most especially "The Cleannesse of Sowle" and *Il Dialogo*.

Flete wrote some letters to his brethren in England long after he had chosen an ascetic and hermetical life in Italy, a letter to Raymond of

Capua about Catherine of Siena, a short document recording a vision of Catherine (known as the *Documento Spirituale*, which will later be translated into English and circulate as "The Cleannesse of Sowle"), and a loving sermon in memory of Catherine (written a year after her death), but the *Remedies against Temptations* is the main written record we have by William Flete, and the only one of his early intellectual life before his ideas are further codified and shaped by an ascetic and hermetical withdrawal from the world.[9] As far as most medieval readers apparently knew, however, Flete did not exist. The *Remedies* is attributed to Walter Hilton in at least six manuscripts; while Hilton knew and drew from the *Remedies,* it is clear he is not its author.[10] Other manuscripts name Richard Rolle as the author and one (Trinity College Dublin, MS A.6.12, c. 1400) will become the basis for three early printed versions of the text – all attributed to him in its first line: "Here after folowes a deuoute counseyl and tretace made by þe holy fader Richarde Rolle hermyte of hampul, marvelous comforthable and necessary to all suche that have takyn upon thayme gostly lyffe. Whiche mater is called þe remedys againe þe trowbylls of gostly temptatyouns."[11] Of course, Rolle and Hilton are the usual suspects for misattribution – Barry Windeatt notes that "reception of Rolle and Hilton would long be swayed by variously plausible and implausible misattribution to them of a whole hinterland of apocryphal works, fakes, and pastiche."[12] In fact, only one manuscript (Cambridge University Library, MS Ii vi 30) names Flete as the writer, but its date and provenance (and markedly different styles from either Hilton and Rolle) have convinced scholars that this is the rightful attribution.[13] Hackett notes that the *incipit* and *explicit* of the Cambridge manuscript, one with Augustinian connections, both name Flete as its author ("tractus compositus a Fratre Willelmo Flete") and because Flete "meant nothing in English spiritual circles of the late fourteenth and fifteenth centuries," the attribution is very likely correct.[14]

William Flete and the Landscape of English Spirituality

In total, the *Remedies* is extant in a remarkable forty manuscripts in both Latin and English, with at least five others known of but now lost.[15] Nearly all of these are English or of English provenance, suggesting most strongly that Flete wrote the treatise before his 1359 departure to Italy and his renunciation of the academic life.[16] It is helpful to talk about the content of the *Remedies* with a few notes on its manuscript tradition and the manuscript circulation of the text.[17] There are two major recensions of the Latin text, one deriving from the other. Early on, Flete's text was subject to addition, conflation, and expansion, so it is difficult, if not impossible, to isolate what was actually Flete's. However, the fact that the text does invite the kind of constant recomposition and conflation that it does, seems to speak to the way in which it represents so soundly something essential in English devotional culture. It becomes the backdrop from which many other texts are added (not to mention those which are originally composed but directly influenced by the work itself). In 1373, not long after Flete has left England for Italy, a version of the *Remedies* circulates with a significant excerpt from Bridget of Sweden's *Revelations* attached to it.[18] The derivative Latin recension rearranges some passages, omits others, and adds new material. One of these texts was owned by a canon in Suffolk and continued to remain in the hands of secular clergy for at least half a century after his death. When translated into English, there were three main versions of the text (identified as Middle English I, II, and III). Some of these recensions bear little relation to the surviving Latin versions, suggesting that there were even further Latin versions of Flete's text in circulation. The second of these recensions is subsequently printed by Wynkyn de Worde, erroneously named as a part of Rolle's "Form of Living."

This varied and extensive manuscript tradition raises the problem all too familiar to scholars of medieval and early modern texts as to what constitutes authorial content and how to speak of an author's voice when that voice has been redacted, rearranged, conflated, and enhanced. I am interested in two divergent elements concerning Flete and his remedies, and both call for a different kind of reading process and analysis. First, I am interested in how the *Remedies against Temptations* comes to define a particular and crucial kind of devotional vocabulary and sentiment in late medieval England. For this, I intend to embrace the *mouvance* of the text and describe the *Remedies* as it was understood by its readers – with its interpolations and alterations, as well as its misattributions. However, I am also interested in what is at the core of these texts, Flete's "original" words, which invite the kinds of changes the text undergoes and the spiritualities it comes to embrace and represent. How do these ideas and related ones get absorbed (and later reflected back) by Catherine of Siena?

Flete's text both defines and is defined by a particular English quality of devotion. Flete's contemplative manual for combating the temptations that assail those trying to live good Christian lives is often copied, but remains within an English milieu. As appealing as it is to its English readers and compilers, it does not leave for the Continent. It remains an English text. Ultimately, what determines the landscape of medieval spirituality – both in the late Middle Ages and as we understand it now – is the diffusion of manuscripts. This may represent more of a reflection of interest in the spiritual life than the practice of it, but it demonstrates a kind of ideal devotional life. The more a work is copied, shared, and translated, the broader its audience, and the more likely it is to be redacted, reinterpreted, read, heard, and incorporated into one's spiritual life. Flete's text survives at such a high number that it clearly was a text that circulated in many different areas. That seven manuscripts (some lost but whose references remain) were linked to Syon Abbey or Sheen Charterhouse indicate that the texts were firmly in the Carthusian pipeline of textual transmission and production (a pipeline that included Hilton's *Scale of Perfection*, the *Cloud of Unknowing*, and Nicholas Love's *Mirror of the Blessed Life of Jesus Christ*, among other major devotional texts of the time, including, as discussed in chapter 1, Catherine's *Il Dialogo* and Stephen Maconi's letter concerning her canonization).[19]

The influence of the *Remedies* spreads well beyond its own manuscript tradition, though, further demonstrating its crucial place near the centre of late medieval and early modern devotional culture in England. Its influence can be clearly seen in the works of Walter Hilton, and it was known to have been read and studied by Thomas More and by the seventeenth-century Benedictine mystic Augustine Baker. Hackett expands on this list:

> Direct or indirect quotations appear in the *Discerning of spirits* and *Speculum Christiani*, both of the fourteenth century, and in the *Of the direction of a man's life*, *Fervor amoris* or *Contemplations of the dread and love of God*, *Speculum spiritualium* and *Donatus devotionis* – all fifteenth-century compilations. At least one spiritual director around 1400 drew heavily on it for a letter of counsel to a client, and complete texts of the treatise were acquired by priests, religious and laity.[20]

This litany shows to what extent Flete's text was representative of devotional life in England from the fourteenth century through to the Reformation. His ideas were either directly or indirectly disseminated, consistently, through these texts and those who preached from them. His words are co-opted into both didactic and mystical spiritual guidance, covering the varying landscape of English contemplative literature and forming the backbone for major works of English devotion.

Translation, Dissemination, and Audience of the *Remedies against Temptations*

Another significant marker of the scope and importance of Flete's *Remedies against Temptations* in English devotional culture is the state of its translated texts. Many of the translated copies of the *Remedies* were addressed to either women specifically or laypersons generally in their introductions. The text was not only for the Latin-literate; again and again it was seen as appropriate spiritual food and reflection for the novice.[21] Of the extant manuscripts, some are clearly written for women or were housed at women's communities. One may have been at the Benedictine house of Cambrai,[22] another was definitely with the Bridgettines at Syon,[23] one was owned by the prioress of the Cistercian convent at Swine,[24] and another has been linked to the Benedictine Barking Abbey.[25] A fourth manuscript has also been at Barking, with a suggested provenance showing a transmission from religious to lay readers. Its editors, Edmund Colledge and Noel Chadwick, write that from the abbey, "it passed into the possession of Elizabeth, daughter of Richard Scrope and successively the wife of William Beaumont and John Vere, thirteenth earl of Oxford, who died in 1537. She had several relatives by blood and by marriage who were nuns at Barking, and it may be that she acquired this volume from one of them."[26] Another fifteenth-century manuscript, with no clear provenance, has as its only other text a prayer written by a medieval nun for the edification of her sisters.[27] One of the surviving Syon manuscripts was donated by Joan Buklonde (d. 1462) and has what Vincent Gillespie calls "the most explicit donation notice of any surviving Syon book."[28] Although the anthology is not directed to women, and indeed, Gillespie speculates that it was "a commission or sponsored purchase,"[29] the fact that it has a woman donor is of note. Flete may not have necessarily intended his work for a female audience, but his text appealed to English female spirituality and this is largely the spirit in which it was translated and transmitted.

Flete's text lays out practical advice and, from the beginning, rather than presenting a chastisement or terrifying outlook on sin, promises comfort even in its first line: "Here seweth a souereyn and a notable sentence to comforte a persone that is in temptacion."[30] Both the tone and approachability of Flete's text, coupled with its serious concerns about spiritual health and sin, appealed to spiritual directors and their charges alike. This affinity for lay piety sheds light on the relationship between Catherine and Flete, as well. Catherine herself was a layperson, and given that she was introduced and drawn to Flete at the beginning of her spiritual formation, he may have eased her into her own and more complex theological understanding of sin and penitence. The lay audience for Flete's work in England also illuminates the dissemination of Catherine's texts as, later, when they arrive there, they would have much the same audience; indeed, Flete's and Catherine's texts would be juxtaposed in more than one late medieval manuscript.[31] But the fact that so many manuscripts, both in Latin and English, find their provenance in multiple monastic and conventual circumstances underscores that this was not simply a text for the laity, but one that blurred the lines between lay and religious readers. The compilers and translators are responsible for moulding the text into the context they find most fit for their audiences.

While many of the texts directed at women had a mystical aspect, such as Richard Rolle's work, it is worth noting that Flete is not a mystic. Flete's writing is contemplative and emotional, but the *Remedies* is not experiential, it is not describing a contact with or personal understanding of the divine. If anything, the language of the text is almost that of a religious rule or a handbook on pastoral care. The compilers who put parts of the *Remedies* in manuscripts directed at lay audiences are offering a more practical understanding of spiritual penance. Flete directs his readers to biblical examples, and explains the importance of asking for mercy in order to be relieved of temptation and its consequence:

> And if it so be þat ȝe haue consentid and fallen in ony temptacion, beth sory, and crieth god mercy þerof, and beth not discomforted þerfore. Þenke wel on the þe grete mercy of god, how he forȝaf Dauid his grete synnes, and Petir and Maudeleyn, and not only hem but also alle tho þat haue be or mow be and schulen ben contrite for here synnes and cryen god mercy.[32]

Despite this clear and straightforward language, however, in even its earliest iterations, Flete's writing is attributed to writers who are frequently considered mystical – Richard Rolle and Walter Hilton.

The quality and content of the *Remedies* – trusting in God's mercy, the fact that redemption is always attainable – speak to Flete's audience in the same way these other writers do as well. It is useful here to shift the terminology of mysticism and to think of the nature of spiritual contemplation and desire for self-knowledge that these writers share. Nicholas Watson calls attention to the myriad problems of identifying a writer or text as "mystical," not the least of which is that the term is broadly used and hard to define. He suggests that an alternate, or at least an accompanying, term to "mystical" may be "contemplative," and that the latter term allows for the process of both "the activity of contemplation itself, and with the writing that developed, in England and elsewhere, around that activity."[33] With Watson's suggestion in mind, it is useful to categorize Flete's text as a work of contemplation rather than mysticism. Flete emphasizes that within every man and woman is a war between good and evil will, and that self-knowledge and reliance on God's mercy will lead the reader to find the good within: "Þe yuel wil cometh of the sensualite, the which is euere downward enclynynge to synne, and þe good cometh of grace, þe which is alwey vpward enclynynge to alle goodnesse."[34] Flete is most interested in introspection, in turning away from the worldly and the sensual, and it is perhaps this interest that spurs him to ultimately eschew the academically engaged Cambridge Augustinians.

Shortly after writing the *Remedies*, Flete would leave England for an ascetic life of contemplation when he chose to be a hermit in Lecceto, but it is clear from the text that Flete did not think a spiritually devout and contemplative life was only the purview of the religious man. This outlook puts him in closer contact with Hilton than the actual substance or style of his writing does, and this shared outlook may point to the misattribution of Flete's writing to Hilton. Watson explains:

> In *On Mixed Life* (1380s), Hilton … makes the argument that the highest forms of contemplation require a commitment only possible for professional contemplatives: an argument whose validity is born out by the fifteenth-century revival of contemplative texts for nuns, especially the Birgittines of Syon Abbey, as well as by the enthusiasm with which Carthusians copied and studied his own works. Yet *On Mixed Life* is famously clear that Hilton, too, considers the laity capable of contemplation. What is more … Hilton periodically lets slip his awareness of a view that would have seemed absurd before the twelfth century, but to which the increasing tendency to distinguish sharply between "inner" and "outer" states of being had given plausibility: that the laity's very lack of "outer" signs of contemplative activity – the signs that distinguished professional contemplatives from others – might make them in a perverse (or spiritual) sense better suited to true contemplation than monks and nuns, because they were less susceptible to religious formalism and the hypocrisy that is its inevitable result.[35]

Flete's text is remarkably easy to comprehend in its straightforward language and practical advice; it is no wonder that it was so swiftly and consistently translated into the vernacular, because it clearly serves the purpose even in its design of spreading well beyond a religious context. This sensibility, coupled with Flete's own rejection of the academic life and theological study, point to an outlook such as the one Watson describes – that the laity are prepared for deep contemplative activity, in some ways more than the professed religious.

Flete's main topic, temptation, of course situates at its centre an appropriate shared point of reading for both lay and religious alike. All Christians are tempted, all fall, and – most necessarily – all should engage in an act of penance. As Nicole Rice has discussed:

> The required practice of penance linked all Christians, regardless of status, as a minimal religious discipline … The penitent, having expressed contrition for sin, was required to accuse herself and then, separately from the priest's absolution (increasingly given before any satisfaction was performed), to reform her own internal dispositions in order to produce a reformed self.[36]

Flete intuits this in the text itself, directing his "remedies" to those both inside and outside the cloister, detailing the kinds of sins into which both worldly and monastic readers could fall (such as believing that their actions are good when they are in fact not, or putting aside obligations to God in favour of other worldly obligations). Temptations (and the penance for failure to resist them) will also be central points to Catherine's own doctrine of faith exemplified in her letters, her *Dialogo*, and her *Legenda major*. This emphasis on penance is profoundly orthodox, giving a valance of conventional spiritual contents to the miscellanies and anthologies that contain Flete and the other texts therein (such as Catherine's, as we will see in the following chapter).

Part of what helps define *Remedies* as particularly English is the way in which it both responds to or incorporates elements of some of the major works of English spirituality (*Stimulus Amoris, Ancrene Wisse*) and the ways in which it will be co-opted into others. A clear example of how Flete is adapted and conflated is the version of the *Remedies* that appears in British Library, MS Royal 18.A.X. This fifteenth-century Middle English anthology is made up almost exclusively of devotional texts, including the segment of Catherine's vision known as "The Cleannesse of Sowle." One of the texts is entitled *A Good Remedie aȝens*

Spirituel Temptacions, which has been demonstrated to be a combination of two different versions of Flete's text, as well as passages from *De Pusillanimitate* (*On Small Mindedness*), a treatise misattributed to Hugh of St Victor that had both a Latin and Middle English circulation.[37] The compiler prefaces his text with an address to the woman for whom he writes:

> Dere sister, I haue in partie vnderstonde by thyn writyng of diuerse temptaciouns and taryinges that thu hast suffered, and ʒit suffrist, formed and maad be malice of the olde serpent, enemy to mankynde; ageynes the wilken temptaciouns I write the here some remedies, the wheche I haue fownde in the writynges of holy doctours. If thu wilt leue thyne owne fantasies and do after this writynge, I trowe to God thu schalt ben esed of all thyne deseses. Amen.[38]

This personal appeal bridges the private individual reader of the text with a broader reading audience who imagines him/herself in that space of the tempted, suffering the devices of "the olde serpent," and wanting desperately to be "esed" of all the "deseses" such temptations cause. The address also subtly scolds the reader for having "fantasies," a word frequently used to describe the visions of women, and to turn instead to "holy doctours."

The text that follows this incipit begins with Flete, but is then interspersed with the compiler's/translator's own thoughts before returning to Flete. F.N.M. Diekstra lays out the ways in which the author clips, rearranges, and intersperses Flete's text among his other major source, creating a new text from this pastiche.[39] Chapters are relayed out of sequence and are often interrupted by long passages from *De Pusillanimitate*. In this way, Flete's ideas and examples are reshaped into a new text, one with a female audience. The opening to this letter cited above, the preface to the text, provides important clues as to how the text was meant to be read by its English audience. It is both personal (in its use of the singular sister, the "thu" of the address, clearly indicating a single reader), but of course it is public by its very nature as a manuscript. It is presented as an individual text, but also shown to be a compilation that is conflated and rewritten. It is authoritative and offers a clear prescription: "do after this writynge." The writer does not see the reading as the act of devotion itself, but the doing according to the reading. Julia Boffey has speculated that the manuscript belonged at one point to well-connected female religious, possibly the abbess at

Aldgate, and that it is "essentially … an anthology catering for the spiritual concerns of women religious."[40] The opening to the *Remedies*, its prominent position, and its careful conflation with *De Pusillanimitate*, show the text as chosen specifically for women readers' concerns about their sinful thoughts and how to ameliorate that damage to their souls. Church concerns about women's "fantasies," visionary or otherwise, are given a corrective in this conflated version of Flete's text.

Flete's *Remedies* notably also draws from works such as the *Stimulus Amoris* and the *Ancrene Wisse*, both major spiritual texts that find their way into many mystical and devotional treatises and compilations. The last substantial section of the *Remedies*, in which Flete encourages his readers to see God as a loving mother, a metaphor Catherine will later employ, is taken directly from chapter 6 of the *Stimulus Amoris*. As mentioned earlier, one version of the text has sections of Bridget of Sweden's *Revelations* appended to it, perhaps indicating the affinity for women's mystical writing that Flete's texts will also show with Catherine's (Hackett estimates that Bridget's text is added around 1373).[41] Regarding the afterlife of the *Ancrene Wisse*, so too we can read in William Flete's *Remedies*. Denis Renevey has written:

> Its comfortable after-life is attested by the number of borrowings from *Ancrene Wisse* in devotional and contemplative texts in the fourteenth and fifteenth centuries. The nature of the borrowings and their new contextualization show how the anchoritic model (used metaphorically) became a trademark for exemplary religious life, both for the more laicized and urban devout public and the (male) monastic public of this later period.[42]

Another way to see Flete as representing a particular strain of late medieval spirituality in England is to further explore the constant misattribution to two of the major English devotional writers of the time: Richard Rolle and Walter Hilton. The former attribution will persist well into the Reformation and beyond, aided by the Wynkyn de Worde editions of Flete, which name Rolle as the author (indeed, which name *the Remedies* as part of Rolle's *Form of Living*). Rolle's *Form of Living* had its own wide circulation in the Middle Ages and as it, too, is concerned with recognizing sin and finding penance, we can see where the confusion may lie. Wynkyn de Worde does his part to solidify this confusion by choosing a manuscript that has conflated part of the *Form of Living* with the *Remedies*, beginning with what is, indeed, part of Rolle's text, and then following it with Flete's. The set up for the entire text, however, names Rolle as the author and the *Form* as the source, even though only the first paragraph is taken from Rolle's work: "Here after foloweth foure proufytable thynges to haue in mynde which hath be taken out of þe thyrde chapiter of a deuoute treatyse and a fourme of lyuinge that the dyscrete & vertuous Richard hampole wrote to a deuoute & an holy persone for grete loue."[43] Not until twentieth-century scholars take up Flete's text are the attributions to Hilton and Rolle disproven.[44] That Flete's text comes to stand in for some of the most important English devotional writing of the age is further exemplified in the fact that, as mentioned previously, Thomas More seems to draw on it in his 1534 *Dialogue of Comfort against Tribulation*, written during his imprisonment, and that the seventeenth-century contemplative Augustine Baker transcribes it and incorporates it (attributing it to Rolle) into his influential *Anchor of the Spirit*, written for English Benedictine nuns who are exiled at Cambrai after the Reformation.[45]

Flete's influence on English spirituality does not end with his *Remedies*, nor, as I shall continue to explore in the next chapter, with the ways in which his ideas return to England through Catherine's texts. In May 1380, Flete writes three letters to the Augustinian friars he has left behind in Cambridge. He urges his brothers to embrace a solitary and hermetical life, he asks them to eschew study and honours, he urges charity and hospitality, emphasizing that frequent confession should be undertaken for spiritual health:

> I am writing now for the common good of England. See that it is preached throughout England that all should undergo conversion and confess frequently for this is the will of Christ ... Let it be preached or told to every religious, prelate, monk, friar, priest, canon that they have for each other mutual and continuous charity, so that the whole English Church may be one spirit in God; let it reform itself; *doctor, heal yourself* (Luke 4:23).[46]

Flete was concerned with the reform of behaviour at all levels, sending his letters to several different members of the order, including the provincial.[47] Although Flete had left his English brethren for the solitary life of Lecceto, they were not far from his thoughts, nor was the formation of the souls in their care. This concentration on reform, penance, a sick Church in need of healing is, of course, central to Catherine of Siena's theological outlook and ministry. Her most enduring legacy is her influence and desire to move the papacy from Avignon back to Rome. Flete's letters show that his outlook went beyond what was happening in the papacy and in Italy and his eye was turned towards the home to which he would never return.[48]

One of Flete's primary concerns manifested in the letters is the spiritual health of the Augustinian novices, reinforcing his desire to speak beyond the high theological learning he has deliberately eschewed. He warns against the danger of study, linking it to a secularism that pulls the young monk away from his primary task of meditation on God:

> For the sake of God see to it especially that the novices, even older ones, during the time of their novitiate should not go out either for pleasure or for temporal gain, but only because of the most pressing need: they enter one day, they go out the next! They should not study, however apt they may be, during the time of their novitiate, except for regular observances or grammar or chant: it would be better not to receive them. By making excursions outside the monastery they become seculars in attitude; *they return* quickly *to their vomit* (Prv 26:11). When they are put to study or deal too closely with the professed, they become proud and so bold that they have no care for due order. See to it that everywhere they are well treated, that they are well provided with what is necessary, but take care that no one has anything of his own nor anything in the hands of seculars.[49]

Flete's bias for the life of contemplative meditation and asceticism he has enjoyed at Lecceto is evident in these lines, seen in his insistence that leaving the monastic environment is the beginning of a spiritual downfall – but they also betray a real anxiety about the future of the Church, his order, and his countrymen. Flete's concern with temptation and the chaos it engenders that began as a student in Cambridge has followed him into his old age. No doubt it was at the centre of his many discussions with Catherine, and his concerns can be read back, too, in her works. For Flete, as for Catherine, what matters in the end is one's authentic relationship with God, not the hierarchy or even the theology that surrounds it.

Writing William Flete: Catherine of Siena and Flete's Influence

When William Flete rejected England for life in Siena, he ostensibly left his academic ambitions behind. Indeed, no more writings other than the occasional letter and official document would come from his hands. However, his ideas about temptation and its remedies no doubt remained at the centre of his spiritual understanding and counsel, and these were most likely passed on to Catherine when he became her adviser. Flete and Catherine both had lived through terrible bouts of plague in their respective homes, and this shared experience no doubt mutually influenced their approach to death, sin, and redemption, reflected in both their surviving writings.[50] In his book on Catherine and Flete, Benedict Hackett attributes the growth of Catherine's confidence and the finding of her own spiritual voice to Flete's mentorship and guidance. He argues that she is clearly influenced by an Augustinian outlook that will continue to permeate her theology throughout her life.[51] Indeed, it would be hard to ignore the authority he must have had as her primary spiritual guide during her formative spiritual years, soon after she chooses a religious life over the married one for which her parents had hoped. We can see this in the ways that the *Dialogo* reflects back some of the tenets that Flete underscores in the *Remedies*.

Catherine's *vita* makes clear that she suffered under the weight of her own sensual temptations, the very issues Flete addresses in his text. Raymond of Capua describes Catherine's battle against temptation, describing Catherine as a tower fortified by God against the enemy's vicious attacks:

> The kynge of Babylone, our ghostely enmye the fende, wyth alle hys cursyd companye come and byseged thys blessyd toure thorough the sufferaunce of god rounde aboute wyth many wretchid temptacions. But fyrst he began to assayle this mayde by flesshely temptacions, whom not oonly he tempted by thoughtes withinforthe ne by yllusyons and fantasyes in her slepe, but by opyn vysyons wakyng, both in seyeng and herynge and seyng, he tempted her in many maner off wyse by takyng vppon hym a body off the eyre. Shame it is to here in how foule flesshely synne he tempted her, and therfore I shall not reherse theym.[52]

Raymond explains that the temptations which assailed Catherine were corporeal; these enticements are neither illusions nor fantasies, but actual physical bodies that she could see and hear. So foul are the temptations, which Raymond more than hints are sexual in nature – "foul flesshely synne" – that he cannot detail them through any further description. The point, of course, is not that Catherine is bombarded with terrible temptations, but that she overcomes them, and this is reiterated throughout this section of the *Legenda major*.

Although Catherine is frequently described as having the temptations more common to saints – thinking trivial sins are mortal ones, for example – Raymond of Capua is careful to emphasize that Catherine had carnal temptations, and that these were linked to her youth. The seductive demons speak directly to Catherine, criticizing her decision to remain unmarried and chaste; one demon tells her that she can still be holy while married and a mother, as did the biblical Sara and Rebecca, among others:

> Yet hast thou tyme that now for to have ioye in the worlde; thou arete yonge and therefore thou mayst the sonner recouere thyne strengthe of thy body agayn, notwythstondyng thyn grete penaunce that thou hast doo. Lyue as other wymmen doo, take an husbond and brynge forthe chyldren to encrece of mankynde. Yf thy desyre be to plese god, trowest þou that holy wymmen haue not be weddyd? Thynke on Sara and Rebecca, Lya and Rachell, how they were weddyd and brought forth chyldren and yet were hooly wymmen! Wherto hast thou take vppon the a syngular lyf, that thou mayst in noo wyse contynue.[53]

When the devil finds these temptations are ineffective, he turns to more explicitly sexual ones, no longer appealing to Catherine's reason (that holy women can still marry) and addressing her very corporeality: "[The devil] brought afore her the likenesse of men and wymmen medlyng togyders in the fowlest wyses that myght be deuysed, spekyng to-gyders foule dyshonest wordes; in soo moche that this cursyd company ranne aboute her wyth yellyng and cryeng for to stere her to suche abhomynable synnes."[54] Catherine's torment is heightened when her frequent visits from Christ are halted as she is repeatedly assaulted by these images and words.

Hagiographically, this "temptation section" sets Catherine's story up for her eventual miraculous and mystical marriage to God; she does choose a bridegroom, just not an earthly one. The sexual scenes are torture for her to witness – not so much because she is tempted to join them, but because they are so abhorrent to her eyes. Although Catherine's temptations do not surface much in her life, her desire to have people combat their own inclination to sin is a central concern to her *Dialogo*. It is clear that in her approach to temptation and in her desire to advise her readers to overcome it, Catherine is greatly influenced by Flete's thoughts on the matter as expounded in his *Remedies*. Both Flete and Catherine address how doubt can cloud one's relationship with God and the necessity of preserving faith in order to maintain a relationship with him. They both also believe, and stress, that to be tempted, to be tested, strengthens the relationship and purifies the soul when those temptations are overcome. Indeed, for faith to be true, it needs to have been tested.

For Flete, the making of faith *is* the testing of it. The third English version of the *Remedies* reads: "For as the goold is purged and pured be fier, and a knight is hard batail is proued good but if he suffre hym selff to ben ouere come, right so is a man be temptacion preued for good but if he suffre hym self to ben ouere come, þat is to seye but if he consente ther to be deliberacion."[55] By using two secular images (forging gold and fighting a battle), Flete perhaps opens up his philosophy to the laity while still maintaining the biblical allusions (here to the books of Peter and Job).[56] With this as the text's premise, Flete returns again and again to the idea of a tested faith as a necessity. Interspersed through his description of both the kinds of temptations one faces and how to overcome them, he reminds his readers that in the facing and overcoming one is actually enacting faith. Sometimes, he even deliberately returns to the quotation with which the text began: "But these fondynges or vyolent temptynge and angwischis ben but purgynges and preuynges of the soule, for as I sette and seyde at the þe feir purgeth gold, and a knyght also is preuyd good and hardy be bataile, right so temptacions and trubles preueth and pureth þe rightful man."[57] Flete methodically reminds his audience that this is the refrain of his *Remedies*. The effect of this repetition is calming: the temptation is necessary; it is not the fault of the reader; it can (and must) be combated.

Catherine's *Dialogo* holds this same core tenet, that temptation is part of one's spiritual formation, but she does not tell her readers this until after a lengthy and rather terrifying section devoted to the many assaults of the devil and the terrible pains awaiting sinners in hell. While Flete's treatise is – as titled – a text about remedying the temptations one faces and falls prey to, Catherine approaches from a position that sin is not a fait accompli, but rather should be avoided at all costs for the peril it causes the soul. But when she does acknowledge the burden of temptation, she, too, turns to the philosophy with which Flete opens his treatise. In *The Orcherd of Syon*, God (here, the "I") explains the workings of the devil, temptation, and the necessity of faith to Catherine:

> The feend is a mynystre ordeyned of my riȝtwiisnes to turment soulis whiche greuously offended me. And I ordeynede hem in þis liif þat þei schulden tempted and do greuaunce to my creaturis; not for my creaturis schulden be ouercome, but for þei schulden ouercome þe feend, and

þat þei schulden resceyue of me þe glorie of victorie þoru þe vertu þat is preuyd in hem. And þerfore no man schal drede þe temptaciouns of þe feend for ony batel þat schal falle hym, for I haue ordeyned men to be strong, and I haue ȝoure wille is ioyned to ȝou of me wiþ a free choys.[58]

For Catherine, overcoming temptation is necessary to prove one's strength of faith in God. The temptations are part of the process of achieving faith, not a blockade to such an act.

These ideas are, of course, not unique to Catherine and Flete; indeed, Flete himself draws the parallel to the biblical quote from James 1:2–3: "My brethren, count it all joy, when you shall fall into divers temptations; Knowing that the trying of your faith worketh patience." But both Catherine and Flete couch the notion of overcoming temptation to that of winning a battle, armored against the fiend, and of proving oneself like metal in fire as victory. The place of this idea in both texts is telling, however. As Flete's opening statement, it governs his entire treatise and serves as a touchstone of hope to its reader. For Catherine, this is not her natural outlook on sin or temptation. It comes nearly in the middle of her lengthy text, after much discussion about the various punishments for sin that await the sinner. She has absorbed Flete's outlook, but not made it entirely her own. This different take will hold through both texts – Catherine is less forgiving of the sinner than Flete. For Catherine the temptation can always be overcome, the tempted cannot and should not lapse into sin. For Flete, there is an understanding of the genuine personal struggle that needs to be overcome in order for the sin to be vanquished.

Both authors also take pains to outline for the reader the kinds of temptations that they will face – ones that are tailor-made to the person. Flete divides his temptations into different categories, those who are tempted by sensuality, by envy, or by the fiend when he comes "somtyme vndir þe coulour of goodnesse to disseyuen hem þat fayn wold doon wel."[59] Catherine, too, reminds her readers: "Þe feend whanne he seeþ a man so blyndid þoru his owne propre loue, he putteþ to hym dyuerse colours of sum profyte or of sum vertu of goodnes," continuing to say, "And þat he putteþ to ech man after his staat and aftir þe principal vicis in þe whiche he knowiþ ech man after his disposicioun moore ready to falle."[60] Catherine and Flete each want their readers to be ever vigilant against the tempting fiend, ready to go into battle, in order to prove themselves worthy of their faith. They also wait to remind the reader that the temptation is specifically for her – the devil knows what her weakness will be.

Again, the common language between the two is remarkable – the fiend comes under "the colour of goodness" for Flete, "in diverse colours" for Catherine. This common vocabulary of spiritual devotion is precisely what appeals to late medieval English readers who accept Catherine so readily into their circulating texts. Just as medieval art draws from recognizable iconographical symbols that convey additional meaning to its viewer, many English devotional texts share phrasing, allusions, and words that expand the meaning on the page. This is particularly true in translated texts where what may have been a nuanced term in its original language gets flattened into a more recognizable word for its audience, and intentionally stripped of language that could be misinterpreted by a lay reader. The similar diction between Flete and Catherine draws their texts together even though generically they are so different. Although *The Orcherd* is in itself a visionary text, recounting Catherine's mystical dialogue with God, it does not have the language of mysticism that is much more common among continental women writers like Mechthild of Hackeborn or Marguerite Porete. Even Julian of Norwich's and Margery Kempe's tones are more overt in their mystical and visionary components than Catherine's, which could be read through the generic lens of spiritual instruction or didactic literature. *The Orcherd* fit neatly into the category of contemplative devotional literature where Flete occupied an already expansive space.

There is one place where Catherine and Flete readily depart from one another, and this is the idea of how to *remedy* the temptations with which one is faced. For Flete, the remedy to which he returns throughout his treatise is wise counsel. Here, in discussing the temptation to make a deadly sin seem like a venial one, Flete returns to this point: "Þe remedy of þis temptacion and of all other is þat þei gouerne hem be here confesseur, or be some good discret persone, and rule hem fully aftir hym, and not aftir here owne blynde mysruled conciens."[61] Flete reiterates throughout his text that sinners are blinded to their own sins, or are convinced that their sins are for the greater good, or that the ends of good justify the means of sin. The sin festers, Flete explains, when it is not shared with someone who can see it for what it is and counsel the sinner. It is notable that Flete does not only couch this in terms of a formal confession but also in terms of advice. This may be because he was writing shortly after the Black Death when a lack of priests and empty churches led to a decline in the availability of sacramental confession.[62] Indeed, as Alistair Minnis has described, the English Church had to adapt quickly to this problem and "proved remarkably robust and resilient" by allowing some extreme contingencies.[63] Ralph of Shrewsbury, who was then the bishop of Bath and Wells, "orders his clergy to publicize the fact that, in these extreme situations, confession to a layman, 'even to a woman if a man is not available,' is perfectly valid."[64] Of course, Flete most frequently calls the exchanges he describes in *Remedies* as counsel, and not confession, but given the climate within which he is writing, an intentional slippage between the two is suggested.

Flete's repeated imperative that the tempted should find a counsellor relates to another reiterated point throughout the text: sinners cannot recognize their own sin and need help to recover from its temptation. He explains that there are three remedies – to avoid being alone, to seek counsel, and to trust God:

> And for as myche as many men kunne not in tyme of temptacion ne woln not see it, but ben sory and dredeful of complexion, þerfore to alle suche men thre thynges ben nedeful. The firste is þat thei be not myche alone. The secunde is þat they þenke not ne seche no þing deeply, but fully reule hem, as I seyde afore, be some good discret persone; and þou3 þei wold beholde here counsell, thei owen to taken non heed in suyche þou3tis and sterynges, ne charge hem. Take thei non heed of suyche ymaginacions or sotyl conseytes, for it may neuevere turne hem to dampnacion, the counseil of wise man, þat is 3ouen to hem for here sauacion … The thredde remedy is this, þat for as myche as the fend traueileth faste to make a man dredful and sory, þanne þat he to þe worchep of god and in troust of his helpe, and to schame and confusion of the fend and right in dispyct of hym, þat he strengthe hym self to be glad and mery, þou3 it be a3ens herte.[65]

Although in some ways this is odd advice from a soon-to-be hermit, Flete stresses the fact repetitively that one person alone is no match for the devil's snares, and that "never being alone" and "seeking wise counsel" will both help the reader see the sin for what it is. Only then can the sinner move to the next step outlined in Flete's *Remedies*, that is to combat the temptation in both thought, deed, and attitude (to be "glad and merry" despite one's self). This advice would particularly resonate with a lay reader or novice who might feel ill-equipped to rise to the spiritual and behavioural standards of the age; it gently encourages conversation, community, and spiritual comfort.

For Catherine, conversely, the onus rests almost entirely on the sinner herself to recognize and remedy the sin. She argues that faith clears the sight of the sinner and leads the way out of temptation: "This þat I seye is for hem þat ben maad cleer in siȝt with þe liȝt of verry feiþ and whiche kitten awey for my loue þe venym of her owne propre sensualyte wiþ a swerd of tweye poyntis, þat is to seye, with haate of vicis & loue of vertues, and whiche wiþ þe liȝt of resoun kepten and geeten gold in þe world."[66] Once the sinner recognizes the venom (of sensuality, of sin, or desire for worldly goods) and casts it from her mind, then she should turn to confession – not for advice, as suggested by Flete, but for cleansing and absolution:

> But I sey of þe venym of þe wickid wil of man, þe which poiseneþ þe soule, bryngynge yn deeþ, but it cast out haastily wiþ al maner desier of þe herte by deuoute confessioun. Þe which confessioun is þe moost souereyn medicyn þat delyuereth a man fro sich venym, þouȝ it seme riȝt bitter in þe sensualyte.[67]

After years under Flete's wing as his advisee and penitent, she no doubt had heard Flete's suggestions for combating the temptations that assailed her, as described by Raymond in his *vita*, but she has reshaped these ideas into a harder line, into her own view of combating temptation. Catherine's *Dialogo* is not the only place where these views can be found. Raymond, too, summarizes them in his text that Catherine knew all temptations could be fought through faith.[68]

In many ways, Flete's text is kinder to the sinner, more comforting in its repetitive reminder that it is never too late to repent and that even the greatest sinner can be saved through penance: "For þouȝ oo man hade do alle the synnes þat euer were don and euer schullen bee do, þouȝt and seyd in to þe day of judgement, and he were contrite and asked god forȝeuenesse, and mekely lowned hym to þe sacramentis of holy cherche, he schuld haue mercy and forȝeuenesse of all his synnes."[69] No matter how egregious the sins, the sinner can find repentance and penance through faith in God and Church. Forgiveness is always within reach. Perhaps this gentle quality, coupled with the insistence on seeking wise counsel, encourages so much copying (and conflating) of Flete's work, which finds its way into so many English convents, monasteries, and homes. Catherine's more spiritually rigorous outlook has a more discreet circulation. However, as the two are frequently juxtaposed, together they give a sense of redemption, temptation, and penance that encompasses the devotional needs of its English readers.

The Legacy of Flete through Catherine

Catherine of Siena and William Flete had a very public falling out towards the end of her life, well documented in her letters to him. After Pope Gregory XI moves the papacy back to Rome, a move for which Catherine had fought and for which she had been largely credited, Catherine realizes her work in shaping and advising the Vatican was not over. Less than a year later, Urban VI became pope in Rome, causing a new schism in the Church with the installation of Clement VII as the "antipope" in Avignon. Catherine suggests a council of advisers to Urban VI, including Flete. However, when he is summoned to the Vatican, Flete refuses – appealing to his desire to remain a hermit and live out his life at Lecceto. Catherine's letters to Flete during this time are clearly angry. She even abandons writing her letters to Flete himself and writes instead to his scribe:

> Now it seems, from the letter Frate William has sent me, that neither he
> nor you will be coming. I don't intend to respond to his letter. I'm really
> sorry for his simple-mindedness, since little honor for God or edification
> for his neighbors will come of it … One's spirit is rooted pretty shallowly
> if it would be lost simply by going to another place! It would seem that
> God is partial to locality and can be found only in the woods, and not
> somewhere else in time of need.[70]

Although it is unclear whether they ever formally reconciled before her death, Catherine forgives him as she puts the care of her *famiglia*, her band of followers, in Flete's hands.

Flete, too, forgives Catherine. Two years after her death Flete writes a lengthy sermon extolling her virtues and grieving her loss. Evident in this eulogy is Flete's love and respect for Catherine and the reversal of roles that took place during their lives. He may have begun as her adviser and confessor, but at her death he considered himself her follower. Through his sermon, he invites his listeners to do the same and place themselves as Catherine's pupils:

> She once said to me: "God is patient in himself, but not in his servants."
> There is no doubt but that God will at some time punish her sons who are
> neglecting her teaching. Let us put aside all sluggishness; let us always
> be advancing, never faltering, and certainly never turning aside from her
> teaching or from devotion to her. She said: "Let us begin today, every day."

Therefore, that she may not rebuke us, let us follow her example and be always in the east and never in the west, for we have seen this star in the east; that we may never falter through negligence let us always remember that she endured intolerable sufferings for our sins; let us remember how daily a new eagerness and fervor was kindled in her to give her life for us, a hundred times a day were it possible, and how many graces we have received from her mind.[71]

He emphasizes that Catherine has been a teacher, and he, among others, her student. The heavily allusive text (practically no sentence goes by without some biblical reference) serves less as a *vita* than a memorial. This is true, as well, in a letter to Raymond of Capua that Flete wrote after her death. In it, he speaks against anyone who would discount Catherine because of her gender, extensively quoting Augustine on Saints Perpetua and Felicity. He even compares her at length to St Paul, suggesting that she should be called "Paula," a defender of the faith. Carolyn Muessig notes that this shows he saw that Catherine "not only possessed the classic hallmarks of female asceticism but was also presented as a preacher, a writer, a strong papal supporter, and a denouncer of schismatics."[72] Significantly, he speaks of the import of her letters and how they affected him and will influence others, pointing to a textual legacy for Catherine that is entwined with her spiritual one:

O most devout mother, your arrows, that is your letters, are sharp and people fall under you (Ps 45:6). Many proud and stubborn people who once spoke ill of you have been laid low and continue to be laid low by the darts of your letters: they fall at your feet overcome by your inexpressible humility and patience. Not only people of this generation, but many others also will fall down before you, many generations of unbelievers, renouncing their unbelief and accepting the faith.[73]

Although Catherine's letters are not the words that reach England, Flete is prescient in recognizing that Catherine will live on in words, narrative, and text, and that it is through this process that she will wield the most power.

For Flete, Catherine's legacy is not the papal return to Rome, marred as it is by the "antipope" and the schism that appears after Urban VI's ascendancy. Rather, Catherine's written words, the texts that she leaves behind, will be the foundation for her future fame and appreciation.

Although Flete's sermon and letter to Raymond of Capua do not have circulation that we know of in his English home, Flete was most likely responsible for the circulation of one of the most copied and anthologized texts concerning Catherine – the Middle English excerpt known as "The Cleannesse of Sowle." As we shall see in the next chapter, although Flete is never credited with authorship or indeed with any relationship at all to either "The Cleannesse of Sowle" or nearly all versions of the *Remedies*, English readers frequently place them together in the same anthologies and miscellanies, implicitly drawing a connection between the spirit, substance, and audience of the two.[74] This juxtaposition seems to be coincidental, as it is clear the compiler would not have known who Flete was, much less know of his relationship to Catherine, but the anthologizers see them as speaking to the same concerns and the same audience. These frequently neighbouring texts, more than anything else, demonstrate that in order to fully understand how Catherine is read and received in England, one must first understand William Flete.

Chapter Three

Catherine Excerpted: Reading the Miscellany

Catherine Excerpted: "The Cleannesse of Sowle"

While *The Orcherd of Syon* is certainly the most impressive of surviving Catherine texts in medieval manuscripts – so lengthy that a volume such as New York, Pierpont Morgan MS 162 is a sizable codex with 186 leaves[1] – there were, in fact, several more bits and pieces of excerpted Catherine's texts circulating in medieval manuscripts than *The Orcherd,* which is extant in only three fifteenth-century manuscripts,[2] including some passages from *The Orcherd,* as well as some from her *Legenda major*. However, no text demonstrates just how Catherine is adapted to so many different purposes than the excerpt that is now known as "The Cleannesse of Sowle." Unlike Stephen Maconi's letter's survival in Douce 114, discussed in chapter 1, "The Cleannesse" is not frequently part of a clearly well-thought-out and planned anthology. In its entirety it is only a few pages, and when excerpted, it is merely a paragraph; as a result, "The Cleannesse" appears in many different contexts but is seen most frequently in the miscellany (as are the few other circulating sections from *The Orcherd* and her *vita*). These collections truly do give the broadest view of medieval English devotional culture, and by examining how Catherine is framed, to what she is juxtaposed, and the manner in which she is excised, we may see how her texts serve many readers.

"The Cleannesse" is by far Catherine's most visible presence in medieval England. It is all the more notable because William Flete is responsible for its existence – perhaps explaining why its circulation is especially prominent in England as it may have originally arrived in one of Flete's missives to his native friary. Indeed, the Latin version of the text has a post script added by the Dominican champion of Catherine's canonization, Thomas Caffarini, that notes, "The above-mentioned servant of God, Brother William, added the following: 'If this discourse were published and disseminated throughout the whole of our Order I think that it would do great good."[3] This is a relatively unknown text on the Continent and among Catherine studies, partly because Flete is overshadowed after Catherine's death by more active and visible supporters such as Caffarini himself, Stephen Maconi, and Raymond of Capua. Known as Catherine's *Documento Spirituale*, a name given to it by Girolamo Gigli in his early eighteenth-century Italian edition of Catherine's *Il Dialogo,* the text survives in only three manuscripts in Latin.[4] As far as I know, there is no documented circulation of the text outside of Italy and England; however, its easy misattribution to either the *Dialogo* or the *vitae* may be obscuring its existence in other vernaculars. Only one of the surviving Latin manuscripts has the complete version of the *Documento* that is attributed to Flete, while the other two are excerpts and are misattributed to Maconi.[5] With such a small Continental circulation, the text's survival in England represents its most robust presence.[6]

Catherine went to Lecceto to visit Flete shortly after Gregory XI decided to move the papacy back to Rome, the crowning achievement of what had effectively been a political career for Catherine. In early January 1377, Catherine dictated to Flete and other accompanying priests a summary of her theological beliefs; this is before the *Dialogo* is set down and prior to all of her surviving letters, thus an early codification of her spiritual outlook. This *Documento Spirituale* made its way to England and remains extant in Middle English, in several versions and many different manuscripts, known (if entitled at all) as "The Cleannesse of Sowle." Curiously, the Middle English translation of Catherine's *vita* introduces another moment in Catherine's life, where she dictates a doctrinal thought to Raymond, as if it were "The Cleanness"; the translator writes that she dictates a "doctrine" for those called to "cleanness of living," although this phrasing – and indeed the entire introductory sentence – is not evident in the Latin text:

> Another tyme this holy made rehersyd in presence of her confessour Maister Reymound and to many other that wer called to clennes of ly-uyng, a full notable doctryne and a vertuous, the whiche is good for pure maydenes to knowe, whos chast lyuying is full specyally to god, and the more ye ben met ner to god by swete meke maydenhede the sonner ye maye vnderstonde that vertuous doctryne. And it is this: that a sowle the

whiche is vertuously i-mette to god, as it is rehersed afore, as moche as it hath of the loue of god, soo moche it hath of the hate of her owne sensualyte. For of the loue of god naturally cometh hate of synne the whiche is done agaynst god, the sowle therefore, consyderyng that the rote and the begynnynge of synne regneth in the sensualyte and there pryncypally is roted, she (is) meued and steryd hyghely and holyly wyth alle her mythes agaynst her owne sensualyte, not for to vtterly destroye the rote – ffor that may not be (so) longe the sowle dwelleth in the body, lyuyng in this lyffe; but euer it shall be lefte a rote namely of smale venyall synnes.[7]

This is most likely *not* the dictation of the *Documento Spirituale* that will become "The Cleanness." Raymond does not mention Flete (nor, for that matter, any of the other witnesses that included another major follower of Catherine, Stephen Maconi), but the translator has shaped this moment into that dictation. Catherine recites a "full notable doctryne" that sums up ideas that Raymond will repeat throughout the *vita* and that Catherine herself will reiterate in *Il Dialogo*, but neither of these redactions have the immediacy and the succinctness that Flete's record of the event contains. However, this change of an added title seems to anticipate a familiarity with Catherine's "The Cleannesse" from the readers of *The Lyf* of Catherine, and may speak to how well known "The Cleannesse" actually was. Significantly, this passage is excerpted and forms one of the few pieces to circulate of the *Legenda major* on its own, and will later be anthologized by Henry Pepwell in a printed volume.[8]

The critical history of "The Cleannesse" is slightly complex in that it has been consistently misidentified as an excerpt from Catherine's *Dialogo*, and thus largely ignored as part of something that had already been circulating in England and not an additional text concerning Catherine.[9] In addition, Flete's influence on Catherine has been discounted, both as to her beliefs and theology (see chapter 2), as well as to the possibility that he may have been responsible for sending word and texts of Catherine back to his home country.[10] It is understandable why "The Cleannesse" has been so easily misidentified, as it covers the same ground that Catherine goes over both in her *Dialogo* and through Raymond of Capua in her *Legenda major*, often with very similar language and metaphor, but the fact that this text is filtered through an English Augustinian friar who potentially sent his *Documento Spirituale* concerning Catherine to his brethren in order for edification and dissemination is worth careful consideration.[11]

As with Flete's *Remedies*, "The Cleannesse" undergoes many conflations, adaptations and alterations in its dissemination. Of all of the extant insular Catherine texts, it demonstrates how one piece served different readers, compilers, and codices: "The Cleannesse" ends up in grand, expensive devotional anthologies with named aristocratic owners and in small grubby preachers' handbooks; it is scrawled on the last page of a potentially Wycliffite codex that otherwise contains a beautifully produced *Pore Caitif*; and is found in traditionally "orthodox" compilations with Nicholas Love's *Mirror*.

"The Cleannesse of Sowle" has a long version, which I will discuss in detail later in this chapter (surviving in only one manuscript, British Library, Harley 2409), but for the most part it circulates as a small paragraph, devoid of mention of Catherine at all.[12] P.S. Joliffe had identified three different versions of "The Cleannesse" (including the full version of Harley 2409), which he labelled as Versions A, B, and C.[13] Each of the three versions strays from the original text of the *Documento Spirituale*, although Version C is the closest to the Latin. Because the extract is so short, it exists solely in relation to the other texts in a codex (unlike *The Orcherd*, which is so lengthy it takes up an entire manuscript when copied). In addition, because this text has for so long been misidentified as being an extract from *Il Dialogo* or the *Legenda major*, it is crucial to look at this text as one that had its own independent circulation and that may very early have been divorced from Catherine herself as she is identified in only two of the eight extant manuscripts, an anonymity which both disseminates her work more thoroughly and yet erases her presence in doing so.

At its simplest version, "The Cleannesse" is just a paragraph. The excerpt here is taken from Harley 2409, which is the most faithful to the Latin version laid out in Siena, Biblioteca comunale degli Intronati, T.II.7, which contains the longer version of the text and which attributes authorship to William Flete.[14] It begins by God's voice, directing the listener, clearly a woman ("my doghter"), but not identified as Catherine, that he will lead her to "the cleanness that she desires" if she follows three points, which are enumerated and explained:

> My doghter if you wil haue þe clennes þat you desires, ye nedes forto be
> parfitely oned unto me þat am souereyn clennes.[15] And þat [shalt þu] be if
> you kepe þies þre poyntes þat folowes: þe first poynt is if you so ordeyne
> þine entent unto me þat you make me þe ende of al þi werkes & euermore
> besy þe forto haue me befor þi sight;[16]

þe second poynt is if you vtterly forsake þine owen wil and no hede
takyng to mannes wil in al þing þat be falle þe onely take hede vnto my
wille þat wil þi holynes. For noyther I wil no I suffre any þing falle vnto þe
bot for þi gode and profite.[17] And if you take gude hede here to, þer shal
no þinge make þe sory, þou shal no while be wrothe with any man.[18] Bot
raþher you shal late þe be holden to þam þat does þe wrong. And ouer þis
you shal deme no man bot if you openly se his synne.[19] And þan wiþ wite
you shal be wroth & of þe man you shal haue pite;

þe þridde poynt is if you deme þe wirkynges & þe dedes of my seru-
antes noȝt efter þi felyng bot efter my dome for you knowes wele þat I
saide sumtyme þat in my faders house er many dwellyng stedes.[20] And
þerfore sen þat þe place of blysse is aunsweryng vnto þe desseert of þis
lyfe it folowes þat riȝt as þer er dyuers places of blisse in heuen so þer er
dyuers wayes of dessert in erthe. Wherfore al þe werkes & þe dedes of my
seruants as long as þai er noȝt expresse agayns my lore þou shal haue þam
in reuerence and be no way misdeme þem.[21]

The three points seem to overlap, but every redaction of "The
Cleannesse" returns to this formulation: The first point is that the reader
must be united with God and that God should always be foremost in
the reader's mind; the second is that the reader's will must be completely denied in order to submit to the will of God, which is the only
consideration; the third is that any judgment of fellow Christians must
be according to God's law not the judgment of the reader herself. The
text is clear that this purity of soul is not only achieved through one's
relationship with God, but also with one's interaction and judgment of
her neighbour. Keeping these tenets in mind will lead the reader to a
life of cleanness and virtue.

The passage concludes with a summary of what following these
rules will yield, beginning with self-regulation, a virtue about which
Catherine was especially adamant. "Cleannesse" involves keeping
vices at bay, and faith in God will insure that:

If you kepe þies iii poynts you shal be wele rewled in þi selfe. And þu shal
be wele rewled onentes me be þe first poynt. And onentis þi neghbore
both gode & ille you sal be wele reueled be þe second & þe þridde. And so
you shal noȝt go be vices oute of þe ordre of vertues And more ouer you
shal parfitely kepe þe clennes þat you desyres, my grace always wirkyng
þies þings in þe.[22]

The text is completely faithful to the Latin, reiterating the points that Catherine will bring up again in her *Dialogo* and that Raymond will bring up throughout her *vita*. For Catherine, and for her readers, the desire for purity, or "cleannesse," will only come with annihilation of self and uniting (becoming "oned") to God. Although the text comes to be known as "The Cleannesse of Sowle," the phrase itself does not appear here, but rather a desire for "cleannesse" in and of itself, implying all of its meanings in Middle English: purity, chastity, modesty, and integrity.[23] Although not specifically outlined here, the word had many connotations that included a kind of sexual purity, although this is not what the text is stressing about Catherine's revelation.

Truly, it is a small piece that has something for everyone, and when it gets divorced from Catherine and attributed instead to a "sely soule," as it is in most manuscripts, it becomes adaptable to nearly every reader. Because of its short length, the text solely exists in medieval miscellanies, most of them devotional in theme, but others more far reaching. It is worth noting that the shorter Latin version, erroneously attributed to Stephen Maconi, is the same shortened version that is found in all English codices save Harley 2409, indicating the possibility that two separate versions of the *Documento Spirituale* were translated into English – the full version and the already excised one. It is the latter that has its strongest presence in English miscellanies.[24] In her study on Mechthild of Magdeburg, Sara Poor notes that the appetite for devotional anthologies, especially as a form of pastoral care for female readers, contributes to an instability of the text as it gets further redacted and its authorship becomes removed from the text, as it does here with Catherine. She writes that this "volatile system of production and transmission has little room for named authors unless they bear an authority that can exert pressure on the production or reception of the books in one reforming direction or another."[25] Catherine is not named because her name would politicize the text by associating her with visionary activity; with her name gone, it becomes a less authoritative text about spiritual growth.

I am using the term "miscellany" here as a capacious term, meant to include the more deliberate idea of an anthology and something that seems truly random, although it may have a design and purpose. Julia Boffey and A.S.G. Edwards remind us that even the terms "anthology" or "miscellany" are not truly useful terms for thinking about medieval "assemblages," which include so many layered possibilities of intent behind creation, copying, and dissemination. They note:

Very probably in many instances what was brought together within the book was what was immediately available. Materials in such circumstances were not shaped to a controlling design in their compilation. To acknowledge this is to resist the purposive implications of such terms as "anthology" or "miscellany" and to set strict limits on forms of interpretation based on the evidence of content.[26]

In examining these varied manuscripts that contain excerpts from Catherine, we can in some places glean the intent of the compiler (from incipits, explicits, or other textual clues), and in other cases only read the text in relation to those around it, seeing the manuscript as a whole document in its final form.

The content of the miscellanies that contain "The Cleannesse" hint as to how we should read the piece itself and what aspects of Catherine's revelation are being stressed. Ralph Hanna reminds us that, in order to understand the medieval reader, we must first understand the miscellany, which modern editing practices cannot duplicate, noting that "works were infrequently transmitted shorn of a context. And that context directed reading experience in ways the modern library edition must ignore."[27] With this in mind, one sees how Catherine herself gets separated from "The Cleannesse." The author is irrelevant here, as is its means of transmission, instead, what we are to take from the text is how it fits into those around it, indeed, into the very landscape of late medieval English spirituality. The devotional compilation then shifts our attention away from who wrote the text to who is reading it. Hanna continues:

> Medieval books, in their contextualization of works, demonstrate quite other interests, ones more readily assimilable to our concept *theme* than to our concept *genre*. And we can retrieve these (often diverse) thematic readings only through attention to the codicizing gestures undertaken by the producers of medieval books.[28]

Neighbours to "The Cleanness" in the miscellanies range from the orthodox pseudo-Bonaventuran *Meditationes Vita Christi*, to the lollard-leaning *Pore Caitif*, to other women's mystical writings such as those by Bridget of Sweden, to Walter Hilton's *Scale of Perfection*, and, in several cases, to William Flete's *Remedies against Temptation* (suggesting a common Augustinian milieu). Neighbouring texts are most often in Middle English, but not infrequently in Latin. They have recorded provenance of monastic houses, aristocratic families, male and female owners, as well as long-lost ownership and transmission. These miscellanies, in short, represent a vast array of English spiritual literate practice.

Different Manuscripts, Different Readers

The textual neighbours of "The Cleannesse of Sowle" may very well determine how it was read and for what purpose it was compiled. As suggested above, in order for this kind of reading of the text to work, one must abandon the "miscellaneous" aspect of the miscellany, and instead see the codex as a "whole book." As Kimberly K. Bell and Julie Nelson Crouch have suggested in their study of Bodleian Library, MS Laud Misc. 108, "the notion of the manuscript as a 'whole book' argues against the assumption of miscellaneity in a codex that contains diverse texts, assuming instead that an 'organizing principle' informs the order and context of the book and points to a writerly or a readerly agenda."[29] Even with the additions of later texts and different scribes, the book is a living thing reshaped each time by its changing contours. For the Catherine texts, the case of Bodleian Library, MS Bodley 131 is an especially interesting one when read in this light. Bodley 131 contains Nicholas Love's translation of the Pseudo-Bonaventuran *Meditationes Vitae Christi*, known as *The Mirror of the Blessed Life of Jesus Christ*, as well as William Flete's *Remedies against Temptation*, both immediately preceding "The Cleannesse" in the manuscript. Its scribe John Morton was "a knight and wealthy bibliophile," who, along with his wife "were the recipients of letters of confraternity from William, prior of the York Austin Friars."[30] The letter itself is also contained in Bodley 131. John Friedman suggests that Morton was not a professional scribe, but rather a "man of substance" who made the book, among others, for his personal use.[31] Morton's connection to the York Austin friars points to a possible route for the *Remedies* and "The Cleannesse" as both arriving in England through Flete's Augustinian connections.

The manuscript's impressive first text, the *Mirror*, which takes up the first 121 folios, casts a light of orthodoxy on the texts that follow, since Love's text was sanctioned by Archbishop Arundel, who was otherwise wary of vernacular theology.[32] The *Remedies*, itself fairly orthodox in content and message, cements this. When "The Cleannesse" follows, especially without a reference to Catherine as its source, the passage loses its mystical and visionary components, seeming instead a lesson in finding purity of soul. "The Cleannesse" is followed by an equally short passage from Bridget's *Revelations*, also seemingly stripped of its strong visionary features, and then the manuscript closes with several saints' *vitae* in Latin. As a text of personal devotion, the manuscript invites the reader to first meditate on the life of Christ, before turning inward through the texts of Flete, Catherine, and Bridget, each of which suggests a kind of internal reflection on how to fight temptation and achieve peace and purity of self through complete faith and devotion to God. Following these texts, at the heart of the codex, are saints' lives, offering contemplation and *exempla*. The reader meditates into the heart of the devotional anthology, is offered explicit instructions and paths to follow in the middle, and meditates her way out of the text as well. Owned by a lay reader, albeit one clearly connected to the world of monastic life, the codex offers a glimpse into personal devotion and the role that Catherine's words may have played.

A very different reader is anticipated in British Library, MS Royal 18 A. X., a manuscript clearly compiled for a female audience and one very focused on the topic of sin. At first glance, this codex may seem like a truly unplanned miscellany (as opposed to a more thought-out anthology); it contains, among its many texts, a translation of the first portion of *Somme le Roi*, part of the life of St Edmund, *The History of the Three Kings of Cologne*, and a disputation between the body and the soul. However, it also has Flete's *Remedies against Temptation*, Catherine's "The Cleannesse" (again, unattributed to Catherine), and a confession formula for a woman. The redaction of William Flete's *Remedies*, a conflation with Pseudo Hugh of St Victor's *De Pusillanimitate*, directly follows "The Cleannesse" and begins with an address to a nun who is struggling against the weight of temptation.[33] As discussed in the previous chapter, the text opens with a direct address to the reader about her struggles with temptations which are leading her away from God. This prelude to Flete's text, which just follows Catherine's, is nestled in a manuscript that continually refers to women readers, indicating a female audience both highly literate and invested in spiritual matters. In this codex, "The Cleannesse," as with Bodley 131, is not a mystical or visionary text. It is a remedy, like that offered in William Flete's *Remedies against Temptations*, and it addresses real concerns of impure living and temptations, as outlined especially in the *Book of Vices and Virtues*, or the first chapter of the *Somme le Roi*. While directed explicitly to a woman, this is a very different reader than the one who is invited to see the visionary implications of Catherine's text (most obvious in Harley 2409, which I will get to shortly). "The Cleannesse" is prefaced here as "a good question to god," followed by "a sely soule askid of god oure stedefast lord clennes of soule." The fact that "god apperid to here" to give the answer is not highlighted, so the visionary aspects, while there, are subsumed by the question the "sely soule" asked.

The reader of "The Cleannesse" in MS Arundel 197 has a very different experience. This manuscript, eventually owned by Henry Howard, a seventeenth-century Duke of Norfolk (1628–84), has no recorded medieval provenance. The small volume has many small texts assembled together (of which "The Cleannesse" is one), and is followed by *Contemplations of the Dread and Love of God*, which is itself followed by short pieces. As Margaret Connolly has pointed out, "what is curious about this otherwise unremarkable collection of devotional pieces is that the text of each work has been subjected to extensive revision, with lengthy additions and omissions, and many corrections to individual words and phrases."[34] "The Cleannesse" is no exception to this, and part of the scribe's seeming revision program is that he does not delineate the separate texts but has them somewhat run together as a complete whole. The opening line seems to address the reader directly, with a second-person address before moving to the third-person narrative of "The Cleannesse": "A þu sely sowle, if þu wilte aske of owre lorde Jhesu Criste any thynge aske clennes of þi sowle, for God aperyd to her & sayde." Connolly surmises that the text "was produced in a monastic rather than commercial context, and that its conflated and corrupt texts are the results of active intellectual engagement."[35] In this case, the reader in that context sees a living text and reads "The Cleannesse" as part of its growth and change. Later, the aristocratic reader – perhaps the Duke of Norfolk – may read this as a more coherent whole than it had ever been or was meant to be.

The Cambridge, Trinity College MS 336 (B.14.53) is another slim and beautifully produced volume that clearly had aristocratic owners. It was eventually owned by scholar and translator Philemon Holland (1552–1637), whose father had been a Protestant exile.[36] As its later owners were Protestant, its earlier owners may have had lollard sympathies, as the main text of the manuscript, *Pore Caitif*, has been linked to Wycliffite manuscripts and revisions. Indeed, M. Teresa Brady has identified this manuscript's copy of the *Pore Caitif* as one of the versions that shows "evidence of Lollard infiltration," and Kalpen Trivedi has argued that the very genesis of the text is lollard in nature.[37] If this is owned by a Wycliffite, or at least a layperson with lollard sympathies, it does challenge a reading of "The Cleannesse" as strictly orthodox. "The

Cleannesse" is added in a second hand, so cannot be clearly linked to any lollard leanings of the first scribe, but the manuscript has only a few short additions in what is otherwise dominated by the *Pore Caitif* (folios 1–129 are the *Pore Caitif,* while folios 130–40 are the remaining few texts, including "The Cleannesse"). "The Cleannesse" is the last piece in the codex, reminding readers to place their faith and fate fully in God's hands.

Not all of the English manuscripts that contain "The Cleannesse" subvert the visionary qualities of the text. Two manuscripts pair "The Cleannesse" with Walter Hilton's *Scale of Perfection* and Richard Rolle's *Form of Living,* both texts written by notable English male contemplatives. The first codex, Bodleian Library, MS Rawlinson C.285, was written as a true devotional miscellany by four scribes over several decades with both unbound and bound folia added. The Catherine segment is added by a second scribe, who takes excerpts from many texts (Walter Hilton, *The Prick of Conscience,* and Richard Rolle) and appends them to the more substantial work done by the first scribe. Hanna notes of this second scribe's additions that "his addenda are clearly somewhat unplanned and adventitious, including not only some Hilton materials already copied into the preceding booklet by scribe I, but also a piece of Rolle that the scribe must have recognized he had copied only a few folios earlier."[38] The Catherine excerpt may have been placed in the manuscript because it fit the space the scribe had, or, it was one of several segments he wanted to write down in one place. Either way, it does not appear to have been a well-thought-out progression or placement. However, it becomes the template for at least one other manuscript, Cambridge University Library, MS Ff.5.40, and at that point is no longer arbitrarily chosen but by design.

Both the Rawlinson and the Cambridge manuscripts have the only surviving copies of "The Cleannesse" known as Version B, an extremely unusual and "corrupt" version of the original text, if we measure corruption as distance from the Latin original. Indeed, the text is so shortened and different than Versions A and C (and such a far cry from the Latin), that it seems more likely that Version B is, in fact, not a version of "The Cleannesse" at all, but rather a redaction of the same ideas as presented in *Il Dialogo.* In Rawlinson C.285, Version B reads as follows:

It was a saul and askyd clennes of saul of oure lorde. And he sayd to hir: "What-sa þou dose, luke I be þi cause. Gif þe eghe of þi saul vnto me, and be aned vnto me. Luk nogth efter ylke a mans wile to do it, bot luk whilke es myne & do þat. Deme nane of my creaturs bodyly ne gastly. A thogth of a vertu es a dyke before þe eghene of þe ryghtwys domes-man; ffor when a man vnthynkis hym of þat gud he has done, he hegys hym-self in hym, and þan he fallis agaynes þe maker of mekenese. Our lord Ihesus sayd to his discipilis þis wordis: 'Whene ȝe haf donne alle wele, says þat ȝe er vnprofytable seruandes.' Amen."[39]

While the passage is clearly related to the main passage of "The Cleannesse," with the lord responding to a woman's request for purity of soul, it loses some of the predominant features of the passage as well – the three enumerated points, for example, as well as their explanations. However, the fundamental points are the same: self-annihilation and utter dependence on God's will and judgment will lead to the desired pure state.

"The Cleannesse of Sowle" in itself is in many ways Catherine's spiritual beliefs in a nutshell, and it is possible to recognize how it came to be originally misidentified as a passage from *Il Dialogo*; indeed, the fact remains that Version B may actually be from the *Dialogo* rather than Flete's *Documento*, as is clearly the case with Versions A and C, which can further explain the confusion. There is a remarkable similarity between "The Cleannesse" and one passage in the *Dialogo*, but it is not as expansive or detailed. The passage is found in a section where God advises Catherine to see human sin not through a lens of judgment but through that of compassion. It is translated from the Latin as follows:

So if you would attain the purity you ask of me, there are three principal things you must do. You must be united with me in loving affection, bearing in your memory the blessings you have received from me. With the eye of your understanding you must see my affectionate charity, how unspeakably much I love you. And where the human will is concerned you must consider my will rather than people's evil intentions, for I am their judge – not you, but I. If you do this, all perfection will be yours.[40]

Throughout the chapter (and the book as a whole), God is offering Catherine similar advice, frequently invoking the "three things you must do" formula, and truly nothing distinguishes this section from the others. When this passage is translated into *The Orcherd*, however, its similarity to "The Cleannesse" in sentiment and language becomes more evident. *The Orcherd* section in which this passage appears falls under a subdivision, found in at least one of the Latin manuscripts, so it is likely not the invention of *The Orcherd*'s translator: "Of þe þridde and moost parfiȝt liȝt of resoun; and of þe werkis þat a soule dooþ whanne it is come to þat estaat. And þere is ischewid a fair visyoun which þis soule hadde, in the which visyoun is schewid fully of þe maner of comynge to parfiȝt purite of þe soule."[41] This subtitle gives almost a paragraph-by-paragraph summary of the many points Catherine will hit in this section of her *Dialogo*. This is not an easy feat as the text itself is very circular, repetitive, and in places confusing (due to the fact that the *Dialogo* was dictated over many months in Sienese, then quickly translated into Latin), but the subtitles force a kind of order on a disordered text.

The last of these points, "And þere is ischewid a fair visyoun which þis soule hadde, in the which visyoun is schewid fully of þe maner of comynge to parfiȝt purite of þe soule," gives prominence to the section, further highlighting its importance. The text appears as follows:

> And þerfore it is ful needful to þee, þat desirest for to come to þat purite which þou axist of me, for to do þese þre principalle þingis. Oon is, þat þou oone þee to me by affecioun of loue, for meruelous loue þat I haue to þee and to alle creaturis. Anoþir is, þat þou deeme not in þe wille of a man my wille. And þe þridde is, þat þou deeme neuere aftir þi witt þat my wille schulde be her wille, for I am oonly þe doomesman, and not ȝe. And if þou kepe wel þese þre principalle þingis, al perfeccioun schal falle to þee.[42]

Note that the second of these three things has changed. In the *Dialogo* it appears as "With the eye of your understanding you must see my affectionate charity, how unspeakably much I love you," but in *The Orcherd* it reverts to another comment on God's will (not seeing it in the will of man). Version B of "The Cleannesse" adheres more closely to the Latin: "Gif þe eghe of þi saul vnto me, and be aned vnto me."

The fact that there are essentially two different versions of "The Cleannesse," very likely from two different sources, demonstrates the reach of this particular idea of Catherine's. As with Flete's *Remedies*, these two versions offer a prescription for the sinner, steps one can follow to achieve the stated devotional goal. Both the manuscripts that contain Version B also contain Walter Hilton's *Scale of Perfection*, as well as Richard Rolle's *Form of Living*. Written in a distinct northern dialect, they demonstrate the reach of the Catherine tradition, and also how its small and concise form lends itself to the devotional anthology.

Here, coupled with clear mysticism in Rolle, and near-mysticism in Hilton, "The Cleannesse" Version B is imbued with its own mystical qualities – the "eye of the soul" that the reader sees gestures towards a visionary eye, a revelatory one, bringing the reader – who does not know that the speaker is Catherine of Siena – into the realm of a visionary woman, regardless.

Reading Harley 2409: Framing "The Cleannesse"

The most complete English version of "The Cleannesse" is in a manuscript that has the testament in full, as well as the prologue and epilogue to the *Documento Spirituale* – Harley 2409. This manuscript as a whole reflects a range of medieval devotional readers through its provenance and contents: religious, lay, female, male. Inscriptions in the book indicate it was once owned by Maud Wade, the prioress of the Cistercian house of Swine in Yorkshire (c. 1473–82), who gifted it to another woman, Dame Joan Hyltoft, who was a nun at another Cistercian house, Nuncoton (in Lincolnshire). Another hand marks that it is then owned by Jorge Hiltoft and Sir Simon Hiltoft, male relations of Dame Joan. Later, another woman's name shows up as the owner: Elizabeth Lockton.[43] The Catherine section follows directly after "Walter Hylton," which, on closer examination, turns out not to be one of Hilton's texts at all but instead is Flete's *Remedies against Temptations*. This raises the tantalizing possibility that Flete's text and the *Documento* may have circulated together at some point, perhaps through Flete's English Augustinian connections. If they did not, it further demonstrates the spiritual compatibility between the two texts as anthologizers think to juxtapose them without any sense that they are written by the same author.[44] Swine was also known to house the works of Bridget of Sweden and Mechthild of Hackeborn, making its readers, perhaps, particularly attuned to women's mystical writings.[45]

The prologue to "The Cleannesse" in the manuscript names a date of the testament (it states 8 January 1386, rather than the correct date of 7 January 1377).[46] Flete is not himself named but rather is identified as "a special familiere" who takes the dictation, although the Latin to which it is closely related does identify that the dictation was to Flete.[47] Both of these qualities lend a grounding, a realness to the revelation that are not present in the excerpted versions. In a mid-fifteenth-century manuscript, the date "1386" would not seem so very far away to its reader. Harley 2409 is also one of only two surviving manuscripts that clearly identifies that the vision is Catherine's – its title states "Here folowes how þe holy mayden Kateryne of Seen first began to sette hyr hert fully to god warde."[48] The prologue, which precedes "The Cleannesse," is fairly lengthy, and the fact that no other manuscript reproduces it indicates that early translators/adaptors noted it as an unimportant aspect of the text. One of the guiding questions of this project is how well Catherine was actually known in England, especially since a far more famous saintly Catherine was depicted so heavily in English iconography and art, St Katherine of Alexandria. "The Cleannesse of Sowle" is in itself an interesting test case for what common knowledge there was about this saint. The introductory line in Harley 2409 seems to clearly point towards a common knowledge – there is no explanation of who the "holy mayden Kateryne of Seen" is, or what the result of her setting her heart towards God may be. On the other hand, the utter lack of a reference to Catherine in all the remaining manuscripts, where she becomes known simply as a "sely soule," may indicate an apathy towards Catherine. Her name is apparently not needed (or may indeed detract from) the lessons that "The Cleannesse" has to offer on its own.

The prologue and epilogue to the *Documento* are clearly offset from the paragraph that will become "The Cleannesse," told more from the perspective of the scribe and witness, Flete, than from Catherine herself. The fact that all other versions of "The Cleannesse" are missing this prologue is telling. This third-person narration leading up to Catherine's revelation divorces the vision itself from a purely mystical context. It is not God's voice, speaking unprompted, but rather Catherine's own asceticism, denial, and self-rejection that lead to her revelation. The prologue sets up an extended metaphor – that of the "rock of self-knowledge" – that Catherine will divide up in order to prepare herself for the purity for which she is praying. For Catherine, self-knowledge (her rock) is something to be destroyed, literally annihilated, until she realizes that there is no self-knowledge, there is only God. In Harley 2409, the translator remains faithful to the Latin, explaining Catherine's process of turning inward, until she finds only hatred of self and love of God:

> Spekand of hir self as it had bene of a noþer person, þat in the begynnyng of hir turnyng to godward. And of hir enlumynynge she set agayne þe lufe of hir owen person as for a sadde grounde of hir lyuyng, þis stoon of knowyng of hir selfe. Þis stoon she departed in thre parties: þe first part is consideracion of hir first makynge, how þat she had no beyng of hir selfe bot of god who boþe made hir of not & kepid hir and al þis dide he

onely of grace, and noȝt of hir dessert; þe secunde part is consideracion of þe beynge of mankynde be þe whilk efter þat we had destruyd oure wele beyng and loste grace of fyne and fervent lufe. Crist boȝt vs agayne wiþ his awen dereworthy blode, þe whilk luf mankynd neuer deserued; þe third part is consideration of þe synnes þat she had done efter that she had receyued þe grace of baptyme, be þe whilk synnes she had deserued endeles dampnacion. Where for she merueyled of þe euerlastyng godenes of god, þat he comanded noȝt þe erthe to deuoure hir. Of þies þre consid-erations þer grew in hir so grete a hate until hir selfward þat she coueyted no þing to be done efter hir wil bot al efter þe wille of god.[49]

All of the hallmarks of traditional mysticism and a visionary world view are present here: Catherine is so outside of herself that she speaks as if she were speaking about another person (this may bring to mind Margery Kempe's own insistence on referring to herself as "this crea-ture," for example), she annihilates the self in favour of oneness with God, and she despairs at her own sinful state of mortality. The opening is explicitly mystical in a way that many circulating English texts are not. Indeed, some of the few English texts that address women's mysti-cism openly (such as Margery Kempe's *Book*) have little to no evidence of circulating among the laity at all, while "The Cleannesse" clearly did. The prologue continues to explain that it is this twofold recogni-tion, of self and of God, that spurs Catherine to realize that in order to live a holy life she must only do things that are the will of God, not her own will.

Flete continues to explain that Catherine's entire world view becomes inverted. What had been pleasurable to her is now shunned, what she had rejected is now embraced. She flees from the caresses of her mother as if they were venomous and embraces her enemies:

For why þe dauntyng of hir moder in þe whilk she was wont fortil haue grete likyng she fled as a swerd or venym. And al enmytees she suffred with likyng. Temptacion of the fende boþe she lufed þam & she despised þam. In als mykel as þei broght hir until feleable lust, she despised þam; in als mykel as þai trubled hir, she lufed þam.[50]

It is interesting to note here that the translator has reversed the order of the phrase as it appears in the Latin, where Flete has written that she embraced the troubles caused by the devil and despised those that brought her pleasure. Here, Catherine's pleasures are subsumed by her troubles, as this is where the emphasis of the sentence ends. It is in this state of mind that Catherine asks God "þat he woulde vouche safe forto graunte her parfit clennes."[51]

The manuscript Harley 2409 also contains an epilogue to "The Cleannesse" that is in the Latin *Documento*, but does not appear in any of the other Middle English versions of the text. In it, Flete summarizes Catherine's vision, expounding on the meaning of the three points and the path to purity it reveals, explaining that love of self is the cause of all sins – both sensual and spiritual. The voice throughout the ending seems much more Flete's than Catherine's, echoing as it does some of the sentiments about sin and its temptations that he has outlined in his own *Remedies against Temptations*; he summarizes Catherine's revelation in similar terms:

> Þe furst luf is cause of alle fleshely synnes and of alle oþere open wrechednes þat er done for lufe of creatures, as when for þe lufe of þem þe comande-ments of god er despised & broken. Þe seconde lufe þat is called propre lufe gostely is þat ilke þat efter forsakyng of erthely þings and of al creatures and also of propre will, it makes men forto folow so mykel þer owen gostely ap-petite and þer owen dome þat þai wil notther serue god, no walke in goddes wayes bot efter þer owen list and þer owen felynge.[52]

While Catherine's revelation explained how to achieve purity, Flete's explanation centres – as does much of his *Remedies* – on what the sins look like from which the reader must turn. The self-love of the flesh causes the fall not only into fleshly sins but also "alle oþere open wrechednes þat er done for lufe of creatures." What Flete terms spiri-tual self-love causes one to follow one's own will rather than the will of God, making him destined to fall: "And for als mykel as god wil þat a man forsake his owen wil, þerfore no swilk man may long stoond in goddes way bot hym most nedes falle for he folowes more his owen wil þan þe wille of god."[53] The man who cannot relinquish his own will to God is destined for sin; one's own will must be subsumed into the divine one.

Flete chastises those who strictly follow one religious practice, falling into despair when they can no longer sustain it: "Also swilk men er al þo þat conceyue ouer mykel lufe until sum o gostely dede as unto fastyng or any oþer swilk and make þat as it war þe ende of þar wirkyng. And if þai happen forto lose þat, anone þai sal falle to despayre and seese of alle oþer gode dedes." Ironically, this is exactly what Flete is accused of by Catherine when he refuses to leave his life as a hermit in order to serve the pope, as noted in the previous chapter. As noted earlier, Catherine is too angry to write to Flete himself, instead turning to his secretary in a letter dated January 1379, admonishing,

> He said that if you ... should come, you would lose your spirit and so be unable to assist the holy father with prayer or stand in spirit with him. One's spirit is rooted pretty shallowly if it would be lost simply by going to another place! It would seem that God is partial to locality and can be found only in the woods, and not somewhere else in time of need.[54]

In a further irony, adherence to strict religious practice is precisely what many scholars have identified as a likely cause of Catherine's death – starvation due to extreme fasting. Flete closes by reiterating that one's will must be immolated in favour of the will of God in order to be both a good Christian and a good neighbour, closing with the line: "If you umbiþink þe þus: bitter þings shal seme vnto þe swete."[55] This line seems to echo some of the words of the "Discernment of Spirits," the selection which follows "The Cleannesse" in the codex, perhaps indicating what caused a compiler to juxtapose the two pieces.

Discerning Spirits: Lessons from a Visionary

Harley 2409 does not merely contain the most complete version of "The Cleannesse." Appended to it are sections taken from the *vita* that also have independent circulation in England. As with "The Cleannesse," itself, these have been traditionally identified as coming from Catherine's *Dialogo*, but a close examination shows that they are directly from Raymond of Capua's *Legenda major*, pointing to a Middle English circulation of the life before the 1493 de Worde edition (although the translations appear to be independent of one another). The first part that follows "The Cleannesse" is, surprisingly, not one of the many places in the *vita* where Catherine discusses the same subject – purity of soul. Rather, it describes how a vision may be determined to be from God or be demonic, a genre known as *discretio spirituum*, or the "discernment of spirits." This is a subject that Catherine herself discusses at length in *Il Dialogo*, but the condensed version appearing in Harley 2409, as well as the fifteenth-century compilation known as the *Speculum Devotorum*, is more direct than these circuitous discussions, perhaps because it has been filtered so firmly through Raymond of Capua.[56] For the compiler of Harley 2409, this section is inextricable from "The Cleannesse." There is nothing – other than the start of a new paragraph – that indicates that this section is separate from "The Cleannesse" that precedes it or another section taken from the *Legenda major* (which does not have any surviving independent circulation) which follows it, so it is not clear how it came to be appended. Was it taken from another scribe's compilations of Catherine's texts? At some point, someone took these two disparate elements of Catherine's dictation to Flete and parts of Raymond's *Legenda major* and juxtaposed them. The question surrounding Catherine's "Discernment of Spirits," the title I will use to distinguish this excerpted section of the *Legenda major*, remains: How does this come to circulate on its own? Further complicating matters, another section of Catherine's writings about discerning spirits is also found in another manuscript, Oxford, University College, MS 14, but that text is taken from *Il Dialogo*, not the *Legenda major*. While the words are very different, the sentiment is the same – a good vision will remain sweet while the evil one will turn bitter. As with "The Cleannesse" and the possibility that Version B comes from *The Orcherd*, two extremely similar passages of Catherine's texts circulate, coming from two disparate origins.[57]

The popularity of Catherine's "Discernment of Spirits" points to one of the conflicting currents of spirituality circulating through late medieval England, particularly women's spirituality. The kind of visionary experience encouraged and so oft reported on the Continent (see, for example, the nuns at Helfta) is rather subdued in England. This is evident in the reaction to Margery Kempe's professed visions, as well as the careful language that Julian of Norwich uses to describe what she has seen. The fact of a vision – particularly one experienced by a woman – seems always suspect, especially when it blurs the line between a visualization (say, of the Passion of Christ), a divinely directed vision, or, most alarming, a prophecy. There were several concerns that arose around the visionary: first, that this would somehow create a superior relationship to the divine than the men who were by necessity their superiors (most frequently as confessors and administrants of the Eucharist); second, that the visions were not actual visions but flights of fancy and imagination caused by the susceptible female mind; and third, that the visions were not divinely inspired but rather demonic in origin. The tradition of *discretio spirituum* dates to St Augustine's writings, but it is in the fifteenth century where the genre is scrutinized and linked explicitly with women's visions and prophecies.[58] While the first concern about female authority is rarely plainly expressed, this anxiety is present in much of the male-authored texts about female mystics and their abilities. As Barbara Newman has explained, one of the primary opponents to Bridget of Sweden's canonization, Henry of Langenstein, focused more specifically on the second concern, the dangers of the misled visionary: "Clearly ... one should not quickly or easily believe a spiritual person who labors continually in fantasy and contemplation, imagining that she is supernaturally moved by a good or evil spirit in all the impulses she feels, or in everything that happens to her unexpectedly."[59] This is written in his 1383 *De discretione spirituum*, only three years after Catherine's death. While Henry may have been speaking out explicitly against Bridget here, as Newman suggests, he surely knew of Catherine and the claims surrounding her as well.

Jean Gerson also wrote against the canonization of Bridget and implicated Catherine as well, by focusing on the veracity of her visions in his later *De Probatione spirituum*, following on the heels of his c. 1400 *Discretio spirituum, De distinctione verarum revelationum a falsis*, on whether a revelation is true or false.[60] Although Gerson does not go so far as to invalidate Bridget's sanctity, he casts considerable doubt on the truth of her visions.[61] For Gerson, contemplation was the closest one could get to understanding the divine. These concerns about the nature and source of religious visions (men's as well as women's, although these concerns are more frequently directed towards women than not) persist well into our own day in scholarship on the subject. One need only look at some of the literature on Margery Kempe and the source of her visions to see that the line between what is imagination and what is "real" is a border constantly being scrutinized. Catherine's treatise addresses the third of these concerns, however, taking as a given that the visions are real, she advises how to determine the origin of the vision.

Most significantly, the "Discernment of Spirits" is cited nearly *verbatim* in the fifteenth-century *Speculum Devotorum*, which is "part translation from the *Meditationes* [*vita Christi*] and part-compilation from other sources."[62] As the *Meditationes* themselves encourage a kind of visualization process and what Newman calls "opportunities for a reader to create her own variants on a standard script, but not for free-form visionary invention," the author of the *Speculum Devotorum* may have seen it as especially useful to have this small segment from Catherine inserted among his texts.[63] Catherine covers this question of discerning the spirits a few times in *Il Dialogo*, but the part that is excerpted and circulated separately had been filtered through Raymond of Capua for his *Legenda major* of Catherine and is condensed. In this excerpt, Raymond tells his readers (through Catherine) that the primary difference between a divine vision and a demonic one is that of feeling – a divine vision begins with fear and awe, but as it continues will be given to comfort and sweetness. Alternatively, the demonic vision is the reverse, feeling sweet at the start and moving to a bitterness of the soul:

> Anoþer tyme our lord Jhesu apered vnto þis same forsayde Dame Keteryne & sayde vntil hire þus: "Doghter sum clerkes seyne & soþe it is, þat þe visyons þat cum fro me þai begynne wiþ ferdnes, bot euer þe lengear þai laste þe more comforte þai gyfe & sykernes; for þai begynne sum what wiþ bitternes bot euer þai waxe swetter & swetter. Bot þe visions þat cum fro þe enemy, þai haye þe reuerse condicion. For at þe begynnyng þai seme forto gyf sum gladnes and swetnes & sykernes, bot euer þe lengar þai last þe more drede and bitternes waxes in þar soules þat sees þam. Þis is soþe for my wayes er knowen & departed fro his wayes be þe same difference."[64]

It is notable that Jesus's first words to Catherine are to validate the opinions of what "some clerks say," confirming that Catherine's visions are in line with orthodox arguments on the matter. This advice on discerning spirits apparently comes to Catherine in a vision itself, with Christ appearing before and speaking directly to the saint. Raymond then links the analysis of visions to a more general view of good Christian behaviour: "For þe way of penaunce & of my comandements in þe begynnyng semes harde & sharpe, bot euer þe more men go þarinne, þe more esy & swete it semes vnto þam. Bot þe way of vices in þe begynnyng semes likand, bot euer þe lenger men goos þerinne þe more it waxes bitter and dampnable." As with the visions, penance and following commandments start bitter and end sweet, unlike sin which holds the reverse process. Raymond's recasting of the visions as an analogy to good Christian living makes the *Legenda major* more applicable to all readers, softening the mystical aspects.

The segment ends again with some more directives as to how to distinguish the good vision from the bad. Here, Catherine stresses that the divine vision leads to an intimate knowledge of the soul and also to self-knowledge, a recurring theme in her *Dialogo* and the *Legenda major*. One cannot know one's self without knowing God, and in that mutual knowing the soul will be humbled through the vision, the self will be dissolved. A true vision leads to the meekness of the soul while a false one leaves only pride in its wake:

Bot ȝit þer is a more siker token þan is þis: For wite you for certayne þat I am verray sothfastnes, euermore be þe visions þat cum fro me þe soule profites in more knowyng of sothfastnes. And for als mykel as sothfastnes is riȝt nedeful to þe soule, boþe for þe knowyng of me & of þe self, of þe whilk knowyng cums þat it despises þe selfe & worshipes me þe whilk es þe propre office of mekenes. Þerfore it is nedeful þat þurgh þe visions þat cum fro me þe soule be made more meke þan it was and also more knowyng and despysyng þe owen writchidnes. Þe reuers here of falles in þe visyons þat cums fro þe enmy. For sen þat he is fader of lesyngs and kyng over alle þe childer of pride and may noȝt gyf bot þat he has euer more of þe visyons þat cum fro hym þer waxes in þe soule a wele latyng of þe selfe. Þe whilk is þe propre office of pride and dwelles stiff bolned & blowen ful of þe wynd of vanite. Wherefore if you besily examyne þi selfe you may liȝtly perceyue fro whens þe visions cums, wheþer fro sothfastnes or fro lesyng. For sothfastnes alway makes þe soule meke and felyng makes it proude.

The text stresses that the visions from Satan are rooted in pride and vanity, the vices waiting to take down all good Christians. The solution to which Catherine returns is the debasement of self, the giving over of will entirely to God. As with "The Cleannesse," the direction to deny oneself completely is the governing philosophy here. Although the de Worde version of Catherine's *Legenda major* clearly has a separate translator, where word choice is notably different as is syntax, a similarity between this fifteenth-century manuscript and sixteenth-century printed text demonstrates how closely the "Discernment of Spirits" adhered to the *Legenda*, even when it had an independent textual life.[65]

The other Catherine text concerning *discretio spirituum* survives in Oxford, University College, MS 14. Although in this codex the section is taken from Catherine's *Dialogo*, not the *Legenda major*, it is very similar in design and language. Lengthier than the *Legenda* excerpts, this selection is situated between Latin texts rather than vernacular ones, and is contained in a manuscript that also houses *The Cloud of Unknowing*. The manuscript's content and context strongly point to an intended clerical audience. Interestingly, this manuscript was later owned by the Protestant bishop of Salisbury, John Jewel (1522–71), whose inscription is on the last folio. Jewel was a humanist and a friend to Thomas Cranmer, exiled when the Catholic Mary Tudor took the throne. The passage from *Il Dialogo* begins by clearly naming Catherine as the recipient of the visionary advice: "Here folo þe doctrine schewyd of god to seynt kateryne of seene, of tokynes to knowe vysytacions bodyly or goostly vysyons whedyr þei come of god or of þe feende." Catherine covers the same ground that Raymond does in the *vita*, but in the much more discursive and recursive style that marks the *Dialogo*. The gist of the advice is the same, however – visions from God will bring sweetness, those from the devil will bring bitterness: "Aftyr tyme such haue receyued a grete loue in receyung of goostly comfortis or vysyons in what wyse þat euyr þei come þei fele a ioye for þei haue þat þyng þe whych þei louyd and desyred and þis may ofte tyne come of þe fende." The vision ends with God's direct address to Catherine, explaining how she has been gifted with good visions and the ability to discern them: "Loo dow3tyr my endles goodnes hath preuydyd þus for parfyte and inparfyte in what state þat þei stand for to knowe þe deceyte of þe fende in tyme of visiouns & visitacious þat þei be not deceyuyd." This passage is very similar to the translation in *The Orcherd of Syon*, and may be taken directly from one of those manuscripts.

Of course, Catherine's (divinely dictated) treatise on the discernment of spirits serves a purpose in her *vita* and her *Dialogo* that it no longer does when it is separated from the complete works: validation of her own visionary and prophetic experiences. In context, Catherine's text signals the reader that she understands the difference in visions and has had the validated ones. In the *Legenda major*, Raymond of Capua also gestures to his clerical readers that he has done his job as spiritual director whose primary function "is to examine the spiritual life of the visionary and to assess the nature and content of vision and revelation."[66] In the context of his narrative, it is clear that not only this passage but the visions that surround it are validated and approved by the hagiographer. These rhetorical moves were conscious decisions on Raymond of Capua's part. As Nancy Caciola has noted, Catherine's "hagiography is brimming with defenses of her spiritual gifts against detractors who murmured that she was a simulator of sanctity if not demonically possessed."[67] With Catherine, the questions of a vision's (and specifically her visions') validity follows her after her death. As previously noted, Jean Gerson criticized Gregory XI for his attention to the visions of both Bridget of Sweden and Catherine. As Dyan Elliot explains:

[Gerson's] critique of confessors who sponsor their female penitents' cults is followed by an admonition to clerics against ceding authority to women and half-wits. This point is punctuated with the example of Gregory XI who, in extremis with his hand on the consecrated host, bemoaned his own adherence to certain mystics whom Gerson refrains from naming, though clearly alluding to Bridget of Sweden and Catherine of Siena, whose deluded advice precipitated the papal schism.[68]

Although Raymond of Capua is writing the *vita* before Gerson's written criticisms, he is no doubt aware of the accusations and questions surrounding a visionary as politically visible as Catherine. Gerson is merely representing the culmination of suspicion that had followed Catherine during her life and well after her death.

Out of context of the *Legenda major* or the *Dialogo*, as Catherine's "Discernment of Spirits" is here (appended to "The Cleannesse"), in the *Speculum Devotorum* or alone in a devotional anthology in Oxford University College, MS 14, the text is read in an entirely different light. It does not reflect back on the author or subject, but functions rather as advice to the reader. Separated entirely from Raymond or Catherine, the *auctoritas* needs to be reflected in the first sentence that "sum clerkes seyne & soþe it is," a much weaker validation of the text's veracity than coming from a cleric himself citing doctors of holy church. The way it has been anthologized changes its meaning entirely, but it also enters into a much wider discourse of *discretio spirituum* that circulated in many forms throughout the medieval Christian west (starting with St Paul's letters to the Corinthians, moving through St Augustine, and culminating in Jean Gerson's writings among those by other prominent late medieval theologians).[69] Rosalynn Voaden notes, "As a discourse, *discretio spirituum* both facilitates the articulation and understanding of the visionary experience, defines its dangers and limitations, and controls what are deemed to be deviant forms of that experience."[70]

As with "The Cleannesse" itself, via the philosophies of William Flete, Catherine is mirroring an already familiar English spiritual fascination. Note, for example, the very similar language in the fourteenth-century contemplative text *The Cloud of Unknowing* (which is coupled with the "Discernment of Spirits" in Oxford University College, MS 14):

For as fast after soche a fals felyng comeþ a trewe knowing in Gods scole. For I telle þee trewly þat þe deuil haþ his contemplatyues, as God haþ his. Þis disseite of fals felyng, & of fals knowyng folowyng þer-on, haþ diuerse & wonderful variacions, after þe dyuerste of states & þe sotyl condicions of hem þat ben disceyuid; as haþ þe trewe felyng & knowyng of hem þat ben sauid.[71]

The language puts the "Discernment of Spirits" very much within the reader's power – it is a feeling, a knowing that is already there. For Catherine, this is described in terms of either comfort or bitterness that will make themselves apparent after the vision has passed. Bridget of Sweden, similarly, has a *discretio spirituum* in her *Liber Celestis*, where the Middle English version of her text reads: "At þe bygynnyng, he comes as he were a frende and comfortour, bot, at þe last, he byttes as it were a hound, and is about to gildir a man … Bot when þe gude spirit commes, sai to him, 'Kindell þe lufe of God in mi hert. And all if I be unworþi to haue þe, neuerþelesse I haue mikill nede of þe.'"[72]

What does it mean that these texts get excerpted from the larger Catherine pieces and circulate on their own, particularly in miscellanies, the way it is included in the devotional compilation represented in Harley 2409? As we have seen, visionary culture or even the expectation of a vision was far from the norm in England and did not have the same kind of currency it held on much of the Continent during the late Middle Ages. What does the reader of this text see in Catherine's description as to discerning the origin of a vision? In the *Legenda major*, it serves a larger purpose of validating much of what Catherine describes that she has seen and knows through her own visions, but to the English reader who sees it out of context, it seems to gesture towards a hidden spiritual life that has less extant textual presence. Clearly, the anthologizers/excerpters felt the passage holds an important, maybe even crucial, lesson. But that assumption is predicated on the belief that readers experience visions and need to understand how to parse them. For the reader who may not have encountered a vision, it almost permits that experience to happen, giving the reader concrete guidelines and a tacit permission. One can imagine a reader like Margery Kempe thrilled to come across this text and the lessons therein.

Marrying Christ: Divine Knowledge as Self- Knowledge

In Harley 2409, the "Discernment of Spirits" is sandwiched between "The Cleannesse" and another excerpt from Raymond of Capua's *Legenda major* of Catherine. At first glance, it seems neither connected to "The Cleannesse" nor the "Discernment of Spirits." Here, Catherine returns to the theme of divine knowledge as self-knowledge, again relaying a visionary conversation with Christ:

Forþer more oure saueour sayd until hir: Doghter knowes you who I am & who þou art? If þou know þies ii verraily, þou shal be a blissed woman.

Þu ert she þat ert noght. And I am I þat am. If þou haue þis knowyng in þe, þine enemy may neuer begyle þe bot you shal ascape alle his snares. And þou shal neuer consent to þings þat es agayn my bidyng. And alle grace & all vertue and al charite you shal gete with outen difficulte.[73]

The passage hits some of the main points of traditional mystical discourse of the disavowal of self in the face of God: "You are she who is nought, and I am I that am." The marginal comment made by a contemporary reader is placed next to the text of "I am that I am," reading *"ego sum qui sum."* It is one of the few pieces of marginalia in the entire manuscript, but confirms a Latin-literate reader, who cites Exodus 3:14: "God said to Moses: I AM WHO AM. He said: Thus shalt thou say to the children of Israel: HE WHO IS, hath sent me to you." It is never clear with a clerical amanuensis like Raymond whether the biblical nods are his or Catherine's, but the sense of self-annihilation as the path to self-knowledge is certainly hers, a theme that recurs through the text and in her letters and other documents. Notably, this excerpt will reappear in the history of Catherine's texts in England. It is in British Library, MS Royal 17 D.V., a late fifteenth-century manuscript that contains several Middle English excerpts from Catherine's *Legenda major*. These will be reprinted in 1521 by Henry Pepwell as some of Catherine's "Divers Doctrines." Although the translation is somewhat different, it is very close to the text (and is even closer to de Worde's 1492 edition), indicating a common source text that had Catherine's *Lyf* in the vernacular.[74]

The final part of Harley 2409 appears to be a slightly looser translation of a passage from the *Legenda major*, not as clearly identifiable as the "Discernment of Spirits" or the section on self- knowledge, but still close enough to insure that it comes from Raymond of Capua's narrative and not from another document concerning Catherine such as *Il Dialogo*. It recounts one of the major mystical moments of Catherine's life and legend, her marriage to Christ. In this scene, Catherine desires a sign of her faith from God who grants her a wedding as a sign of devotion. When it is time for the ceremony, Jesus appears with Mary, Paul, and St Dominic, among others:

Þis Dame Kateryne asked on a tyme of our lord þat he wolde vouche safe fortil eke hir faith. And our lord aunswerd & saide, "Doghter, I wil wedde þe in faithe." And oft tymes when she praied for þe same grace, our lord aunswerd hir with same wordes. And efter þat she had besied hir feruently in wakyng fastyng and praying, at þe laste oure lord apered until hir and saide: "I haye sette and ordeyned a feste day of solmpne

weddyng of þi soule to me as I haf behette forto wedde þe to me in fay-
the." After þis opon a tyme oure lord Jhesu wiþe his moder Mary, Johan
þe Wangelist, Paul þe Apostle, and saynt Domynyk, and David þe proph-
ete apered vntil hir."[75]

This section is somewhat shortened from the fuller Latin description
but keeps the essential dialogue and elements. The Wynkyn de Worde,
however, includes a full translation of the Latin, indicating a more judi-
cious editing hand that has spliced and compiled these texts as one.

Catherine's mystical marriage to Christ, along with her reception of
the stigmata, are the most demonstrably mystical elements of her *vitae*,
and again it is notable that this is excerpted and translated in England,
where such texts and their contents were less popular; indeed, there
are no descriptions of her received stigmata in any surviving English
texts, and this appendix to "The Cleannesse" from the *Legenda major*
only survives in this one manuscript, indicating perhaps a small circulation. The wedding is explicitly described, with an exchange of vows
and rings to validate it:

And oure lady pyttande forth þe right hand of Dame Kateryne. Criste putte
þar on a ryng and saide: "I wedde þe to me þi maker and þi saueoure in
faithe, þe whilk shal euer be keped wiþ outen wemme until þe tyme þat
yu make þine endles weddynge feste wiþe me in heuen. And þarfore my
spouse loke þat you wirke now strongly and be noȝt in doute, for all þings
þat er nedful vnto þe for soule or for body þurgh myne ordynaunce and my
peruayance shal redily be broght vnto þine handes. And be þe myght of þe
faithe in þe whilk þou ert now armed, þou shal selily ouercome alkyns adu-
ersite." And when þis was sayde þat ioyful visyon vnapered. And þe ryng
abode stiff on hir fynger, Deo Gratias.[76]

With the marriage, Catherine is given the strength through God to
overcome all of her earthly adversaries and awaits her death for the
wedding feast in heaven. In Catherine's letters, she describes the wedding ring as made from Jesus's foreskin, but this is not in her *Legenda
major*, seemingly intentionally omitted by Raymond of Capua.[77] Dyan
Elliot points out that for Raymond, this moment is the cornerstone
of Catherine's spirituality and that he "emphasiz[es] the experience
more than Catherine does herself in the course of her writings."[78] Its
significance clearly resonates with the compiler of Harley 2409 who
appends it to "The Cleannesse" and the "Discernment of Sprits." With

its addition, "The Cleannesse" takes on a new valence as a discussion between Christ and a Bride of Christ, a more mystical and definitely female understanding than the text offers on its own.

Although Margery Kempe never explicitly mentions a familiarity with Catherine's story, the actual wedding ceremony as it is described here resonates so strongly with Kempe's own description of her mystical marriage to the Godhead, complete with witnesses (Mary, John the Evangelist, St Paul, St Dominic, and David), a wedding ring and "vows," that it seems unlikely she was unfamiliar with this moment in Catherine's life:

> And than the Fadyr toke hir be the hand in hir sowle befor the Sone and the Holy Gost and the Modyr of Jhesu and alle the twelve apostelys and Seynt Kateryn and Seynt Margarete and many other seyntys and holy virgynes wyth gret multitude of awngelys, seying to hir sowle, "I take the, Margery, for my weddyd wyfe, for fayrar, for fowelar, for richar, for powerar, so that thu be buxom and bonyr to do what I byd the do. For, dowtyr, ther was nevyr childe so buxom to the modyr as I schal be to the bothe in wel and in wo, to help the and comfort the. And therto I make the suyrté." And than the Modyr of God and alle the seyntys that wer ther present in hir sowle preyde that thei myth have mech joy togedyr.[79]

The moment of the "mystical marriage" between God and Catherine finds its way into many Continental artistic representations of Catherine and, with the exchange of hearts she makes with God and her stigmata, marks her iconographically. It also identifies her as a visionary and mystic in a way that no other moment does as clearly. This portion of the *Legenda major* could not simply be excerpted, without reference to Catherine herself, as it is in "The Cleannesse" when it circulates separately; the marriage is especially Catherine's and serves as a model for other visionary women. Such a vision conversely casts her into a category of suspicion among her sceptics.

In closing, I would like to look at how these excerpts all function together in the manuscript Harley 2409. Outside of one other late fifteenth-century manuscript (British Library, Royal MS 17 D v) that contains parts of Catherine's *Legenda major* in translation, there is no other evidence in addition to Harley 2409 that the *Legenda* had much circulation in English before the de Worde edition in 1492. However, the way that the elements are selectively clipped and placed together after "The Cleannesse" suggest that the complier had access to a complete

Legenda in translation (there is no indication that the compiler is also the translator in the manuscript). Written in one hand, owned by women religious, the codex seemed to have been assembled for a particular reader – and the Catherine segment is one of only four texts, with one of the remaining three being William Flete's *Remedies against Temptations*.

Within only a few pages of Harley 2409 (the Catherine sections appear from folios 70r to 75r), four different texts related to Catherine are collated into one short passage – all under the title, "Here follows how þe holy mayden Katheryne of Seen first began to sette her here fully to god warred." They are concluded with the line "Here endes þe forsayde visions of Dame Kateryne Seen." It functions almost as a mini-anthology in itself, where the compiler took what he felt were four essential elements of Catherine's life and placed them together: her treatise on "The Cleannesse of Sowle," the "Discernment of Spirits," how self-knowledge is reflected in knowing God, and the description of her mystical marriage to Christ. If this was the entirety of Catherine's story that the reader ever knew, two of her most important accomplishments – the writing of her own *Dialogo* and the political influence she held in her dealings with the papacy – are completely erased in relation to her more mystical, visionary qualities. Catherine has been excerpted into a kind of guidebook for the near-visionary or aspiring visionary – a very different Catherine than the short "Cleannesse" Catherine who appears in nearly all the other manuscripts that house that text. There, she provides guidelines for sinless living without the context of discerning visions or an accounting of her mystical marriage.

These excerpts, more than the complete versions of Catherine's texts, demonstrate the ways in which different compilers may shape Catherine into the kind of textual authority that they need for the purposes of their anthologies or readership. The selections of "The Cleannesse" and the *Legenda major* instead shows a carefully curated selection to convey a demonstrated interest in women's visionary literature and the woman mystic in medieval England. They also demonstrate the ways in which Catherine can be clipped to accommodate different strands of late medieval English spirituality – as in turn pedantic, methodological, visionary, or mystical. Who Catherine is and the purpose she serves is not inherent in the text itself, but rather in the pen of the compiler.

Chapter Four

The Orcherd of Syon: How to Read in the Convent

Syon Abbey and Medieval Devotional Reading Culture

Throughout medieval Europe, Catherine of Siena and Bridget of Sweden were often mentioned in the same breath. These near contemporaries (Bridget lived from 1303 to 1370, Catherine from 1347 to 1380) did indeed have some similar profiles. They were both politically active, engaging particularly with Gregory XI hoping to move the Avignon papacy back to what they considered its righful and holy place in Rome. Both were visionaries and had powerful male Church members supporting their visions and its implications. Both wrote letters, books of revelations, and prayers that were copied, disseminated, and spread their words far beyond their native homes.[1] They certainly knew of each other, working in similar ways through powerful political and religious circles, and Catherine had some connections with Bishop Alfonso da Vadaterra, Bridget's confessor, after Bridget's death. Catherine and Bridget were not always positively known in tandem, however. Important members of the Church constantly questioned and criticized their visions, their power, and the implications of their advice.[2] Despite the cases against them and their visionary status, it is worth noting that they are the only two visionary laywomen who became saints in the Middle Ages; Bridget's disputed canonization took place three times, by three popes, before it was permanent (1391, 1415, and 1419), and Catherine was canonized in 1461, nearly a century after her death and after a long campaign for her sainthood. But while Catherine's presence in medieval England is notable, Bridget's had a firmer hold largely due to the prominence of the Bridgettine convent Syon Abbey. Catherine's connection to both Bridget and to Syon Abbey significantly shaped her tradition and the English interpretation of her texts. Bridget functions as a kind of palimpsest on Catherine, guiding the reader to understand the latter through the lens of Bridgettine influence and thought.

Bridget had established her own order of nuns, and Syon Abbey was not only Bridgettine, it was the most important house for religious women in fifteenth-century England.[3] Established in 1415, less than fifty years after Bridget's death, the professed nuns of Syon were not so far removed from their founding mother who had imagined an international network of Bridgettine houses of both brothers and sisters. Vincent Gillespie explains the founding of Syon:

> The English house, when finally established by Henry V early in 1415, cost many thousands to build and continued to cost thousands to maintain and develop as it moved and grew in the course of the fifteenth century. Syon … was envisaged as part of a network of three houses (the others were the Charterhouse of Jesus of Bethlehem and an unachieved foundation of Celestines). The scale and prestige of Henry's plans for these houses, all intended to nestle close to the royal palace at Sheen, undoubtedly sent signals about the ambition and purposefulness of the new king (he had been on the throne less than two years when he laid the foundation stone for Syon in February 1415).[4]

Henry's establishment was meant to stand as a monument against heresies, capitalizing on the feeling that Bridgettines were "guardians and protectors of the faith."[5] And Bridget's role in bringing the papacy from Avignon to Rome, like Catherine's, stood as rebuke to the French during and after the Hundred Years' War.[6]

But the connection between Catherine and Bridget was not only English. Even in Catherine's native Italy, Bridgettine nuns would prove instrumental in the proliferation of Catherine's cult and dissemination of her texts. Since Catherine herself was not a professed nun – although the *mantellatae*, the Dominican third order of which Catherine was part, flourished after her death – strict adherents of Catherine's philosophy may have been drawn to a more rigorous religious or enclosed life. A Dominican convent seemed a natural fit for Catherine devotees, and, indeed, many women who venerated Catherine were Dominican nuns. Gabriella Zarri points to at least one Italian convent, San Domenico of Pisa, that held Catherine's *Legenda major* in its library and most likely her *Dialogo* as well. But Zarri also writes that this convent had a deep commitment to Bridget of Sweden and that "devotion to this Scandinavian prophet, who had shared Catherine's commitment to bring the Holy See back to Rome, was deeply rooted in the leaders of the Dominican observance."[7] More significantly for the transmission of texts to England, Catherine's texts were known and copied at the Bridgettine double monastery in Florence known as "Paradiso." Zarri notes that at Paradiso, the nuns were scribes and disseminators of Catherine's texts: "In addition to St. Birgitta's *Rivelazioni*, the nuns copied and disseminated the *Dialogo*, and the *Lettere* of Catherine of Siena."[8] And one preacher closely associated with the convent, Feo Belcari, wrote a *lauda* in Catherine's honour that explicitly draws from *Il Dialogo*.[9] Indeed, it is possibly through this connection that the *Dialogo* found its way to Syon Abbey in the first place (rather than through the Carthusian connection linked to Stephen Maconi as has long been assumed). Paradiso ran into trouble around 1421, which may have led to Martin V's papal legislation abolishing double monasteries, a legislation that brought a delegation from Syon to Rome in 1423 in order to overturn it (the delegation was ultimately successful).[10] While in Italy, the English Bridgettine scribe and translator Symon Wynter had material copied – possibly from Paradiso – that he subsequently brought back to Syon. Catherine's *Dialogo*, to become *The Orcherd of Syon*, may very well have been one of them.[11]

Calling Catherine's *Dialogo* by the title *The Orcherd of Syon* places her text firmly within a Bridgettine context and in some ways protects the contents of the text through this association. Syon's connection to power, and particularly royal power, persisted through to the Reformation. The abbey is exiled abroad in 1539 during the dissolution of the monasteries enacted by Henry VIII but returns to England under Mary Tudor when the country returns to Catholicism. Mary even made provisions for Syon Abbey in her will, demonstrating its close connection to her Catholic identity, pointing out that she had revitalized the foundation upon her ascension to the throne. Mary is concerned with both the re-establishment of the house, using the will to denounce its dissolution, and the religious who lived there:

> And whereas the Howses of Shene and Sion ... the oon of Monks of th' order of Carthusians and th' other of Nunns Ordines Stae Brigittae wer in the tyme of the late Scisme within this Realme clerly dissolv'd and defac'd, which sayde howses are lately by my said dere Lord and husband and by me reviv'd ... and we have restor'd and endow'd them severally with

diverse Mannors, londs, tenements and hereditaments, sometyme parcell of ther severall possessions. For a further increase of their lyvyng … I will and give unto ether of the said Religious howses of Shene and Sion, the summe of fyve hundred pownds of lawfull money of Englond.[12]

She closes this section of the will asking that the houses of Sheen and Syon "praye for my Soulle … and for the Soulle of the said good and vertuous Quene my Mother, and for the Soulles of all other our Progenitours, and namely the said Kynge Henry 5 as they were bounden by the ancyente Statuts and ordyenances of ther Severall foundacyons."[13] In this way, Mary looks back to the founding of Syon and forward to a future where she imagined a Catholic England would rise again. Mary's view of Syon as a lynchpin of this kind of future attests further to its importance in English devotional culture.

At the centre of both that culture and of Syon stood the practice of devotional reading. Bridget, known for her learning and writing, has a chapter of her *vita* solely devoted to her reading practice; it notes that "when she was not occupied with manual labor, she was continually rereading the lives of the saints and the bible, which she had caused to be written out for herself in her own language."[14] This centrality of vernacular devotional reading is made part of the Bridgettine Rule at Syon and other houses. *The Myroure of Oure Ladye*, an early fifteenth-century devotional guide used by the sisters of Syon, describes both the elements of divine service as well as the office used by the sisters, giving in great detail the different kinds of reading expected of the nuns. In his prologue, the translator portrays the care needed in selecting the appropriate books, the state of mind one needs to attend to contemplative reading, and the various ways of reading – aloud, repeatedly, meditatively. The writer explains:

> For some bokes ar made to enforme the vnderstondynge. & to tel how spiritual persones outghte to be gouerned in all theyr lyuynge that they may knowe what they shall leue. & what they shall do, how they shulde laboure in clensyng of theyr conscyence. & in gettyng of vertewes how they shulde withstonde temptacyons & suffer trybulacyons. & How they shall pray. & occupy them in gostly exercyse. with many suche other full holy doctrynes.[15]

The translator details that there are books of uplifting joy, books that describe the horrors of sin, books that require inward reflection, books for the mind, and books for the heart; the pious sister can find a book for each occasion, a remedy for every concern.

"The Syon Additions," a supplement to the Bridgettine Rule added specifically for the English sisters, also describes both public and private reading among its adherents and suggests its novices should have their own books, implying that those entering the abbey should come with a background in learned reading (although the rule does make room for unlettered nuns):

> If any kepe her ȝere of profe in the courte with, outeforth, and be not of power by no mene to pay for her borde, skole, and other costes, perteynyng to her profession, sche oweth to be founde of the monastery. If sche or els her frendes, be of power to fynde her, it is reson that þei pay for alle her necessaryes, and for all the costes, in the day of her profession, purueyng for her bokes, beddynge, profession rynge, dyner, offerynge, and suche oþer.[16]

This emphasis on learned women is apparent in the choice of leadership at Syon Abbey's founding. Its first abbess, Matilda Newton, came from Barking Abbey – a convent with a long history of women's learning, reading, and book production.[17] Newton was later dismissed from her post for refusing to accept modifications to the Bridgettine rules that were not Bridget's herself. Rebecca Krug describes how Newton's close and learned reading of the rule is at the heart of her insubordination and dismissal: "Having been recruited to head a Bridgettine monastery, Matilda had become intimately acquainted with Bridgettine writings and believed that legislation composed by the order's patron constituted the only 'rule' that the community should follow."[18] Even with Newton's departure, reading and book production (either by Sheen monks with an intended Syon audience or by Syon brothers) remains at the heart of Syon Abbey. Between 1415 and 1630, 13 per cent of the nuns are known to have had personal copies of books.[19] There is also some compelling evidence of limited scribal activity at Syon by the nuns there, so there may have been some culture of copying and writing among the sisters as well.[20]

A Sienese Inside Syon and Out

Books written and copied at Syon Abbey were not meant just for the nuns who professed there. Its close connection to the Charterhouse at

Sheen already showed a vibrant back and forth between the books and manuscripts of the two houses, and the early English printers William Caxton and Wynkyn de Worde found much of their material from Syon. The Carthusians at Sheen, in particular, were known as book producers and joined in Carthusians on the Continent in the distribution of devotional materials both in Latin and the vernacular. Significantly, this may be due to the influence of Stephen Maconi, one of Catherine of Siena's most fervent followers.[21] As noted in chapter one, Stephen Maconi had implemented a program of translation and dissemination of important devotional texts throughout the Carthusian order. With Sheen founded only four years after Maconi stepped down as prior and ten years before his death, it is highly probable that some of Catherine's texts made their way to English libraries through these Carthusian channels. The texts may also have come via Bridgettine contacts, such as the Syon delegation's visit to Rome and opportunity to copy books from Paradiso's library. With both Maconi's and Bridget's connection to Catherine, it is no wonder that her texts were so firmly rooted at Syon.

In this highly literate context we find texts about Catherine of Siena that assume an audience deeply familiar with Bridget, implicitly drawing an intimate connection between the two women. Nancy Bradley Warren compares Catherine and Bridget with Julian of Norwich, explaining how they all interact within an English devotional and literary context, pointing out that all three women are interested in an embodied piety and that this infuses their visionary texts.[22] Catherine and Bridget are most closely aligned, however, because of their political activism regarding the papacy's move back to Rome and social engagement with the world around them. While Julian's book may have not been intended for a wide audience, Bridget's and Catherine's writings always were. Once at Syon Abbey, many texts were directed outward – to other religious houses and, significantly, to the laity. Syon, more than Sheen, Vincent Gillespie writes, "may deliberately have functioned as a source of copies of orthodox and approved texts of vernacular devotional and para-mystical materials, whose impacts would have been enhanced by the abbey's close links with Westminster and London, and its popularity with gentry and noble clients who turned to the house for spiritual guidance."[23] The books at Syon, then, always had a twofold purpose – to be private devotional readings and publicly shared texts.

One book with probable Syon ties is the previously discussed *Speculum Devotorum*, a fifteenth-century compilation of the *Meditationes Vitae Christi* interspersed with other texts. Paul Patterson has noted the *Speculum* has strong ties to Syon Abbey.[24] In the preface to the text, the author writes that he has "browgth inne othyr doctorys in diuerse places, as to the moral vertuys, and also summe reuelacyonys of approuyd wymmen."[25] These "approuyd wymmen" turn out to be Mechthild of Hackeborn, Elizabeth of Hungary, as well as, notably, Catherine of Siena and Bridget of Sweden; their approval eliminates any suggestion of heresy or even heterodoxy in a Church suspicious of some vernacular devotional literature.[26] However, merely labelling the women as "approved," calls attention to the fact that many women (and their literature) in circulation is likely "unapproved." The author introduces Catherine's short excerpt as follows, "How a man or a womman mygth knowe a goode vysyon fro a badde, and whenne they be of God and of an euyl spyryt, oure Lorde taugth Kateryne of Sene a prophytable lore."[27] Catherine's section is about discerning good visions from demonic ones, reassuring her readers about her (and by association in this text, Bridget's) veracity. This *discretio spirituum* is the same passage that circulated in Harley 2409 appended to "The Cleannesse of Sowle," indicating that it had independent circulation in medieval England.[28] The fact that Catherine's *discretio spirituum* is tied to Syon, whose very existence is predicated on the visions of Bridget of Sweden, points to the paradox surrounding visionary women's literature and the wisdom it has to offer religious and lay readers, especially other women.

Another manuscript, the Latin fifteenth-century codex Sloane 982, is at first glance merely a copy of Bridget's *Revelations*. Its title, both in the manuscript in a contemporary hand and now in its library catalogue, is "Revelationes Beate Brigitte," though this is not the sole or even the first text in the codex. However, the *Revelations* forms the central and overarching text of the book, interspersed with other meditational material (notably those by Anselm of Canterbury, Gregory the Great, and Mechthild of Hackeborn). The Bridget section has parts that are largely intermixed with texts from various traditions, while maintaining an overall narrative of the *Revelations* – its purpose is not accuracy but meditation. Although the manuscript is not explicitly linked to Syon Abbey, Ann Hutchinson has noted that its apparent devotion to Bridget along with that to the Holy Name mirrors other manuscripts that are definitely of Syon provenance (such as Cambridge, Corpus Christi College, MS 141).[29] So, the evidence is strong that this may be a Syon book, but even if that were not so, it is "Bridget's book" and its readers held it to be so. However, when the Latin text of Bridget's *Revelations* end, and before the next text (a treatise from John the Evangelist) begins, there is a Middle English prayer, unattributed, and seemingly the *coda* to Bridget. However, it is actually Catherine of Siena's "The Cleannesse of Sowle," discussed at length in the previous chapter. There is no indication that this is not Bridget, and its placement and wording would certainly lead the readers to believe it was, pointing to the similar flavour of the two women visionaries. This is one of only two vernacular texts (the other equally short and attributed to Mechthild) in an otherwise Latin manuscript, so there is a clear indication that the text is different than that which precedes it (Bridget's *Revelations*). However, the "devout woman," although Catherine, is not identified at all. The compiler clearly sensed she belonged with Bridget and Mechthild, but a reader could easily understand the subject to be Bridget or one of her nuns. Catherine gets subsumed here and erased of her individual identity. The piece's vernacularity indicates it comes from a different source entirely than the Bridget text. Rosalyn Voaden has looked closely at the Mechthild excerpts interspersed throughout this codex, and concludes that the framing of potentially disruptive women's visionary texts (Bridget, Catherine, and Mechthild) is validated and authorized by the male authorities and fathers that surround them.[30] In the same way, this vernacular excerpt from Catherine is validated by the Latin *Revelations* of Bridget that surround it as well. None of the texts concerning Bridget have the same central interest in self-annihilation and denial that the Catherine texts do. "The Cleannesse of Sowle" is in many ways an encapsulation of Catherine's theological philosophy and relationship to the divine. Nestled as it is in Sloane 982 among the Bridget texts, it offers its readers a new aspect of their private relationship with God and to their devotional reading.

Bridget's textual legacy in medieval England, Roger Ellis writes, can fall into three categories: "Those that contained a prophetic element, or described the requirements of the spiritual life, or provided information about the life of Christ and the Virgin."[31] If we take Catherine's English corpus as a whole most of the works that circulated fall into this second category, the requirements of the spiritual life. This is the place where texts by and about Bridget and Catherine most clearly intersected and are most often paired. Bridget has a much wider circulation of her *Revelations* than Catherine does of her *Dialogo*, which is shorter and does not contain nearly as much of the prophetic element that Bridget's do. However, it is Catherine's most revelatory text, *Dialogo*, that becomes associated with Syon Abbey, *The Orcherd of Syon*. This text most clearly demonstrates that there was an interest in the description of visionary moments and a discouragement of the practice of them. The translation is specifically set up to highlight this disconnect for its readers, both in the convent and later for lay consumers when the text gets printed by Wynkyn de Worde.

If *Il Dialogo* came to England initially through the hands of nuns at Paradiso, the role they played has been erased, and instead the male translator/scribe becomes the guiding voice and hand of the *The Orcherd*. Courtney E. Rydel has written about a similar phenomenon in the transmission of Mechthild of Hackeborn's *Booke of Gostlye Grace* from its origins to its English version. In that case, two nuns acted as the scribes for Mechthild, and then worked with her afterward to edit and shape the book. Rydel argues that a "translator bringing Mechtild's text into the vernacular for a fifteenth-century English audience that included women would have been highly motivated to change the text to emphasize clerical authority and supervision of women's religious experiences."[32] She writes that the translator apparently changed the number and gender of the scribes in order to fit a vision of male authority, effectively erasing the women's participation. As with Mechthild, so we can see with Catherine. For example, Virginia Bainbridge speculates that an Italian nun at Syon, Sr. Magdalena Baptista Boeria, may have helped prepare the 1519 Wynkyn de Worde edition of the text.[33] Likewise, Catherine's known female scribes (mostly noted as scribes in letters) are not mentioned in Raymond's *Legenda major*, as are most of Catherine's other scribes and followers, and here, potentially, the female Paradiso scribes of the *Dialogo* are written over by the English male translator of *The Orcherd*.

Reading *The Orcherd in Syon*

Catherine's *Il Dialogo* details her visionary understanding of Christ. Dictated to her followers, who then knew it by a number of titles, including *Il Libro* and *Il Dialogo della Divina Provvidenza*, the book describes a dialogue with Christ and Catherine and includes at its core a complex metaphor of Christ as a bridge connecting humanity and the divine. Completed in 1378, Catherine's "book" (as she called it) circulated after her death in Italian and in Latin with three distinct translations executed by different followers: Cristofano di Gano Guidini, Stephen Maconi, and Raymond of Capua.[34] The surviving Middle English translation is based on Guidini's Latin version, and is almost certainly related to the only complete extant Latin version of Catherine's *Dialogo* in Britain, the fifteenth-century codex Edinburgh, MS 87 (D b IV 18), itself likely owned by the Dominican convent near Edinburgh dedicated to the saint.[35] The Latin shares with all three of the Middle English translations (themselves clearly interrelated) a short prologue and some phrasing not found in the Italian versions. The Middle English translation of *Il Dialogo* is a massive, important work. Known in its Latin forms in England as Catherine's *Liber Divine Doctrine* or her *Revelations*, the text is reimagined by its anonymous Middle English translator as specifically for the nuns of Syon and becomes known as *The Orcherd of Syon* due to an explicit in one of the surviving codices (other manuscripts entitle it *The Book of Divine Doctrine*); this is also the name that Wynkyn de Worde would give his edition of the book. *The Orcherd* survives in both manuscript and print copies attesting to some significant circulation.[36] While there was clearly a Latin circulation of Catherine's *Dialogo* in England – for example, the aforementioned Edinburgh copy,[37] another is found among the list of books that John Blacman (a Fellow of Merton College, Oxford, and a spiritual adviser to Henry IV) bequeaths to Witham Charterhouse, named the "Revelaciones Sancte Katerine de Senis"[38] – most codices are in the vernacular.[39] Another Blacman book donated to Witham, containing Henry Suso's *Horologium*, has a marginal notation concerning Catherine's *Revelations*.[40] The brethren of Syon Abbey did own at least one Latin version, but it is now lost to us; it is mentioned twice in Thomas Betson's *registrum* of the Syon brethren (c. 1500–c. 1524).[41] Its continental circulation, too, seemed to be primarily in the vernacular.[42]

Il Dialogo is a difficult text in Latin, and translating it was a Herculean endeavour. The modern-day translator of Catherine's book, Suzanne Noffke, notes that "the task of translating Catherine is not an easy one. In the torrent of her thought she frequently loses sight of her pronominal antecedents, her tense sequence, even sometimes of the fact that she has left in mid-air the sentence with which she began, while getting lost in a whole series of parentheses."[43] And yet, not only is the text translated, there are three complete extant manuscripts, all from the fifteenth century. As Phyllis Hodgson and Gabriel M. Liegey, the editors of the only modern edition of *The Orcherd*, write, "All three manuscripts are large, finely written, elaborate, and contain a full and faithful paraphrase of *Il Dialogo*, itself estimated to be about 130,000 words."[44] Needless to say, these manuscripts are hefty tomes that are not for the faint-hearted scribe or reader. The translation of the *Dialogo* into *The Orcherd* was a major project with the Syon nuns as its intended audience, a commentary on just how intense and centred their reading was meant to be. The translator remains unknown to us, although he no doubt had extremely close connections to Syon – either a Syon brother himself or a neighbouring Carthusian at the Charterhouse of Sheen.[45]

As the Middle English translation of the text explains, Catherine dictated her book in a mystical state:

> Here begynneþ þe boke of diuine doctrine, þat is to seie, of Goddis techinge, ȝouen bi þe persone of God þe fader to þe intellecte of þe glorious virgyn, Seint Katerine of Seene, of þe Ordre of Seint Dominike, which was write as sche endited in her moder tunge, when sche was in contemplacioun inrapt of spirit, and sche heringe actueli and in þe same tyme tellinge tofore meny what oure Lord God spake in her.[46]

This prologue, not present in the Italian but preserved in the Latin version represented in Edinburgh, MS 87 (D b IV 18), is already deeply invested in both the mystical process and how it is disseminated.[47] Catherine – in a state that is either fully outside herself (in rapture of spirit) or fully inside herself (given by God directly to her intellect) – hears and dictates in her Tuscan tongue what she understands from God.[48] The simultaneity of the hearing and telling is stressed here, as is the sameness of the language – there is no gap from God to what the scribes put to paper, stressing both the immediacy and the vernacularity of Catherine's connection to the divine. The version before the reader – edited, translated into Latin, translated into English, resituated for its Syon readers – is a far remove from that moment of rapture/hearing/telling, but this prologue succeeds the English translator's preface and is placed just prior to the text itself, bringing the reader directly to that moment when Catherine was "inrapt of spirit."[49] In looking at slightly later Carmelite nuns' visionary texts and experiences, Nicky Hallett has pointed out that the senses are the place where body meets mind, and that the visionary experience (and, indeed, the reading experience of that visionary) is pointing to a "sensory capacity and those areas that language, like bodies, cannot apprehend: the extra-sensory that so structures their approach to meaning."[50] *The Orcherd* is a text that is both inside and outside of language, just as Catherine in her moment of rapture and dictation is both simultaneously inside and outside of herself. The translator is aware of these contrary tensions and is attempting through his prologue to somehow guide the reader through the disorienting experience that the text confers.

In *The Orcherd*, a soul (Catherine) offers God four petitions: that she be allowed to suffer in atonement, that the Church be reformed, that Christians live in peace, and that God grant the world divine providence, mercy and justice according to his will. These requests lead to a layered dialogue where Catherine returns, circularly and repeatedly, to the same points with various elaborations. The centre of the book, both literally and metaphorically, is her understanding of God as a bridge of truth. The bridge's three stairways correspond to the feet, side wound, and mouth of Jesus, and as souls ascend these stairways they relinquish their sinful lives, engage in virtue, and ultimately end in union with God. This metaphor is the touchstone of the book, describing God as the way to oneness and unity with truth, life, and mercy. Phyllis Hodgson notes that the use of this recurrent imagery "is not to be found earlier in English mystical writings. The opening vision of *Piers Plowman* has comparable vastness and sublimity, but it is surpassed in dynamic force by the Bridge, which through its manifold interpretation is essentially a symbol of movement – the Way, the Truth, the Life."[51] Catherine's metaphoric language is complex and learned, reflecting what she has shown elsewhere in letters and conversation with followers: Catherine is keenly aware of the intersection of her gender and her role as visionary.[52]

Although *The Orcherd* is not a title given by the translator, he imposes the orchard metaphor in a remarkable prologue, suggesting that the reader see more than a book in front of her. In this excerpt, the translator describes the metaphor to his readers, writing that the book is an orchard and the wisdom within it are fruits to be picked and eaten. These fruits are sometimes sweet, sometimes medicinally bitter, but they should be savoured slowly and truly digested:

> Þis book of reuelaciouns as for ʒoure goostly comfort to ʒou I clepe it a fruytful orcherd. This orcherd by Goddis grace my wil is to deuyde into seuene parties, and ech party into fyue chapitres, as ʒe mowe se and rede in þe kalender folowynge. In þis orcherd, whanne ʒe wolen be conforted, ʒe mowe walke and se boþe fruyt and herbis. And albeit þat sum fruyt or herbis seeme to summe scharpe, hard, or bitter, ʒit to purgynge of þe soule þei ben ful speeful and profitable, whanne þei ben discreetly take and resceyued by counceil. Therfore, religiouse sustren, in þis goostli orcherd at reesonable tyme ordeyned, I wole þat ʒe disporte ʒou & walke aboute where ʒe wolen wiþ ʒoure mynde & resoun, in what aleye ʒou lyke, and namely þere ʒe sauouren best, as ʒe ben disposid.[53]

While the original *Dialogo* has subdivisions, but no overarching chapter divisions, *The Orcherd* is divided into seven parts of five chapters each, which, the translator explains, are "xxxv alleyes" where the reader may choose to walk, taste, and chew the advice offered there. The image of reading as "walk[ing] aboute where ȝe wolen wiþ ȝoure mynde & resoun" demonstrates an active and engaged reading that the translator is espousing; choosing what to read, reading it, and understanding it are all given active corporeal metaphors (walking / tasting / digesting). However, this division imposed on the text and the encouragement of excerpted reading rather than taking in the whole of the book may have the effect of limiting a program of immersive reading in the visionary text by forcing a logic, an order, and a method to a text that otherwise is convoluted and free-flowing. Whereas a reader of the Italian *Dialogo* can literally get lost in its words, finding oneself in a maze of repeated ideas and images, the reader of *The Orcherd* is frequently stopped, given a summary, and, as the translator encourages, meant to dwell on what has been read in small "digestible" pieces.

In translating the *Dialogo*, the translator does not merely change the language of the text. His preface and chapter divisions direct and change how the text is read. He translates Catherine into a Bridgettine context. He translates Catherine from an Italian saint into an English mystic. He also requires a consciousness about one's reading practices and environment because the translator is so insistent about the ways in which the text must be read. There are several demands on the various readers' imaginations here. Rebecca Krug notes that this "approaches the distractions of living among other people explicitly" and that the "*Orcherd* in fact pointedly juxtaposes its private universe with the busyness of monastic life."[54] The medieval Syon nun is actively imagining herself out of the cloister and into the vineyard. She is also simultaneously reinforcing her own connection to the Bridgettine order. Hodgson notes what an apt metaphor the translator has employed, writing, "This framework is appropriate ... for Syon Abbey, for a comparable vision – 'I will plant a new vineyard and will surround it with the hedge of my grace' – had inspired St. Bridget to found her Order."[55] The translator is also pointing to the importance of trees in medieval devotional understanding – the *hortus conclusus*, tree of life, the tree of Jesse, the crucifixion tree.[56] The metaphor gestures to the desert (often the "forest" in Middle English texts), and even Catherine's desire to be a kind of desert father, but ultimately an orchard is cultivated, manmade, and controlled.

The metaphor of the orchard may additionally have its origins in Catherine's own work, and the fact that the translator opens her *Dialogo* this way indicates a familiarity with her *vita*. In discussing Catherine's penance and austerity, Raymond of Capua utilizes a very similar construction so that his readers may choose what *exemplum* of Catherine's to follow in that regard. Raymond of Capua writes:

> This [narrative] will enable the reader to pluck already for his own use some of the choicest fruits and some of the finest flowers from that garden of the soul which he later will enjoy in all its length and breadth if he reads on to the story of her life. I shall not hesitate to draw attention once more to the same choice fruits when I come, please God, to the proper place as my narrative unfolds.[57]

As with the translator's *The Orcherd*, Raymond's metaphor anticipates a reading practice of picking and choosing, savouring certain lessons over others. Interestingly, the Middle English translation of the *vita* omits this sentence entirely.[58]

In the prologue, the translator directs his readers to understand that the text may be "scharpe, hard, or bitter," as it demands intense introspection and self-examination. Here, he acknowledges not the pleasures of the text or of reading, but the strenuousness a difficult theological treatise may demand. Conversely, however, he also suggests that the reader's first task is "to assaye & serche þe hool orcherd, and taste of sich fruyt and herbis resonably aftir ȝoure affeccioun, & what ȝou likeþ best, aftirward chewe it wel & ete þereof for heelþe of ȝoure soule."[59] Although the codex is a complete translation of the book, the translator is effectively describing the process of assembling a spiritual anthology or miscellany, with the reader as the compiler. This acknowledges the richness and length of the book, and again speaks to a kind of personal reading experience and devotion. Although meant for the nuns who also had a program of open and public reading assigned by superiors (during meals, for example) that were intended for everyone to understand, the translator is describing an individualized kind of reading, one that assumes an interiority and theological sophistication not frequently ascribed to female readers.[60] Rather than claiming that he has already vetted the text and chosen what is appropriate (a trope reiterated by so many translators for a female and lay audience), he deliberately acknowledges the ability of the sisters to discern for themselves what will be best for the "health of their souls."

The translator attempts to create order out of the disorder that is the text by imposing the divisions, but in some ways the metaphor of the orchard is his biggest accomplishment, allowing for the choosing and parsing that he describes. The text is so multilayered, folding back on itself in ways that baffle a reader used to more obvious groupings or clearly articulated devotional texts. This elliptical form, however, replicates the mystical and visionary experience itself: not linear, disorienting, unclear, attempting to convey feeling as much as information. In addition, Catherine stresses the ongoing and immediate nature of Christ's death for sins, echoing the affective piety of the time and bringing the reader into a state of witness. God tells Catherine that baptism is a state of continuity, not a static event of the past:

> Therefore it is callid a contynuel baptisme, whereynne a soule may baptize
> hersilf euere and alwey, if sche wil, vnto þe laste day of departynge fro þe
> body, as I haue seid. Þou knowist þerfore in þis baptisme þat my wirking
> by passioun of my sones cros was fynyte, but þe fruyt of þat payne þe
> which ȝe han reseyued of me is infynyte.[61]

As Christ's death and the sinner's baptism is an ongoing process, so, too, is that of reading and experiencing Catherine's text. Each reading reiterates Catherine's mystical process, and the reader is taken along with her.

The visionary mysticism that seemed to sweep the Continent seems at first to be largely absent from the medieval English context. This is surprising given how exchange, both material and philosophical, existed between England and the Low Countries, where such expressions were prevalent (most clearly among the practice of the beguines and other celebrated lay religious women). Although Julian of Norwich certainly qualifies as "visionary," as does Margery Kempe, it seems that the practice or encouragement of women visionaries, if not their texts, was limited. A woman religious reader had to turn to continental models, for examples, of active and articulated narratives of female visionaries. In addition to Catherine's book, Syon Abbey's libraries included, naturally, the revelations of Bridget, as well as Mechthild of Hackeborn's *The Book of Gostlye Grace*.[62] Alexandra Barratt points out that it is Philip Repingdon, the Bishop of Lincoln, who first suggests to Kempe that she write down what she is experiencing, that Kempe "must have seemed a fascinating home-grown variety of a species with which he, as a late medieval Latinate and cosmopolitan cleric, would have been familiar:

the European woman mystic."[63] Kempe will, of course, embrace these Continental models as she is exposed to them, but for the readers of Catherine, Bridget, and Mechthild of Hackeborn in English, the texts are explaining a foreign kind of piety.[64] The process of translating these texts into English and placing them in the Syon readers' hands effectively translated Catherine into a kind of English mystic, a model for what that would look like.

Catherine and Bridget are both exposed to the deepest mysteries, the places accessed only through mystical communion, a commonality that would not have been lost on those who read them in tandem. God tells Bridget that he cannot reveal his Godhead to man because "if a man lyfyng here saw my godhede, þe whilke, wythoute comparison, is brighter þan þe son withoutefurthe, his body wald melt and relent as wax dose agayn þe fire, and þe saule suld haue so grete ioy þat þe body suld turn to askis."[65] The texts of these women are truly revelations; they expose divine secrets. Bridget's revelation tells her that should a man view God, that man only would dissolve, melting like wax. The intensity of that encounter is so searing that it cannot be withstood by humans. God explains to Catherine a similar fervour in the instant of mystical union, where the mystic literally loses her senses and ability to speak:

> Whanne alle þese myȝtis of þe soule ben gaderid togyderis, ooned and drenchid by loue in me, þe body leseþ his feelyng, for þe iȝe seynge seeþ not, þe eere heerynge heereþ not, þe tonge spekynge spekeþ not, but as I suffre it sumtyme to speke aftir þe abundaunce of þe herte of siche þingis þat it feelith for glorie and laude of my name. So þouȝ it speke, it spekeþ not, þe hand also feelynge feeliþ not, þe feet goyinge goon not. Alle þese lymes & feelinges of þe body ben bounde and ocupied by þe inward sencible feelinge and boond of loue, by þe which boond of loue þei ben so knytt and subiecte to resoun wiþ affeccioun of þe soule þat alle þei crien wiþ oon vois to me, eendlees fadir, in wille for to be departid, þe body fro þe soule, and þe soule fro þe body, þe which in in maner aȝeins kynde.[66]

In this moment of encounter and effacement, Catherine's body has no feeling, her eyes have no sight, her tongue no longer speaks, and God is endless and everywhere. The outer world shuts down and Catherine can only turn inward, the only place that there is feeling – love. Catherine stresses the division of the body and the soul, and reminds her readers that only one of these matters to God. For the reader, the passage brings awareness of one's own senses engaged in the moment, but also remind her that reading is inward, too, that the words on the page are serving to ignite the "sencible feelinge" inside. As Hallett explains, the body and mind are meeting in an extra-sensory space here; where is the experience? In the mind? The words? The body? Catherine is describing a moment that combines and explodes all of these simultaneously.

In the light of this ineffability, this numb unspeakableness of the mystical experience, *The Orcherd* can and must be as layered and convoluted as it is. It is confused because the experience is confused. It has lacunae because the moment of divine union does as well. And this acknowledgment of language and what it lacks is profoundly different than other devotional texts directed to women readers. As Karma Lochrie has explained,

> The crisis of language experienced by Catherine of Siena is caused by her entrance into the "unleeful" (unlawful) domain of God's mysteries. The mystic transgresses the lawful limits of language only to find her speech overwhelmed by "marvelous communication" and her own desire. Her speech is continually disappearing, but this makes divine speech possible. Her silence is not the silence of discretion advocated for women by such devotional treatises of women as Hali Meidenhad, Ancrene Wisse, or De institutione inclusarum. It is a silence inspired by "unleeful" knowledge of God's secret showings – those tastings and savoring into which language disappears.[67]

These texts create a new space for English spiritual devotion. While some male authors' works would resonate with the themes and language of *The Orcherd* – Richard Rolle and Bernard of Clairvaux, for example – this woman's voice speaking the unspeakable is, although not entirely rare, mostly limited to the small group of "approved women" of Bridget, Mechthild of Hackeborn, and Catherine. Some of the texts that will soon accompany *The Orcherd* among English mystical writins, such as those by Walter Hilton and Julian of Norwich, follow models that are seemingly originated in Catherine's text.[68] Margery Kempe, who does not mention Catherine specifically, but does demonstrate the strong influence of Bridget of Sweden's revelations, is also an inheritor of this small but powerful group of English mystics (or, in the case of Catherine, a mystic made English). It is not a coincidence that Hope Emily Allen, who first rediscovered and researched Margery Kempe's *Book*, is also responsible for bringing *The Orcherd* to modern critics' attention; they are generically closely related.[69] In Catherine of Siena's *The Orcherd of Syon*, the readers have a new model of mysticism that is outside of text and outside of body, but based on feeling, speech, personal prayer, and union with God.

This slippage of inner/outer, public/private also disrupts the temporality of the mystical text. Is the reader witnessing the divine voice in the moment it is delivered? Are they witnessing the mystical moment? Are they being guided into their own visionary and immediate experience? As Patricia Dailey writes, "This process of allowing the inner to be translated into terms applicable to the outer is part of a process of reading and interpretation that ensues with the event of a vision and continues beyond the event itself."[70] The process of reading that a mystical text demands is different than other devotional reading of the time. A reader must be aware of her own interiority and exteriority, of her spirit and her materiality, and especially of the presence of a mediated divine voice. Precisely because this is a disrupted temporal experience, the translator's advice to select and taste the fruit of the words, both bitter and sweet, proves an effective method for reading.

This may seem unavoidably gendered – a woman's text, a woman's devotion, a women's house – but the evidence of all three surviving manuscripts demonstrates that it was not. The provenance of MS Harley 3432, for example, shows the men through whose hands it passed: Wiliam Tarboke, George Horde, Roland Gosenell, Walterus de Evereux, through to the late seventeenth-century owner, John Battely (1647–1706), the Archdeacon of Canterbury.[71] Cambridge, St John's College, MS 75 passed from Robert Baxter to William Cranshaw to Henry Wriothesley, the Earl of Southampton.[72] Likewise, Pierpont Morgan, MS 162, one of the three surviving manuscript copies of the text, shows a series of owners' names, all male – John Crosse,[73] Joseph Ames,[74] and Richard How Aspley Beds.[75] Before it was ultimately acquired by Pierpont Morgan, the manuscript was owned by the pre-Raphaelite poet and artist William Morris (1834–96). This manuscript, estimated to be written around 1470, is small at 21cm x 14 cm with only one column of writing: a handbook to read privately. Whatever the manuscript's origins and the intent of the translator, its effect is to translate the female continental mysticism into an English context and make it an integral part of the English devotional reading experience.

Misattributing *The Orcherd*

Until recently, the excerpt "The Cleannesse of Sowle" has been mis-identified as being taken from *The Orcherd of Syon,* or translated from another version of Catherine's *Dialogo.* So, too, the passages from Catherine that are in the *Speculum Devotorum* have been consistently misattributed to *Il Dialogo.*[76] It is understandable why this is so – *The Orcherd* clearly replicates the messages of other Catherine texts. Like "The Cleannesse of Sowle," Catherine's *Dialogo* reveals an emphasis on maintaining purity through closeness to the divine. For example, these words of God's to Catherine are extremely close to the discussion of "cleanness" in William Flete's *Documento Spirituale,* the text from which "The Cleannesse" is actually taken: "For I am most souereyne and eendelees purite. And also I am þat feer þat purifieþ þe soule. And þerfore þe moore a soule drawiþ and cleueþ to me, þe moore purer it is; and þe ferþer þat it gooþ fro me, þe moore vnclene it is."[77] It takes the reader through Catherine's own self-annihilation in order to reach that pure state. She also echoes how to discern a divine vision from a demonic one, very close to the "Discernment of Spirits" excerpted in the *Speculum Devotorum* and elsewhere that is taken from her *Legenda major.*[78] As described in chapter 3, this similar section of the *Dialogo* has its own separate circulation.[79]

These misattributions have led scholars to believe that *The Orcherd* may have had a wider circulation in manuscript form than it actually may have had. At the very least, it was not excerpted nearly as much as was believed, and it is notable that while there are three whole and complete codices of *The Orcherd,* there are really only two known excerpts: the "Discernment of Spirits" in Oxford University College, MS 14, and a small section regarding penance found in Manchester, Rylands MS Latin 395, fol. 70v. This latter manuscript, c. 1500, is a devotional miscellany that contains prayers and lyrics. In addition to the excerpt from *The Orcherd,* it contains small extracts from Bridget of Sweden and Latin passages of Mechthild of Hackeborn's revelations. Interestingly, it contains a shortened life of Katherine of Alexandria, who is often confused, but rarely coupled, with Catherine of Siena. The scribe, deliberately noting not only Catherine but her text, identifies the selection from *The Orcherd* as coming from "Þe Reveulacione Katrine de Senis, ij parte, capitulo iij" (although it is actually from part 1, chapter 3):[80]

I tell the that no penauce which a dedly body may suffre. That is to say
that payne oonly is [not] sufficient to make satisfaction for the synne & for
payne ffor synne but it be onyed or ioyned with desire or with affection of
cheritee. And not verray contricoun & not displesaunce of synnes which the
penaunce is knytt to thereto that þe penaunce maketh satisfaccion, not by
the vertue oonly of actuell peyne which a man suffrith but for the sorowe
which a man hath for synne, and for the merite of his charitee which charite
a sohle hath purchaced with a right herte and with a liberal and a free lyht of
intellecte beholdynge in me which am that charite.[81]

Echoing elements of "The Cleannesse," the passage encourages a
unity with God (here, described as synonymous with charity) in order
to achieve a purity of self, without sin. The fact that the part and chapter are listed as part of the heading in this miscellany is curious, clearly
indicating to the reader that this excerpt comes from a larger work
and not allowing it to stand on its own – as nearly every other excerpt
does. Serving almost like a modern-day footnote, it invites the reader
to find the passage in a whole and to read its context and surround-
ings. This may indicate at least some familiarity with *The Orcherd* as a
complete book rather than something merely to be cut up and anthologized. As the manuscript evidence suggests, this is mostly how it circulated as well.

Wynkyn de Worde and Lay Readers outside the Abbey

The Orcherd's association with Syon would stay with it even as it
definitively leaves the cloister. In 1519, Wynkyn de Worde – the
printer who is William Caxton's successor (discussed in more detail
in chapter 5) – publishes an edition of *The Orcherd of Syon*, taking
its title from the explicit of MS Harley 3432, which appears to have
been its basis.[82] The preface of the book explains that the steward of
Syon, Sir Richard Sutton, discovered the manuscript at the abbey and
funded its publication. This was the first of several devotional texts to
come out of Syon, and C. Annette Grisé has noted that "by the 1520s
Syon's reputation as a supplier of texts for the printed book market
was cemented. The 1530s see the Syon authors become their most prolific ... publishing advice for living a good Christian life, justifying
the monastic life, and drawing connections between lay piety and the
monastic life."[83] With each of these movements, the reading environment changes: from a communal library manuscript to a privately

owned book, from a location-specific text to one that resides beyond the abbey, from inside a religious institution to outside it. Catherine is at *The Orcherd*'s centre, but Bridget is always at its margins, as she is synonymous with Syon Abbey.

The text opens with a title page stating, "Here begynneth the orcharde of Syon in the which is conteyned the reuelacyons of Seynt Katheryne of Sene, with ghostly fruytes & precyous plantes for the helthe of mannes soule."[84] Underneath is a woodcut of Catherine in a moment of mystical rapture with God above her. Catherine is kneeling on what appears to be a *prie dieu*, but she is outdoors as the mystical vision opens the world in front of her, a book open on her lap with the Godhead looking on from above (very reminiscent of Marian annunciation images). This collapse of inside and outside, Church structure and God are all indicative of the text that is to come. Usually, the Syon texts showed a woodcut of Bridget receiving a vision – a conscious and pointed image placed there by the brethren responsible for the books' publications. Indeed, no fewer than eighteen printed books in the early sixteenth century show a woodcut image of Bridget at her desk, an image used by at least four printers in addition to de Worde.[85] Alexandra da Costa posits:

When the Syon brethren decided to preface the majority of their printed books with a woodcut of St. Bridget receiving her Rule from heaven, rapt in mystical communication, they projected a contradictory image of the Abbey as a contemplative centre. The woodcut suggested that, while Syon offered pilgrims preaching, confession, and indulgence, this co-existed with a profound commitment to the contemplative life and the potential for mystical experience of God: the pilgrim staff is to the right of the woodcut, but St Bridget in rapture is in the centre, just as her visions were central to the Bridgettine order.[86]

The image in *The Orcherd* similarly invites a sense of potential visionary experience and identification; the picture of Catherine is demonstrably her – with a Dominican habit and stigmatic hands – and she is not represented as writing or reading, but in a famous mystical moment from her *Legenda major* where she and God exchange their hearts. Further, the placement of Catherine where one typically expects to see Bridget further aligns the two women and shows how central Catherine and her text were to the devotion of the women of Syon.

The second page of the volume also has a woodcut of a nun, accompanied by a group of attentive sisters. Although the image is clearly of Catherine, it gestures more towards Bridget who does have nuns who follow her by following the Bridgettine rule at Syon, making the image serve as kind of a fusion between the two women. In the image, the Catherine/Bridget figure has the same habit and crown of thorns that the image of Catherine does in the first woodcut. She is holding a heart in her right hand (the heart that she just exchanged in the previous image), and is trampling a demon underneath her feet. Martha Driver notes that "this blurring of identity … argues that the artist of *The Orcherd of Syon* woodcuts was intimately connected with Syon, imposing a familiar model, St. Bridget, on a new subject, St. Catherine."[87] The juxtaposition of images is clear: God speaks to Catherine, Catherine speaks to professed women, and with the clear connection to images of Bridget, Syon women specifically. For the Syon nuns, this makes sense, even if they are not the nuns pictured (the nuns have Dominican habits, not Bridgettine), Catherine is speaking to them. The middlemen (Catherine's scribes, the translator) are omitted here. And yet, as the book is printed by de Worde, it demands an audience outside of Syon Abbey and one beyond the nuns pictured. There are woodcuts throughout the book, introducing each major section. Driver surmises that *The Orcherd*'s eight woodcuts are unique in style and not typical of de Worde's other books, writing, "They look closest to Spanish woodcuts of the period, and I suspect the artist might possibly have been a nun of Spanish or possibly Italian origin living at Syon, given the book making and binding activities going on there in the late fifteenth and early sixteenth centuries."[88] In both images, Catherine holds a book, reinforcing that at the heart of the text and of Syon lies the process of writing and reading, a literate relationship with each other and with the divine.[89]

The lay reader of de Worde's book must imagine herself twice into Syon Abbey: as the initially intended audience and then for the "discovery" of the book in her hands. The last page of the book reads:

Master Rycharde Sutton, Esquyer, stewarde of the holy monastery of Syon, fyndynge this ghostely tresure, these dyologes and reuelacyons of the newe seraphycall spouse of Cryste, Seynt Katheryne of Sene, in a corner by it selfe, wyllynge of his greate charyte it sholde come to lyghte, that many relygous and deuoute soules myght be releued and haue conforte therby, he hathe caused at his greate coste, this booke to be prynted, trustinge that moche fruyte shall come therof to all that shal rede or here of it, desyrynge none other thinge therfore but onle be rewarde of God & theyr deuoute prayers for helthe of his soule.[90]

The image of Sutton finding this valuable manuscript "in a corner by it selfe" invites the visualization of this lost treasure uncovered, of its movement from the darkness of the abbey library to the light of the "relygous and devoute soules" soon to be comforted and educated by Catherine's words. Although the 1519 de Worde edition is printed within decades of the latest surviving *Orcherd* manuscript, its printed form, illustrated with handsome woodcuts rather than illuminated initials, speaks already to its different medium. Copies of several de Worde editions of Syon's books were made primarily for the nuns of the abbey, moving the reading experience out of a communal place like the abbey library and into private cells. The Bridgettine reader of the early sixteenth-century Wynkyn de Worde may imagine her earlier sister reading as she too reads the text translated for her abbey's inhabitants, but her situation is different. She, by nature of her private reading and individually owned book, does not need to imagine herself apart from the activities of the monastic life; she is already separate.

However, even though the text immediately appeared to have a life outside of the abbey, it always, in a sense, brings its reader back to the nuns for whom the words were translated. A lay reader – either medieval or modern – is reminded of the "first reader" of the translated text, as it were, almost immediately:

> Religyous modir & deuoute sustren clepid & chosen bisily to laboure at the house of Syon, in the blessid vyneȝard of oure holy Saueour, his parfite rewle which hymsilf enditide to kepe contynuly to ȝoure lyues eende vndir þe gouernaunce of oure blessid Lady, hir seruise oonli to rede and to synge as hir special seruauntis and douȝtren, and sche ȝoure moost souereyne lady and cheef abbess of hir holy couent.[91]

Here, the reader is told that she is a sister labouring at the house of Syon, and that she should see the Virgin Mary as the abbess overseeing her toil. Before moving into the "orcherd" of the text, the reader is reminded of the "modir & deuoute sustren" who are cultivating the "blessid vyneȝard of oure holy Saueour," emphasizing that this is a religious text intended for the conventual audience.

Once through the translator's introduction and into Catherine's revelatory text, both the lay reader and the cloistered nun are invited into what Krug suggests is a kind of mystical experience by proxy. She writes, "In the century after Syon's founding, books became both media through which the reader could experience God's presence (an anglicized version of continental mystical experience, perhaps) and physical icons that gave readers direct, material connections to the divine and to other believers."[92] The manuscript of the *Orcherd* very clearly serves this textual connection for nun and lay reader, for medieval and modern ones. The provenance of one of de Worde's editions shows just how fluid this movement from religious to lay may have been. The first recorded owner of New York Public Library Spencer MS 1519, a Wynkyn de Worde *Orcherd of Syon*, had been Elizabeth Strickland, a nun of Syon, in 1542. Written on the last page of the book is "Thys perteynyth to Syster Elyzabeth Strykland, professyd in Syon," followed by the note "That I Sur Assheton of Arydylton knight executor vnto my lady Strykland decessed have giffen thys boke vnto my lady my wyffe." Mary Erler posits that after the dissolution of Syon, Strickland had gone to live with her sister and brother-in-law. After her death, and her sister's, the book becomes that of his second wife.[93] A later recorded owner is also a woman, with the charming inscription on the first page: "Katheryn Sacheurall, my right owner, 1554 15 May." Katheryn Sacheverell was the daughter of a knight and later wife to Thomas Babington, an important Derbyshire landowner and Justice of the Peace there. Unlike the surviving manuscript codices, which show almost exclusively male ownership, this example of the de Worde edition demonstrates how the printed book came back to its first home in Strickland's possession and then out into lay women readers' hands.

The printing of *The Orcherd*, a Syon text meant for a lay audience in addition to the sisters, is at first an anomaly for the brethren and sisters of Syon. As Alexandra da Costa has noted, the first books that come out of Syon are mostly meant for a religious readership; an anxiety about an untrained layperson reading theologically complex work hampers a more robust publication program. However, as the threat of the Reformation and its implications begin to loom over England, Syon considerably steps up its output of devotional literature:

> Apart from the *Orcherd of Syon*, which was printed by the lay steward of Syon for a wide audience, the brothers made only token gestures of inclusion towards secular readers: the *Right Profitable Treatise*, the *Rule of St. Augustine*, and the *Pilgrimage of Perfection* were all directed towards a

religious readership and their adaptation to the mixed market only went so far as the title-pages. Writing in English was perceived as a necessary evil for instructing unlearned religious, especially women, and there was significant anxiety about the unwanted readers this might also attract for relatively advanced material. However, between the time when the evangelical Thomas Arthur and Thomas Bilney first came to the authorities' attention and when Bilney was executed in 1531, Syon became radically invested in the support of lay faith, as its anxiety about lay readers' over-curious enquiry into the contemplative life was displaced by a more acute anxiety over their potential interest in heresy. This encouraged a bolder use of the vernacular to address the laity directly.[94]

This change means that the way a book owner reads *The Orcherd* may depend greatly on when they own the book. As the years proceeded from the book's 1519 printing, the name of Syon Abbey would carry more meaning and thus shift the weight of the text's import. An early owner sees it as a glimpse into the religious life, carrying with it the weight of a potentially mystical Syon Abbey and the women who are professed there. A later reader carries with her many more implications to the name of Syon and sees it as a centre of devotional publishing and Catholic theological thought. A post-Reformation reader may hold the book as a symbol of resistance, a link to a Catholic faith no longer welcome in England, to a convent that was forced from its home, and an homage to the martyr Richard Reynolds, a Bridgettine monk at Syon, who was executed for treason in 1535 for opposing Henry VIII's marriage to Anne Boleyn.

No matter what, the reader of *The Orcherd*, even when outside of Syon, must still imagine herself into that Bridgettine context as the reader is so explicitly named in the prologue and title. Bridget herself is never mentioned, but the name and place of Syon Abbey carries her meaning. A 1540 reader of the book, such as Elizabeth Strickland's sister and brother-in-law, would understand Syon to be a locus of vernacular faith, particularly in the face of an uncertain future of devotional life in England. In this sense, an added prologue to the de Worde edition seems prophetic. Directly after the woodcuts, and before the translator's prologue with which the manuscripts begin, the book includes a passage that it attributes to Marcus Ciuilis, an Italian, written to Paule Sauche of Aragon. It is attached to some Latin versions of Catherine's *Dialogo*, although none of the extant Middle English manuscripts have it. In this prologue, the writer explains how he is moved after reading

Catherine's words as an example of the perfect religious life and that corrupt monastics should follow her example. He notes that her efforts have been "greatly edyfyenge of crystes chyrche,"[95] and he advises the readers, similarly as does *The Orcherd* translator, to "fede you here with the swete meet of ghostly counsayll þat cometh fro heuen."[96] Ciuilis is not a cleric, and as such, C. Annette Grisé argues, transforms Catherine into "a figure for the reader outside the monastery who deplores monastic corruption (but likely still supported the monastic life) and the inaccessibility of knowledge and learning to those who are not clerics."[97] Almost anticipating the religious unrest to come, the book shows itself as orthodox from the outset.

Mysticism: Proceed With Caution

Catherine and Bridget travel together outside of Syon as a pair in various manuscripts and even some artistic representations. For example, as noted in the introduction, an early sixteenth-century screen at Horsham St Faith's in Norfolk shows what appears to be Catherine and Bridget opposite one another in two panels.[98] Eamon Duffy surmises that these "highly unusual choices" were likely commissioned by the donor William Wulcy because of his interest in women's devotional writing.[99] He additionally notes that "their presence is difficult to account for except through the contact of the donors with Syon or at least the literature emanating from there."[100] It is surprising, given *The Orcherd of Syon*'s popularity and its content, that the nuns of Syon, or indeed anywhere in England, were not at all known for visionary and ecstatic activity. When this ecstatic response does happen – as in the case of Margery Kempe, or, as we shall see in the conclusion, in the case of Elizabeth Barton, the English Church hierarchy mostly frowns on the behaviour. Denise L. Despres suggests that part of the translator's agenda in suggesting the method of reading outlined in *The Orcherd* prologue is to limit this kind of "unsupervised mystical reading."[101] By not allowing the whole of the text to subsume the reader, to get literally lost in Catherine's convoluted circularity and repetition, the reader is forced instead to "taste" the fruits of Catherine's labour in small digestible pieces. The order that the translator tries to impose on the text is resisted by the text itself, though, as it does not lend well to chapters and divisions; it is too elliptical, too recursive. A reader could follow *The Orcherd*'s translator's advice, picking and choosing parts, but the invested reader cannot help but get lost in the text – more labyrinth than orchard. It is precisely this kind of reading experience, losing oneself entirely in God's revelation that may encourage a reader's own visionary response.

And what does this text do for the lay reader, even less likely to be in a community where a visionary life may be possible? Grisé suggests that *The Orchred* along with the other great Syon publication, *The Myroure of Oure Ladye,* constructs a vision of the ideal Syon nun:

> [She is] studious, serious, peaceful and gracious … [enforcing] the monastic ideals of humility, obedience and chastity in order to regulate religious practices inside the monastery. Yet they also serve a function outside Syon Abbey, by illustrating ideals suitable for emulation by other readers, ideals which attempt to regulate devotional practices and especially vernacular reading practices in the growing audience for the devotional literary tradition in late medieval England.[102]

In this way, the lay reader, male or female, reads not only the text but the construction of the ideal nun. They place themselves into that position of religious labourer in the vineyard, exposing themselves to the mystical text and the visionary word, but simultaneously reining themselves in so that it is an inward process, not an external one. Grisé further points out that the "labour" described in the prologue is decidedly classed – they are reading (a learned activity) and strolling through an orchard.[103] Here, two erstwhile leisure activities become the activity of contemplation. This preface does not describe the corporeal and physical experience of the mystic, but the cultured, aristocratic body of the Syon nun.

This juxtaposition, the paradoxical ideas of the visionary and the obedient contemplative, charges a tension in *The Orcherd* both as manuscript and printed book, and indeed in Syon itself. These conflicts between preface and text, translation and original, demonstrate how, on the one hand, the reading of the experience was encouraged but, on the other, the actual practice was limited. Vincent Gillespie notes that Syon had a deep interest in the visionary, but was also steeped in the discussions surrounding the validity of one:

> As an order founded by a visionary woman whose authenticity was frequently and repeatedly challenged, even at the Council of Constance, Syon also had a particular interest in contemplative, prophetic, and visionary

materials, and in the processes of their discernment (one of the most serious faults to be confessed by the brethren was "if any afferme the reuelacions of saynte birgitte as dremes, or els deracte hem," so the issue remained live even inside the house). Its massive brethren's library, and the documented book holdings of the nuns show a systematic and continuing interest in contemplative experience and its discernment. Syon's involvement in the 1530s with the political visionary Elizabeth Barton was a late (and politically highly perilous) example of a constitutional fascination that had marked the house throughout its life.[104]

As Gillespie points out, the brethren at Syon learn to live with a fundamental tension between real scepticism as to women's visionary experiences (Jean Gerson, for example, a major critic of Bridget's revelations, holds a prominent position in the library) and their devotion to an order founded on such a vision. The Syon Additions for the sisters, too, lists the same warning that it is a "greuous defaute" to state that Bridget's visions were not authentic.[105]

This tension is part of the Syon name, the brand with which the Syon books are printed and disseminated, and none more clearly than *The Orcherd of Syon* itself. Catherine of Siena, who seems to be firmly on one side of this ecstatic visionary/obedient religious divide, is, upon closer inspection, more ambiguously situated. God's words to Catherine clearly indicate that her knowledge is outside of learning and text, that she knows the truth simply because he has spoken to her:

> Lo, riȝt swete douȝtir, al þis haue y toold þee þat þou myȝtist knowe þe perfeccioun of þe state of vnyoun, where þe iȝe of intellecte is rapte by þe fier of myn eendelees charite, in þe which charite is resceyued liȝt aboue nature, wiþ which liȝt I am loued, for loue renneþ aftir vndirstonding. And þe moore a soule knoweth, þe moore it loueth; and þe moore it loueþ, þe moore it knowiþ, þat oon norischiþ þe toþir.[106]

Here knowing, loving, feeling are achieved because of Catherine's perfect union with God. There is no intermediary – no priest, no scribe, no text. On the other hand, though, a good portion of *The Orcherd* is devoted to God's description of the absolute importance of the Holy Church, in all its earthly incarnations, and that obedience to that hierarchy is effectively obedience to God. Following sections where God (through Catherine) describes the faults of priests (who still administer a pure sacrament), and a section on the good in priests, he tells Catherine:

Now, my dere dou3tir, I haue schewid þee a lytil sparcle of þe excellence
of hem…I haye also toold þee of her dignyte and worþines, in þe which
dignite I haue put hem, siche as I haue chose to my specyal mynystris….I
wil þat þei haue hem in dew reuerence, not for hemsilf but for me, þat is,
for þe auctorite þat I have 3oue hem. And þat reuerence schulde neuere be
menvsid, þou3 vertu be menusid in hem.[107]

No matter what doubts or faults the priests and the hierarchy of
the Church may have, they are to be revered and obeyed; that reverence should not be diminished ("menusid"), even if the virtue of the
clerks is lacking.[108] They are the final word. Should there be any doubt
where the ultimate authority of the text lay, it is put to rest (repeatedly, I would add) throughout *The Orcherd*. God may speak directly to
Catherine, but her earthly responsibilities are to men. The Syon nuns
and the lay readers of *The Orcherd* are similarly reminded that whatever unorthodox reading the text espouses, it does not overrule the
Church's words.

Finally, the effect of the triple prologue (first Ciuilis, then the translator's, then the opening of the text) and the triple conclusion (Catherine's,
the translator's, and the epilogue describing the book's discovery and
recovery in Syon Abbey), is to demand imaginative leaps of its readers to different times, locations, bodies. In the space of the book they
are lay readers of Catherine's devotion, they are priests who lovingly
transmit the text to their charges, they are custodians of Syon who recognize its lost treasures, they are nuns, and – in the centre – they are the
mystical body of Catherine, the inner mind, the one at union with God.
The effect of that travelling to the centre of the text, however, is that it
removes the reader from that visionary core. She is reading about the
experience, and the glosses on that experience, but she herself is not
fully immersed inside it. *The Orcherd*'s set up fully expresses England's
ambivalence about women visionary texts and the reading of them. The
reader is not prompted to her own ecstatic and mystical moment. The
prologues and epilogues box the text in, containing its power.

Chapter Five

Catherine in Print: Lay Audiences and Reading Hagiography

From the Radical to the Orthodox: *The Legenda major* in England

Raymond of Capua opens his *vita* of Catherine with a prologue directed at the reader, expounding on her holiness, her angelic nature, her learning, her astounding capacity to rapidly dictate letters to two or three scribes simultaneously with different recipients intended, and her vast inner strength and knowledge. He acknowledges that such an encompassing list of attributes is hard to believe in any one person, especially that there was "such a capacity in that weak woman's body of hers, worn out as it was by vigils and fasting … a sign that it was miraculous and supernaturally infused, and no mere natural talent."[1] He further anticipates the readers' unasked question as to whether or not Catherine was capable of writing her *Il Dialogo*: "If we turn next to the *Book*, which she composed in her own vernacular, manifestly at the dictation of the Holy Spirit, who could imagine or believe that it was the work of a woman? Its style is so sublime that it is quite a task to make a corresponding Latin version equal to it in sublimity."[2] This latter note is interesting in so few works of translation comment on the movement from the vernacular into Latin, but rather the reverse. These musings on Catherine's gender and her exceptionality, however, do not make it into English, neither in the medieval translation nor in the early modern one, as both versions skip the preface entirely.[3] Raymond's rhetorical surprise acknowledges that there is something exceptional about a woman like Catherine, and that she may be unsettling to her readers for her abilities and accomplishments. By removing this preface, the Middle English *The Lyf of Saint Katherin of Senis* becomes more matter-of-fact. Catherine's exceptionality (especially that of her gender) is muted. Although the fifteenth-century Wynkyn de Worde edition of Catherine's *The Lyf* seems to be a straightforward translation of Raymond's *Legenda major*, on closer examination it is clear that it is as shaped by its language, readers, and circumstance as are earlier Catherine manuscripts.[4] One of de Worde's very first publications, the book reinscribes its audience in a way that will soon become familiar to late medieval readers but is at this point very new: taking a text that was in the private, mostly religious domain, and moving it into the public sphere of the laity. Although there are radicalizing and subversive moments in the text, *The Lyf of Saint Katherin of Senis* paradoxically advanced a lay social identity that is sanitized and orthodox for the new audiences it reached through its printing.

Although several texts circulating after Catherine's death were considered her *vita*, the *Legenda major* by Raymond of Capua was the basis for many of them and considered the most authoritative. Raymond was Catherine of Siena's spiritual director and confessor from 1374 until her death in 1380, and became extremely important to Catherine's life and after-life legacy. He was not only one of the scribes, disseminators and translators of her *Dialogo*, but he also began her *Legenda major* shortly after her death in 1380 (most accounts place the beginning of his composition at 1385), although it took him nearly ten years to complete it, recording the details of her life and spiritual growth.[5] Raymond had to balance many conflicting elements in the *Legenda major*, and the tensions of these conflicts are small fissures throughout the text. He wanted to portray Catherine as an obedient, meek, and humble woman who was chosen by God as a vessel for his works and words. However, this Catherine conflicts somewhat with the real Catherine who had ecstatic visions, an outspoken political engagement, and an influential and vast network of correspondents and followers. F. Thomas Luongo notes that Raymond's resistance to portraying Catherine in her full political and social engagement

> was probably heightened by the resistance among some theologians and highly placed clerics to the canonization of Birgitta of Sweden, as a reaction against what was seen as an excess of influence by allegedly prophetic women and a criticism of Birgitta's role in promoting the return of the papal court to Rome – a charge ... that was eventually lodged against Catherine.[6]

The *Legenda major* became influential in promoting her cult abroad and in Italy, even though her canonization would be long after Raymond's death. There was a supplement to her life written by

Thomas Caffarini, known as the *Libellus de Supplemento*, and a shortened version of Raymond's *vita* also by Caffarini called the *Legenda minor*, both which actively promoted her cult and canonization (and more effectively than Raymond's *Legenda major* had), but there is no evidence that these were ever translated into Middle English and scant evidence that they made their way to England in Latin.[7] The Caffarini texts highlight Catherine's miraculous and visionary nature much more sharply than does Raymond, whose interest is less in the sensational and more in the spiritual.

As far as the English reader knew, the *Legenda major* written by Raymond of Capua was the definitive account of Catherine's life. The only complete version that survives from medieval England is the one printed by Wynkyn de Worde in 1492, shortly after he takes over William Caxton's printing press. The fact that de Worde would later publish *The Orcherd of Syon* allows for a fuller picture of Catherine than most readers would get of a woman mystic or saint, usually limited to either a *vita* or her personal writings. Generally, the *vita* works to mitigate some of the mystical and rapturous aspects of the visionary, giving her a wider audience, or as Chiara Frugoni notes, the hagiographer couches the mystical "in terms of everyday experience and thereby rendered accessible," and this is certainly the case with Raymond's text as well.[8] While no other full manuscripts of the *Legenda major* survive, either in Latin or English, the evidence demonstrates that it had some circulation before its printing. There are several extant Continental manuscripts that were circulating, both in Latin and the vernaculars, increasing the likelihood that more than one would arrive in England.[9] As discussed in chapter 3, translated excerpts of the *Legenda major* have survived in at least three manuscript compilations (the devotional anthology Harley 2409, the book of spiritual direction known as the *Speculum Devotorum*, and British Library, MS Royal 17 D.V., which was later printed in a compilation by the printer Henry Pepwell in 1521). The existence of these translated excerpts indicate that there were at least some Latin versions of the full *Legenda major* in manuscript circulation, and likely a complete Middle English version as well.[10] The translations in the de Worde are similar enough to some of the earlier manuscript excerpts to indicate a possible common translated source.

Printed first and in its entirety by de Worde and later in Pepwell's excerpts, the *Legenda major* exposes Catherine to a new audience of medieval readers who may not necessarily be linked to a monastic or conventual community, or who may not circulate in a particularly aristocratic milieu. De Worde reprints *The Lyf* a mere eight years after its first printing, indicating an ongoing demand, and the follow up by Pepwell in 1521 further indicates an unwavering interest in Raymond's text.[11] In this way, *The Lyf* reflects more widely what is happening to medieval devotional manuscripts. Texts that are seemingly public, like those in convent libraries for shared purpose, are in actuality very cloistered, frequently intended for quiet reading and meditation. However, with the printing press, these texts are taken out of their monastic settings and opened up to a wider audience – a lay readership or for individual ownership by nuns and priests. While the reading may remain meditative and private, it becomes part of a public shared spiritual vocabulary and a powerful possession symbolizing piety. These changes also affect how the texts are read – the de Worde edition opens with an incipit invoking a female reader, but in its printed form anticipates a much wider audience than its original form. The expectation of a cloistered gendered reader persists in the printed version, placing the reader – whether religious or lay, female or male – in that imaginary subject position just as it would for *The Orchard of Syon* (see chapter 4). That subject position is one of orthodox piety, interested in but not imitative of the radical subversion implied in Catherine's *The Lyf*.

Catherine had a rich political and public life that is mostly excised from Raymond's *Legenda major*. However, even Raymond of Capua and Catherine's relationship was, at its core, a political one; Raymond was assigned to Catherine by the papacy to aid in her work of promoting the Crusades, among other concerns. And as Luongo has pointed out, Raymond necessarily plays down Catherine's political and social life in order to paint the picture of an ascetic saint.[12] Without access to Catherine's letters and supplementary hagiographies, the reader of Raymond's translated *Lyf* is given a more conventional view of this unconventional saint than some of her Italian contemporaries would have understood. The Catherine that Raymond gives his readers is a pious, ascetic, and visionary Catherine. For English readers, this is the Catherine they already know through *The Orchard of Syon* and "The Cleannesse of Sowle." The example of the visionary woman, if not the practice, is preferable to that of the politicized woman. This Catherine may have been mystical, but she is also orthodox, apolitical, and subservient to God. Looking closely at the English *Legenda major* allows us to see how one text moves from the cloister to the laity and what meaning is created by its context and readers. The *Legenda major* is the only Catherine text to extend into and persist after the Reformation, demonstrating its importance in defining Catherine in the medieval devotional world view.

Wynkyn de Worde, the Gendered Audience, and *The Lyf of Saint Katherin of Senis*

Wynkyn de Worde published *The Lyf of Saint Katherin of Senis* as one of his first projects at the helm of his press. William Caxton was the first and most important printer in fifteenth-century England, exerting an influence over what books should be printed, which had a marked effect on forming a medieval canon. When he died in 1492, his shop and its accompanying business went to de Worde. In those early years, de Worde printed five books, some still using Caxton's device, woodcuts, and his seal.[13] Some of these are still clearly Caxton's (such as a reprinting of *The Golden Legend*) and some are new – this includes Catherine of Siena's *Lyf*, printed in 1492, still with Caxton's seal and type. Indeed, while many of the texts in that first year after Caxton's death appear to be reprints of works that Caxton had already done, or texts requested by his heirs, de Worde began making his mark right away with a penchant for publishing devotional books and pamphlets, leading with Catherine's *Lyf*.[14] The growth of readers and printed works was symbiotic – there was a growing demand for books either created by or spurring on the printing of the same. Many devotional and spiritual works were more readily published under de Worde than they had been under Caxton. George Keiser speculates that de Worde developed commercial relationships with clergy that Caxton had not had, allowing for a clear pipeline of religious texts that appealed to particular religious houses or monastic networks.[15] In the landscape of English printing in the early 1490s, de Worde's only legitimate rival was Richard Pynson, and both printers dominated different markets. Devotional texts were largely in de Worde's purview, right from the beginning of his career. For example, another of de Worde's very first books printed was *The Chastising of God's Children*, which was coupled with William Flete's *Remedies against Temptations*, demonstrating that the earlier reading audiences which had linked Flete's text and Catherine's continued to do so into the era of the printing press.[16]

If de Worde was Dutch, as has been speculated, his understanding of medieval devotion would be decidedly different than an untravelled Englishman. As Lotte Hellinga writes, a Low Countries' upbringing would have made de Worde familiar with the reform movement known as *Devotio Moderna*, which emphasized a mystical lay piety and was an active form of devotion in the medieval Low Countries.[17] This is a significant departure from English piety which, while embracing some "approved women" and visionary texts, does not encourage a practice of mysticism, which the *Devotio Moderna* allowed more freely. De Worde's familiarity with the movement would have enabled him to look at texts that may have been suspect under Arundel's Lambeth Constitutions in a new light and deemed worthy of wide dissemination through his press.[18] Caxton's career would have started under religious strictures that eventually relaxed, but de Worde would have been facing new reservations about texts that held a whiff of Lutheranism, the new heresy raising its head throughout Catholicism. De Worde's alignment with Syon Abbey, for example, may have given him some cover in publishing texts that otherwise may have been suspect, and allowing him, for example, to publish many more books about female spirituality than had his predecessor. In addition to *The Lyf* and, later, *The Orcherd of Syon*, he also published *The Fifteen Oes*, apocryphally attributed to St Bridget, as well as extracts from the *Book of Margery Kempe*.[19]

Both Caxton and de Worde had close relationships with important aristocratic women who commissioned works and supported the printing press. Most significantly, de Worde followed Caxton's lead in having Margaret Beaufort as a patron who commissioned specific works of spirituality to be printed. De Worde could hardly have asked for a more visible and important champion of his press than Margaret, mother to King Henry VII, and she proved to be instrumental to his book trade as a patron, promoter, and even a translator of religious texts.[20] Although Margaret does not appear to be responsible for the publication of any of the Catherine texts, she certainly was for closely related devotional ones, including *The Fifteen Oes* printed in 1491, just before *The Lyf* of Catherine, and one of the last texts commissioned under Caxton before his death. Margaret had important connections to Syon Abbey and was interested in promoting books that had relevance to the nuns and priests there, as well as to the connected Carthusian Charterhouse of Sheen.[21] *The Lyf* may have been printed with Bridgettine audiences in mind. Booklists show that the Bridgettine convent of Syon owned a Latin *vita* of Catherine, and similar texts like *The Fifteen Oes* and Catherine's *The Orcherd of Syon* come from an explicitly Syon source.[22] The life of what appears to be Elizabeth of Töss (1294–1336) is also included in the de Worde edition, although she is called Elizabeth of Hungary (c. 1207–31), a saint with whom she was most likely confused.[23] Alexandra Barratt has suggested that this is another clue to its potential Bridgettine connections, writing that the nuns at Syon may have "suggested the Elizabeth text to de Worde."[24] Alternatively, the Dominican house at Dartford may have been a source, particularly since Cecily Neville gave her granddaughter, Bridget, a nun at the Dominican convent of Dartford, a copy of *The Lyf*.[25] Cecily died in 1495, although the ordinance concerning her is possibly earlier, indicating that she gave either a written manuscript to Bridget or had the de Worde book soon after its 1492 publication. Cecily also gave a copy of Bridget's *Revelations* to her grandchild Anne de la Pole, who was the prioress of Syon. As noted in my introduction, the fact that both books come from Cecily's library and are bequeathed to nuns shows how intertwined the religious and lay readership of these texts were, as well as the movement of books between women readers.

At this point in England, any shadow cast by the issuance of the Lambeth Constitutions of 1409 would have passed, and with it a fear about printing vernacular devotional texts. Indeed, the English printing press with its appetite for religious literature was itself largely responsible for a new appreciation of vernacular devotional works.[26] But the idea of a heretical lollardy is not entirely lost in the early sixteenth century, and is felt more acutely with Lutheran sentiments abroad, requiring a certain level of caution for both readers and printers of vernacular devotional texts, and some self-consciousness about which ones are chosen for wider dissemination. In October 1524, de Worde, along with other printers, was warned by the bishop of London against printing heretical material.[27] More importantly, a new kind of heresy would arise with the Reformation and the printing press would be centrally placed in its conflicts.[28] The wide lay audience and easily reproducible nature of a printed devotional book (markedly different from a written codex that required much more time and labour to copy) made its possibilities for heresy and heterodoxy greater than ever before.

Where a reader previously may have been at the mercy of the compiler and anthologizer – and as we have seen with Catherine of Siena, many of her texts were disseminated in an excerpted manner – the expanding print market of the sixteenth century allowed a reader to have Catherine's *Lyf* in its entirety. The de Worde edition, which also had the much shorter *Revelations* of Elizabeth of Hungary (or Elizabeth of Töss) appended to it, spans 192 pages. A manuscript version of the same would be prohibitive in terms of the labour required and the cost of materials for one copy, but with the press, *The Lyf* found an audience in convents and aristocratic homes, and in the hands of women readers like Cecily and her granddaughter Bridget. Many of the devotional books that are printed in the late fifteenth and early sixteenth century persist as the stalwarts of English spirituality up until the Reformation, demonstrating how important the books chosen and printed at this time would be in establishing what would be considered a canon of Catholic orthodoxy.[29]

We can absolutely speculate that there was a prior vernacular circulation of *The Lyf* in the absence of any surviving codex. One excerpt, discussed in chapter 3, survives in three fifteenth-century manuscripts – Catherine's treatise on the "Discernment of Spirits"; two of these are in copies of the *Speculum Devotorum*, and the third, British Library, MS Harley 2409, additionally contains other excerpts from *The Lyf*.[30] A fourth fifteenth-century manuscript, British Library, Royal MS 17 D.V., has several excerpts from *The Lyf* (including a short passage also in Harley 2409 on self-knowledge and knowledge of God), and these would be reprinted almost verbatim by Henry Pepwell in his 1521 devotional anthology (discussed in more detail later in this chapter). The closeness in language between all of these versions suggests a common source translation and indicates that there most likely was a vernacular version of *The Lyf* in circulation from which de Worde drew his edition. While some have interpreted the "I" in the prologue to the text, discussing the translation and its purpose, as de Worde himself – or Caxton, who had a reputation as a translator – it seems more likely that this derives from a prologue in a manuscript written by an anonymous translator and copied down by de Worde as part of the edition.

Unlike Wynkyn de Worde's other major printed text concerning Catherine, *The Orcherd of Syon*, *The Lyf* names neither its provenance nor, as mentioned above, its translator. Because there are no comparable surviving manuscripts, answers as to translators and provenance are limited to speculations based on analogous texts. C. Annette Grisé argues that the printing of the text is "inspired by contemporary Italian editions," noting that it is "the first edition of Catherine's life and / or works to be published outside of Italy."[31] Jane Chance and Nancy Bradley Warren both suggest that the translation was possibly done by Thomas Gascoigne, who translated the *vita* of Bridget for Syon Abbey, but there is no real proof that he also did the translation of Catherine's *Legenda major*.[32] We know that at least by the time Thomas Betson did his early sixteenth-century *registrum* of books in Syon Library, the *Vita sancte Katerine de Senis* is listed, but whether this is Raymond of Capua's *Legenda major* or another of the several *vitae* about Catherine is simply unknown.[33] There is, however, a prologue that clearly identifies the text as having been translated for a specific audience, with some telling information. It opens with a line familiar in many a medieval manuscript, addressing an imagined female reader: "Here, doughter, and see fructuous example of vertuous liuinge to edyfycacion of thy sowle and to comforte and encrese of they gostly labour."[34] The first paragraph goes on to describe that as the translator, he is performing an act of worship in order to aid the reader and "al other of thi gostely susteren," and concludes with "here I purpos by our lordis mercy only in his worshyppe wyth truste of his grace and leue by helpe of your prayers to translate in englysshe tongue the legende and the blessid lyf of an holy mayde and virgyn, whiche was and is called Katheryn of sene."[35] The "doughter" and "ghostly susteren" of the address indicate a conventual audience, but he continues with a trope more readily used in prefaces anticipating a lay readership. While translating, he explains, he excised concepts beyond the understanding of the reader, gesturing towards a lay audience unschooled in the finer points of theology:

> In this translacion I leue of the two prologues whiche in the begynnyng the same clerke made in latyn – the whiche passeth your vnderstondyng, and touche alle maters only that longeth only to your lernynge, by-cause that moche maner of her vertuous lyuyng shall be rehersyd in especial in chapytres of this boke whiche in generall wordes he toucheth shortely in his prologue; I leue of also poyntes of diuynyte whiche passeth your vnderstondyng, and touche only maters þat longeth to your lernyng.[36]

With the translation of a female saint's life comes the written assumption of a female reader, coupled with the anticipation of a reader who needs guidance in what is appropriate spiritual matter. This description of a translator omitting the difficult passages, beyond the comprehension of the laity in general and women especially, is repeated in many translators' prologues. Here, the translator points to the distinction between "understanding" (the capabilities of the reader) and "learning" (the literate background of the reader). The implication here is that both of these categories are limited and inadequate in the female reader.

However, the female reader also serves as a trope in order to justify translation, a way of reaching a wider lay audience, male and female both. By claiming the presumably religious female reader, the translator has also shaped a text that he sees as appropriate for the unschooled laity. With the preface naming a female reader, the actual reader – whether male or female – takes on the gendered subject position that necessarily posits a power dynamic between translator/authority and reader. Alexandra Barratt writes that this power-play, one that we may read as analogous to that between a male confessor and a female penitent, is encoded into the text itself:

> By means of translation, men teach women and in various ways acculturate them into the gender roles they want them to fill. Men have the linguistic knowledge; they have access to the texts, both physically and metaphorically; they also have the leisure to translate … The dynamics behind these translations are therefore complex. Seen from one point of view, it is female desire for translation that stimulates male response. But that female desire, of course, arises from female lack – of knowledge, of Latin, usually, their being either completely nonexistent or deficient.[37]

Indeed, the often-repeated translator trope that the text has been excerpted and shaped in order to fit the (lesser) understanding of the female reader automatically conveys these gender and power differentials. Because the text opens with this trope, it governs the text entirely; each page is doubly alienated from the Latin from which it is translated and from the complexities the original contained.

This edition of *The Lyf* may easily apply to the religious and enclosed reader, say at the Bridgettine convent of Syon or the Dominican Priory at Dartford (where records reflect ownership of Catherine's *Lyf*), who look specifically to Catherine as a model of piety and sanctity. But how does this translate to the lay reader? Although there is little specific evidence regarding the circulation of Catherine's *Lyf*, the fact of a second edition shows that there was demand for it, and comparable texts have been shown to be owned by lay readers, and not only aristocratic ones.[38] Devotional texts were consistently willed and passed down, objects of status and representative of piety.[39] *The Lyf* of Catherine would not be out of place among these books, and was most likely both owned and bequeathed by readers in a variety of different positions of late medieval England. The prologue, although addressed to a female reader, no doubt spoke to an audience who could read in Raymond's redaction of Catherine's life a model of piety for her own. But therein lies another tension of the text: on the one hand, the intimacy of Raymond's understanding of Catherine encourages a personal knowledge of his subject and her actions; on the other hand, the mediated text that has been reshaped to "touche only maters þat longeth to your lernyng," discourages that full embrace.[40] Read, do not imitate. Learn, but do not fully understand.

Parsing the Layered *Lyf*

Raymond's Latin *Legenda major* of Catherine follows the more or less prescribed generic conventions of late medieval hagiography. The saint's early life takes up the first part, here describing Catherine's birth, her vow of virginity, her familial persecutions, and ending with her taking of the Dominican habit (as a tertiary) and her mystical marriage to Christ. A second part follows Catherine's more public life, although focused more on her charity, miracles, visions, and prophecies than her work to move the papacy back to Rome or her interest in promoting crusades to the Holy Land. A final part describes her death and the miracles that followed it. To the medieval reader, all the expectations of a hagiographic account are fulfilled. In addition, unlike many hagiographers piecing together stories and legends well after a saint's death, Raymond knew Catherine and knew her well, a relationship that is evident in the *Legenda major* as it unfolds. He was not only her biographer, but her confessor, and that secret knowledge about Catherine's inner life is revealed throughout the text.

However, Raymond is very aware that he is also painting a picture of himself along with that of Catherine throughout his narrative, and this self-consciousness leads to a slightly more restrained narrative than those upon which he is building. This may be because Raymond is also trying to promote the Dominican order along with Catherine, and he is writing his *vita* with a broader audience and agenda in mind than a simple hagiographic account. This breadth serves to bring the text outside of fourteenth-century Siena, and makes it an accessible read to the Middle English lay readers who receive its translation a century later. Although Catherine herself was mired in the politics of the day (especially the papal schism), the hagiography is not overtly concerned with these details, focusing more on the visionary subject herself. Raymond is also explicitly aware that he is constructing a hagiography in a tradition of Dominican holy women's texts. Raymond had his own political motivations as well, and writing a *vita* associating him so firmly with a powerful saint is a large part of that.[41] By the time this reaches English hands, Catherine's Dominican ties and the general promotion of the order are firmly in place, so the effect of Raymond's focus on Catherine's independent visionary and ascetic tendencies no longer serves the order as a whole, but instead moves the focus onto the individual Catherine. Indeed, what Raymond intended as a nod towards orthodoxy seems somewhat subversive against the backdrop of an even more orthodox canon of English devotional texts, which primarily stressed didacticism, meditation, and church hierarchy.

After the brief translator's prologue, *The Lyf of Katherin of Senis* follows the format of the *Legenda major* with some closeness, although cutting out many biblical allusions and shortening some of the descriptions. The translator notably cuts some of the more gruesome ones about Catherine's self-mortification, although *The Lyf* still has extended descriptions of Catherine's ascetic practices, far more than indicated in her own writings or *Dialogo*. Maiju Lehmijoki-Gardner notes that this may partly be the gendered expectations Raymond has of his readers, as well as the demands of the hagiographic genre that highlight the suffering of the saint.[42] There are also some clear moments of rephrasing or editing – for example, in the Latin, Raymond refers to himself in the first person throughout, but the Middle English amends this to a third person narration about "her confessour,"[43] emphasizing his clerical and sacramental role. The reader in Middle English, without the Latin for comparison, would not notice any disjointed narrative or lacunae.

The Lyf opens with Raymond's description of seven-year-old Catherine's first realization that she would devote her life to God during a vision she had while walking with her brother. The vision of Christ, accompanied by Peter, Paul, and John the Evangelist, looms over the Dominican church near her home: "And when she behelde alle thys, she was fyrst astonyd; but by a-vysement stably she stode styll and wyth a louyng herte deuoutly she loked on her sauyour bothe wyth bodely and gostely eyen."[44] Her brother pulls her away from the vision to Catherine's dismay, and Raymond describes her chiding her brother for breaking the vision, but also draws attention to the fact that Catherine had been especially chosen to see it: "She anon cast doune a lytyll her eyen, as she hadde awaked of an heuy slepe, and sayde: 'A, yf thou sawe that I sawe, thou woldest not haue lette me from this holy vysyon."[45] Catherine is a visionary from the start, both in her life and her *Lyf*. Even though the vision fades, the effect on a young Catherine is lasting: "Soo that anone was shewed that the fyre of dyuyne loue was kyndeled in her herte, by the whiche vertu her intellection was made clere, her wyll was feruent, her memorye was comforted, and alle her outward werkyng shewed in alle thynges the rewle of goddes lawe."[46] This early in the *Legenda major*, Raymond already makes his case for Catherine's link to the Dominican order. Her vision takes place above its Church and is followed by Catherine's statement that she knows – not through any reading, teaching, or hearing – about the lives of important saints,

"and specyally the lyfe of Saynt Domynyk."[47] The trope of saints finding their religious calling in childhood is integrated into many hagiographical accounts, but Catherine's immediate link to a particular order
is notable, especially since she does not actually profess as a Dominican
nun. Raymond's secondary agenda of promoting the Dominican order
is evident throughout the *Legenda major*.

These revelations are then representative of Catherine's lifelong desire
for a religious life that imitates the holy fathers and the Dominicans
especially. Raymond describes her piety as bodily and spiritual, encap-
sulating the devotional practice she would continue throughout her life.
He writes that she would self-flagellate with "a little scourge," as part
of her routine in prayer: "For after that tyme she sought oute where that
she myght haue a pryue place to abyde in preuely whanne she wolde
vse bodely affeccyons and whanne she wolde occupye hyr in prayer
and holy medytacyons; In that place at certeyne tymes she scourged
her lytell tender body with a lytell scourge."[48] Catherine is still just a
seven year-old girl in this story, with a "lytell tender body," and part
of her spiritual education is that she embraces an ascetic life as much
as a devotional one. It would seem that this episode would not serve
as *exemplum* for its readers, but the *Lyf* explains that Catherine inspired
many of the "damsellys" of Siena who similarly "scourgyd hem-selfe
as she dyde."[49] A surviving Alsatian manuscript of Catherine's *Legenda
major* depicts this scene in an illustration, graphically showing a child-
like and naked Catherine dripping with blood next to a crucified Christ,
speaking to the power of this textual moment.[50] This ascetic experience of Catherine's childhood is followed by a charming anecdote that
young Catherine, desiring for the wilderness of the desert fathers, runs
away to a cave at the edge of town, which she feels must be the desert
she had heard about. In this way, Raymond skillfully moves back and
forth from moments of deep piety to some levity and a reflection of the
personality he is trying to convey.

Raymond quickly follows the story of Catherine's first vision with
her desire to remain a virgin. Notably, the translator omits a section
heavy on numerical theology about the perfection of the number six
(Catherine's age at which she makes this request) and how this relates
to the perfection inherent in her name. The translator excises it from
his text, likely seeing this theological construction as beyond the comprehension of his readers.[51] Raymond segues Catherine's request for
virginity into a lesson for all his readers to eschew the material world
in favour of the spiritual: "Loo, maydens that rede thys, Loo here ye

may se how ordynatly alle the yeftes and vertuous werkyng and dedys of thys holy mayde were dysposed and ordeyned by that euerlastyng wysdome, whyche myghtely dysposeth alle thynges in softnes!"[52] Rather than urging the readers to also choose virginity and chastity, Raymond's rearticulation of Catherine's desire into one for a spiritual life over a material one can translate and appeal to any reader.

Indeed, the Latin in the above section speaks to any "lector," but it is the English translator who calls the reader a "maiden," a term usually reserved for women, speaking to its expected audience.[53] The translator does this several times throughout the text – just like Raymond's *Legenda major* loses its first person narration to a third, the ungendered readers become clearly female "maidens," altering how it is read by either gender. For the female reader, the text becomes much more identified with gender, and Catherine's femaleness and *exemplum* are foregrounded. For the male reader, the text becomes less personal, alienating him from some of the universal messages of the original. There are several places throughout the translation where, similarly, unlike a language that may indicate a gender-neutral reader, the English has translated or feminized it in a way that makes the audience seem more "female." For example, the Latin describes Catherine, fresh after her vow of virginity, as being galvanized like a recruit in the army of Christ, a masculine metaphor. The English translator has removed that reference entirely.[54]

Overall, however, Catherine's *Lyf* does support a gender-neutral reading of her text despite the specifically addressed "doughter" in the prologue. Catherine's first desire is to enter the Dominican order, but not as a nun, nor as a tertiary (her eventual path), but, remarkably, as a priest:

> From that tyme forward there wext a grete desyre in hyr sowle to go vnto that ordre, that she myght profyte mannes sowle wyth other brethern of that ordre. But by-cause she sawe a grete obstacle in that she was a woman, therfore she thought to folowe Saynt Eufrosyen – as men clepyd hir – in childhode wonderfully as for a pronostycacion, that ryght as saynt Eufrosyn feyned hyr a man and went in to a monastery of monkes, in the same manere thys mayde is purposed to feyne hyr a man and go in ferre contree, where she was not knowe, and take the abyte of the ordre of pre-chours: where she myght helpe sowles and saue them from perysshyng.[55]

The fifth-century saint Euphrosyne of Alexandria dressed as a man in order to avoid the marriage her father wanted for her. She entered a monastery, eventually attaining the role of abbot. Catherine and her circle would have likely known of the saint through the *Vite dei Santi Padri*, circulating in Tuscany in the early fourteenth century.[56] The English audience may have been less familiar with Euphrosyne. There is an anonymous Anglo-Saxon version of her life, however, as well as one in Middle English found in the late fourteenth-century Vernon manuscript, so there is some genuine possibility that the English reading audience was familiar with the analogy that Catherine makes here.[57] If not, Raymond gives enough context to understand that Catherine's first desire is to live as a monk, not a nun, and that this necessarily means living life as a man. Raymond explains that although this desire burned in Catherine for a long time, it was representative of her desire to serve God – which did come to pass, just not in the way that Catherine had initially hoped.

While Raymond says no more of the gender implications of the desire, although it mirrors his own articulated surprise at Catherine's abilities despite her femaleness, he does speak to the kind of saint Catherine envisions herself to be – one who is engaged politically and socially with the world, not just meekly receiving divine grace or imparting visions. Catherine had grown up in a Siena that actually had a substantial number of female recluses living in and around her environs, so her desire to live as a male is even more interesting.[58] Catherine understands that this is not the role ascribed to her gender, so she must "feyne hir a man" in order to behave this way. She believed firmly that the Church needed to fulfil a crusade, and her letters attest to the lengths she went through to secure these activities for the pope. In fact, Catherine's main connection to England and the English, other than her relationship with William Flete, was with John Hawkwood, an English mercenary for hire whom Catherine tried to convince to go on a Crusade (rather than exacting a ransom from Siena in exchange for peace, a bargain he had made with Florence).[59] She writes to him, "You find so much satisfaction in fighting and waging war, so now I am begging you tenderly in Christ Jesus not to wage war any longer against Christians (for that offends God), but to go instead to fight the unbelievers, as God and our holy father have decreed."[60] It is Raymond of Capua who delivers Catherine's letter, showing how firmly he was invested in her dual roles as visionary ascetic and political activist, even though this latter aspect of her life is not very evident in the *Legenda major*.[61]

Catherine's *Lyf* may offer something to the lay reader that the traditional hagiographical account does not. One appealing aspect of the narrative is its proximity to the reader in time and culture; the Siena of the late fourteenth century does not seem so different from the England of a century later. But, even more significantly, Catherine was a layperson herself and lived a public life out in the world. The seeming contradiction that Raymond of Capua points to in his preface with which I opened this chapter, that Catherine is both extraordinary and female, is excised from the translation but inherent in the very construction of the text. Catherine is a lay woman, and yet Raymond is her champion, writing her story. This somewhat conflicting image of the mystical or visionary woman teaching the learned man develops its own tradition through the hagiographies of the thirteenth and fourteenth centuries.[62] Much has been written on the intimacy that develops between a confessor and his female charge, and the strange dynamics that arise due to power imbalances associated with gender, church hierarchy, and spiritual abilities. But the relationship that develops between the male confessor and spiritually gifted penitent is also precariously balanced, taking into account power associated with the confessor's ability to absolve the sin of the penitent, when she, in fact, may be spiritually superior to the confessor. Catherine's access to God allows her to know secret things about her confessor, just as he is exposed to her private thoughts through the act of confession. Raymond is constantly walking the fine line between exposing too much about what he knows of Catherine and her private moments with God, presumably revealed during confession, and proving Catherine's sanctity.[63] Some of these moments become erotically charged merely because Raymond is relaying Catherine's hidden thoughts and actions, often imbued with vulnerability and a kind of voyeurism as they describe Catherine's most intimate moments. Hagiographers describing a "bride of Christ" cannot escape the eroticism already permeating their subjects' relationship with God, and this translates into how they are described after their death while the hagiographer recounts private moments that are now revealed in the glorification of the saint. Dyan Elliot argues that this eroticism initially comes from the thirteenth-century beguine *vitae*, but is picked up in Italy when these narratives disseminate there.[64] Certainly, Raymond would be deeply familiar with the *vitae* of beguines written by his Dominican predecessors James of Vitry and Thomas of Cantimpré, who both utilize erotic metaphors to describe their subjects. As Catherine is a *literal* bride of Christ, as described in chapter 3, Raymond already has that erotic vocabulary integrated into his text. Notably, in the Latin *Legenda major*, Raymond admits that he is now telling Catherine's secrets because she is dead when he describes her reluctance to marry and to be seen in a sexual way by men.[65] The English translation relays only the confessional discussion, omitting Raymond's comments that Catherine's secrets are now meant to be told in order to magnify her sanctity: "He asked … whether she dyde it [dressed and wore make up] to the plesaunce of ony man in speciall or to the plesaunce of all men. She answerd and sayde, ther was none so moche payne to her as to beholde men or to be seyne of men or to be there men shold fynde her."[66] The translator's omission, coupled with the third-person change of Raymond's narrative, makes the descriptions of Catherine's confessions seem even more starkly exposed.

For Raymond, his intimacy with Catherine is also evident in the moments he uses to illustrate her exceptional piety. For example, he describes in detail the conditions of her bed and the austerity of her nighttime bodily mortifications.[67] He writes that she started to use a hair shirt, but then progressed to "an yron chayne next her body" that "endented the skynne and made a marke there-vpon as it hadde be fobrennyd."[68] More intimately, he describes one of Catherine's moments of self-inflicted penance as taking a painfully hot bath, one that burns her skin:

> Whan she came to the bathe, she founde a new maner bathyng in hyr sowle how that she shold tormente hyr body amonge the delycyous bathes: she went to the condyte there the hote water cam inne to the bathe, and there she satte all naked and suffred pacyentyly the hote water brenne hyr tender naked flesshe; the whyche was more payne to hyr thenne when she bete hyr wyth a cheyne.[69]

In order to tell the story, Raymond must imagine a naked Catherine (indeed, her "tender naked flesh") burning herself in the water, a pain akin to when she beat herself (also, presumably, naked) with a chain. Both of these intimate, bodily scenes are known to Raymond because he is her confessor, about which he explains to the reader:

> Now shall I tell you how hyr confessour knew it: in a tyme hyr moder Lapa tolde mayster Raymond afore hyr doughter how they went for to be bathed, and how wysely she asked leue of hir moder, whan she was there, that she myght be bathed by hyr-self whan all folke were gone; ffor

she wyst well, yf hyr moder had seen hyr, she myght not do as she dyd. And thenne hyr confessour axyd hyr how she myght suffre so grete hete wythout peryll of deth. Thys mayde answerd to hym and sayd full symply, that whan she satte in that bathe, she thought besyly vpon the paynes of purgatorye and of hell, prayng to our lord, whome she had so hyely offended, that he wolde wouchesauf to torne mercyably tho peynes that she had deserued in to that temperall payne that she suffred gladly.[70]

This description gives further insight into the complex relationship between Catherine and Raymond. Here, it is Catherine's mother who tells Raymond that Catherine asked to be alone for her bath (and that this was indicative of a secret behaviour); Raymond, in turn, speaks to Catherine about what transpired during the bath. Only then are we given the spiritual lesson of the story, which is that Catherine believes her sins are so great that she deserves the extreme pain of hell, but that God's mercy allows her to suffer the earthly pains in its stead. The translator omits the direct speech of Catherine's that the Latin contains, instead moving her to third-person narration in Raymond's voice, further emphasizing the role of the confessor as mediator between Catherine's actions and the readers.

For the lay English reader, Catherine's life and text may feel very immediate both due to this intimate narrative tone and its actual temporal proximity. Unlike the hagiographies of the classical virgin-martyrs, such as St Katherine of Alexandria – a saint whose life is widely venerated in late medieval England – whose refusal to deny her faith results in her torture on a spiked wheel and her eventual beheading, Catherine of Siena lives a recognizable life to her readers, lay and religious alike. She lives and operates in a Christianized world, and rather than addressing the pagan-Christian clashes and controversies of her foresisters, instead concerns herself with the politics and activities of the Church itself (heresies, the schism, the Crusades). These issues are not far removed from her readers' minds, and indeed will become more prominently analogous to their lives and concerns during the Reformation. Each of Catherine's English texts postulate an ideal reader, which may or may not be the original text's intended one. In the late fifteenth century, neither Catherine's canonization nor the direction of the Dominican order remains issues of concern, both reasons that had driven Raymond in his authorship of the *Legenda major*, but in *The Lyf*'s new iteration as the de Worde volume it instead espouses a particular kind of female piety. Significantly, the second part of the

Legenda major, which contains most of Catherine's political and external life, is heavily edited by the translator, betraying a wariness about this aspect of Catherine's life that strays from the traditional view of a meek and humble woman as visionary. A lengthy preface, which describes Catherine as a public spouse to her bridegroom – indicating that Catherine was not only a "Mary" (as described in the first part of the *Legenda major*), who represents contemplation and pious prayer, but also a "Martha," who serves God in a social realm – is completely absent from the translation.[71] Instead, the translator simply tells his reader straight out that he wants her to "see fructuous example of vertuous liuinge to edyfycacion of thy sowle and to comforte and encrese of thy gostly labour in all werkis of pyte."[72] Reading Catherine's life is a lesson to be learned, but it is clear that the English translator plans to shape that lesson as much as he can.

Unruly Readers: The Visionary Reader and Catherine of Siena

Margery Kempe's *Book*, frequently used as a source to understand which devotional texts were circulating among lay readers in late medieval England, surprisingly, does not mention Catherine of Siena. This despite the fact that there is some clear evidence that many around her would have known the saint's story quite well. For example, William Bakthorpe, the prior of Kempe's hometown of Lynn, exchanged correspondence with Raymond of Capua in the 1390s.[73] In addition, Margery frequently alludes to Bridget of Sweden, who is repeatedly linked to Catherine, as well as Marie of Oignies, whose Dominican adviser Jacques de Vitry served as a model for Raymond of Capua in his own *vita*-writing. Nevertheless, Kempe can give valuable insight into how Catherine might have been read by looking at how she read analogous works, such as the *Revelations* of Saint Bridget.[74] Roger Ellis remarks that Kempe clearly models herself after Bridget, and for at least one reason that would not work with modelling after Catherine: "Like Birgitta, Margery faces rejection as often as acceptance at the hands of her contemporaries; like Birgitta, Margery appeals to divine speakers who can give her the unqualified confirmation of her spiritual gifts that she needs."[75] Catherine is rarely portrayed as being doubted or rejected, right on up to her audience and influence with the pope (although Bridget had the same), but she does seek and receive confirmation of her spiritual gifts. Bridget, of course, is also famously a mother of eight – as Kempe was a mother of fourteen – and the fact that she manages to combine her sainthood despite her familial obligations may be something that appeals greatly to Kempe, who, at least as she is presented in her *Book*, is trying to achieve the former and eschew the latter.

It is worth imagining, however, the kind of reader of the *Lyf* that Kempe would have been and to speculate the way Catherine's texts could have been read by an Englishwoman inclined towards mysticism or attracted by the visionary elements of these narratives. What would reading Catherine like Margery entail? Kempe had a knack for choosing the most subversive elements of the visionaries' texts to which she was exposed, and then reinterpreting these into her own brand of devotional theatre. For example, Marie of Oignies is described as crying out loud when moved by Christ's suffering, and Kempe cites Marie in relationship to her own weeping; Kempe understands her own body through a lens of the devotional literature to which she has been exposed. She writes of how her confessor understands her better after reading about Marie's tears:

> And yet owr Lord drow hym agen in schort tyme, blissed mote he ben, that he lovyd hir mor and trustyd mor to hir wepyng and hir crying than evyr he dede beforn, for aftyrward he red of a woman clepyd Maria de Oegines and of hir maner of levyng, of the wondirful swetnesse that sche had in the word of God heryng, of the wondirful compassyon that sche had in hys Passyon thynkyng, and of the plentyuows teerys that sche wept, the whech made hir so febyl and so weyke that sche myth not endur to beheldyn the crosse, ne heryn owr Lordys Passyon rehersyd, so sche was resolvyd into terys of pyté and compassyon.[76]

But Kempe's tears take on a life of their own in her *Book*, and her uncontrollable wailing at seemingly inappropriate moments is a point of much consternation for Kempe's companions and family.[77] Catherine of Siena, too, is described as weeping uncontrollably, beyond the comprehension of her confessors until God allows them to understand, demonstrating how firmly this trope is incorporated into the stories of visionary women.[78] As described in chapter 3, Kempe's mystical marriage to Christ is remarkably similar to the one described in Catherine's *Legenda major*, complete with witnesses and audience made up of various prophets and biblical figures. Kempe, certainly, would have seemingly loved this description of the pearl-and-diamond wedding ring Christ bestows on Catherine – "[He] brought forth a Rynge, arayed rounde aboute wyth four precious margarete stones, and in the ouer parte off the rynge was enclosyd a ryght fayre dyamant stone"[79] – a detail lacking from her own account of her marriage.[80]

Other sections that may have appealed to Kempe and readers like her are those which refer to Catherine's visionary abilities and her corporeal understanding of Christ. Raymond is consciously writing against condemnation of Catherine (and Bridget of Sweden) and their claims of divine visions. In England, Raymond's description of Catherine's visions would certainly stand out against the relatively sparse landscape of visionary literature (although not as starkly as *The Orcherd of Syon* does as an entirely visionary text written by a woman). Raymond's account of Catherine's life is literally interspersed with her dialogues with God, where he consistently reveals truths to her about his word and mankind. It is this implied divine authority that has readers such as Jean Gerson so infuriated at the power of the words spoken by women like Bridget and Catherine. Raymond himself admits that prior to knowing Catherine he had doubts about visions, specifically those by women:

> For thenne came too his mynde of ypocritis the whiche regnyd in his dayes, and that he founde many dyscetys, and namely amonges wymmen, whom þe deuyll dysceyued with þat vyce aboue all other creaturs; hyt came also in to his mynde how þe fyrst womman Eue was deceyued, and many suche other: and therefor he doubted the more of this holy mayde.[81]

Although Raymond is ultimately convinced of Catherine's sanctity and the legitmacy of her visions, this expression of doubt is a necessary part of his convincing process as he anticipates the same objections in his readers. Reading the *Legenda major* closely, one can see why visionary women were so threatening to many in the Church hierarchy and likewise so attractive to some readers. The power they wield by claiming a direct understanding of God can be either beneficial or destructive, depending on whose ear and support they have. During the Reformation, Elizabeth Barton, the disruptive "Holy Maid of Kent," would be accused of using Catherine as a model for her visionary and political activities. As we will explore further in the next chapter, she is executed for such imitations.

Catherine's visions are as corporeal as they are spiritual. She receives the stigmata from Christ (visible only to her) and when offered the crown of thorns from Christ, she takes it and thrusts it "vpon hyr hede wyth a maner of vyolence, that the thornys percud hir hede rounde

about as hir thought, in so moche that she had a peyne long afterward in hyr hede by prykynge of thornys."[82] What is Catherine's body
and what is Christ's collapse, forming a blurred line that epitomizes
the mystic's singular devotional viewpoint. In more than one vision,
Catherine drinks from Christ's side wound, demonstrating the kind of
divine intimacy she envisions: "He helde hys arme of hyr necke and
brought hyr mouth to hys blessyd wounde in hys syde and sayd to
hir thus: 'Drynke doughter, out of my syde the drynke of helthe, by þe
whiche thy soule shall be fulfylled wyth so moche swetenesse, that it
shall rebounde in to thy body, the whiche thou hast so meruayllously
despysed for my loue.'"[83] Later, she specifically describes the wound
like a breast that a mother teasingly withholds and then gives to her
child, eventually handing it over for full satiation. This metaphor
moves from Christ as father/spouse to Christ as mother, nourishing his
children through his pain, and brings the sacrament of the Eucharist
into very literal terms:

> Trewely, as a moder serued hyr lytell soukyng chylde, whom she loueth
> tenderly. A moder suffred other-whyle hir chylde stonde a-ferre from hyr,
> whyle she sheweth hym hir tete of hir breste, and suffred hym to wepe
> longe tyme after hit, but all that tyme she lawhed; at the last, whan she
> hath suffred it to wepe long tyme, she gothe ther-to wyth a lawhyng chere
> and beclypped it in her armes and kyssed it and soo gyueth it hyr brest
> or the tete. Ryght so ferde our lorde wyth me: that day he shewed me hys
> blessyd wounde in his side.[84]

The image of Catherine drinking from Christ's side is illustrated in
surviving Continental *vitae*, which graphically demonstrate this physical moment. Jeffrey Hamburger describes one such image as:

> Lunging forward, [Catherine's] action accelerated by the broad brush-
> strokes in the background, Catherine thrusts her tongue deep in the gap-
> ing hole in Christ's side. The saint's conjoining with Christ may often have
> been depicted with more grace, but hardly with greater intensity. Looking
> at the image, it is not difficult to imagine why reformers seem to have
> preferred that most manuscripts of Catherine's *Vita* remained without
> illustrations.[85]

Indeed, the de Worde *Legenda major* contains few woodcuts and
none of the surviving English manuscripts about Catherine contains
illustrations.

This same extreme bodily manifestation and understanding of Christ's suffering and the spiritual salvation of his blood represents the kind of incarnate understanding of Christ's life that permeates Kempe's text. These images, too, may recall another English visionary – Julian of Norwich. She, like Catherine, sees Jesus as a mother, feeding from his breast:

> The moder may ley her childe tenderly to her brest. But oure tender mother Jhesu, he may homely lede us into his blessed brest by his swet, open syde, and shewe us therein perty of the godhed and the joyes of heven, with gostely sekernesse of endlesse blisse. And that shewde he in the tenth, geving the same understanding in this swet word where he seyth, "Lo, how I loved thee," beholding into his blissed syde, enjoyeng.[86]

While Julian's is a more literal interpretation of the wound-as-breast, Catherine's text mirrors both Julian and Kempe in their bodily understanding of Christ and their visceral interpretation of his love.[87]

Catherine and Kempe are also quite alike in their rebellious behaviours, desire to preach, and social aspirations. Jane Chance writes that it is especially in their dialogues, their conversations with God, that one may locate their subversions to the norm.[88] Catherine explicitly questions God throughout the *Legenda major* about the status she holds as a visionary woman. In one of her conversations, Catherine professes her amazement that God has chosen her as a vessel for his revelations, even though she is a sinner, so lowly, and, worst of all, a woman. She asks him:

> But yet I praye the, lord, in what maner of wyse may this be that þou seyste now, that I wretche that am soo freell shold be soo profytable to mannys soule? Thou knowest well, lord, that men setten lyttll store by womens wordes, speke þe neuer so vertuously, as it were not semely, ne lyuest thou that wymemen sholde be more conuersaunt amonges men.[89]

Catherine's query reflects both her understanding of her position as a politically savvy woman in a man's social realm and Raymond's awareness that her validity was questioned. Women are not supposed to speak, she reminds him. They are not believed. His response is immediate, addressing both Catherine's humility and the men who condemn her:

Am not I he the whiche hathe made mankynde bothe man and woman and the shappe of euery eyther; and where that I wyl enspyre myn grace, al is one to me both man woman? Neuertheles by-cause thou spekest thise wordes not of none vnfaythfulnesse but only of mekenesse, therfore I wyll þat thou knowe that in thyse dayes soo moche pryde and elacion aboundeth in the worlde, and namely of men that holden them-self lettred men and wyse men, that myn ryghtwysnes may not lenger suffre it, but nedlynges I muste shame them endelesly at the daye of dome for her cursed pryde.[90]

Men and women are equal, he reminds Catherine (and her readers), despite what "lettered men" (i.e., clerics) may think. God furthermore explains to Catherine that waiting for judgment day for these men's education may not be sufficient, so in the meantime he will shame them on earth by forcing them to hear his words through the mouths of women, "all-be-it that they be freell vessels."[91]

This message that women are equal to men, that Catherine's words are truth, and that lettered men are drowning in their own mistaken pride repeats throughout the text. These are clearly radical words, ones that Raymond tempers by reminding the readers that Catherine is the exception, not the rule; however, the message she is conveying, through God's words, is undeniably radical for the medieval reader who may not question the frailty of women or the infallibility of lettered men. Excised from the Latin in this section is perhaps the more subversive notion that not only does God see no man or woman but that classes – lower and upper – are also equal in his eyes, saying "all stand equal in my sight, and all things are equally in my power to do."[92] This translator, at least, is more attuned to reaching a gendered audience than one concerned with class. The *Lyf* lacks the apologetic tone of Julian of Norwich's *Vision*, where she specifically points out her inadequacy as a conveyer of the visions she has seen because she is a woman, "lewd, febille, and freylle," and her statement that ultimately the clerics have the final voice: "Bot in alle thinge I lyeve as haly kyrke techis."[93] Instead, Catherine's criticism of the Church and her denial of the limitations of her femaleness better reflect the defiance inherent in Margery Kempe's *Book*, written at her behest and consistently demonstrating how she steps around the clerical hierarchy by virtue of her own relationship to God. The seemingly orthodox hagiographical account of Catherine's *Lyf* allows for this same slippage and contradiction.

Later Readers: Anthologizing Catherine in the Pepwell Edition

Modern readers are not the only ones who draw a line from Margery Kempe to Catherine of Siena, nor is it only the subversive or radical elements of these women that link them. Excerpts from the *Legenda major* of Catherine again appear in print in the early sixteenth century, this time in a volume with excerpts from Margery Kempe's *Book*, naming her as a holy anchorite – one of the only vestiges of her *Book*, in fact, until the manuscript was rediscovered in the early twentieth century. Henry Pepwell, one of de Worde's printing rivals (and also, presumably, friend, as he was named one of the executors of his will), printed a collection of mystical texts in 1521, which included several excerpts from the *Legenda major*.[94] The Catherine excerpts appear to be taken directly from British Library, MS Royal 17 D.V., a late fifteenth-century manuscript that contains translated excerpts from Catherine *Legenda major* alongside a copy of *The Cloud of Unknowing*. The excerpts are nearly identical in translation to the analygous sections in the de Worde edition of Catherine's *Lyf*, suggesting a common source, and since the manuscript upon which the text is based precedes the de Worde, serves as evidence that a translated version of Catherine's *Lyf* was in circulation before de Worde set it down in print.[95] This is further supported by the existence and apparent circulation of the vernacular extracts concerning the "Discernment of Spirits," the text on self-knowledge, and Catherine's mystical marriage to Christ (discussed in chapter 3).

Pepwell did not leave a terribly large corpus behind. Alexandra Gillespie notes that only "sixteen books survive that were printed by or for Pepwell between 1518 and 1539."[96] Two of these are works of fiction, but a great many of them were didactic and humanist texts. Unlike de Worde, Pepwell does not appear to have powerful patrons interested in devotional literature or any particular interest in Catherine. The Catherine excerpts survive in a rather surprising volume of mystical texts that Pepwell apparently collated himself. The title that the fifty-page 1521 volume apparently carried refers only to the first selections of the book, those of Richard of St Victor: *Here Followeth a Very Devout Treatise, Named Benjamin, of the Mights and Virtues of Man's Sowle, and of the Way to True Contemplation, Compiled by a Noble and Famous Doctor, a Man of Great Holiness and Devotion, Named Richard of Saint Victor*. While a few have suggested that this book is a *Sammelbänd*, a collection of pamphlets that are bound together by a book owner as a personal volume, Ralph Hanna has demonstrated that it is deliberately printed as an anthology.[97] Hanna suggests that the items were collected from a London Carthusian house which "underwrote the production."[98] Looking at it as a purposely constructed anthology further gives us a real sense of the transition from medieval manuscript to printed page. Because the Catherine text is taken directly from the segment that is represented in Royal 17 D.V. (and may have been taken directly from this manuscript) and the Kempe text is taken from the earlier de Worde printing, we can see a process of assemblage for a printed devotional work that is not relying on one exemplar, but pulling excerpts from various places and putting them together. As Margaret Connolly and Raluca Radulescu note in the introduction to their volume on English miscellanies, *Insular Books,*

> Medieval manuscripts of all types have continuous history of ownership and use (and sometimes reuse), and their most vibrant period of textual afterlife was during the sixteenth and seventeenth centuries, when they were valued and used primarily as reading resources, prior to their transformation into objects of antiquarian curiosity and profit.[99]

Pepwell's excerpt from Catherine has been chosen and edited for him by a medieval reader and scribe, his selection from Margery Kempe similarly excerpted. He is not doing the real work of an anthologizer here, but is doing the work of a compiler and assembler. We can see through his choices just how texts were put together to create something new. A reprint of the book edited by Edmund G. Gardner in 1910 carries the less cumbersome title *The Cell of Self-Knowledge,* and further demonstrates how the choices of a medieval compiler may continue to create meaning for readers well beyond their intended audience.[100] In addition to Catherine and Richard of St Victor, the anthology also has portions from Margery Kempe's *Book,* Walter Hilton, and *The Cloud of Unknowing.* The Catherine section is preceded by a lengthy title of its own: "Here followeth divers doctrines devout and fruitful, taken out of the life of that glorious virgin and spouse of our Lord, Saint Katherin of Seenes. And first those which our Lord taught and shewed to herselfe, and sith those which she taught and shewed unto others."[101] The woodcut image underneath this heading shows the image of Catherine's heart being exchanged for God's, one of the detailed incidents of her *Legenda major.* The woodcut is identical to the opening woodcut in *The Orcherd of Syon.*

Pepwell opens with Catherine's text on self-knowledge that we have seen previously in Harley 2409 (see chapter 3 for more on this). Although the translation in Harley 2409 is slightly closer to the de Worde edition than the Pepwell, they are all close enough to further support a common manuscript source of Catherine's *Lyf* circulating in the vernacular. Here, the opening words are God's to Catherine: "Knowest thou not, daughter, who thou art and who I am? If thou know well these two words, thou art and shalt be blessed. Thou art she that art nought; and I am He that am ought."[102] This idea of having the self subsumed by God and God's will is centrally thematic to almost all of Catherine's texts. Grisé writes that the *Doctrines* distills Catherine "into small lessons the reader can consider individually or together" that reflect on the larger *Lyf* as well.[103] Indeed, many of Catherine's main points are touched on here in addition to the idea that self-knowledge can only come with self-annihilation and complete love of God; the *Doctrines* also stress that sensuality is the root of sin (and must be destroyed) and in prayer there is power. As for sin and sensuality, the portion extracted from the *Lyf* is to the point, and this time in Catherine's voice, not God's. The translation omits much of the glossing and biblical allusions present in the Latin:

> A soul which is verily mete to God, as much as it hath of the love of God, so much it hath of the hate of her own sensuality. For of the love of God naturally cometh hate of sin, the which is done against God. The soul, therefore, considering that the root and beginning of sin reigneth in the sensuality, and there principally is rooted, she is moved and stirred highly and holily with all her mights against her own sensuality; not utterly to destroy the root, for that may not be, as long as the soul dwelleth in the body living in this life, but ever there shall be left a root, namely of small venial sins. And because she may not utterly destroy the root of sin thus in her sensuality, of the which displeasaunce springeth an holy hate and a despising of the sensuality, by the which the soul is ever well kept from her ghostly enemies. There is nothing that keepeth the soul so strong and so sure as doth such an holy hate.[104]

Catherine again espouses a self-annihilation, a "holy hate" that despises all of the sin either enacted or even thought of in the sinner's mind. Truly, Catherine says, one must hate one's own humanity in order to serve God, because it is part of the human condition to be a sinner. Excerpted from the *Legenda major*, these sections elevate Catherine seemingly above sin by omitting what her struggles actually were. In the *Lyf*, not long after this passage, we are told that Catherine was assailed by temptations and invitations to sin that she needed to combat. Raymond writes that the temptations themselves are too foul even to write down: "Shame it is to here in how foule flesshely synne he tempted her, and therfore I shall not reherse theym; but to clene sowles it is delectable to here how this holy maude ouercame suche foule delusyons, and therefore that shall I reherce."[105] Without this postscript to Catherine's exhortation to "holy hate," the reader does not see that Catherine can summon such a magnitude of hate for sin because it is the only way to combat the desire to sin which assailed her.

The Pepwell volume also speaks specifically to its readers about the value of prayer, and the difference between mental and vocal prayer as Catherine sees it, also pointing to the different and developing practices of reading aloud or silently:

> For she said that was ever her business, to give herself to the exercise of prayer, so for to win the continual habit of prayer; for she did see well that by prayer all virtues are increased, and made mighty and strong; and, without prayer, they wax feeble and defail. Wherefore she induced her disciples that they should busy them to prayer perseverauntly; and therefore she told them to two manner of prayers: Vocal and Mental. Vocal prayers, she said, should be kept certain hours in the night and in the day ordained by holy Church; but mental prayer should ever be had, in act or in habit of the soul.[106]

This distinction of vocal and mental prayer, which seems well suited for the cloister, finds a new audience as it speaks to an emerging devout laity who is both keeping liturgical hours and extending their piety beyond the prescribed prayers and moments the Church provides.

The Catherine section of Pepwell's volume closes with a passage from the *Legenda major* that is reminiscent of "The Cleannesse of Sowle" (discussed in chapter 3). It reminds the reader that purity of soul is only achieved by replacing one's own will with God's will, by not judging others and leaving the judgment to God:

> Also she said, for to get and purchase purity of soul, it were right necessary that man kept himself from all manner of judgments of his neighbour's deeds; for in every creature we should behold only the will of God. And therefore she said that in no wise men should deem creatures; that is, neither despise them by their doom nor condemn them, all be it that they see them do open sin before them, but rather they should have compassion on them and pray for them, and despise them not, nor condemn them.[107]

The selection of this passage for the volume, taken along with "The Cleannesse of Sowle," and the similar section taken from *Il Dialogo*, shows how firmly the concept of annihilation of will in order to achieve purity was understood as central to Catherine's theological doctrine. It serves as one of Catherine's core tropes to be selected and repeated in different venues for different readers.

The section following Catherine's excerpts in the Pepwell volume is that of Margery Kempe. It is identical to the de Worde publication of Margery Kempe, printed in 1501, that identifies her as an "ancress of Lynn."[108] As Karma Lochrie has noted, particularly about the way Kempe is excerpted and presented in these texts,

> It is important to remember that, while the patronage and readership of sixteenth-century England enjoyed the type of piety rendered in the editions of de Worde and Pepwell, the monks of Mount Grace were reading and commenting on the more ecstatic and boisterous text of Margery Kempe. Perhaps the greatest irony is that Kempe, who was designated to be a mirror among sinners, should find her readership not among the lay population to whom she appealed but within an order of monks dedicated to strict seclusion and austerity.[109]

Just as there are two Catherines known to readers at this time – the full visionary, political Catherine and the aphoristic Catherine presented here – so are there two Margeries. And, as with Margery, the readers who know the full texts are apparently the religious readers, while the broader reading public is given a stripped down, more pious version of these women.[110]

There appears to be little general, contemporary knowledge of Margery Kempe outside of these excerpts (and indeed they are just small, seemingly orthodox and devout snippets of her book); but this "shorte treatyse of contemplacyon" had some wide readership in that it was printed twice. Grisé writes,

> Kempe explicitly aligned herself with the tradition of holy women from the Continent, and Henry Pepwell's interest suggests that he sees Kempe as a native example of this tradition as well, since she is included in a collection of devotional treatises that also contains selections from Catherine of Siena. In a sense, then, Kempe acts as the English link in this collection between the texts by the male mystical writers Hilton and the *Cloud*-author and the extracts from the continental female mystic Catherine of Siena.[111]

Even Gardner, whose early twentieth-century edition of these extracts precedes the modern discovery of her *Book* by some three decades, writes that Kempe's excerpt "is enough to show that she was a worthy precursor of that other great woman mystic of East Anglia: Juliana of Norwich," showing how different the woman portrayed in these snippets is from the picture painted in her full *Book*.[112]

The Pepwell volume opens up with a woodcut showing an "Image of Pity," an image of the crucified and risen Christ often used on indulgences and so linked strongly to that practice; indeed, the words asking an indulgence and pardon surround the woodcut. Jennifer Summit suggests that this opening serves to guide the readers to see the entire book and its parts as a form of an indulgence, for what they read will "excite readers' belief in the ritual efficacy of reading and the salvific power of the book."[113] While Summit's focus is on Margery Kempe's excerpts throughout her discussion of the Pepwell volume, the Catherine text, too, neatly fits into this paradigm.[114] Framed by the more local Margery, Catherine's text speaks to individual piety and devout reading (silent prayer in addition to vocal, the self-regulation of sin in its idea of "holy hate," the annihilation of self in order to serve God's will). Summit shows that the Pepwell volume retained significance to its readers even after the Reformation by looking at the only surviving copy, British Library, C.37.f.19. The woodcut "Image of Pity" with which the book opens is somewhat defaced, with the texts of the indulgence beneath the image scratched out. This is a common fate of books after the 1550 *Act against Superstitious Books and Images*, but Summit notes that only the use of the books as an indulgence is marked out.[115] What remains is still an anthology of devotional texts, untouched, with Margery Kempe and Catherine of Siena at its heart.[116]

The last section of Pepwell's book is, notably, "A Devout Treatise of Discerning of Spirits, Very Necessary for Ghostly Livers." This is not either of the two treatises concerning the topic that come from Catherine's texts but rather one that is associated and circulated with *The Cloud of Unknowing*.[117] The excerpts from both Catherine and Kempe in the Pepwell volume are, of course, taken from texts that are literally saturated with the visions of the two women. Both Catherine and Kempe have texts that are heavily dependent on their visions of God, their dialogues with him, and their understanding granted by their special relationship with the divine. However, neither of the Pepwell excerpts contain much visionary language or text of these women at all. The fact that the ending chapter is about discerning the quality of the vision stands as an almost ironic counterpart to the women's texts that precede it, pointing out by its presence the earlier absence.

The Pepwell volume serves as an appropriate *coda* for the medieval Catherine texts and transition to the new Catherine who will appear in the early modern era, as it stands on the cusp of the Reformation. The ecstatic visionary Catherine of "The Cleannesse of Sowle" and *The Orcherd*, who had already been somewhat tamed and sanitized for Raymond's *Legenda major*, is even more stripped of her eccentricities and made more palatable for a lay reading audience in these bite-sized aphorisms. Pepwell's readers do not have the option of finding the radical or the subversive within her text; it has been excised completely. What is offered instead is a kind of controlled and restrained spirituality. If the text had been commissioned by a Carthusian house as Hanna hypothesized, it also moved firmly back into the realm of private male reading. In the text's movement from convent to printing house to monastery, Catherine becomes indistinguishable from the equally altered Margery Kempe, blurring the self-written to the written-about, the mystic with the lay, the Continental with the English, and the exceptional visionary with the merely devout.

Reforming Reading: Catherine of Siena in an Age of Reform

Syon Abbey, Elizabeth Barton, and Catherine of Siena: English Spiritual Identity and the Reformation

Catherine of Siena is not swept aside or forgotten during the dissolution and subsequent Reformation in England. In fact, she may have been more important to Catholic English readers than she had ever been in the century prior, standing in as a powerful symbol of adherence to Rome and the papacy. Catherine herself was, of course, a reformer. Reform of the Church was one of the central tenets of her doctrine and in her *Il Dialogo*; it is the prayer to which she consistently returns. For Catherine, reform was strictly orthodox – bringing the papacy back to Rome, spreading Christianity throughout the world by any means possible (including the brutality of the Crusades), and demanding the importance and centrality of penance and confession in everyday life. Among many changes ushered in by the Reformation were very different views about women's spirituality, particularly in relation to the idea of women's visionary or mystical status. Thomas Cranmer, the Archbishop of Canterbury under Henry VIII and a leader in the Reformation, did not believe in the authority of visions at all, overturning even the most sceptical of previous theologians, such as the previous century's Jean Gerson, who at least suggested that they *could* be true.[1] And at the centre of nearly every debate concerning Lutheranism or Catholicism was the question of book ownership and reading; the printed word served metonymically for the inner soul of the reader.[2]

In and among these debates and changes, it became increasingly difficult for a visionary woman to a have a visionary life; women who claimed visions were met with mistrust and suspicion rather than embraced by public and Church alike. Euan K. Cameron has pointed out that mysticism generally "thrives ... in the times when dogmatic debates have least impact on the political stability of the church. It loses most credibility, or exposes its adherents to greatest suspicion, in those epochs where disputes over doctrine cast the cohesion of the ecclesial community into doubt."[3] In this light, we can see why Catherine's visions are always interrogated at historical crossroads – first the aftermath of the schism, later during controversies surrounding lollardy, and then at the Reformation. However, despite this questioning, Catherine's visionary voice survives and gets politicized in new ways. One of the defining spiritual philosophies of the English Reformation was access to scripture for the laity, calling into question many of the mediations that the Catholic Church required of priests. Genelle C. Gertz has noted how this shift fundamentally changes the public view of the female visionary:

> Looking back on visionary women of the late medieval period (and it was mostly women who were visionaries), what becomes clear is that the visionary–confessor relationship achieves a kind of protection, as well as patronage, for the visionary. Under Protestantism's revision of a priest's role, and especially, its elimination of confession, there is no mechanism for 'discovering' a woman visionary and bringing her to the attention of the ecclesiastical hierarchy.[4]

The woman visionary, always skirting a subversive line, had been dependent on the protection offered by the validation of powerful men throughout the Church. She loses those safeguards when the clerical role itself is deemed suspect.

In this final chapter, and as conclusion to this study, I would like to examine how Catherine is used as a porous figure that can be appropriated for any age and for different agendas, especially among the changes and turbulence of the Reformation in England. Catherine is used by the advisers to Elizabeth Barton, an English visionary who spoke out against Henry VIII's desire to divorce his wife and marry Anne Boleyn, as a comparative model for Barton's political activity. Catherine is in turn used by critics of Barton to condemn her in a sermon against her prior to her execution. Barton is at exactly the crossroads that Gertz suggests above: she is a woman prophet who has the protection of priests and confessors just at the moment when their protection no longer has meaning. In addition, Catherine finds new reading audiences in this era. The recusants will turn to Catherine in a new translation of her *Legenda major*, published abroad and distributed to exiled Catholic nuns. Conversely, the Protestant apologist and author John Foxe will use Catherine to justify the rightness and inevitability of the fall of Catholicism. Through Catherine's appropriation and use in the Reformation, we can see the complex issues and emotions at work – at times reactionary, resistant, or resigned.

As theologians and members of the Church became increasingly more sceptical of women's visionary activities at the time of the Reformation, a positive public attitude towards mystical and contemplative works remained strong. As we have seen, texts concerning Catherine were being printed by de Worde as late as 1520, and *The Myroure of Oure Ladye*, the vernacular translation of the Bridgettine office (given to Bridget of Sweden in a vision) was printed in 1530, just four years before the *Act of Supremacy*, which is widely considered the defining break with Rome in the English Reformation. As a centre of women's learning and orthodox thought, Syon Abbey is a natural place to examine what happened to women's reading and devotional life leading up to and after the dissolution of the monasteries starting in 1536 (Syon was dissolved in 1539). As the original site of *The Orcherd of Syon* and very probably *The Lyf*, as well as Catherine's close connections to Bridget of Sweden, Catherine and the nuns of Syon Abbey are inextricably linked; what happens to the nuns and their associated texts after the dissolution happens, to some extent, to Catherine of Siena as well. In addition, the abbey was a locus of counter-Reformation activity and was intimately associated with the English visionary Elizabeth Barton who would play an important role in the events that were unfolding around Henry VIII and his desire to divorce Catherine of Aragon and marry Anne Boleyn.

Catherine of Siena had long been closely associated with Syon Abbey through her frequent juxtaposition to Bridget of Sweden, and as such we can read how the two are discussed in tandem and used as a way of talking about the Reformation indirectly, especially at the time of the dissolution. The Bridgettine priests of Syon continued to have a robust publication program and helped shape the market for devotional texts into the mid-sixteenth century; it was additionally one of the visible centres of anti-Lutheran publications and arguments. Many of the books published and championed by Syon in the years leading up to the dissolution were intended as direct attacks on the threat of Protestantism and heresy that the brothers and nuns saw circling around them. As Alexandra da Costa has noted, this reputation is perhaps what leads William Tyndale, a leading scholar in the fight for a Protestant England and influential English translator of the Bible, to speak out directly against Syon in his *Exposition of Matthew*, where he claims the abbey is a place "wherein the tonge and lyppes laboure and all the bodye is payned, but the harte talketh not with God."[5] The "payned" body references the self-mortification and ascetic practices of some Catholics, and a practice frequently attributed to women visionaries, Catherine of Siena among them. This division between what is said by tongues and lips and what is felt in the heart gets directly at the questions of what constitutes genuine devotion in the eyes of God – the questions at the centre of the Reformation. By naming Syon directly, even if meant as a wider metaphor for the Roman Catholic Church in England, Tyndale demonstrates how the abbey is firmly placed in opposition to any Protestant reform.

John Fewterer, who was the Confessor General of Syon in 1534, owned books that showed an interest in affective piety and mystical devotion of the fourteenth and fifteenth century, reflecting not only his personal taste but also the kinds of books he may have championed for printing.[6] In addition, the Abbess Agnes Jordan would have had to approve the books that went out from Syon. Together, Jordan and Fewterer would have overseen the Syon corpus.[7] Other Bridgettine priests from Syon, such as William Bonde and Richard Whytford, were publishing orthodox and widely read texts right through the dissolution of Syon, laying out in a public and printed dialogue their opposition to any Lutheran reform. Catherine of Siena, while never central to this publication program, was consistently at its margins and her link to Syon Abbey remained firm. For example, the *Dyetary of Ghostly Helthe*, a Syon pamphlet published by Wynkyn de Worde in 1520 (and later again by Pepwell), reused the woodcut image of Catherine from *The Orcherd of Syon* preceding an image of Bridget. Both women are shown rapt in the midst of a visionary experience. The image of Bridget reminds the reader that the text is from Syon Abbey, as a woodcut of her precedes so many of the books that originate there; as discussed previously in chapter 4, the woodcut points to Syon as a contemplative centre and hints at the possibility of the abbey as a place for mystical activity, serving as a symbol of the "Syon" brand of book.[8] The purpose for the image of Catherine in the *Dyetary*, however, is less clear. The text does not reference her at all, but her very recognizable iconography – in her Dominican habit, crown of thorns, her stigmata, and holding the Sacred Heart – would not be confused for another saint. Part of the text – a list of rules for the sisters of Syon in order to participate in "good living" – notes that "it is very good to haue a synguler deuocyon to some specyall sayntes in whom we haue grete confydence to be your aduocates helpers & defenders at all nedes to call on them."[9] Although neither Catherine nor Bridget are named, the fact that this book opens with the juxtaposed woodcut images of the two saints indicates that these are the "special saints" worthy of devotion by its readers. Seeing Catherine here, as an unnamed but recognizable double for the seemingly more prominent Bridget, reveals that she is an essential model and intercessor for the Syon readers (both the religious in the abbey and the laity outside of it).

Catherine's influence at Syon can also be seen through the publications of the Syon brother Richard Whytford. He was a prolific author who wrote texts specifically for use by religious readers (such as a translation of the *Rule of Saint Augustine*), as well as books he intended for the laity, published by Thomas Godfray and Wynkyn de Worde.[10] Friends with both Erasmus and Thomas More, Whytford was part of an intellectual Catholic elite who, in many ways, helped define the Reformation through his opposition. He not only printed his works as small pamphlets but also brought them together in a collection, consciously engaging in a program of publication linked to Syon Abbey. Brandon Alakas notes that "by bringing books into the vernacular and by printing them in order to ensure the widest circulation, Whytford challenged reformers not only by engaging with them directly on doctrinal issues but by attempting to reach larger audiences who may have had access to spiritual literature that straddled the line between orthodox and heterodox."[11] One of Whytford's latter texts was entitled "A Dayly Exercyse and Experyence of Dethe," which he had begun to write two decades prior at the request of Elizabeth Gibbs, then Abbess of Syon. Directed to the nuns of the abbey in his preface, he also is clear that he has chosen print for the medium in order to have a wider reach. Printed by the Catholic printer John Wayland in 1537, Whytford's text opens by detailing the tedium of having to write something out as opposed to the ease of printing, and the new audience this change in medium anticipates:

> This lytle treatie, or draght of deth, dyd I wryte more than .xx. yeres ago / at the request of the reuerende Mother Dame Elizabeth Gybs whome Iesu perdon / then Abbes of Syon. And by the oft callyng vpon / and remembraunce of certeyne of hyr deuout susters. And nowe of late I haue ben

> compelled (by the charytable instance and request of dyuers deuout per-
> sones) to write it agayne and agayne. And bycause that wrytynge vnto me
> is very tedyouse: I thought better to put in print / wherunto I was the rather
> moued / that I perceyued by the printers: you haue thankfully taken suche
> other poore labours: as we before haue sende forth. Rede this I pray you
> ones ouer and after ass you lyke it is but very short.[12]

Whytford's preface is a miniature description of the kind of writing
and reading that was habitual at Syon Abbey and how it moved outward. His "lytle treatie," which details how one can best be prepared
for death when it comes, was written initially for the Abbess at Syon –
presumably as a guidebook for the sisters and brethren under her care.
The pamphlet gains a reputation, which Whytford implies goes beyond
the Syon community (to "dyuers deuout persones"), perhaps through
Syon's status as a pilgrimage destination or through the aristocratic
and powerful connections that Syon maintained, and he is enjoined to
copy the piece "agayne and agayne." Whyftord is not only relieved of
the tedium of writing (and rewriting) the text, but now has the opportunity to "sende forth" the book to a wider anticipated audience, who
may purchase it because of Syon's reputation for printed devotional
material – a reputation he also alludes to in this opening when he notes
that the printers who have undertaken the printing of this book have
"thankfully taken suche other poore labours."

In "A Dayly Exercyse and Experyence of Dethe," Whytford writes
that the visionary deep in contemplation is practising for death, prepar-
ing herself for her actual death when it comes. The contemplative is, in
fact, the model of one prepared for a good death – both ready in body
to depart the world and ready in spirit to embrace heaven. He uses
Catherine of Siena as his example of this "experte … in deth," displaying a real sympathy for the woman reader in deep contemplation and
near mystical transcendence:

> Many a holy person (as saynt katheryne of Sene and dyuers other) hath
> ben so depe in contemplacion that the body (for the tyme) was with-
> out the senses, so that whan they were prycked with pynnes, or nedles,
> they nothynge felte. So than this exercyse, standeth al in contempla-
> cyon, which thniig who dayly vseth shall be so experte, and practysed
> in deth / that whan so euer it shall approche and come, it shall be no
> new thyng vnto the person. For betwyxt naturall deth, and this deth of
> contemplacion, is lytle difference … So doth the person, that is deed in

contemplacyon for that tyme / leaue the body as a lumpe of claye without any mynde, care, or thoughte thereupon / or vpon any other bodely or worldly thyng / wherfore whan dethe commeth (as I sayd before) it shall nother be newe, nor straunge vnto the person that hath thereof, and often practysed the same.[13]

The language Whytford uses to describe transcendence recalls the Catherine described by Stephen Maconi (discussed in chapter 1) as standing still, unmoved as a jealous woman stabs her feet with a needle in order to disprove her transcendent state: "she stode stille vnmoued, for so hadde she stonden thof she hadde cut of the fete." Maconi uses this example to demonstrate how deeply in prayer Catherine could be and also uses it to demonstrate the veracity of Catherine's holiness, what wonders he had witnessed. The contemplative Whytford speaks of here is likewise so deep in a meditative state that "whan they were prycked with pynnes, or nedles, they nothynge felte." In both cases, neither Maconi nor Whytford is actually focusing on what the content of Catherine's prayers or visions are, but instead they are solely fixed on the external body. There is nothing dangerously heretical here; deep contemplative prayer, while frequently the external marker of the mystical's internal state, violates no boundaries of orthodoxy.

The depiction of the body and the senses entirely divorced from one another is a typical trope of the mystic in rapture, and, as Whytford points out, "dyuers other" saints could fit the description offered. The fact that he points to Catherine of Siena as the prime example underlines both her importance at Syon and her recognizability as a saint known for mystical activity to the lay audience he intends to reach through his book. Note, too, Whytford's use of a gender-neutral "they" even though Catherine of Siena is the only named "holy person" in his example. This has the effect of both speaking directly to the nuns of Syon and to the outside readers of both genders. Although he does not encourage the visionary experience of the mystic for his readers, keeping in line with English theologians and with the seeming ethos of Syon Abbey, he does invite his readers into the kind of transcendent mystical meditation that allows the world to drop away and have the woman be only with herself, God, and her prayer. This, Whytford argues, creates a kind of death that will make an actual death easy, peaceful, and rehearsed. His more or less casual reference to Catherine of Siena (he does not cite her, nor point to a specific instance in her texts) shows an expected familiarity of his audience with the saint and her life.

Whytford and other writers at Syon were explicitly reacting to the anxiety and unease in the air surrounding the threat of Luther and the Protestant fervour in parts of the Continent. In addition to Whytford's pamphlet with its subtle championing of Catholic sainthood and its practices, the brethren were publishing works that were a much more vocal defence of orthodoxy. For example, Whytford's *The Pipe or Tun of Perfection*, printed by de Worde in 1532, defends the monastic life point by point in response to criticisms raised by Lutherans.[14] Shortly thereafter (1533), Fewterer publishes *The Mirror of Glass of Christ's Passion*, a translation of Ulrich Pinder's *Speculum Passionis Domini Nostri Jesu Christi*.[15] A meditation on Christ's Passion, the *Mirror* included *exempla* that validated the visionary and her prophecies. For example, the text includes a redaction of the life of Marie of Oignies – a Low Countries' mystic whose *vita* by James of Vitry had some small circulation in Middle English in the codex Bodleian Library, MS Douce 114, which also contained Stephen Maconi's letter concerning Catherine discussed in chapter 1.[16] Marie was practically a prototype of a visionary, mystical woman and, indeed, is used this way by her hagiographer James of Vitry, who sees her as the first in the grouping of religious women known as the beguines. Her *vita* includes descriptions of extreme asceticism, self-mortification, deep private communication with God, and the power of prophecy.

The importance of including women like Marie of Oignies and Catherine of Siena in texts coming out of Syon cannot be underestimated. They are championing a kind of devotion that is quickly falling out of favour as Protestant pressures bear down on the Catholics of England; pressures felt most keenly at houses which so recently had held political, religious, and financial favour as had Syon. Both sides of the religious divide were invested in Henry VIII's marital decisions. If he could not get his marriage to wife Catherine of Aragon annuled, as he hoped to, he threatened a break with the Church in order to marry Anne Boleyn. Syon, more than any other religious house, was thrust into the centre of this debate. First, it had been actively and vocally orthodox, defending Catholicism at all turns. Second, it was closely associated with Elizabeth Barton, the "Holy Maid of Kent" who claimed visions, particularly damning political ones, about Henry VIII and Anne Boleyn.

Although not professed at Syon Abbey, Barton stayed there frequently and was strongly associated with the abbey and its brothers. Barton was supported, if not exactly championed, by Thomas More, who had become for much of England the symbol of Catholic resistance to Henry VIII's religious actions. Barton's condemnation was public, and her execution in 1534 meant to be an example to any who would speak out against the king. The fact that her execution takes place only a year after Fewterer's text is printed brings into focus more clearly the significance of its including an account of the life of Marie of Oignies. Here, the life of a woman mystic and her troubling prophecies is celebrated, while Elizabeth Barton, a contemporary mystic, is condemned for speaking out. As Alexandra da Costa notes:

> The similarities between Maria of Oignies' life and Elizabeth Barton's ... brought into question the government's sentence by emphasizing its bias and determination to twist the evidence. The point was not that Elizabeth Barton was an irrefutable mystic – even the Syon brethren had their doubts – but that there was nothing in her physical or spiritual experiences that was dangerously different from other models of female mysticism. Indeed, Elizabeth's obedience to her superiors and her taking of vows placed her within acceptable limits. As [Thomas] More notes, her humility was one of the things which most recommended her to others and it is not surprising that the Syon brethren were eager to see her as God's messenger.[17]

Fewterer translated the text prior to her execution, but it shows how open the Syon brethren had become to the idea of female visionaries and mysticism in a way that is not evident in earlier writings from the abbey. As the Catholic Church felt a constriction all around it, its readers reached for more exuberant and visionary models in its past.

Shortly after her death, a book of Elizabeth Barton's visions was published and circulated widely in England along with additional accounts of her activities written by her followers. It is a sign of how disruptive King Henry and his government found these texts that they were aggressively censored and destroyed, leaving no known extant copies of what was purported to be around 700 documents. Had Barton's texts survived, they surely would be read with the same interest that Margery Kempe has generated.[18] As a result of this effective censorship, Barton's words are mostly reconstructed from sources opposing her activities, such as the letters of Thomas Cromwell and Thomas Cranmer, and a significant public sermon spoken against Barton before her execution. From what contemporary evidence we can glean, we know that – like Kempe – Barton shaped who she was and what she saw through the lens of what she read (or what had been read to her). In this case, Catherine of Siena plays an important role as both visionary and outspoken political critic. Barton rises because of the circumstances of her time and the inflammatory nature of her visions, but she may also rise because of an increased interest in women visionaries and the kind of ecstatic, affective religion they represent.

In 1533, the year before Barton's execution, the bishop-elect of Bangor, John Capon, is chosen to speak across England against Barton; his speech is given once at Paul's Cross in November and again at Canterbury in December of that year. *The Sermon against the Holy Maid and Her Adherents* serves the dual purpose of publicly accusing Barton of her crimes and, lest she have any remaining supporters, stand as a warning. Barton and her condemned followers were present as it was preached.[19] Capon speaks firmly against the validity of her visions, damning her to the execution that will soon follow. He pointedly addresses both Barton and her spiritual adviser, Edward Bocking, drawing attention to her feigned asceticism, which would certainly bring Catherine and other mystical women models to listeners' minds:

> Among [her followers] she (being herself fat and ruddy) caused some to fast so much, that the sharpness of their bones had almost worn through their skin. Some did wear hair; some chains of iron next their body; and suffered other marvellous penance in their bodies at her commandments, to prepare themselves to be worthy to preach and declare her false and mischievous revelations. By which all this realm, if the falsehood of them had not been espied, might have been brought to utter confusion and destruction.[20]

The deliberate dismissal of the kind of corporeal and affective piety inspired by women's visionary literature (hairshirts, extreme penances, revelations) indicts not only Barton, but Cartherine too, as well as any of their analogues.

Ultimately, though, the blame falls on the texts that Barton was reading and her susceptibility to them. And these texts are now familiar ones to us – the revelations of Bridget of Sweden and Catherine of Siena. Capon is as damning of her models as he is of Barton, and the parallel is clear. She has confessed that her revelations are made up, as are likely the models on which she based them. While incriminating Barton, Capon explicitly implicates Catherine, too:

And that all her revelations contained in the said great book be falsely imagined, feigned, and contrived without any ground of truth, you shall understand that she herself, examined by divers of the King's Grace's council, without any fear or compulsion, hath confessed: that she had never in her whole life any revelation from God but that they were of her own feigning, wherein she used much craft to make and devise them consonant and agreable to the minds of them who were resorting unto her, with the help of Dr. Bocking, her ghostly father. Who daily rehearsed matter enough unto her, out of St. Bridget's and St. Catherine of Senys revelations, to make up her fantasies and counterfeit visions, and moved her very often and busily to make petition to God to have revelations in manifold matter. And when she ceased any while of shewing new revelations unto him, he was wont to say unto her: "How do you live now? Virtuously? Meseemeth God hath withdrawn His grace from you, that ye have no revelations this season." Whose words caused her to feign many more revelations than she else would.[21]

According to Capon, the blame for Barton's visions rests squarely on the fact that she had a daily diet of Bridget and Catherine read to her by Bocking, who expected the same kind of "output" from his charge as these women had produced. These are not randomly chosen texts, either. Both Bridget and Catherine are politically motivated saints who interfered in the politics of their time. Barry Windeatt notes, "It was the model of St. Birgitta and St. Catherine as political prophets that empowered Barton to enter that more public sphere as a visionary and a prophet – dispatching warning letters to the pope and admonishing senior churchmen for their shortcomings – which was to be her undoing."[22] Barton's "fantasies and counterfeit visions" are not harmless, and she was leading the country to "confusion and destruction" through them. This charge is not unlike Jean Gerson's charge against Catherine of Siena and Bridget of Sweden when he places the blame for the schism on what he claims were their false prophecies.

The casual reference of the two women saints here demonstrates the audience's familiarity with Catherine, and its coupling with Bridget further solidifies how the women were understood in tandem throughout England in a way that is not necessarily the case on the Continent. In England, Bridget is central because of Syon Abbey and Catherine is pulled along by her popularity. By mentioning Bridget, specifically, Capon is also reminding his audience that Syon Abbey shares blame, showing it as a site of resistance against the king, which it was until its dissolution. After Barton's death, Thomas Cranmer writes a letter whose recipient is a commissioner charged with administering the oaths of succession, stating that he "would gladly know who shall take the oaths at the religious of Syon," knowing that their opposition and symbolism were both especially strong.[23] Indeed, in 1535, Richard Reynolds declined to take the oath and was executed, in his religious habit, along with other dissenting clerics. His mangled body tied to the abbey's gates immediately marked him as a Catholic martyr of the Reformation and powerful symbol of dissent.[24]

Although there seems to have been plenty of contemporary doubt about the veracity of Barton's visions, priests and nuns did rally around her and she garnered support from a variety of Church members. Diane Watt has suggested that this, too, may be an imitation of Catherine of Siena and her *famiglia* of followers, who see her as a politically and spiritually important leader.[25] Clearly, Barton's advisers were familiar with Catherine as a political prophet and if that is not how she saw herself, it is surely how many understood her role. At least one vision attributed to Barton seems to have been drawn directly from the life of Catherine. This vision encompasses a Eucharistic miracle where a host, about to be given to Henry VIII at Calais, is taken from him and instead immediately transported to Barton in Canterbury. As Diane Watt points out, this vision mirrors a moment in Catherine's *Legenda major* where a host flew directly to Catherine from a chalice on an altar.[26] We can see in this account the tensions of the pre-Reformation moment in England: Henry VIII is not viewed as rejecting the Church, but rejected *by* the Church as the Eucharist flies out of his hands into Barton's, and the female visionary, so long out of fashion in English devotional practice, is made central by imitating the kind of female piety championed in the high Middle Ages – a last gasp of Catholic power in England.

Barton's professed visions, however, did not sit well with those in favour of Henry's break with Rome and those opposed. Indeed, Thomas More, the symbol of orthodox resistance to Henry VIII's reforms, was clearly uneasy about Barton's notoriety and the visionary power she represented. In a letter to Thomas Cromwell, considered the chief architect of Henry VIII's turn from the Church and marriage to Anne Bolyen, More casts doubt on Barton's revelations, the account of the miracle of the Eucharist, as well as a later vision Barton had regarding the salvation of the late Cardinal Wolsey's soul, writing:

> I wott well when or where so euer I harde [the miracle], me thoughte it a
> a tale to mervelous to be trew, and verye likely that she had tolde some
> man her dreame, which tolde it oute for a reuelacion. And in effecte, I litle
> doubted but that some of these tales that were tolde of her were vntrew;
> but sithe i never harede them reported, as spoken by her owne mouthe,
> I thoughte never the lesse that many of them mighte be trew, and she a
> verye vertuous woman to; as some lies be peraduenture wrytten of some
> that be sayntis in heaven, and yet many miracles in dede done by them
> for all that.[27]

More is walking a thin line between publicly opposing the king's plans
to defy the pope by marrying Boleyn, the position represented in Barton and her visions, and indicating his own scepticism of her actions
and his loyalty to Henry. He acknowledges that her accounts are "to
mervelous to be trew" and blames the visions on a "dreame" that gets
wrongly received and interpreted as a revelation. However, he stands
firm that "many of them mighte be trew" and that even saints have
stories surrounding them that are fiction, nevertheless their miraculous
actions stand. Ultimately, it is this precipitous balance that More cannot
maintain and he is executed for treason to the Crown when he refuses
to take the oath of succession that Henry required of his subjects.

More also writes directly to Barton, warning her to stop speaking
publicly; he is acutely aware of the damage that she was doing both to
the Catholic cause and to herself by proclaiming the prophecies concerning Henry VIII:

> I no thinge doubt your wisedome and the spirite of God shall keepe you
> frome talkinge with any persons speciallye with ley persons, of eny suche
> maner thinges as perteyne to princes affairs, or the state of the realme,
> but onelye to common and talke with eny person highe and low, of suche
> maner thinges as maye to the soule be profitable for you to shew and for
> them to know.[28]

More specifically warns against speaking to the laity concerning the king
and kingdom, and he tells Barton that her speech should be restricted
to discussing the health of the soul. The warning betrays his anxiety for
himself, but also for Barton and her perception by those around her.
The letter also demonstrates the divisions that More sees in the society
around him and how these influence Barton: the lay and the religious,

those who have something to do with the "prince's affairs" and those who do not. It is not Barton's devotion or piety that is the problem, it is her political engagement and the troubled status of her revelations.

In the absence of Barton's own text, we cannot be sure how she herself read and understood Catherine of Siena, or even with which texts she was most familiar – *The Orcherd of Syon* or *The Lyf*. Both had been printed by de Worde in the fifty years leading up to the Reformation, and with Barton's connections to Syon there is no doubt that she could have had access to both. Catherine provides both a model of visionary mysticism and public activism, a combination that Barton and her supporters saw in her as well. It is, of course, the latter that eventually doomed her. While the visionary life was not fully embraced, it had some place in English society and at Syon Abbey. The woodcut of Bridget in rapture that preceded most Syon books reminded its readers that there was something special about the abbey, that it held a privileged relationship with God, founded upon Bridget's affective and revelatory piety. The English tolerance for women's visions was further seen in Margery Kempe who, although frequently suspected of lollardy and unorthodox intentions, was always cleared of heresy and ultimately has important supporters. Julian of Norwich was accepted enough to have at least two versions of her book copied and circulated. In 1422 a nun, simply known as Margaret, probably from the convent of St Mary's Winchester, had a revelation of purgatory that was copied and disseminated.[29] There was a limited but accepted history of women visionaries in England, and Barton could have fit into this tradition if her visions were solely about God. None of these English visionary women, however, ever challenged the king or the Church directly. Barton's pointed attack on the king and his marriage made any acceptance of her revelations just too dangerous for a country in such upheaval. Acknowledging that the visions held any validity would have negated the king's right to marry Anne Boleyn, so all that Barton saw had to be roundly and definitively condemned. Barton had to be silenced, and with her execution, Henry VIII condemned her foresisters as well. Catherine of Siena's texts soon held more than a hint of heresy as they represented both a Catholicism now being suppressed throughout England and the troubling devotion of visionary women.

Resistant Catherine: A *Vita* for the Recusant Reader

Most convents and monasteries were unable to survive the dissolution enacted through Henry VIII's *Suppression of Religious Houses Acts* in 1536 and 1539, which effectively disbanded all of England's religious houses and put their lands and money in the Crown's control. The movement of the nuns of Syon Abbey during this time was both representative and exceptional of other contemporary English religious women. In order for a religious house to survive, it required finances and support abroad so it could move its community out of England, and Syon Abbey had both of these. At first, many of the nuns returned to their familial homes in England at Syon's suppression. With the dissolution, much of the community subsequently moved in pockets throughout England, then to the Netherlands, and then to France, finally moving to Lisbon, Portugal, where it remained for over two hundred years before returning to England. Other religious houses did the same, but in the absence of funds many were completely disbanded, so the nuns returned to families or joined other communities abroad.[30] Jenna Lay has recently argued that this female recusancy abroad is particularly responsible for maintaining a sense of English Catholic faith in England despite the Reformation at home.[31] Syon in its exile, especially, becomes a symbol of English nuns abroad. When Mary Tudor took the throne, restoring Catholicism to England and trying to rebuild what had been destroyed by her father, Henry VIII, much of the Syon community was in Dendermonde, in the Low Countries. Syon was among her priorities for the restoration of Catholicism in England, and the abbey is momentarily returned there (one of only six religious houses that were). However, with Mary's death and Elizabeth I's ascendance to the Crown in 1558, the Bridgettine nuns again move to the Continent.

By the early seventeenth century, England was divided into the competitive ideological identities of "Protestant" and "Catholic." The turmoil of the sixteenth century, with Henry VIII's break from Rome, Mary Tudor's brief queenship (and the equally brief return of the country to Catholicism), and Elizabeth I's long powerful reign had taken its toll. For example, Guy Fawkes's Gunpowder Plot of 1605 was very much in the popular imagination and minds of the English and was "proof" of the existence of a Catholic conspiracy. Many recusant Catholics were abroad, but others lived throughout England and a vibrant if shadowy community of Catholics continued to operate. One Syon document, "The Life and Good End of Sister Marie," recounts the life of Mary Champney who returned to England from Syon when the cloister no longer seemed safe abroad. Her life describes an intellectual and relatively vibrant communication network of what Ann Hutchinson calls "the Catholic underground of London."[32] As with the Reformation itself, print culture was important to the marking of these Catholic and Protestant boundaries.

Frances Dolan explains that, well into the Reformation, Catholics were portrayed as more interested in spectacle than reading, and that this became gendered with an "assumption that women were more likely than men to stick with Catholicism, or to convert to it, [which] often corresponded to the assumption that women were illiterate and unlearned, and thus were loyal to a religion that coddled their incapacities, or, in the case of converts, were vulnerable to one that preyed on their ignorance."[33] In this way, the souls of women were particularly important to Protestant and Catholic writers alike, and books published at the time show a concerted effort to court these readers.

Women's religious leanings were understood to be separate from their husbands' or families' affiliations, but those affiliations also protected them legally. Lay notes that women were shielded by coverture laws, so women with nominally Protestant husbands were able to remain Catholic in a way that gave them some political, religious, and literary outlets they would not have otherwise had.[34] Both sides published books with an eye towards propaganda, dismissing the opposition, and supporting their own agenda. It is in this environment that a new translation of Catherine of Siena's *Legenda major* was published abroad, translated specifically for recusant women, and entered into a thriving but often dangerous book trade catering to and rallying Catholic English readers. For example, in 1622, the English writer Thomas Robinson's pamphlet *The Anatomy of the English Nunnery at Lisbon in Portugall* discusses a salacious Syon Abbey abroad where the nuns are now low born and suffering from the clap from their "vnchaste practices," that would "make the Christian Reader blush at them."[35] Notably, the nuns at Syon wrote a rebuttal, portraying the Reformation in the evil light that they saw it. Just as the Catholics wanted to hold the abbey up for its resilience, the Protestants wanted to make a different example of it.

The dissenters who now populated parts of the Low Countries and France, the Syon nuns included, played a vital role in maintaining a readership of English Catholic texts, particularly those that embraced mysticism and visionary women. Some of these books were made specifically for the English nuns abroad. For example, William Peryn's 1534 book *Spiritual Exercyses* was written for Katherine Palmer (who would become Abbess of Syon upon its return to England under Mary Tudor) and Dorothy Clement, a Poor Clare. Mary Erler writes that the book "provided a synthesis of new Ignatian spirituality and still-powerful Flemish mysticism influenced by the Devotio Moderna. Its influences were Jesuit, Flemish, female-oriented, mystical."[36] Augustine Baker compiled books particularly for the nuns exiled at Cambrai, including Dame Gertrude More, the great-great-granddaughter of Thomas More, who would later include a list of his suggested books in her own book of suggested devotions among which Catherine's texts are included.[37] As noted earlier, at least one of Baker's writings drew on William Flete's *Remedies against Temptations*. He also invoked Catherine of Siena as a model more than once in his *Sancta Sophis, or Directions for the Prayer of Contemplation*.[38] Books published for the recusants abroad found their way to recusants in England, serving the dual purpose of keeping the Catholic faith alive under its suppression and nurturing the English Catholic identity on the Continent. Ceri Sullivan explains: "There were two ways in which the Church could publish such texts: through a secret press in Britain, or by using a Continental press and then importing the books. The latter method was less expensive than the former, where capital costs were incurred more frequently than under normal trade conditions."[39] In a reversal of what had been true only a few years' prior – Protestant books (such as Tyndale's *Bible*) being smuggled from the Continent to Catholic England – Catholic books were now produced continentally and brought to England illegally.

Printing these texts was not without its risks, especially in their movement from the Low Countries or France back to England. Each act in the process was an act of rebellion: the writing, the printing, the selling, and the reading. Each book was a small victory against an English Protestant hegemony, a stitch in knitting the recusant community together. Queen Elizabeth I took many measures to counter the book trade, recognizing the power this community of writers and readers created. These efforts, as A.C. Southern describes,

> included the appointment of special customs officials to the port of London for the examination of all books that came into the custom-house; careful watch at other principal ports and creeks by hired "promoters" and "waiters," who searched all incoming vessels; an order to all booksellers who sold foreign books in England to supply the Commissioners with a list of such books before any sales were effected; munificent rewards for informers or, for any who should turn Queen's evidence, pardon and reward; systematic search of the houses of known Recusants, as also of those suspected of leanings towards recusancy; and finally the careful examination of all those in custody on charges of recusancy.[40]

Clearly, these texts represented more than simply reading material for exiled English religious. They served to continue an important tradition of English Catholic thought and provide a continuity for contemplative reading. The reading material produced abroad for this specific group of readers bore the weight not only of its medieval contemplative history but also the hope for a future of a Catholic England. It was reactionary and revolutionary at once.

John Fenn, chaplain of the Augustinian House of St Monica's in Louvain, reintroduced his English readers to Catherine of Siena in this milieu. Fenn was well aware of the risks of his overt Catholicism and printing dangerous books. His younger brother, James, also a priest, had been martyred for his faith in 1574. Fenn had associations with several recusant nuns living abroad, notably at St Ursula's in Louvain, St Monica's in the same city, and Syon Abbey when it was at Dendremonde. Under Mary Tudor, Fenn, a Jesuit, had been a Fellow at New College, Oxford, and master of a school at Bury St Edmunds, but was stripped of his jobs when Elizabeth I became queen. Fenn became a prolific translator and author of recusant texts, including a book for the Syon nuns entitled *Spiritual Treatises Collected from English Writers*, but he was most well known for his co-authorship of *Acts of the English Martyrs*, a decidedly political entry into the corpus of texts made available for English Catholics. In 1609 he became the first chaplain of St Monica's (a house of Augustinian Canonesses) and in the same year translated Raymond of Capua's *Legenda major* of Catherine of Siena for them.[41]

Unlike the earlier Wynkyn de Worde version, this version of *The Life* of Catherine was translated by Fenn from the Italian (not the Latin). Its lengthy title tells its reader for and by whom the text was translated: *"The Life of the blessed virgin, Saint Catharine of Siena. Drawne out of all them that had written it from the beginning. And written in Italian by the reuerend Father, Doctor Caterinus Senensis. And now translated into Englishe out of the same Doctor, by Iohn Fen priest & confessar to the Englishe nunnes at Louaine."*[42] Translating anew from Lancellotto de' Politi's abridged Italian version of Raymond of Capua's *Legenda major*, Fenn seems unaware of the earlier de Worde edition of the text, not surprising given the anti-Catholic sentiment in England and the considerable amount of time between the last publication of de Worde's edition (over a century). De' Politi, in addition to translating the *Legenda major* of Catherine into Italian, had authored several anti-Lutheran treatises, demonstrating how Catherine's story had been linked to orthodoxy and a definitive response to the Protestants.[43] The title's double use of the word "English" (as the language of translation and the nationality of the nuns) emphasizes that this translation of Catherine is made for a recusant audience, exiled from their English home to be living their faith in Louvain.

Fenn published his book with the printer and bookseller John Heigham who it seems had worked with William Wrench, who ran a secret English Catholic press in Whitefriars.[44] He was the most productive English Catholic printer of the early seventeenth century, and he suffered for it. He was imprisoned in London in 1597 and his press was destroyed, causing Heigham to leave England for the Low Countries in 1603.[45] Heigham translated a number of texts himself and made several important Catholic devotional books available for the recusant audience, including the Tridentine primer and Psalters. It is Heigham, rather than Fenn, who prefaces the translation of *The Life* with a lengthy dedicatory address to a specific, unnamed female reader, addressing her misery of being in exile from her country in order to practise her faith: "Madam, It is now long since that my hart hath had, not only a verie inward compassion of your miseries, but also a vearie earnest desire to present vnto you some godlie Treatise, which might both be consolatory vnto you amidst your discomforts, and a patterne for your conformitie vnto the life of Christ."[46] Here, the bookseller engages in a kind of false construction where the printed, public text lays claim to a personal, private reader. The "Madam" of the address calls to mind a solitary reader, a specific woman whose "miseries" and "discomforts" include exile from her native land and language. Those who purchased this text were clearly an expected readership, but this address gives them the impression of peering into someone's private devotion, of having access to a version of Catherine that was meant perhaps for someone else.

The preface continues where Heigham tells his reader that although the hardship she suffers seems in vain, it is in fact like water to the roots of a tree that will ultimately bear fruit. This analogy recalls the controlling metaphor of the translator's preface in *The Orcherd of Syon* where Catherine's book is the orchard and the fruit her words and advice:

Wherefore, good Madam, nether let your longe afflictions seeme tedious vnto you, nor account that lost which you haue left for Christ. If we cast water about the roote of a fruitfull tree, we doe not thinke that water lost, because we expect great aboundance of fruite; euen so, that which we forgoe for the loue of Christ, is not lost, for we shall gather of that tree, the fruite of enternall life. Rather reioyce herein, that by this your patience

and sufferance you preserue your soule in the grace and fauour of al-
mightie God.[47]

It is clear that the printer views the text as a kind of salve for the pain the
"woman" (standing in archetypically for all readers of the text) suffers
at the exile from her homeland for her faith. Invoking Job, Heigham encourages fortitude in the face of her struggles. The passage is poignant
in that it addresses a real hopelessness that a recusant nun feels at having "lost" what she knew and had to choose to leave behind. Heigham
does not indicate that what has been lost will be regained, but rather
that it is a kind of penance on earth whose reward will be heavenly.

At first glance, Catherine may seem an unusual choice as *exemplum*
for the recusant reader. She did not suffer for her faith: she was neither
persecuted nor martyred. Indeed, Catherine was wholly integrated
into the religious and political fabric of her country and her Church,
never truly disenfranchised despite her gender or lay status. However,
Catherine's turn towards God despite her parents' opposition mirrors the kind of resilience that the author calls on for the nuns. When
Catherine is relegated to working as a servant in her family's home, she
makes of that job a kind of worship:

> When she sawe, that her father and mother had appointed her to doe all
> the workes of drudgerie in the kitchen, and other places of the howse, she
> neuer repined at it, but turned all that basenes to her great commodtie &
> merite, by this holie imagination. She had this conceite with her selfe, that
> her father, represented in the howse, our Sauiour Christ; her mother our
> blessed Lady; her brethren, sisters, and others of the familie, the Apostles
> and disciples of Christ. The kitchen she imagined to be the innermost tab-
> ernacle of the temple called *Sancta Sanctorum*, where the most principal
> burnt sacrifices, were dight and offred vp to God.[48]

Catherine's persecution by her family may be more analogous to the
exiled religious reader than a more extreme virgin martyr's account of
persecution where dying for one's faith looms large. The English nun
seemed safe and had the support of a community abroad; it was not
home, but it was not ostensibly perilous either.[49] Like Catherine, she
had to make the best of what she had.

De' Politi's abridged version of the *vita* contains accounts of
Catherine's extreme bodily mortification that was excised from the earlier de Worde edition, and Fenn does not move to excise them here.

Perhaps appealing to a more rigorously orthodox audience in the recusants or one more accustomed to religious violence after the brutal martyrdoms of the Reformation, *The Life* has detailed accounts of Catherine's ascetic practice:

> The holie virgin, hauing a great desire to folwe the steppes of *S. Dominike*, vied for a long space to beate her selfe, three tymes euery daie with a chaine of yron ... And while she was in this exercise, laid on so sore vpon her bodie, that her mother being one tyme neere vnto the chamber, & hearing the noise of the strokes, was inwardly moued with motherlie pitie, and so entred in sodainly vpon her. But when she sawe the maner of it, when she beheld presently with her eyes, the roughe yron chaine, wher with she beate her selfe, the bodie of [her] daugher miserably rent and torne, the bloodie streames, that ranne downe to the grownd on all sides, being ouercome with natural compassion, she cried out like a woman besides her selfe.[50]

Catherine's mother's screams draw the house members who then witness Catherine's battered body, which Raymond explains is "rigorous iustice, and bloodie reuenge ... for the synnes of others."[51] The extreme suffering that Catherine self-imposes mirrors the kind of suffering a sinner would ultimately receive. A familiar trope in hagiographical accounts of mystical or visionary women, the saint takes on earthly suffering in order to relieve purgatorial pains for those in agony. This, too, serves as a rallying cry for the intended readers – sins would be punished, suffering was not in vain.

Most significantly, Catherine was also credited with bringing the papacy from Avignon to Rome (the later schism, just soon after this happens, of course, is not mentioned anywhere in her *vita* or its later redactions). The final section of Catherine's *Life* is titled, in Fenn's edition: "How the holie maid was endued with the spirite of prophecte, and foretold, what calamities should happen to the Church, and likewise, how it should be restored againe."[52] This section is replaced (at the beginning of a section rather than the end) and extremely truncated from the original *vita* in which Catherine's prophecies concerning the Crusades looms large. De' Politi was reworking his text in response to a Lutheran threat and Fenn in response to the Reformation, and Catherine's prophecies regarding the papal schism (which was to happen right before her death) mirror the anxieties of their age. In this passage, Raymond of Capua laments to Catherine about lay rebellions against the papacy of Gregory XI:

> Father, said she begynne not to weepe so soone: for all this is but honye
> & mylke in comparison of that, that shall come hereafter … Father, all
> that ye see hitherto, is done by the common laie people: but you shall see
> hereafter an other maner of rebellion, then this is, contriued and practised
> by the clergie. When Doctour *Raimundu* heard that, he was meruelously
> astonied for a tyme. At the lengthe he asked her, whether she thought it a
> thing possible, that the clergie should rebell against the Church. Yea, said
> she, it is possible: and you shall see it. For, when our holie Father the Pope
> shall goe about to reforme their maners, then shall they set them selues
> vp against him, and make a schisme in the Church.[53]

The Catholic reader of Catherine's life is here twice comforted by the
past and by her words. First, there is a sense that historically the Church
has had its trials and has overcome them. Catherine lived through more
than one of these trials and recognized that the Church would prevail.
Second, it feels as if Catherine predicted the schism, which came to pass
in 1378, the effect of Luther's theses in 1517, and Henry VIII's separation from the Church a little more than a decade later. The shock with
which Raymond reacts to the idea of a clerical schism may still resonate
in Fenn's 1609 edition.

Catherine continues her prophecy about the unsettling future of
the Church, promising even more trials to come, but leaves Raymond
hopeful with the idea of a Church made stronger and more pious by its
persecutions. Fenn even includes the word "reformation" in his translation, aware of all its implications, but in a context that clearly refers to
a new orthodox and Catholic regime:[54]

> Father, said she, almightie God hath determined thus to purge his Church
> by calamities and tribulations. The which when he hath once done, he will
> raise vp a new spirite in his chosen seruanted, and send such godlye Pas-
> tors and Curates ouer his flocke, that my hart reioyseth within my bodie to
> thinke vpon that goodlye Reformation, that shall insue in all states of men.
> And as the Church of Christ seemeth now poore, deformed, and naked; so
> shall it then be seene in a verie glorious and beautifull state, clad with the
> seemelie ornamentes of vertue & Godlines.[55]

To the reader of Fenn's volume, it is not Catherine's Church that is
"poor, deformed, and naked," but the state of the Church in England.
Significantly, this is a passage that the Protestant author John Foxe
will use for the opposite purposes. The Reformation for which Fenn's

reader awaits is not the Reformation that has taken place, but a future one where England is again Catholic. Catherine's prediction gives that reader hope. In this sense the woman reader is encouraged not to read Catherine as an example of persecution and patience, as it may seem from the preface, but to see her as an inspiration for fighting against oppressive forces, for resisting persecution. As Catherine returned the Church to its home, there is the hope that she will return the readers' home to its rightful Church. Catherine's texts will from here on form a central part of English Catholic nuns' identity and understanding, perhaps more so than her writings ever did in medieval England where Bridget was more often the focus.[56]

The Jesuits, founded in 1540, became one of the centres of the Counter-Reformation, working throughout England and the Continent in order to secure Catholicism. Writings by members of their order in the sixteenth- and seventeenth-century publications also invoked Catherine again and again. Many of these were translated into English, presumably for recusant readers both at home and abroad. These Continental authors, the Italians especially, may have had far more familiarity with Catherine of Siena and what she stood for, but as these texts were translated into an English defence of the Catholic faith, new readers are introduced to her teachings. For example, the Jesuit Fulvio Androzzi (1523–75) suggests Catherine as a model of meditation, focusing on her metaphor of the bridge and the destruction of her own will in order to follow God's. He writes, "The conformitie of her will with that of God, by which she would haue become the ladder (as S. Catherine of Siena writeth) that by it Christ might goe vp to the crosse, so to saue the whole world."[57] Likewise, the Jesuit Étienne Binet (1569–1639) writes in a discourse on purgatory that Catherine had chosen to suffer purgatorial pains on earth.[58] Another Jesuit writer, Girolamo Piatti (1545–91), writes extensively of Catherine in *The Happines of a Religious State*, reflecting the sentiments in her "Discernment of Spirits" about the nature of divine revelations: "And we reade of *S. Catharine* of *Siena*, that our Sauiour sayd the same to her almost in the same words, to wit, that she should seeke after *bitter* things, as if they were *sweet*; and refuse *sweet* things, as if they were *bitter*. Which *Truth* itself spake indeed to these two Saints; but we may take it as spoken to euerie bodie."[59] Finally, the English Jesuit John Sweetnam (1579–1622), who had left Oxford for Spain in 1602 (and was arrested upon his return in 1616), wrote about Catherine in his book about Mary Magdalene and the path for sinners to redemption.[60] Here, he writes that Catherine saw Mary Magdalene in a vision and esteemed her greatly, noting, "Neither is it much that this Blessed Saint *Catherine* did so greatly esteeme her, and call her Mother, since the Catholike Church teacheth vs all to do the like."[61] Catherine is here a representative of what all of the Church should do. In the hands of the Jesuit authors, she becomes a saint that Catholic writers referred to again and again, a symbol of purity and of the Church. Never having set foot in England, Catherine had made an indelible mark on its spirituality, even as the Reformation cleaves it apart.

Catherine as Reformer: But Whose?

Catherine, however, did not only serve the recusant cause in the turmoil following the dissolution of the monasteries and the ensuing English Reformation. The Protestant reformer John Foxe (c. 1516–87) wrote several works, among them his important martyrology *Acts and Monuments*, also known as *The Book of Martyrs*, which provides an overview of Church history and focuses especially on England in the years between the lollards and Queen Elizabeth I. The book underwent four editions in the sixteenth century (1563, 1570, 1576, and 1583), and it established an important sense of English Protestant identity through its publication. The second edition is a dramatic departure from the first, entirely revised and rewritten. The remaining two are very similar to the 1570 edition. Drawing heavily on medieval sources, including Matthew Paris's *Chronica majora* and other medieval chronicles, the work was meant to demonstrate the inevitability and righteousness of a Protestant England. Part of Foxe's agenda is to literally rewrite Church and English history with the Protestant cause in mind. For example, he spends several pages retelling the story of the important English martyr Thomas Becket and denouncing him as an object of veneration. Accounts of his post-mortem miracles were lies told by the clergy to influence lay piety, Foxe argues, and thus "if the holy Sainctyng of Thomas Becket, standeth vpon no other thing but vpon his miracles: what credite is to be geuen therunto, and vpon what a weake ground his shryne so long hath stand, by this may easely be sene."[62] The erstwhile heretic, John Wyclif, too, is given a new story and standing by Foxe, who sees him as a precursor to the Reformation and a point of national pride. Wyclif was a man "whom the Lord (with the like zeale and power of spirit) raised vp here in England, to detect more fully and amplye the poyson of the popes doctrine, and false religion set vp by the friers."[63] Through this new history, Foxe attempts to give the

Reformation a sense of historical inevitability and a rightful place in not only the English present but also its past.

It is notable, then, that Foxe writes a significant section on two pre-Reformation saints who are not English and do not bear directly on Protestantism: Catherine of Siena and Bridget of Sweden. Their inclusion, like that of Thomas Becket, indicates their lasting hold on English devotion and perhaps their stubborn resistance to the changes in it demanded by Protestant piety. Foxe writes first about Gregory XI, a pope that he says "vexed this realme of England," and then discusses Bridget and Catherine in Book 5 of the *Acts*.[64] First, Foxe notes Bridget's condemnation of the pope, despite her standing as saint and prophet in the Church:

> About thys tyme, being þe yeare of our Lord. 1370, lyued holy Brigit, whom the churche Rome hath canonised not onely for a saynt, but also for a prophetis: who notwithstanding in her booke of reuelations, which hath bene oft times imprinted, was a great rebuker of the Pope, and of the filth of his clergy, calling hym a murtherer of soules, a spyller, and pyller of the flocke of Christ: more abhominable then Iewes, more crueller then Iudas: more vniust then Pilate, worsse then Lucifer hymselfe.[65]

As we have seen, Bridget of Sweden held a special place in English devotion because of its connection to the important and visible Syon Abbey. Here, Foxe uses her in a clever double way – if you do not venerate her, she is a false prophet, but if you are devoted to her, you must accept the extremely harsh criticism she levels against the Church.

Foxe devotes more space to Catherine of Siena, however, who follows quickly on the heels of his description of Bridget. Rhetorically, he similarly draws the reader into either denouncing the saint as a prophet or accepting that her prophecy about a corrupt Church was true:

> To this Bridget I wyll ioyne also Catherina Senēsis, an holy virgin, which lyued much about the same tyme, an. 1379 … Thys Katherine hauing the spirite of prophesye, was woont muche to complayne of the corrupt state of the church, namelye of the prelates, of the court of Rome, and of the pope: prophesieng before of the great schisme, which then folowed in the churche of Rome, and dured to the councell of Constance, the space of. xxxix. yeares. Also of the great warres and tribulation, which ensued vpon the same. And moreouer declared before and foretold, of this so excellent Reformation of religion in the church now present.[66]

Choosing his words deliberately, Foxe twists Catherine's central aim of more intense orthodoxy within the Church and full obedience to the pope as a desire for the "Reformation of religion." Of course, Catherine was calling for a kind of reformation of the Church, especially one that curtailed abuses of its hierarchy, but Foxe has rewritten this to mean his Reformation, the Protestant one. The complete revision of Catherine's and Bridget's legacies is especially useful to Foxe's Protestant agenda. As Nancy Bradley Warren points out, Foxe "makes these two saints, who were … passionately committed to the cause of the Roman papacy, serve the Protestant aim of undermining papal authority and bolstering English monarchical independence."[67] The prophecies that Catherine made, Foxe argues, bore out: the schism, the wars that followed, and a great Reformation of the Church.

Foxe continues with his description of Catherine and what he understands as her reformist desires, further drawing the reader into a bind. She must either determine that the saint was a false prophet, and thus agree with the Protestant line on Catholic saints, or that her prophecies were true, in which case the great saint had not only foreseen but sanctioned and hoped for the changes that were to come to the Church. He narrates an episode from Catherine's *Legenda major* in which she discusses the Church's future with Raymond of Capua, her hagiographer:

> After this virgin in her going to Rome, had told her brother of the warres and tumultes that should ryse in the countries about Rome, after the schisme of the popes, I [Raymond] then curious to know of thinges to come, and knowing that she vnderstood by reuelation what should happen, demaunded of her: I pray you (good mother) sayde I, & what shall befall after these troubles in the churche of God? And she sayd: By these tribulations and afflictions, after a secrete maner vnknowen vnto man, God shall purge his holy church, and styrre vp the spirite of hys elect.[68]

Foxe includes these opening lines before the substance of Catherine's revelation, because they reveal the authority of Raymond as the recipient of the prophecy. The passage is notably different in translation than what Fenn provides, examined above in the context of the recusant reader, and was clearly used for different ends as Foxe recasts Catherine's prophecy about great change in the Church in a Protestant light:

> And after these thinges shall follow suche a Reformation of the holy church of God, and such a renouation of holy pastors, that the onely cogitation and remembraunce therof maketh my spirite to reioyce in the lord. And as

I haue oft tymes told you heretofore, the spouse which now is all deformed and ragged, shall be adorned and deckt wyth moste ryche and precious ouches and brouches.[69] And all the faythfull shall be glad and reioyce to see them selues so beutified with so holy shepheardes. Yea, and also the Infidels then allured by the swete sauour of Christ, shall returne to the catholique folld, and be conuerted to the true bishop and shepheard of theyr soules. Geue thankes therefore to God, for after thys storme, he wyll geue to his a great calme. And after she had thus spoken, she stayed and sayd no more.[70]

Although this passage originally speaks to Catherine's agenda of returning to a "true bishop," that is, the rightful pope, Foxe has moved the revelation firmly into the realm of the Reformation. The "deformed and ragged" Church will be "conuerted to the true bishop and shepheard of theyr soules." Note that the bishop here is not necessarily the Bishop of Rome, a fact that Foxe knows will be evident to his readers. By using Catherine for this agenda he also casts "Infidels" – who were Muslims for Catherine, invested as she was in the Crusades – as Catholics.

Foxe later addresses what he intuits is the central problem with using a Catholic visionary saint as a spokeswoman for the virtues of the Reformation – the soundness of her visions. Protestant figureheads like Thomas Cranmer had written very clearly against the validity of the woman visionary, but Foxe tries to walk both sides of the line, addressing both Bridget and Catherine and again invoking Catherine's vision of a reformed Rome. On the one hand, he denies that the visions may be true, while on the other, he argues they demonstrate the inevitability (and rightness) of the Reformation itself:[71]

To these speculations of Brigit, I geue no great respecte, as neither I doe to the predictions of Katherine De Senis ... Of the authoritie of this prophetisse, I haue not to affirme or iudge, but rather to heare what the Catholique iudges will saye of this their owne Saint and Prophet. For if they doe not credite her spirite of prophesie, why then doo they authorise her for a pure Saint, among the Sisters of deare S. Dominicke? If they warrant her prophesie, let them say then, when was this glorious Reformation of the Churche euer true or like to bee true, if it bee not true nowe in this maruelous alteration of the Church, in these our latter dayes? Or when was there any such conuersion of Christen people in all countreys euer heard of, since the Apostles tyme, as hath bene since the preachyng of Martin Luther?[72]

Foxe clearly states that he has no respect for the revelations of either Bridget or Catherine, but at the same time plays both sides here noting that their visions do see a future where the Church is greatly reformed. He employs Catherine to serve a dual purpose – to validate the changes of the Reformation, while simultaneously using her to discredit the Catholics. If the Catholics are correct, and Catherine is an important saint and visionary, then she has predicted their own demise. If they are incorrect, then their beliefs are misplaced and false. Either way the Protestants are in the right here. Catherine, the great believer in the authority and importance of the papacy, has been used against it to good rhetorical effect.

However, simply by using Catherine and Bridget as his examples, Foxe is calling attention to their centrality and authority in English devotional culture and the legacy that Catholic saints and piety still had so firmly planted on English ground. Claire Falck has pointed out this same paradoxical use of woodcut images of saints throughout *Acts and Monuments,* which illustrates "false idols, holy preachers, persecuted martyrs" while it simultaneously "celebrates the destruction of images in its accounts of famous English iconoclasts" and "explicitly attacks the Roman Church for its 'veneration of images.'"[73] He doubts the validity of Bridget and Catherine, but uses their words in order to support his own agenda. Foxe enacts the thing he would condemn.

The dean of Exeter, Matthew Sutcliffe (c. 1550–1629), similarly uses Catherine as an example of the fallacies and failures of the Catholic Church.[74] Known for his vitriolic attacks on and denouncements of Catholics, Sutcliffe invokes Catherine in two different polemical tracts. The second of these, printed in 1606, has the wonderfully descriptive and extensive title, *An abridgement of suruey of poperie conteining a compendious declaration of the grounds, doctrines, beginnings, proceedings, impieties, falsities, contradictions, absurdities, fooleries, and other manifold abuses of that religion, which the Pope and his complices doe now manteine, and wherewith they haue corrupted and deformed the true Christian faith.* Sutcliffe uses Catherine like Foxe does, as an example that supports his position: "Catherine of Siena … saith that religious men pretend angels liues, but for the most part are woorse than diuels."[75] Here, Catherine's advice is being used as a reason to distrust the Jesuits and their defence of Catholicism; their religious lives are pretense and they are "worse than devils." Sutcliffe does not seem to note the contradiction in using Catherine as his mouthpiece for this dictum. In an earlier tract of 1602, however, he uses Catherine as an example of the fallacies of belief Catholics hold regarding their saints, "Of Saint Catherine of Siena they say, *that she was betrothed to our sauiour Christ.* All which points are very incredible, and not to be found in any authenticall writing. If then the church of Rome publish and teach these fables and lies; then is she no mistresse of trueth, but of lies."[76] Sutcliffe, like Foxe, is both influenced by and resisting the writings and stories of Catherine of Siena. Here, one of her primary mystical moments – her betrothal to Christ – is used as an example of the falseness of the Church. She is both example and anathema.

Representing these paradoxes after the Reformation, Catherine does not fade away from England. As noted earlier, the sixteenth-century Anglican bishop John Jewel, greatly committed to Elizabethan religious reforms, owned a devotional anthology, which contains excerpts from Catherine's "Discernment of Spirits." Likewise, the seventeenth-century Archdeacon of Canterbury John Battely was once an owner of a copy of *The Orcherd of Syon*. These leaders in the Protestant Church had Catherine's words in their libraries and no doubt in their theological framework as well. However, most vestiges of Catherine in England suffered a more ignoble fate. The 1528 rood screen at St Andrew and the Blessed Virgin, Horsham St Faith, Norfolk in East Anglia, which included an image of Bridget and Catherine, leaves Catherine literally defaced – her head is scratched out completely. The heart in her hand is the only real sign that Catherine was the image there (Bridget is untouched).[77] Other rood screens, such as the image of Catherine in Torbryan Church in Devon show much more half-hearted and pro forma attempts at defacement but leave the image intact. And, as discussed in chapter 4, the Pepwell edition that contained excerpts of Catherine's life had selections on indulgence carefully crossed out, allowing the post-Reformation reader to remain on the right side of heresy while holding onto her devotional texts and visionary women, but even this selective defacement reminds the reader that the whole was subject to scrutiny.

Ultimately, though, it is John Foxe's use of Catherine of Siena in *Acts and Monuments* that demonstrates her persistence within the devotional reading and contemplative culture of Reformation England. She was celebrated and known enough that she needed to be addressed in what would become one of the most important and standard texts of English Protestant thought. It also shows how firmly twinned Catherine and Bridget were in the popular English imagination. Although Catherine arrived in England via William Flete and probably through the Carthusian pipeline, it was not the Dominicans, the Augustinians, nor the Carthusians who are ultimately responsible for Catherine's popularity. It was the Bridgettines. Foxe cannot address one without addressing the other of the two Continental visionary lay women who came to define English women's devotional spirituality in so many ways.

Post Script

Although this book is in many ways about women – Catherine of Siena herself and the readers to whom she is most often solely directed as audience in theory, if not in practice – it is bookended by men. At the start, we have Stephen Maconi and William Flete, men who influenced her spirituality in ways that are difficult to elucidate and who were responsible for the dissemination of her texts, and through them, her cult, in medieval England. At the end, we have post-Reformation attempts at disseminating Catherine – John Fenn who translated her *Legenda major* for the recusant Catholics abroad and John Foxe who reinterprets her prophecies for Protestants at home. But this is at the centre of Catherine's dissemination generally and her life personally, as it is for nearly every visionary woman's text of the Middle Ages, Continental or Insular. The realities of a male-controlled Church hierarchy, a male-dominated literati, and a male-owned printing press are that no matter how exceptional the woman, she must have a man to champion her. While we are fortunate indeed that Catherine had so many (particularly among her tight-knit *famiglia* in Siena), the women she no doubt inspired in England are most likely lost to us. For every Margery Kempe, there are countless unknown inspired readers.

The three centuries in between Flete and Fenn show how a Continental woman's texts – hagiographic, prophetic, visionary, didactic, and political – can be reinscribed for varied English audiences. It seems that there was a Catherine for everybody – for the various readers of devotional miscellanies, for the Carthusians of Beauvale reading about their prior's spiritual awakening and call to their order, for the nuns of Syon, for the lay reading public, for the mother of kings. While the Catherine texts that we know reached England may represent a small sample of all of the texts concerning her (no letters, no *Legenda minor*, no songs or prayers), those that do reach England spread far, demonstrating a real if subtle appetite for the genre of women's visionary literature. After the dissolution of the monasteries, many books that had been in nuns' hands and libraries pass back to secular readers (see, for example, the discussion of Elizabeth Strickland's *The Orcherd of Syon* in chapter 4), which Mary Erler writes "may suggest a continuing attachment on the part of women to older forms of female life, not changing radically or passing from existence."[78] This attachment would have been more than sentimental in the recusant families who held on to Catherine's texts.

The Reformation forever changed the possibility and legacy of women visionaries in England. Although a robust tradition of women mystics and prophets continued throughout Catholic countries, English women really only had such opportunities abroad. For example, the Catholic Englishwoman Mary Ward (1586–1645) left for the Continent where she embraced a third-order religious life very similar to Catherine's, politically and civically minded, opening both an institute and school for poor women in order to educate them both in mind and spirit.[79] David Wallace argues that we can see England as both not having produced its own Catherine of Siena, and yet, having done so either through the figure of women somewhat buried by the remoteness of their past (like the seventh-century Abbess Hild of Whitby) or, in the case of Mary Ward, by their timing (a Catholic in an Anglican England).[80] Mary Ward is not medieval, but she inherited a legacy of women's activity and texts that coincided with the life that she led: Catherine's legacy. However, the evidence shows that England did produce "an English Catherine of Siena," after all: Catherine herself. This Catherine was a textual and symbolic woman who was made into the kind of spiritual model that England needed and who changed according to those constantly evolving needs.

Appendix A

Literary Ancestry Chart

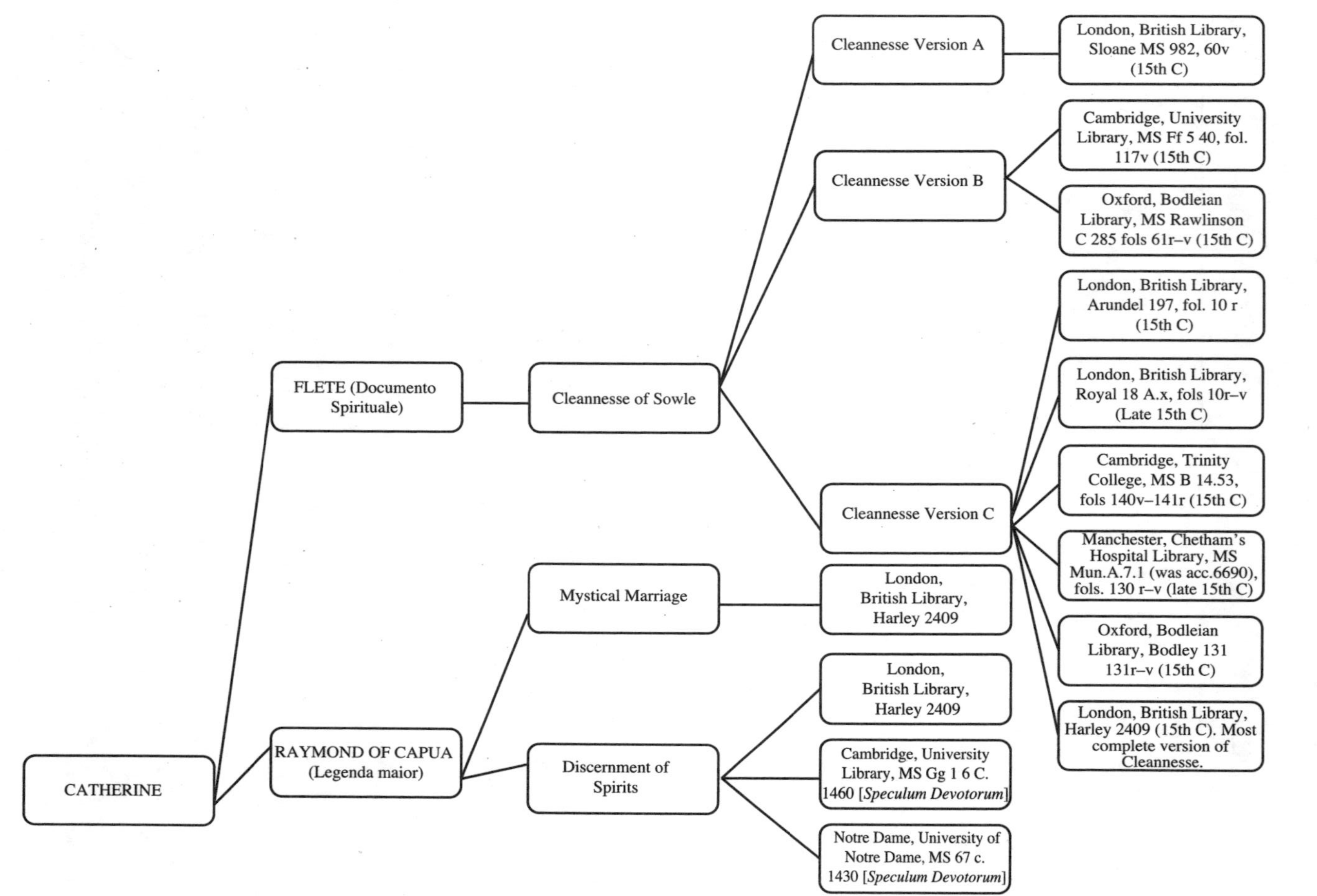

CATHERINE
FLETE (Documento Spirituale)
RAYMOND OF CAPUA (Legenda maior)
Cleannesse of Sowle
Mystical Marriage
Discernment of Spirits
Cleannesse Version A
Cleannesse Version B
Cleannesse Version C
London, British Library, Harley 2409
London, British Library, Harley 2409
London, British Library, Sloane MS 982, 60v (15th C)
Cambridge, University Library, MS Ff 5 40, fol. 117v (15th C)
Oxford, Bodleian Library, MS Rawlinson C 285 fols 61r–v (15th C)
London, British Library, Arundel 197, fol. 10 r (15th C)
London, British Library, Royal 18 A.x, fols 10r–v (Late 15th C)
Cambridge, Trinity College, MS B 14.53, fols 140v–141r (15th C)
Manchester, Chetham's Hospital Library, MS Mun.A.7.1 (was acc.6690), fols. 130 r–v (late 15th C)
Oxford, Bodleian Library, Bodley 131 131r–v (15th C)
London, British Library, Harley 2409 (15th C). Most complete version of Cleannesse.
Cambridge, University Library, MS Gg 1 6 C. 1460 [Speculum Devotorum]
Notre Dame, University of Notre Dame, MS 67 c. 1430 [Speculum Devotorum]

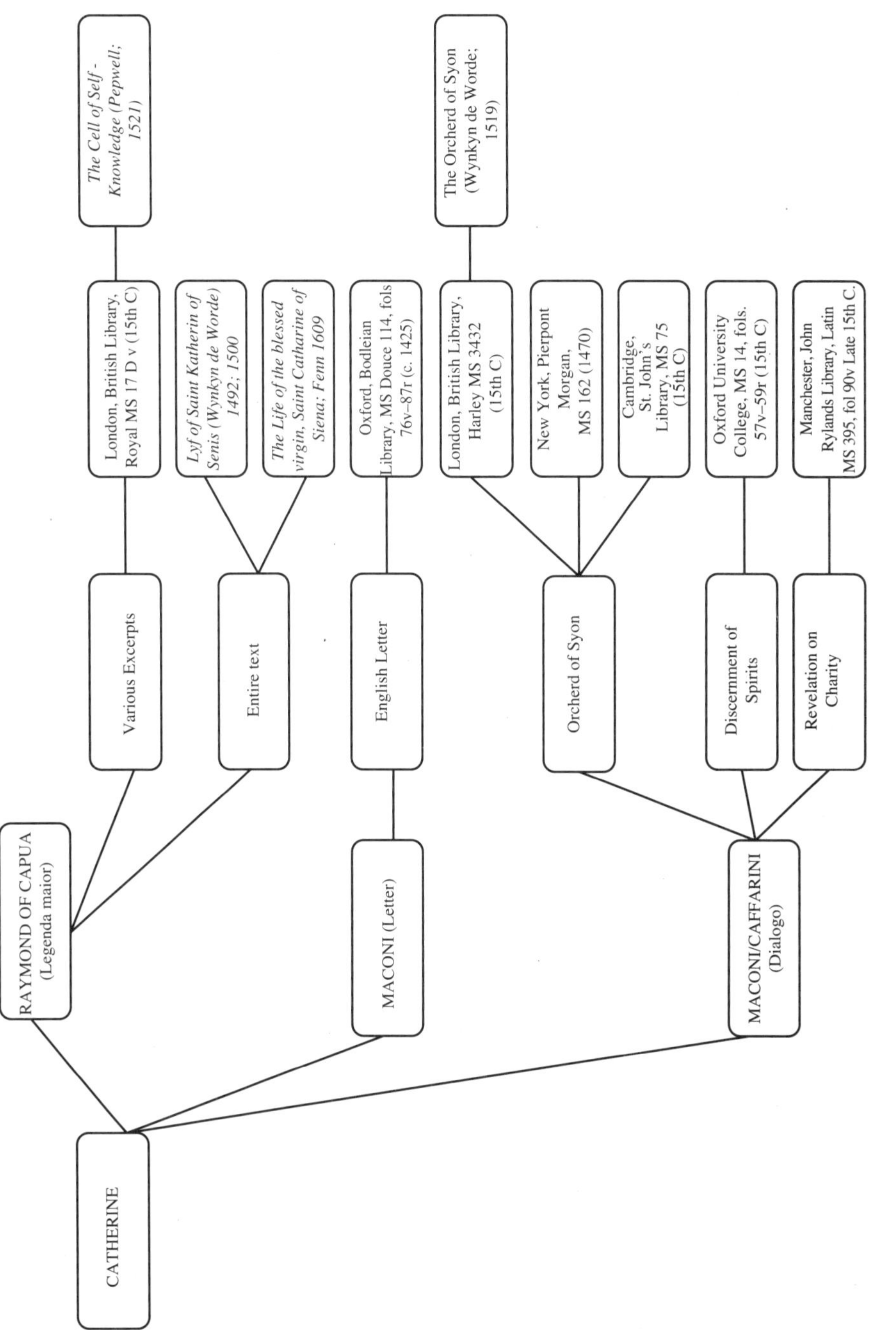

Appendix B

Catherine Texts in England

Catherine Manuscripts

MS/TEXT	DATE	CONTENTS
Cambridge, St John's College, MS 75	15th c.	*The Orcherd of Syon*
Cambridge, Trinity College, MS 336 (B.14.53), fols. 140v–141r	15th c.	"The Cleannesse of Sowle," Version C
Cambridge, University Library, MS Ff.5.40, fol. 117v	15th c.	"The Cleannesse of Sowle," Version B
Cambridge, University Library, MS Gg 1 6	c. 1460–70	*Speculum Devotorum*, contains portions of chap. 9 of the *Legenda major* of Catherine by Raymond of Capua, on the discernment of spirits
British Library, MS Arundel 197, fol. 10r	15th c.	"The Cleannesse of Sowle," Version C
British Library, MS Harley 2409	15th c.	"The Cleannesse of Sowle," longest version (Version C, extended); three excerpts from the *Legenda major* of Catherine by Raymond of Capua. *Also contains William Flete's *Remedies against Temptations*
British Library, MS Harley MS 3432	1st quarter of 15th c.	*The Orcherd of Syon*

MS/TEXT	DATE	CONTENTS
British Library, MS Royal 17 D.V.	Late 15th c.	Excerpts from the *Legenda major* of Catherine (will be printed in Pepwell's 1521 edition)
British Library, MS Royal 18 A.X., fols. 10r–v	1st half of 15th c.	"The Cleannesse of Sowle," Version C. *Also contains William Flete's *Remedies against Temptations*
British Library, MS Sloane 982, 60v	15th c.	"The Cleannesse of Sowle," Version A
Manchester, Chetham's Hospital Library, MS Mun.A.7.1 (was acc. 6690), fols. 130 r–v	mid-15th c.	"The Cleannesse of Sowle," Version C
Manchester, Rylands MS Latin 395, fol. 90v	latter half of the 15th c.	Revelation on charity, excerpt from *The Orcherd of Syon* (part 1, chap. 3)
Pierpont Morgan, MS 162	c. 1470	*The Orcherd of Syon*
University of Notre Dame, MS 67	c. 1430	*Speculum Devotorum*, contains portions of chap. 9 of the *Legenda major* of Catherine by Raymond of Capua, on the discernment of spirits
Bodleian Library, Bodley 131, fols. 131r–v	15th c.	"The Cleannesse of Sowle," Version C. *Also contains William Flete's *Remedies against Temptations*
Bodleian Library, MS Douce 114, fols. 76v-87r	c. 1425	Stephen Maconi's (also known as Stephen of Siena's) letter in support of Catherine's canonization
Bodleian Library, MS Rawlinson C.285, fols. 61r-v	15th c.	"The Cleannesse of Sowle," Version B
Oxford University College, MS 14, fols. 57v–59r	15th c.	"Doctrine" on the discernment of spirits, excerpt from *The Orcherd of Syon* [part 5, chap. 2]

Printed Texts

Title	Year(s)	Printer/STC #
The Lyf of Saint Katherin of Senis	1492, 1500	Wynkyn de Worde, STC 24766, 24766.3
The Orcherd of Syon	1519	Wynkyn de Worde, STC 4815
The Cell of Self-Knowledge (no given title to the book, an anthology, but this is how it has been referred to since its reprinting by Edmund Gardner in 1910)	1521	Henry Pepwell, STC 4830
The Life of the blessed virgin, Saint Catharine of Siena Drawne out of all them that had written it from the beginning. And written in Italian by the reuerend Father, Doctor Caterinus Senensis. And now translated into Englishe out of the same Doctor, by Iohn Fen priest & confessar to the Englishe nunnes at Louaine	1609	John Heigham (alias Roger Heigham), STC 4830

Notes

Introduction – Finding Catherine of Siena in Late Medieval and Early Modern England

1 Unending thanks are due to Kevin Alban who took me on this journey.
2 See Roger Ellis, "Flores and Fabricandam … Coranam: An Investigation into the Uses of the Revelations of St. Bridget of Sweden in Fifteenth-Century England," *Medium Aevum*, 51 (1982): 163–86; James Hogg, "Middle English Translations of the Birgittine Rule," in *The Translation of the Works of St. Birgitta of Sweden into the Medieval European Vernaculars: The Medieval Translator,* vol. 7, Bridget Morris and Veronica O'Mara, eds. (Turnhout: Brepols Press, 2000), 152–69; Rosalynn Voaden, "Rewriting the Letter: Variations in the Middle English Translation of the Epistola solitarii ad reges of Alfonso of Jaén," in *The Translation of the Works of St. Birgitta of Sweden into the Medieval European Vernaculars,* vol. 7, Morris and O'Mara, 170–85.
3 I have opted to use the Anglicized "Bridgettine" rather than "Birgittine" throughout the book, as I am specifically looking at the English context of the order.
4 For more on this, see Jeffrey F. Hamburger and Gabriela Signori, eds., *Catherine of Siena: The Creation of a Cult* (Turnhout: Brepols Press, 2013).
5 There is some tradition of "visions," in late medieval England, but this term can encompass, as Gwenfair Walters Adams writes, "a wide variety of supernatural experiences," including "apparitions or visitations of angels, saints, the Virgin Mary, Christ and Ghosts." The kind of revelatory vision, as seen in Catherine's *Il Dialogo* is much rarer, and really confined to Julian of Norwich and Margery Kempe. In Adams, *Visions in Late Medieval England: Lay Spirituality and Sacred Glimpses of the Hidden Worlds of Faith* (Leiden: Brill, 2007), 214.

6 Phyllis Hodgson and Gabriel Michael Liegey, eds., *The Orcherd of Syon*, EETS 258 (Oxford: Oxford University Press, 1966), 1. [Hereafter, *The Orcherd of Syon*, or *The Orcherd*.]

7 For example, Mary C. Erler's *Women, Reading, and Piety in Late Medieval England* (Cambridge: University of Cambridge Press, 2002) examines book ownership in and out of the convent to map out patterns of book transmission and reading among women, and the recent collection edited by E.A. Jones and Alexandra Walsham, *Syon Abbey and Its Books c. 1400–1700* (Woodbridge: The Boydell Press, 2010), specifically analyses the books that were copied by the clergy at Syon and how these were sent out for aristocratic lay readers. I am also indebted to so much recent work on medieval reading and women's literacies, too numerous to list here in full, but see especially Carol M. Meale, ed., *Women and Literature in Britain 1150–1500* (Cambridge: Cambridge University Press, 1993); Anne Clark Bartlett, *Male Authors, Female Readers: Representation and Subjectivity in Middle English Devotional Literature* (Ithaca: Cornell University Press, 1995); David Bell, *What Nuns Read: Books and Libraries in Medieval English Nunneries* (Kalamazoo: Cistercian Publications, 1995); James Raven, Helen Small, and Naomi Tadmor, eds., *The Practice and Representation of Reading in England* (Cambridge: Cambridge University Press, 1996); Jocelyn Wogan-Browne, *Saints' Lives & Women's Literary Culture: Virginity and Its Authorizations* (Oxford: Oxford University Press, 2001); Diane Watt, *Medieval Women's Writing: Works by and for Women in England, 1100–1500* (Cambridge: Polity Press, 2007); Jennifer Bryan, *Looking Inward: Devotional Reading and the Private Self in Late Medieval England* (Philadelphia: University of Pennsylvania Press, 2008); Jennifer N. Brown and Donna Bussell, eds., *Barking Abbey and Medieval Literary Culture* (York: York Medieval Press, 2012); Elizabeth Salter, *Popular Reading in English c. 1400–1600* (Manchester: Manchester University Press, 2012); and the series of conferences and books on *Nuns' Literacies* (Turnhout: Brepols).

8 For example, several essays in Vincent Gillespie and Kantik Ghosh, eds., *After Arundel: Religious Writing in Fifteenth-Century England* (Turnhout: Brepols Press, 2011) interrogate the boundaries of orthodoxy and heterodoxy, pre- and post-Reformation vernacular devotional writing, as do several of the contributions in Brian Cummings and James Simpson, eds., *Cultural Reformations: Medieval and Renaissance in Literary History* (Oxford: Oxford University Press, 2010).

9 See Thomas Luongo, *The Saintly Politics of Catherine of Siena* (Ithaca: Cornell University Press, 2006); Jane Tylus, *Reclaiming Catherine of Siena: Literacy, Literature, and the Signs of Others* (Chicago: Chicago University Press, 2009); Grazia Mangano Ragazzi, *Obeying the Truth: Discretion in the Spiritual*

Writings of Saint Catherine of Siena (Oxford: Oxford University Press, 2014); Suzanne Noffke, ed. and trans., *The Letters of Catherine of Siena,* 4 vols. (Tempe: Medieval and Renaissance Texts & Studies, 2000–8); Suzanne Noffke, ed. and trans., *The Dialogue of Catherine of Siena* (Mahwah, NJ: Paulist Press, 1980). For an overview of Catherine's life and complete bibliography of sources, see Suzanne Noffke, "Catherine of Siena," in *Medieval Holy Women in the Christian Tradition c. 1100–c. 1500,* Alastair Minnis and Rosalynn Voaden, eds. (Turnhout: Brepols, 2010), 601–22. For a brief overview of Catherine in England, see Jennifer N. Brown, "From the Charterhouse to the Printing House: Catherine of Siena in Medieval England," in *Middle English Religious Writing in Practice: Texts, Readers, and Transformations,* Nicole Rice, ed. (Turnhout: Brepols, 2013), 17–46, and C. Annette Grisé, "Catherine of Siena," in *The History of British Women's Writing, 700–1500,* vol. 1, Liz Herbert McAvoy and Diane Watt, eds. (New York: Palgrave, 2012), 216–22. Other articles concerning Catherine in England worth noting are David Wallace, "Mystics and Followers in Siena and East Anglia: A Study in Taxonomy, Class and Cultural Mediation," in *The Medieval Mystical Tradition in England: VII,* Marion Glasscoe, ed. (Cambridge: D.S. Brewer, 1984), 169–91, and Jane Chance, "St. Catherine of Siena in Late Medieval Britain," *Annali D'Italianistica* 13 (1995): 163–203. Many of these studies build on the work of two of the first Catherine scholars, Robert Fawtier and Edmund Gardner.

10 Sara Poor writes about her own "vertical view" of Mechthild of Magdeburg in her book *Mechthild of Magdeburg and Her Book: Gender and the Making of Textual Authority* (Philadelphia: University of Pennsylvania Press, 2004), xiii.

11 Kathryn Kerby-Fulton, *Books Under Suspicion: Censorship and Tolerance of Revelatory Writing in Late Medieval England* (Notre Dame: University of Notre Dame, 2006), 9.

12 Kerby-Fulton, *Books Under Suspicion,* 15–17.

13 Eliana Corbari, *Vernacular Theology: Dominican Sermons and Audience in Late Medieval Italy* (Berlin: De Gruyter, 2013), 15.

14 MS Harley 2409 is one notable exception, and will be discussed in chapter 3 in detail.

15 See Gabriella Zarri, "Catherine of Siena and the Italian Public," in *Catherine of Siena: The Creation of a Cult,* Hamburger and Signori, 70–1.

16 For a general introduction on the *mantellatae,* see the introduction to Maiju Lehmijoki-Garner, ed. and trans., *Dominican Penitent Women* (New York: Paulist Press, 2005).

17 Suzanne Noffke, ed. and trans., *The Letters of Catherine of Siena*, vol. 1 (Tempe: Medieval and Renaissance Text & Studies, 2000), xv.

18 See Noffke, *The Letters of Catherine of Siena*, vol. 1, xxi; and for a very thorough and astute reading of Catherine's literacy, see Tylus, *Reclaiming Catherine of Siena: Literacy, Literature, and the Signs of Others*, esp. 53–62, and also Tylus, "Mystical Literacy: Writing and Religious Women in Late Medieval Italy," in *A Companion to Catherine of Siena*, Carolyn Muessig, George Ferzoco, and Beverly Mayne Kienzle, eds. (Leiden: Brill, 2012), 155–84, and Tylus, "Writing versus Voice: Tommaso Caffarini and the Production of a Literate Catherine," in *Catherine of Siena: The Creation of a Cult*, Hamburger and Signori, 291–312. See also Luongo, *The Saintly Politics of Catherine of Siena*, esp. chap. 2, "Catherine Enters Tuscan Politics: Networks and Letter Writing," 56–89; and Catherine Mooney's "Wondrous Words: Catherine of Siena's Miraculous Reading and Writing According to the Early Sources," in *Catherine of Siena: The Creation of a Cult*, Hamburger and Signori, 263–90.

19 These can be seen in Italian in Fausto Sbaffoni, ed., *Santa Caterina da Siena: Opera Omnia. Testi e concordanze* (Pistoia: Provincia romana dei Frati Predicatori Centro riviste, 2002), CD-ROM. The letters have been translated into English as well: see Noffke, *The Letters of Catherine of Siena*.

20 See Kimberly M. Benedict, *Empowering Collaborations: Writing Partnerships Between Religious Women and Scribes in the Middle Ages* (New York: Routledge, 2004), 43.

21 *I Miracoli di Caterina di Iacopo da Siena di anonimo fiorentino*. Fontes Vitae S. Caterinae Senensi Historici 4 (Florence: Sansoni, 1936). The author is unknown. It is translated in "The Miracoli *of Catherine of Siena*," in *Dominican Penitent Women*, Maiju Lehmijoki-Gardner, ed. and trans. (Mahwah, NJ: Paulist Press, 2005), 87–104.

22 For a discussion of the iconography of her stigmata on the Continent, see Diego Giunta, "The Iconography of Catherine of Siena's Stigmata," in *A Companion to Catherine of Siena*, Muessig, Ferzoco, and Mayne Kienzle, 259–94.

23 Marie-Hyacinthe Laurent, ed., *Il Processo Castellano. Con appendice di docu-menti sul culto e la canonizzazione di S. Caterina*. Fontes Vitae S. Catherinae Senenis Historici 9 (Milan: Bocca, 1942).

24 Giuliana Cavallini, ed., *Le Orazioni di S. Caterina da Siena*, I classici cristiaini, 287 (Siena: Cantagalli, 1993). In English: Suzanne Noffke, ed. and trans., *The Prayers of Catherine of Siena* (Mahwah, NJ: Paulist Press, 2001).

25 *Il Dialogo* is also sometimes known as *Il Libro*. For dating of *Il Dialogo*, see Luisa Aurigemma, "La tradizione manoscritta del 'Dialogo della Divina

Provvidenza' di Santa Caterina da Siena," *Critica Letteraria* 16 (1988): 237–58.

26 Suzzane Noffke, "The Writings of Catherine of Siena: The Manuscript Tradition," in *A Companion to Catherine of Siena,* Muessig, Ferzoco, and Mayne Kienzle, 327.

27 There are several editions in Italian of Catherine's *Il Dialogo*, but none of any of the Latin versions. The most critical Italian edition is Giuliana Cavallini, ed., *Il Dialogo della Divina Provvidenza: ovvero Libro della divina dottrina,* Testi Cateriniani 1, 2nd ed. (Siena: Edizioni Cateriniane, 1995). There is a modern English edition in Suzanne Noffke, ed. and trans., *The Dialogue*, Classics of Western Spirituality (New York: Paulist Press, 1980).

28 Catherine M. Mooney, "Wondrous Words: Catherine of Siena's Miraculous Reading and Writing According to the Early Sources," in *Catherine of Siena: The Creation of a Cult*, Hamburger and Signori, 263–90.

29 Urban VI (c. 1318–89); Clement VII (1342–94). For more on Catherine's involvement with the schism and the papacy more generally, see Blake Beattie, "Catherine of Siena and the Papacy," in *A Companion to Catherine of Siena*, Muessig, Ferzoco, and Mayne Kienzle, 73–98.

30 Raimondo da Capua, *Legenda maior Sive Legenda Admirabilis Virginis Catherine de Senis,* Silvia Nocentini, ed. (Firenze: Sismel, 2013), or Acta Sanctorum, BHL Number 1702; Tomaso Caffarini, *Libellus de supplemento: Legende prolixe virginis beate Catherine de Senis*, Giuliana Cavallini and Imelda Foralosso, eds., Testi catariniani 3 (Rome: Cateriniane, 1974); Tomaso Caffarini, *Sancta Catherinae Senensis Legenda minor*, Ezio Franceschini, ed., Fontes vitae S. Catherinae Senensis Historici, 10 (Milano: Bocca, 1942).

31 Daniel Bornstein, "Spiritual Kinship and Domestic Devotions," in *Gender and Society in Renaissance Italy*, Judith C. Brown and Robert C. Davis, eds. (Essex: Longman, 1998), 181.

32 See, especially, Zarri, "Catherine of Siena and the Italian Public."

33 See Karen Scott, "Catherine of Siena and Lay Sanctity in Fourteenth-Century Italy," in *Lay Sanctity, Medieval and Modern: A Search for Models*, Ann W. Astell, ed. (Notre Dame: University of Notre Dame Press, 2000), 77–90.

34 See appendix B for approximate manuscript dates. Catherine was officially canonized on 29 June 1461 by Pope Pius II. For more on the process of her canonization and its result, see Otfried Krafft, "Many Strategies and One Goal: The Difficult Road to the Canonization of Catherine of Siena," in *Catherine of Siena: The Creation of a Cult*, Hamburger and Signori, 34.

35 See Krafft, "Many Strategies and One Goal," 37–40.

36 See Jeffrey F. Hamburger and Gabriela Signori, "The Making of a Saint:
Catherine of Siena, Tomaso Caffarini, and the Others – Introduction," in
Catherine of Siena: The Creation of a Cult, Hamburger and Signori, 7–8, and
Thomas Brakmann, "The Transmission of the Upper German Life of
Catherine of Siena," in *Catherine of Siena: The Creation of a Cult*, Hamburger
and Signori, 83–107. See also Jörg Jungmayr, "Die Legenda maior (*Vita
Catherinae Senensis*) des Raimund von Capua in Italien und Deutschland,"
in *"Der Buchstab tödt – der Geist macht lebendig": Festschrift zum 60.
Geburtstag von Hans-Gert Roloff,* James Hardin, ed. (Bern: Peter Lang,
1992), 223–59.

37 There is one fifteenth-century collection of Catherine's letters in Latin:
British Library, MS Harley 3480. It is Italian provenance, written in a
Tuscan hand, and enters the Harley collection in the eighteenth century.
(Note: This manuscript has been misidentified as Harley 3489 in a few
places.)

38 See appendix A for the "Literary Ancestry Chart" of the Catherine texts
that are translated into English and their various forms. See appendix B for
specific manuscript information.

39 There are a few other manuscripts related to Catherine that are not in the
vernacular or do not have English provenance but are now in English
collections: Oxford, Bodleian Library MS Canon ital. 283 is an Italian
manuscript of unknown provenance and contains the beginning of *Il
Dialogo* in Italian; Oxford, Bodleain Library, MS Canon Misc. 205 is a
fifteenth-century Italian manuscript from a convent in Venice. It contains
part of the *vita* of Catherine by Raymond of Capua, William Flete's letter to
Raymond regarding Catherine and his sermon on her, and part of
Catherine's *Dialogo* (translated by Raymond of Capua). See Silvia
Noncentini, "La Tradizione della 'Legenda maior,'" *Legenda maior sive
Legenda Admirabilis Virginis Catherine de Senis*, Nocentini, 54. There is
also a fifteenth-century Latin copy of the *Dialogo*, the Edinburgh, MS 87
(D b IV 18).

40 Carl Horstmann, ed., "The Lyf of Saint Katherin of Senis: nach dem Drucke
W. Caxtons (c. 1493)," *Archiv für das Studium der neueren Sprachen und
Litteraturen* 76 (1886), 33–112, 265–314, 353–400 (STC2 24766 and 24766.3);
Hodgson and Liegey, *The Orcherd of Syon* [STC2 4815]; Edmund Gardner,
ed., *The Cell of Self-Knowledge: Seven Early English Mystical Treatises Printed
by Henry Pepwell in 1521* (London: Chatto and Windus, 1910); John Fenn,
trans., *The Life of the Blessed Virgin, Sainct Catharine of Siena* (Leuven, 1609)
[STC2 4830]. All of these texts are available as a PDF in their original form
through the Early English Books Online database.

41 Hamburger and Sighnori, "The Making of a Saint: Catherine of Siena, Tomaso Caffarini, and the Others – Introduction," 4.

42 See Roger Lovatt, "The 'Imitation of Christ' in Late Medieval England," *Transactions of the Royal Historical Society, 5th Series*, 18 (1968): 97–121; and Michael Sargent, "The Transmission by the English Carthusians of Some Late Medieval Spiritual Writings," *Journal of Ecclesiastical History*, 27 (1976): 225–40.

43 The Augustinian canons were separate from the Augustinian friars, so there would be no connection between Flete and the house of Thurgarton, although this has been erroneously suggested by some scholars; see, for example, Dirk Schultze, "Translating St. Catherine of Siena in Fifteenth-Century England," in *Catherine of Siena: The Creation of a Cult*, Hamburger and Signori, 188n5.

44 See Jennifer N. Brown, ed., *Three Women of Liège: A Critical Edition of and Commentary on the Middle English Lives of Elizabeth of Spalbeek, Christina Mirabilis, and Marie d'Oignies* (Turnhout: Brepols, 2008), 12.

45 Jacques Le Goff, *Saint Louis* (Notre Dame: University of Notre Dame Press, 2009), xxi–xxii.

46 For more on the change in women's book ownership and reading over this period, as evidenced in wills, see Anne M. Dutton, "Passing the Book: Testamentary Transmission of Religious Literature to and by Women in England 1350–1500," in *Women, the Book and the Godly*, Lesley Smith and Jane H.M. Taylor, eds. (Cambrdge: D.S. Brewer, 1995), 41–54.

47 For more on the dating of the ordinance, see C.A.J. Armstrong, "The Piety of Cecily, Duchess of York: A Study in Late Medieval Culture," in *England, France and Burgundy in the Fifteenth Century* (London: The Hambledon Press, 1983), 140n11.

48 "Orders and Rules of the Princess Cecill," *A Collection of Ordinances and Regulations for the Government of the Royal Household Made in Divers Reigns* (London: Society of Antiquaries, 1790), 35.

49 John Gough Nichols and John Bruce, eds., *Doctors' Commons: A Selection from the Wills of Emininent Persons Proved in the Prerogative Court of Canterbury, 1495–1695* (The Camden Society, 1863), 2–3.

50 See also C.A.J. Armstrong, "The Piety of Cecily, Duchess of York: A Study in Late Medieval Culture," in *For Hilaire Belloc: Essays in Honor of His 71st Birthday*, Douglas Woodruff, ed. (New York: Greenwood Press, 1969), 68–91, as well as Andrew Taylor, "Displaying Privacy: Margaret of York as Devotional Reader," in *Cultures of Religious Reading in the Late Middle Ages: Instructing the Sowle, Feeding the Spirit, and Awakening the Passion*, Sabrina Corbellini, ed. (Turnhout: Brepols, 2013), 275–95, about Cecily's daughter's own devotional reading.

51 David Bell notes two surviving MSS from the convent, although neither of
them relate specifically to Catherine in *What Nuns Read: Books and Libraries
in Medieval English Nunneries,* 137. See also Jane Chance, "St. Catherine of
Siena in Late Medieval Britain," *Annali D'Italianistica* 13 (1995): 163–203,
esp. 170n19; and "Convent of St Catherine of Siena," *Edinburgh Southside
Heritage Group,* https://sites.google.com/site/southsideheritagegroup/
the-south-side-story/convent-of-st-catherine-of-siena, accessed 31 July
2015.

52 See Catherine Borland, *A Descriptive Catalogue of the Western Mediæval
Manuscripts in Edinburgh University Library* (Edinburgh: University of
Edinburgh Press, 1916), 46.

53 See Lucy Freeman Sandler, *A Survey of Manuscripts Illuminated in the
British Isles,* Vol. 5, *Gothic Manuscripts (II) 1285–1385* (Oxford: Harvey
Miller Publishers, 1986), 143–5. See, too, Denise L. Despres, "Ecstatic
Reading and Missionary Mysticism," in *Prophets Abroad: The Reception of
Continental Holy Women in Late-Medieval England,* Rosalynn Voaden, ed.
(Cambridge: D.S. Brewer, 1996), 150–1.

54 David Griffith, "The Reception of Continental Women Mystics in
Fifteenth- and Sixteenth-Century England: Some Artistic Evidence," in *The
Medieval Mystical Tradition in England: Exeter Symposium VII,* E.A. Jones, ed.
(Cambridge: D.S. Brewer, 2004), 99.

55 Griffith, "The Reception of Continental Women Mystics in Fifteenth- and
Sixteenth-Century England," 107.

56 See Michael Aufrère Williams, "Medieval English Roodscreens with
Special Reference to Devon" (PhD diss., University of Exeter, 2008), 223,
https://ore.exeter.ac.uk/repository/bitstream/handle/10036/89276/
WilliamsM.pdf, accessed 20 August 2015.

57 Eamon Duffy, *The Stripping of the Altars: Traditional Religion in England
1400–1580* (New Haven: Yale University Press, 1992), 167. In a list of
most frequent saints on rood screens, although many are women, neither
Bridget nor Catherine make the cut. See Christine Peters, *Patterns of Piety:
Women, Gender and Religion in Late Medieval and Reformation England* (Cambridge: Cambridge University Press, 2003), 109.

58 See Denise Despres, "Ecstatic Reading and Missionary Mysticism," in
*Prophets Abroad: The Reception of Continental Holy Women in Late-Medieval
England,* Rosalynn Voaden, ed. (Cambridge: D.S. Brewer, 1996), 86, and
Duffy, *The Stripping of the Altars,* 168. See also Schultze, "Translating St.
Catherine of Siena in Fifteenth-Century England," 192, but note he has
incorrectly cited Duffy at 192n23.

59 She is in Dominican habit, but there is no stigmata or other clear
iconography. See Christopher Norton, David Park, and Paul Binski,

Dominican Painting in East Anglia: The Thornham Parva Retable and the Musée de Cluny Frontal (Woodbridge: Boydell and Brewer, 1987), 36–8; and Paul Lee, *Nunneries, Learning, and Spirituality in Late Medieval English Society: The Dominican Priory of Dartford* (York: York Medieval Press, 2001), 157.

60 See "Ancient Church Is Given a Name – After 900 Years," *Chichester Observer*, http://www.chichester.co.uk/news/local/ancient-church-is-given-a-name-after-900-years-1-1500348, accessed 20 August 2015.

61 Horstmann, "The Lyf of Saint Katherin of Senis," 35.

62 See the Middle English Dictionary, "conversāciǒun (n.)," http://quod.lib.umich.edu/cgi/m/mec/med-idx?type=id&id=MED9627, and the Oxford English Dictionary, "conversation (n)," http://slb.mmm.edu:2177/view/Entry/40748?rskey=XVR0oC&result=1&isAdvanced=false#eid, both accessed 3 August 2015.

63 These included the English Benedictine Adam Easton, who became a Cardinal in 1381 and was ultimately jailed with other cardinals under an accusation that he was plotting against Pope Urban VI. At least six copies of his treatise defending Bridget survive. The Cistercian Abbot Geoffrey of Byland, an unknown "Dr. Anglicus," are also noted defendants of Bridget's legitimacy. See F.R. Johnston, "English Defenders of St. Bridget," in *Studies in St. Brirgitta and the Birgittine Order*, vol. 1, James Hogg, ed. (Salzburg: Institut für Anglistik und Amerikanistik, Universität Salzburg, 1993), 263–75.

64 Brian Stock, *The Implications of Literacy: Written Language and Models of Interpretation in the Eleventh and Twelfth Centuries* (Princeton: Princeton University Press, 1983), 91.

65 Margaret Connolly and Raluca Radulescu, Introduction to *Insular Books: Vernacular Miscellanies in Late Medieval Britain*, Proceedings of the British Academy, vol. 201, Margaret Connolly and Raluca Radulescu, eds. (Oxford: Oxford University Press, 2015), 28.

66 See the introduction to Bryan, *Looking Inward: Devotional Reading and the Private Self in Late Medieval England* for an overview of the changes between aloud/silent and public/private reading in the later Middle Ages.

67 See David Russell, "Religious Mystical Mothers: Margery Kempe and Caterina Benincasa," in *The Medieval Mystical Tradition in England: Papers Read at Charney Manor, July 2011 (Exeter Symposium 8)*, E.A. Jones, ed. (Woodbridge: D.S. Brewer, 2013), 83.

68 See C. Annette Grisé, "Catherine of Siena in Middle English Manuscripts: Transmission, Translation, and Transformation," in *The Medieval Translator/ Traduire au Moyen Age*, Volume 8, Rosalynn Voaden, René Tixier, Teresa Sanchez Roura, and Jenny Rebecca Rytting, eds. (Turnhout: Brepols, 2003), 157.

69 Liz Herbert McAvoy, "'O der lady, be my help': Women's Visionary Writing and the Devotional Literary Canon," *The Chaucer Review* 51 (2016): 76.

70 Barry Windeatt, "1412–1534: Texts," in *The Cambridge Companion to Medieval English Mysticism*, Samuel Fanous and Vincent Gillespie, eds. (Cambridge: Cambridge University Press, 2011), 196.

71 Karma Lochrie, *Margery Kempe and Translations of the Flesh* (Philadelphia: University of Pennsylvania Press, 1991), 60–1.

72 It survives in British Library, MS Harley 612.

73 Alexander Russell, *Conciliarism and Heresy in Fifteenth-Century England* (Cambridge: Cambridge University Press, 2017), 74. Russell posits that "Reginald" is likely Reginald Peacock or Reginald Boulers.

74 Nicholas Watson, *Richard Rolle and the Invention of Authority* (Cambridge: Cambridge University Press, 1991), 1.

1. Compiling Catherine: The Visionary Woman, Stephen Maconi, and the Carthusian Audience

1 A part of this chapter is taken from and building on Jennifer N. Brown, "From the Charterhouse to the Printing House: Catherine of Siena in Medieval England," in *Middle English Religious Writing in Practice: Texts, Readers, and Transformations*, Nicole Rice, ed. (Turnhout: Brepols Press, 2013), 17–47.

2 He is also sometimes known as "Stephen of Siena." In this book, I refer to him as Maconi.

3 See Michael G. Sargent, "The Transmission by the English Carthusians of some Late Medieval Spiritual Writings," *The Journal of Ecclesiastical History,* 27 (1976): 225–40.

4 See Dennis D. Martin, "Carthusians as Advocates of Women Visionary Reformers," in *Studies in Carthusian Monasticism in the Late Middle Ages*, Julian Luxford, ed. (Turnhout: Brepols, 2009), 134–5.

5 Jeremy Catto, "1349–1412: Culture and History," in *The Cambridge Companion to Medieval English Mysticism*, Samuel Fanous and Vincent Gillespie, eds. (Cambridge: Cambridge University Press, 2011), 126.

6 See chapter 4 in ths volume for a fuller account of this speculation. Maconi still may have been responsible for *The Orchend*'s arrival in England. See Roger Lovatt, "The 'Imitation of Christ' in Late Medieval England: The Alexander Prize Essay," *Transactions of the Royal Historical Society* 18 (1968): 108.

7 The letters and testimonies span from 1411 through 1416. See Marie-Hyacinthe Laurent, ed., *Il Processo Castellano. Con appendice*

di documenti sul culto e la canonizzazione di S. Caterina da Siena, Fontes vitae S. Catherinae Senensis Historici, 9 (Milano: Bocca, 1942), ix. The letter is BHL 1703.

8 Brian C. Vander Veen argues in his dissertation, "The Vitae of Bodleian Library MS Douce 114" (PhD diss., University of Nottingham, 2007), 39–41, that the manuscript was likely produced *at* Beauvale.

9 Christina *mirabilis* is also known as Christina the Astonishing or Christina of St Trond.

10 Hand one covers 1r–89v and 7 lines of 90r, then picks up again at 109r line 10, to the end. Hand two is 90r line 7–109r, line 10.

11 For more on Douce 114 and an edition of the Middle English beguine lives, see Brown, *Three Women of Liège.*

12 Barry Windeatt, "1412–1534: Texts," in *The Cambridge Companion to Medieval English Mysticism,* Samuel Fanous and Vincent Gillespie, eds. (Cambridge: Cambridge University Press, 2011), 212.

13 Kathryn Kerby-Fulton, *Books Under Suspicion: Censorship and Tolerance of Revelatory Writing in Late Medieval England* (Notre Dame: University of Notre Dame, 2006), 289–96.

14 Excerpts of Margery Kempe's book do get anthologized by Wynken de Worde, so there was some circulation outside of the cloister, but there is only one complete extant manuscript.

15 This manuscript is now lost, but recorded in British Library, MS Sloane 3548, a booklist from the priory.

16 See T. Webber and A.G. Watson, eds., *The Libraries of the Augustinian Canons* (London: The British Library, 1998), 421.

17 Webber and Watson, *The Libraries of the Augustinian Canons,* 416. Webber and Watson speculate that this version of Catherine's *Dialogo* "is likely to be the translation by Cristofano Guidini, from which the Middle English version, *The Orcherd of Syon,* was probably made" (416). Witham Charterhouse also owned a copy of *Revelations,* but a different translation. See Vincent Gillespie and A.I. Doyle, eds., *Syon Abbey with the Libraries of the Carthusians* (London: The British Library, 2001), 647.

18 Liz Herbert McAvoy, "'O der lady, be my help': Women's Visionary Writing and the Devotional Literary Canon," *The Chaucer Review* 51 (2016): 81.

19 Unless otherwise noted, all transcriptions from manuscripts are my own.

20 See the Middle English Dictionary, http://quod.lib.umich.edu/cgi/m/mec/med-idx?type=id&id=MED8717, accessed 4 August 2015.

21 For example, here the text should read: "here the soth preueth, [preyeth] lowely and meekly ...," but the copier eye-skipped over the word "preyeth" because of its similarity to the word next to it. This would not

happen if translating directly from the Latin, but only happens in copying from an already translated text.

22 Indeed, an analysis of the text does show that it mixes dialects. See Michael Benskin, Margaret Laing, Vasilis Kariaskos, and Keith Williamson, *An Electronic Version of a Linguistic Atlas of Late Mediaeval English* (Edinburgh: University of Edinburgh, 2013), http://www.lel.ed.ac.uk/ihd/elalme/elalme_frames.html, accessed 4 August 2015.

23 For more on this distinction, see Seth Lerer, "Medieval English Literature and the Idea of the Anthology," *PMLA* 118.5 (2003): 1251–67.

24 In "The Vitae of Bodleian Library MS Douce 114," 129, Vander Veen suggests this more strongly than I think is likely.

25 Nicholas Watson, "Censorship and Cultural Change in Late-Medieval England: Vernacular Theology, the Oxford Translation Debate, and Arundel's Constitutions of 1409," *Speculum* 70.4 (1995): 830.

26 See the introduction to Nicholas Love, *The Mirror of the Blessed Life of Jesus Christ: A Full Critical Edition, based on Cambridge University Library MSS 6578 and 6686, with Introduction, Notes and Glossary*, ed. Michael Sargent (Exeter: Exeter University Press, 2005), as well as Michael G. Sargent, "Nicholas Love's *Mirror of the Blessed Life of Jesus Christ*," in *The Wycliffite Bible: Origin, History and Interpretation*, ed. Elizabeth Solopova (Leiden: Brill, 2017), 389–405, where he suggests that Nicholas Love may have encouraged Arundel to issue the Constitutions (405).

27 See Watson, "Censorship and Cultural Change in Late-Medieval England." For some debate on this, see the collection by Vincent Gillespie and Kantik Ghosh, eds., *After Arundel: Religious Writing in Fifteenth-Century England* (Turnhout: Brepols, 2012).

28 Michael Sargent, "The Anxiety of Authority, the Fear of Translation: The Prologues to *The Myroure of Oure Ladye*," in *The Medieval Translator*, Volume 14: *Essays on the Theory and Practice of Translation in the Middle Ages in Honour of Roger Ellis*, René Tixier and Catherine Batt, eds. (forthcoming).

29 See Margaret Harvey, "Adam Easton and the Condemnation of John Wyclif," *English Historical Review* 118 (1998): 321–34, and James Hogg, "Adam Easton's Defensorum sanctae Birgittae," in *The Medieval Mystical Tradition England, Ireland, and Wales: Exeter Symposium VI*, Marion Glasscoe, ed. (Suffolk: D.S. Brewer, 1999), 213–40.

30 For more on these books, see Wendy Scase, "Reginald Pecock, John Carpenter and John Colop's 'Common Profit' Books: Aspects of Book Ownership and Circulation in Fifteenth-Century London," *Medium Aevum* 61 (1992): 261–75. Building on Scase, Ryan Perry has looked at these in relation to the Guildhall Library. Thank you to Ryan for an early look at

his recently published book, *The Material Text: A Study of Middle English Manuscript Cultures, 1380–1440* (Turnhout: Brepols Press, 2017).

31 See Brown, *Three Women of Liège*, 9–14.

32 The problem of clear definition of these terms is well-covered territory. See, for example, the prologue to Steven Fanning, *Mystics of the Christian Tradition* (London: Routledge, 2001); the introduction in Amy Hollywood, *Sensible Ecstasy: Mysticism, Sexual Difference, and the Demands of History* (Chicago: University of Chicago Press, 2002).

33 See on this change, for example, Michael G. Sargent, "Mystical Writings and Dramatic Texts in Late Medieval England," *Religion & Literature* 37 (2005): 77–98.

34 André Vauchez, *The Laity in the Middle Ages: Religious Beliefs and Devotional Practices*, Daniel Bornstein, ed., and Margery J. Schneider, trans. (Notre Dame: University of Notre Dame Press, 1993), 252.

35 For more on these Church-wide tensions and how they manifest in Marguerite Porete's case specifically, see Bernard McGinn, "'Evil-sounding, rash, and suspect of heresy': Tensions between Mysticism and Magisterium in the History of the Church," *The Catholic Historical Review* 90 (2004): 193–212.

36 Michael G. Sargent, "Medieval and Modern Readership of Marguerite Porete's *Mirouer des Simples Âmes Anienties*: The French and English Traditions," in *Middle English Religious Writing in Practice: Texts, Readers, and Transformations*, Nicole Rice, ed. (Turnhout: Brepols, 2013), 49.

37 Sargent, "Medieval and Modern Readership of Marguerite Porete's *Mirouer des Simples Âmes Anienties*," 77.

38 Kerby-Fulton, *Books Under Suspicion*, 276. See also Marleen Cré, "Women in the Charterhouse? Julian of Norwich's *Revelations of Divine Love* and Marguerite Porete's *Mirror of Simple Souls* in British Library, MS Additional 37790," in *Writing Religious Women: Female Spiritual and Textual Practices in Late Medieval England*, Denis Renevey and Christiania Whitehead, eds. (Toronto: University of Toronto Press, 2000), 43–62.

39 For an overview of visionary literature in medieval England, see Gwenfair Walters Adams, *Visions in Late Medieval England: Lay Spirituality and Sacred Glimpses of the Hidden Worlds of Faith* (Leiden: Brill, 2007).

40 For more on mystical texts, see Sargent, "Mystical Writings and Dramatic Texts in Late Medieval England."

41 Kerby-Fulton, *Books Under Suspicion*, 2.

42 London, Lambeth Palace, MS 436, fol. 52. Thank you so much to Sonja Drimmer who looked up and took photos of this manuscript for me. See Theresa A. Halligan, ed., *The Book of Gostlye Grace of Mechtild of Hackeborn* (Toronto: Pontifical Institute of Mediaeval Studies, 1979), 50.

43 Windeatt, "1412–1534: Texts," 212–13.
44 Suzanne Noffke, ed. and trans., *The Letters of Catherine of Siena*, vol. 2 (Tempe: Medieval and Renaissance Texts & Studies, 2000–8), 209.
45 Noffke, *The Letters of Catherine of Siena*, vol. 2, 258.
46 On the complications of Catherine's canonization process, see Otfried Krafft, "Many Strategies and One Goal: The Difficult Road to the Canonization of Catherine of Siena," in *Catherine of Siena: The Creation of a Cult*, Jeffrey Hamburger and Gabriel Signori, eds. (Turnhout: Brepols, 2013), 125–45.
47 See George Ferzoco, "The Processo Castellano and the Canonization of Catherine of Siena," in *A Companion to Catherine of Siena*, Carolyn Muessig, George Ferzoco, and Berverly Mayne Kienzle, eds. (Leiden: Brill, 2012), 188.
48 For more on *Il Processo Castellano*, its impetus, and legacy, see Krafft, "Many Strategies and One Goal," and Laurent, *Il Processo Castellano*, esp. xl–lxx.
49 For a list of extant codices of *Il Processo Castellano*, see Laurent, *Il Processo Castellano*, lxxiii–civ. For the introductory paragraph to Maconi's letter, see Laurent, *Il Processo Castellano*, 257–8.
50 See Laurent, *Il Processo Castellano*, 273.
51 The Latin letter is edited in Acta Sanctorum, "EPISTOLA DOMNI STEPHANI de gestis & virtutibus S. Catharinæ," BHL 1703, Col. 0961C, and in Laurent, *Il Processo Castellano*, ix. I have chosen to use the latter for Latin quotations throughout. The Latin reads "in publica forma, de gestis, moribus et doctrina famose sanctitatis virginis Catherine de Senis," in Laurent, *Il Processo Castellano*, 258.
52 "Post modicum temporis prefata sacratissima virgo mihi dixit in secreto: 'Noveris, dilectissime fili, quia cito implebitur maius desiderium quod habeas.' Quo percepto fui aliqualiter stupefactus, quia nesciebam invenire quid in mundo vellem habere, ymo potius omnia sua recusabam. Ideo dixi: 'Obsecro, carissima mater, quod est maius desiderium quod habeam?' Et ipsa: 'Queras in corde tuo.' Ad quam ego: 'Vere, mater amantissima, nescio in me maius desiderium invenire, quam esse iugiter iuxta cos.' Et illa subito respondit: 'Et hoc erit.' Ego vero nesciebam intelligere modum qualiter commode fieri posset ista propter dissimiles conditiones et statum. Ille vero, cui nihil est impossibile, per modum admirabilem ordinavit ipsam ad Avenionem, videlicet ad dnum Gregorium XI, dirigere gressus, et ita, licet indignus, acceptatus fui comes tam sancet societatis, parvipendens atque derelinquens utrumque parentem, germanos, sororem, aliosque consanguineos, me beatum reputans esse pro virginea presentia et familiaritate" (Laurent, *Il Processo Castellano*, 260).

53 Jessica Brantley offers an overview and analysis of English Carthusian reading practices in *Reading in the Wilderness: Private Devotion and Public Performance in Late Medieval England* (Chicago: University of Chicago Press, 2007). See esp. chap. 2, "'Silence Visible:' Carthusian Devotional Reading and Meditative Practice," 27–77.

54 "Charteus" means Carthusian.

55 "Dum vero laboraret in extremis, ordinavit cum aliquibus quid agere deberent post eius transitum. Postea faciem ad me vertens, ait digitum suum protendendo: 'Tibi autem in virtute sancte obedientie precipio ex parte Dei, ut vadas ad ordinem Cartusiensem, quoniam ad illum ordinem te vocavit et elegit' … Et sicut ore promisit et verbo sic opere perfectissime adimplevit, immo cottidie adimplere non cessat; et ut hec aliquali pateat exemplo, proferam unum ad honorem Dei et ipsius virginis, quamvis ad vercundiam meam accedat: quia quando mihi precepit ex obedientia Dei, ut irem ad ordinem Cartusiensem, ego non optabam illum, vel etiam alium ordinem, sed ex quo migravit ad ethereas mansiones, in corde meo tale desiderium iussa perficiendi succensum extitit, ut si totus mundus mihi contradicere voluisset, ego non attendissem, sicut experientia declaravit, ubi quantum et quid operata iam fuerit et etiam operatur cum filio suo, licet inutili, non est huius temporis enarrare" (Laurent, *Il Processo Castellano*, 261).

56 "Hoc autem intactum preterire non patiar, quia post Deum atque beatissimam virginem Mariam, ego magis me obligatum existimo prefate sancte virgini Catherine quam alicui creature mundi, et si quid boni foret in me, totum attribuo ipsi post Deum, etc. Per suprascripta comprehendi potest aliquibus annis habuisse me supra ceteros familiarissimam conversationem eius, litteras atque secreta sua, et partem sui libri scribendo et ab ore virgineo percipiendo, quia supra merita me nimis affectuouse caritate materna dilexit, ita ut multi filiorum egre portarent et quamdam emulationem haberent" (Laurent, *Il Processo Castellano*, 261–2).

57 For more on dates, see Gerald Parsons, *The Cult of Saint Catherine of Siena: A Study in Civil Religion* (Aldershot: Ashgate, 2008), 16–17.

58 "… et presertim occasione cuiusdam querele facte Venetiis in episcopali palatio circa celebrationem festi sive commemorationis eiusdem virginis" (Laurent, *Il Processo Castellano*, 258).

59 The Middle English Dictionary sees "querele" as a dispute or debate, and the Latin word being translated is "querelæ," meaning "complaint." See "querele," Middle English Dictionary, http://quod.lib.umich.edu/cgi/m/mec/med-idx?type=id&id=MED35552, accessed 25 August 2015.

60 See Ferzoco, "The Processo Castellano and the Canonization of Catherine of Siena," 194.

61 Kerby-Fulton, *Books Under Suspicion*, 24.
62 See Krafft, "Many Strategies and One Goal," 25–6.
63 "Si vero aliquando compellebatur audire facta seculi vel ad salutem
    inutilia, subito rapiebatur in extasim et corpus ibi remanebat absque sensu
    quocumque, velut in oratione sua consistens illo modo cottidie
    rapiebatur, ut ipsi vidimus, non dico centum vel mille vicibus, sed
    valde pluries. Membra sua rigida remanebant inflexibilia, ita ut prius ossa
    frangi potuissent vel a se disiungi quam flecti membra valuissent"
    (Laurent, *Il Processo Castellano* 262).
64 In this passage, "shewed or deuocyone" means "feigned devotion."
65 The meaning of "deed blode" is "dead" or dried blood, demonstrating that
    the wound had been enacted earlier. The Latin is "emortuum sanguinem"
    (Laurent, *Il Processo Castellano*, 263).
66 "Sed illa infelix, sicut existimo, cogitavit quod virgo simularet, unde
    celebrata missa, ostendit ex devotione faciem suam superponere
    pedibus virginis et eam pluribus vicibus in pedibus acerrime perforavit.
    Ipsa vero stetit immobilis, quemadmodum ita stetisset, etiam si pedes
    totaliter abscidisset. Sed postquam omnes abscesserant, virgo redit ad
    sensus proprios et valde cepit dolere pedem, ita quod bene non poterat
    ambulare; et considerantes socie sue viderunt emortuum sanguinem ex
    puncturis illatis, et intellexerunt aperte malitiam illius misere et
    nequissime mulieris" (Laurent, *Il Processo Castellano*, 263).
67 Sarah Macmillan, "Mortifying the Mind: Asceticism, Mysticism and
    Oxford, Bodleian Library MS Douce 114," in *The Medieval Mystical Tradition
    in England*, Jones, 121.
68 "Circa quem extaticum statum eius unum valde mirabile non est
    omittendum, sed cum debita veneratione recolendum, quia precipue
    quando pro quibusdam arduis eius anima ferventius in oratione
    semetipsam excitabat et cum maiori impetu conabatur ascendere,
    gravedinem etiam corporis a terra sublevabat" (Laurent, *Il Processo
    Castellano*, 263).
69 See "rēren," the Middle English Dictionary, http://quod.lib.umich.edu/
    cgi/m/mec/med-idx?type=id&id=MED37022, accessed 2 June 2016.
70 "… absit etiam a sinceritate, serenitate atque puritate conscientie mee,
    ut scienter et contra conscientiam aliquid alienum a simplici veritate
    permiscere vellem in sermonibus quibuscumque meis, quia novi quod
    os quod mentitur occidit animam, neque Deus indiget habere mendacia
    nostra, neque fienda sunt mala ut inde proveniant bona. Certissimum
    igitur habeatis quia meram veritatem protuli supra scripta narrando
    vel veritatem asserere putavi, pro qua non solum expono iuramentum

iuxta petitionem vestram, sed paratum offero me sub quacumque forma
fuerit expediens efficacissime iurare, ymmo quod plus est ..." (Laurent, *Il
Processo Castellano*, 272–3).

71 A notary in Middle English is much like today's meaning of the word, "a
scribe authorized to draw up and authenticate documents and
legal instruments, act as a witness, take depositions." Middle English
Dictionary, "nōtārī(e)," http://quod.lib.umich.edu/cgi/m/mec/
med-idx?type=id&id=MED29873, accessed online 26 August 2015.

72 The Latin does not correspond entirely here. The first part does, "... ut ita
dixerim, pro tali veritate confirmanda et ad honorem Dei et hedificationem,
consolationem atque salutem proximorum sum paratus etiam in igne
ponere manus, ut ille novit qui nichil ignorat, cui est laus, honor et gloria
per infinita [secula] seculorum. Amen" (Laurent, *Il Processo Castellano*, 273).
The latter part, however, is a condensation of several paragraphs.

73 See chapter 3 for more on validating Catherine's visions.

74 For more on this perception and how Catherine's confessor Raymond of
Capua counters it in his *vita*, see F. Thomas Luongo, "Cloistering
Catherine: Religious Identity in Raymond of Capua's *Legenda maior* of
Catherine of Siena," *Studies in Medieval and Renaissance History* 3 (2006):
25–69.

75 "Ego tamen attente cum diligentia magna considerabam verba, mores et
actus eius in omnibus et per singula; et in paucis volendo multa concludere,
super conscientia mea coram Deo et universa ecclesia militante veridice sibi
prebeo testimonium istud, quia licet ego me peccatorem intelligam, tamen
habui, elapsis iam annis sexaginta et ultra, conversationem multorum et
valde famosorum servorum Dei, et numquam vidi vel etiam audivi a
multis elapsis temporibus aliquem Dei servum, qui esset in omni virtute
in tam perfectissimo atque supremo gradu, quare merito reputabatur ab
omnibus virtutem simulacrum et speculum servorum Dei lucidissimum"
(Laurent, *Il Processo Castellano*, 262).

76 "Unde propter tantum fructum, quem ipsa faciebat in huiusmodi, papa
Gregorius XI ei gratiose concessit habere secum iugiter tres confessores
cum auctoritate valde magna, etc. Quandoque tamen occurrebant ei
peccatores aliqui a diabolo tam tenaciter alligati, quod omnino resistebant
ei, dicentes: 'Vere, domina, si mihi diceretis quod Romam irem vel ad
Sanctum Iacobum, infallibiliter adimplerem; super hoc autem articulo
confessionis obsecro parcatis mihi, quia non possum.' Tandem quando per
alium modum ipsa prevalere non poterat, in secreto dicebat ei: 'Si dixero
tibi causam ob quam tu renuis confiteri, numquid postea confiteberis?'
Ille tamquam attonitus atque preventus ita facere promittebat. Et ipsa:

'Dilectissime frater, oculos hominum aliquando latere possumus, oculos vero Dei numquam. Ideo tale peccatum quod in tali tempore et in tali loco fecisti est illud unde diabolus tali modo mentem tuam ita confundit, quod te confiteri non permittit.' At ille videns ita se deprehensum ad pedes eius humillime se prosternebat, cum habundantia lacrimarum veniam exposcens et indilate confitebatur" (Laurent, *Il Processo Castellano*, 266–7).

77 "Noveris quod si scientia illorum trium poneretur in una lance, et in alia poneretur scientia omnium qui sunt in curia Romana, scientia illorum trium valde preponderaret" (Laurent, *Il Processo Castellano*, 270).

78 "Si vero te non miserunt, valde miramur, cum tu sis vilis femella, quia presumis de tanta materia loqui cum domino nostro Papa" (Laurent, *Il Processo Castellano*, 269).

79 See chapter 3 in this volume for more on *Discretio Spirituum*.

80 "[Ei] proposuerunt valde magnas et quamplurimas questiones, precipue de istis abstractionibus eius et modo singularissimo vivendi; et cum Apostolus dicat quod angelus sathane se transfigurat in angelum lucis, ad quid ipsa cognoscit utrum a diabolo sit illusa? Et alia multa dixerunt atque proposuerunt et in effectu disputatio protracta fuit usque ad noctem. Aliquando magister Iohannes pro ea respondere volebat, et licet esset in sacra theologia magister, illi tamen erant ita valentissimi quod in paucis verbis confundebant eum, dicentes: 'Vos erubescere deberetis in conspectu nostro talia proferre. Permittatis eam respondere, quia valde magis satisfacit nobis quam vos' … Postremo recesserunt hedificati pariter et consolati, referentes domino pape quod numquam invenerunt animam tam humilem nec ita illuminatem" (Laurent, *Il Processo Castellano*, 269–70).

81 See Richard Davies, "Richard II and the Church," *Richard II: The Art of Kingship*, Anthony Goodman and James Gillespie, eds. (Oxford: Clarendon Press, 1999), 94.

2. William Flete, English Spirituality, and Catherine of Siena

1 Some parts of this chapter appeared in "The Many Misattributions of Catherine of Siena: Beyond *The Orcherd* in England," *The Journal of Medieval Religious Cultures* 41 (2015): 67–84.

2 Formally known as the convent of San Salvadore di Selva di Lago. There seems to have been a formal connection between Lecceto and the Augustinians of Cambridge. In 1368 an Italian Lecceto friar, Giovanni Tantucci – who would also become one of Catherine of Siena's followers – went to the Cambridge friary for three years. See David Russell, "Religious Mystical Mothers: Margery Kempe and Caterina

Benincasa," in *The Medieval Mystical Tradition in England: Papers Read at Charney Manor, July 2011 (Exeter Symposium 8)*, E.A. Jones, ed. (Woodbridge: D.S. Brewer, 2013), 81–2.

3 See Robert Fawtier, *Sainte Catherine de Sienne : Essai de critique des sources. Sources hgiographiques* (Paris: Boccard, 1921), 53–81.

4 See Suzanne Noffke, ed. and trans., *The Letters of Catherine of Siena*, vol. 1 (Tempe: Medieval and Renaissance Texts & Studies, 2000–8), 155n2.

5 Noffke, *The Letters of Catherine of Siena*, vol. 1, 155.

6 Maiju Lehmijoki-Garner, "The *Miracoli* of Catherine of Siena," in Maiju Lehmijoki-Garner, ed. and trans., *Dominican Penitent Women* (New York: Paulist Press, 2005), 97–8.

7 M.B. Hackett, *William Flete, OSA, and Catherine of Siena: Masters of Fourteenth Century Spirituality* (Villanova, PA: Augustinian Press, 1992), 84.

8 That is, "that [thing] which is not"; M.B. Hackett, "Catherine of Siena and William of England: A Curious Partnership," *Proceedings of the PMR Conference: Annual Publication of the International Patristic, Mediaeval and Renaissance Conference 5* (Villanova: Augustinian Historical Institute, 1980), 34.

9 "The Cleannesse of Sowle" is discussed in detail in chapter 3. The list of Flete's surviving letters are as follows: *Epistola ad rectores civitatis Sensnis, Epistola ad Raymundum de Capua, Epistola ad fratres provinciae Angliae, Epistola ad magistros provincae, Epistola ad provicincialem provinciae, Epistola ad regentes civitatis Senensis*. Although Robert Fawtier believed the sermon, *Sermo in reverentiam B. Catherinae de Sensis*, was misattributed and was more likely that of Thomas Caffarini. See Fawtier, *Sainte Catherine de Sienne : Essai de critique des sources*, 69–75. Carolyn Muessig has recently argued for Flete as the likely author. See Muessig, "Catherine of Siena in Late Medieval Sermons," in *A Companion to Catherine of Siena*, Carolyn Muessig, George Ferzoco, and Berverly Mayne Kienzle, eds. (Leiden: Brill, 2012), 204n3.

10 M.B. Hackett, "William Flete and the *De Remediis Contra Temptaciones*," in *Medieval Studies Presented to Aubrey Gwynn*, F.X. Martin, ed. (Dublin: Three Candles Press, 1961), 330–48 (the manuscript list is on 342–8).

11 As quoted in Hope Emily Allen, ed., *Writings Ascribed to Richard Rolle Hermit of Hampole and Materials for His Biography* (London: Oxford University Press, 1927), 360.

12 Barry Windeatt, "1412–1534: Texts," in *The Cambridge Companion to Medieval English Mysticism*, Samuel Fanous and Vincent Gillespie, eds. (Cambridge: Cambridge University Press, 2011), 197.

13 Hackett, "William Flete and the *De Remediis Contra Temptaciones*," 334. Hackett is so convinced he argues that Flete is the "sole candidate for authorship."

14 Hackett, "William Flete and the *De Remediis Contra Temptaciones*," 334.

15 These are listed in Hackett, "William Flete and the *De Remediis Contra Temptaciones*," 342–8, with some additions in M.B. Hackett, Eric Colledge, and Noel Chadwick, "William Flete's 'De Remedies contra Temptaciones' in its Latin and English Recensions: The Growth of a Text," *Mediaeval Studies* 26 (1964): 3n2.

16 If this is true, it was written just about a decade after the Black Death ravaged England, and this destruction and its aftermath may well have influenced Flete's philosophy of radical forgiveness.

17 Hackett lays out the most important elements of this tradition in his 1961 article "William Flete and the *De Remediis Contra Temptaciones*." His findings are expanded on in Hackett, Colledge, and Chadwick, "William Flete's 'De Remedies contra Temptaciones' in its Latin and English Recensions." Colledge and Chadwick take the subject up further in the only modern edition of the *Remedies,* in "'Remedies against Temptactions': The Third English Version of William Flete," *Archivo Italiano per la storia della pietà* 5 (1968): 203.

18 Hackett, "William Flete and the *De Remediis Contra Temptaciones*," 338. This is Cambridge University Library, Ii.vi.3.

19 See M.G. Sargent, "The Transmission by the English Carthusians of Some Late Medieval Spiritual Writings," *Journal of Ecclesiastical History* 27 (1976): 225–40.

20 Hackett, *William Flete, OSA, and Catherine of Siena,* 120.

21 In the case of Brotherton Collection, MS 501, a Middle English anthology, the *Remedies* addresses a *literal* novice about how and what to confess. See O.S. Pickering, "Brotherton Collection MS 501: A Middle English Anthology Reconsidered," *Leeds Studies in English,* 21 (1990): 152.

22 A house of English Benedictine nuns, known to have female scribes and responsible for one of the surviving copies of Julian of Norwich's *Revelations.* Thomas More's great-great-granddaughter, Dame Gertrude More, was one of its founding members.

23 See Vincent Gillespie and A.I. Doyle, eds., *Syon Abbey with the Libraries of the Carthusians* (London: The British Library, 2001), 231, 257, 281, 293–5. The last MS noted survives as Bodleian Library, MS Bodley 630 (SC 1953).

24 London, British Library, Harley 2409, which also has "The Cleannesse of Sowle" – misidentified as excerpts from *The Life of Catherine of Siena* in David Bell, *What Nuns Read: Books and Libraries in Medieval English Nunneries* (Kalamazoo: Cistercian Publications, 1995) and other places.

25 British Library, MS Harley 1706; Beeleigh Abbey, Miss C. Foyle s.xv. See Bell, *What Nuns Read*, 107.

26 Colledge and Chadwick, "'Remedies against Temptactions,'" 211.

27 Oxford Bodleian Library MS Holkham misc. 41. See Colledge and Chadwick, "'Remedies against Temptactions,'" 210–11.

28 Bodley 630, in Gillespie and Doyle, *Syon Abbey with the Libraries of the Carthusians*, xlii.

29 Gillespie and Doyle, *Syon Abbey with the Libraries of the Carthusians*, xlii.

30 Colledge and Chadwick, "'Remedies against Temptactions,'" 221.

31 This is exemplified in the fact that both Flete's and Catherine's texts will have multiple "editions" or works published by Wynkyn de Worde, whose audience was much broader than a monastic one. See appendix B, which notes the MSS that contain both Catherine's and Flete's texts.

32 Colledge and and Chadwick, "'Remedies against Temptactions,'" 223.

33 Nicholas Watson, Introduction to *The Cambridge Companion to Medieval English Mysticism*, Fanous and Gillespie, 11.

34 Colledge and and Chadwick, "'Remedies against Temptactions,'" 229.

35 Watson, Introduction to *The Cambridge Companion to Medieval English Mysticism*, Fanous and Gillespie, 14.

36 Nicole Rice, *Lay Piety and Religious Discipline in Medieval English Literature* (Cambridge: Cambridge University Press, 2008), 2.

37 A devotional treatise attributed to Hugh of St Victor.

38 Diekstra, "*A Good Remedie aȝens Spirituel Temptacions*," 321.

39 F.N.M. Diekstra, "*A Good Remedie aȝens Spirituel Temptacions*: A Conflated Middle English Version of William Flete's *De Remediis Contra Temptationes* and Pseudo-Hugh of St Victor's *De Pusillanimitate* in London BL MS Royal 18.A.X," *English Studies* 4 (1995): 307–54.

40 Julia Boffey, "Some Women Readers and a Text of *The Three Kings of Cologne*," *The Ricardian* 10 (1996): 392.

41 Hackett, "William Flete and the *De Remediis Contra Temptaciones*," 338.

42 Denis Renevey, "1215–1349," in *The Cambridge Companion to Medieval English Mysticism*, Fanous and Gillespie, 95.

43 EEBO, 20875.5, Remedy; STC 1288.02. The first section of the de Worde edition corresponds with Chapter IV of Rolle's form, although it is somewhat condensed.

44 Indeed, the confusion about what work belongs to whom persists. James Simpson has erroneously noted: "A short extract of Rolle's *Form of Living* was published as *The Remedy ayents the Troubles of Temptacyons* in 1508 and 1519." See James Simpson, "1534–1550s: Texts," in *The Cambridge Companion to Medieval English Mysticism*, Fanous and Gillespie, 253. However, the extract is merely the opening paragraph appended to Flete's text.

45 See M.B. Hackett, "William Flete," *Pre-Reformation English Spirituality*,
James Walsh, ed. (New York: Fordham, 1965), 158; and Hackett, "William
Flete and the *De Remediis Contra Temptaciones*," 341n38.

46 Hackett, *William Flete, OSA, and Catherine of Siena*, 159–60, emphasis in the
original.

47 M.B. Hackett, "The Spiritual Life of the English Austin Friars of the
Fourteenth Century," in *Sanctus Augustinus Vitae Spritualis Magister:
Settimana internazionale di spiritualità agostiniana: Roma, 22–27 Ottobre 1956*
(Rome, 1956), 488.

48 For more context on the letters and how they may have been received, see
Aubrey Gwynn, S.J., *The English Austin Friars in the Time of Wyclif* (Oxford:
Oxford University Press, 1940), esp. 240–5.

49 Hackett, *William Flete, OSA, and Catherine of Siena*, 156.

50 For Flete, the plague was in England, c. 1348; for Catherine, it was in Italy
also in 1348, and then again in 1363 and 1374.

51 Hackett, *William Flete, OSA, and Catherine of Siena*, 86–7.

52 Carl Horstmann, ed., "The Lyf of Saint Katherin of Senis," *Archiv für
das Studium der Neueren Sprachen und Litteraturen* 76 (1886), 79. The
Latin is available through the Acta Sanctorum, BHL Number 1702, and
more recently through Raimondo da Capua, *Legenda maior sive Legenda
Admirabilis Virginis Catherine de Senis*, Silvia Nocentini, ed. (Firenze:
Sismel, 2013). As the latter is a critical edition, I will be using it rather than
the AASS. A PDF of the de Worde may also be accessed through EEBO
STC (2nd ed.), 24766 for the 1492 edition, STC (2nd ed.), 24766.3 for the
1500 edition. "Accedunt illi per detestabiles turmas suas et eam undique
circumdare conantur, ut nemine succurrente succidere ipsam possint a
fundamentis. Primoque inchoant a temptatione carnali, quam non tantum
per cogitationes immictunt interius, non solum per illusiones et fantasias
in somnis, sed per apertas visiones quas, assumptis corporibus aeris,
suis oculis et auribus ingerebant modis sibi multimodis ministrabant.
Horror est prelia illa redicere, sed victoriam audire puris mentibus nimis
delectabile invenitur" (Raimondo da Capua, *Legenda maior sive Legenda
Admirabilis Virginis Catherine de Senis*, 190).

53 Horstmann, "The Lyf of Saint Katherin of Senis," 79; "Melius tibi est ut
hanc stoliditatem dimictas antequam ex toto deficias, adhuc est tempus
ut possis gaudere in mundo, iuvenis es et agiliter recuperabit corpus
vigorem suum. Vivas sicut cetere mulieres, accipias virum et procrea filios
ad generis humani augmentum. Quod, si desideras Deo placere, numquid
non etiam sancte nupserunt? Saram considera, Rebeccam, Lyam pariter
et Rachelem, ut quid hanc singularem accepisti vitam in qua nullo modo

valebis perseverare?" (Raimondo da Capua, *Legenda maior sive Legenda Admirabilis Virginis Catherine de Senis*, 191).

54 Horstmann, "The Lyf of Saint Katherin of Senis," 80; "Effigiat siquidem imagines mulierum et hominum turpissime se invicem commiscentium actusque fedos et verba inhonestissima tam visui quam auditui eius obicientium, sicque turmis tam abominabilibus contra eam discurrentibus ululatibus et clamoribus ipsam ad turpia invitabant" (Raimondo da Capua, *Legenda maior sive Legenda Admirabilis Virginis Catherine de Senis*, 192).

55 Colledge and Chadwick, "'Remedies against Temptactions,'"221.

56 Peter 1:7: "That the trial of your faith (much more precious than gold which is tried by the fire) may be found unto praise and glory and honour at the appearing of Jesus Christ"; and Job 23:10: "But he knoweth my way, and has tried me as gold that passeth through the fire." Douay-Rheims Bible Online (drbo.org), accessed 29 January 2018. All biblical citations are taken from this site.

57 Colledge and Chadwick, "'Remedies against Temptactions,'" 224.

58 Phyllis Hodgson and Gabriel M. Liegey, eds., *The Orcherd of Syon*, Early English Text Society, 258 (Oxford: Oxford University Press, 1996), 100; "Egli è fatto giustiziere mio dalla mia giustizia per tormentare l'anime che miserabilemente ànno offeso me. Ed in questa vita gli ò posti a tentare, molestando le mie creature; non perchè le mie creature sieno vinte, ma perchè esse vincano e ricevano da me la gloria della vittoria, provando in loro le virtú. E niuno in questo debba temere per veruna battaglia nè tentazione di dimonio che lo' venga, però che io gli ò fatti forti e datolo' la fortezza della volontà, fortificata nel sangue del mio Figliuolo. La quale volontà nè dimonio nè creatura ve la puo mutare, però che ella è vostra, data da me col libero arbitrio" (Giuliana Cavallini, ed., *Il Dialogo della Divina Provvidenza: ovvero Libro della divina dottrina*, Testi Cateriniani 1, 2nd ed. [Siena: Edizioni Cateriniane, 1995], 92); corresponds with Edinburgh, MS 87 (D b IV 18), fol. 67v.

59 Colledge and Chadwick, "'Remedies against Temptactions,'" 232.

60 Hodgson and Michael Liegey, *The Orcherd of Syon*, 103; "E però il dimonio, come iniquo, vedendo che egli è accecato dal proprio amore sensitivo, gli pone i diversi e vari difetti i quali sono colorati con colore d'alcuna utlità e d'alcuno bene, e a ogni uno dà secondo lo stato suo e secondo quelli vizi principali nei quali il vede piú disposto a ricevere" (Cavallini, *Il Dialogo della Divina Provvidenza:* 95); corresponds with Edinburgh, MS 87 (D b IV 18), fol. 69v.

61 Colledge and Chadwick, "'Remedies against Temptactions,'" 234.

62 Alastair Minnis quotes some plague era chroniclers to this effect: "The chronicler Henry Knighton follows his obituary for Bradwardine with the general statement that 'At that time there was such a great shortage of priests everywhere that many churches were widowed and lacked the divine offices, matins, vespers, and the sacraments and sacramentals' … In similar vein, in 1349 Ralph of Shrewsbury, bishop of Bath and Wells, spoke of how the plague had 'left many parish churches and other benefices' in the 'disocese without an incumbent, so that their inhabitants are bereft of a priest', and therefore 'many people are dying without the sacrament of penance'" ("1215–1349," in *The Cambridge Companion to Medieval English Mysticism*, Fanous and Gillespie, 83).

63 Minnis, "1215–1349," 83.

64 Minnis, "1215–1349," 83.

65 Colledge and Chadwick, "'Remedies against Temptactions,'" 231–2.

66 Hodgson and Liegey, *The Orcherd of Syon*, 110–11; "Costoro ti dissi che col coltello di due tagli, cioè coll'odio del vizio e amore della virtú, per amore di me tagliavano il veleno della propria sensualità, e col lume della ragione tenevano e possedevano e acquistavano l'oro in queste cose mondane, chi le voleva tenere" (Cavallini, *Il Dialogo della Divina Provvidenza*, 104); corresponds with Edinburgh, MS 87 (D b IV 18), fol. 72v.

67 Hodgson and Liegey, *The Orcherd of Syon*, 113; "Dico che ella avelena l'anima e dàlle la morte, se essa non el vomica per la confessione santa, traendone il cuore e l'affetto. La quale è una medicina che'l guarisce di questo veleno, poniamo che paia amare alla propria sensualità" (Cavallini, *Il Dialogo della Divina Provvidenza*, 107); corresponds with Edinburgh, MS 87 (D b IV 18), fol. 72r.

68 Catherine finds an expression of her own penance through bodily mortification. See Maiju Lehmijoki-Gardner, "Denial as Action – Penance and Its Place in the Life of Catherine of Siena," in *A Companion to Catherine of Siena*, Carolyn Muessig, George Ferzoco, and Berverly Mayne Kienzle, eds. (Leiden: Brill, 2012), 113–26.

69 Colledge and Chadwick, "'Remedies against Temptactions,'" 225.

70 Letter T328/G130, to Frate Antonio da Nizza, at Lecceto, early January 1379. Noffke, *The Letters of Catherine of Siena*, vol. 4, 80.

71 Hackett, *William Flete, OSA, and Catherine of Siena*, 211.

72 Muessig, "Catherine of Siena in Late Medieval Sermons," 205.

73 Hackett, *William Flete, OSA, and Catherine of Siena*, 168.

74 "The Cleannesse" is frequently anthologized with Walter Hilton, who draws from Flete, as well as with the *Fervor Amoris*, which does as well.

3. Catherine Excerpted: Reading the Miscellany

1 It measures 210 x 140 mm.

2 British Library, Harley MS 3432; Cambridge, St John's College, MS 75; and Pierpont Morgan, MS 162.

3 M.B. Hackett, *William Flete, OSA, and Catherine of Siena: Masters of Fourteenth Century Spirituality* (Villanova, PA: Augustinian Press, 1992), 184. For Latin, "Ad haec autem addidit supradictus Dei servus frater Guilielmus dicens: 'si ista lectio esset promulgata et communicata per totum Ordinem nostrum, credo quod magnum faceret bonum," see Robert Fawtier, ed., "Catheriniana," *Mélanges d'archéologie et d'histoire* 34.1 (1914): 93.

4 Girolamo Gigli, ed., *Opere della serafica Santa Caterina da Siena*, vol. 4 (Lucca, 1707–21), 374–6.

5 As with the sermon attributed to Flete, Fawtier suspects that the *Documento* is more likely to be that of Maconi or Caffarini, as it survives in a manuscript in his hand with other texts authored by him. I think this is the reason, actually, to believe it is Flete's – why name him when the neighbouring texts are clearly Caffarini's? It seems more likely that Flete's name is attached because he is, indeed, the author. See Robert Fawtier, *Sainte Catherine de Sienne : Essai de critique des sources. Sources hagiographiques* (Paris: Boccard, 1921), 68.

6 According to Robert Fawtier in his 1914 edition of the *Documento*, the full Latin text is in Siena, Biblioteca comunale degli Intronati, T.II.7. This manuscript was compiled by Thomas Caffarini and also contains a sermon attributed to Flete. See Carolyn Muessig, "Catherine of Siena in Late Medieval Sermons," in *A Companion to Catherine of Siena*, Carolyn Muessig, George Ferzoco, and Beverly Mayne Kienzle, eds. (Leiden: Brill, 2012), 203–26. It also contains a copy of the *Orazioni*, prayers attributed to Catherine. See Suzanne Noffke, "The Writings of Catherine of Siena: The Manuscript Tradition," in *A Companion to Catherine of Siena*, Muessig, Ferzoco, and Mayne Kienzle, eds. (Leiden: Brill, 2012), 295–37. The redacted versions attributed to Maconi are found in Siena, Biblioteca comunale degli Intronati, C.v.24, fol. 253, and Milano, Biblioteca Nazionale Braidense AD.IX.11, fol. 56. For more on these manuscripts, see Fawtier, "Catheriniana," 3–96.

7 Carl Horstmann, ed., "The Lyf of Saint Katherin of Senis," *Archiv für das Studium der Neueren Sprachen und Litteraturen* 76 (1886), 76–7. "Porro ex hac coniunctione doctrix hec discipline Dei unam aliam inferebat, quam non cessabat hiis quos in via Dei volebat instruere cotidie replicare, quod

videlicet talis anima, sicut supra dicimus, Deo coniuncta quantum habet de amore Dei, tantum habet de odio sancto partis proprie sensitive, sive proprie sensualitatis, quia enim ex amore Dei naturaliter procedit odium culpe que contra Deum commictitur. Videns anima fomitem et originem omnis culpe in parte sensitiva regnare, in ipsaque sancto movetur odio contra eam conaturque totis viribus non occidere ipsam, sed fomitem illum radicatum in ea" (Raimondo da Capua, *Legenda maior Sive Legenda Admirabilis Virginis Catherine de Senis,* Silvia Nocentini, ed. [Firenze: Sismel, 2013], 187).

8 See chapter 5 for more on this.

9 For more on this, see Jennifer N. Brown, "The Many Misattributions of Catherine of Siena: Beyond *The Orcherd* in England," *Journal of Medieval and Religious Cultures* 41 (2015): 67–84.

10 See, for example, Dirk Schultze's discounting of Flete's role in dissemination in "Translating St. Catherine of Siena in Fifteenth-Century England," in *Catherine of Siena: The Creation of a Cult,* Jeffrey F. Hamburger and Gabriela Signori, eds. (Brepols, 2014), 188n5.

11 Note here that Flete is an Augustinian *friar* not an Augustinian *canon,* a religious order which also had an interest in Catherine (see the introduction to this volume and the discussion of Stephen Maconi's letter concerning Catherine's canonization).

12 It survives in nine manuscripts: in Sloane 982 (1400–25), Rawlinson C.285 (a.k.a. Bodl 12143) (1400–50), Cambridge University Ff.5.40 (1400–50), Bodley 131 (a.k.a Bodl 1999) (1425–75), Arundel 197 (c. 1400), Royal 18.A.X. (1400–25), Cambridge, Trinity College 336 (B.14.53) (1400–50), Chetham's Hospital Library, MS Mun.A.7.1 (was acc. 6690) (c. 1450), and, most fully, in Harley 2409 (1400–50).

13 Version A includes the MS Sloane 982; Version B is Bodleian Library, MS Rawlinson C.285 (Bodl 12143) and Cambridge University Library, MS Ff.5.40; Version C occurs in the remaining five manuscripts. See P.S. Joliffe, *Checklist of Middle English Writings* (Toronto: Toronto University Press, 1974), 105. Joliffe assumed that the longer version in Harley 2409 was due to additions and expansions made using Catherine's *Dialogo,* rather than a complete version of the primary text, which is why its designation is "C."

14 The Latin edition is in Fawtier, "Catheriniana," 88–95; Hackett translates it into English in *William Flete, OSA, and Catherine of Siena,* 181–4.

15 "Dilectissima filia," or "dearest daughter," in the Latin. See Fawtier, "Catheriniana," 90. This is missing entirely from other manuscripts that address an ungendered "sely soule."

16 The MS seems to have "sal tou" written here, but corrected against other manuscripts, should read "shalt þu" (how it is written, for example, in Arundel 197, 10r).

17 The Latin merely reads "for your good," that is, "pro tuo bono," but this translator has more than once changed this to read "good and profit."

18 The Latin reads that "no one will cause you anger, not even for an hour," "nulli irasceris etiam ad horam," but this is omitted from Harley 2409 and the other English versions of "The Cleannesse." For Latin, see Fawtier, "Catheriniana," 91.

19 The "deme no man" here means "pass judgment on no man."

20 John 14:2: "In my Father's house there are many mansions. If not, I would have told you: because I go to prepare a place for you."

21 Unless otherwise noted, all transcriptions from "The Cleannesse" are my own (with light editing such as punctuation). However, parts of Harley 2409 are available as part of the Middle English Grammar Project at the University of Stavanger, Norway, http://www.uis.no/getfile.php/Forskning/Kultur/MEG/Notts_L0278_OK2.pdf, accessed 10 June 2016. The Latin reads as follows: "Dilectissima filia, si vis haere puritatem quam optas, oportet qui sum summa puritas uniaris; hoc autem fiat si tria servabat: Primum est si totam intentionem in me dirigens in omnibus factis tuis me solum finem constituas et me prae oculis semper habere contendas. Secundum est si voluntatem tuam penitus abnegans et voluntatem cujuscumque creaturae non respiciens, et omnibus quae tibi acciderint solam voluntatem mean quae tuam vult satisfactionem consideres et discernas, nihil enim volo aut permitto nisi pro tuo bono. Quod si attenderis, de nullo contristaberis, nulli irasceris etiam ad horam sed potius reputabis te obligatam omni injurianti. Insuper nullum judicabis nisi manifeste videas peccatum. Et tunc vitio irasceris et homini compatieris. Tertium est si facta servorum meorum non secundum judicium meum judicaveris, nosti enim me dixisse quod *in domo patris mei mansiones multae sunt* et cum mansio gloriae respondeat merito viae sicut sunt diversae mansiones in prima, sic sunt diversae ambulationes in via, propter quod omnia facta servorum meorum dummodo non sunt contra meam doctrinam expresse habeas in reverentiam et ipso nullatenus judices" (Fawtier, "Catheriniana," 90–1).

22 "Si haec observaveris, eris ordinata in te ipsa et erga me per primum, et erga proximum tam malum quam bonum per secundum et tertium ac sicut extra virtutum ordinem; per vitia non exibis et per consequens puritatem perfecte servabis, gratia mea semper hoc operante" (Fawtier, "Catheriniana," 92).

23 See the definitions and examples for "cleannesse" in the Middle English
   Dictionary, http://quod.lib.umich.edu/cgi/m/mec/med-idx?type
   =id&id=MED7963, accessed 18 February 2014.

24 The term "miscellany" is most often used to define a group of manuscripts
   that contains many varieties of texts within one codex, but scholars
   are repeatedly demonstrating that these compilations are, in fact, not
   miscellaneous but by design. I am using the term to underscore the
   amount of texts housed within the same covers, and perhaps not as
   well-planned a collection as an "anthology," but see the groupings
   as more carefully curated than the term generally implies.

25 Sara Poor, *Mechthild of Magdeburg and Her Book: Gender and the Making of
   Textual Authority* (Philadelphia: University of Pennsylvania Press,
   2004), 168.

26 Julia Boffey and A.S.G. Edwards, "Towards a Taxonomy of Middle English
   Manuscript Assemblages," in *Insular Books: Vernacular Miscellanies in Late
   Medieval Britain, Proceedings of the British Academy*, vol. 201, Margaret
   Connolly and Raluca Radulescu, eds. (Oxford: Oxford University Press,
   2015), 279.

27 Ralph Hanna, *Pursuing History: Middle English Manuscripts and Their Texts*
   (Stanford: Stanford Unversity Press, 1996), 9.

28 Hanna, *Pursuing History*, 9.

29 Kimberly K. Bell and Julie Nelson Crouch, "Introduction: Reading Oxford,
   Bodleian Library, MS Laud Misc. 108 as a 'Whole Book,'" in *The Texts
   and Contexts of Oxford, Bodleian Library, MS Laud Misc. 108: The Shaping of
   English Vernacular Narrative*, Kimberly K. Bell and Julie Nelson Croch, eds.
   (Leiden: Brill, 2011), 7.

30 John B. Friedman, *Northern English Books, Owners, and Makers in the Late
   Middle Ages* (Syracuse: Syracuse University Press, 1995), 27. Also thanks to
   Ryan Perry who pointed out the connections to me.

31 Friedman, *Northern English Books, Owners, and Makers in the Late Middle
   Ages*, 27.

32 Exactly how wary is continuously up for debate. See Nicholas Watson's
   major article on Arundel's Constitutions, "Censorship and Cultural
   Change in Late-Medieval England: Vernacular Theology, the Oxford
   Translation Debate, and Arundel's Constitutions of 1409," *Speculum* 70.4
   (1995): 822–64; as well as Vincent Gillespie and Kantik Ghosh, eds., *After
   Arundel: Religious Writing in Fifteenth-Century England* (Turnhout: Brepols,
   2012) for differing views. See also chapter 1 where I discuss this in relation
   to Bodleian Library, MS Douce 114.

33 See F.N.M. Diekstra, "A Good Remedie aȝens Spirituel Temptacions: A
   Conflated Middle English Version of William Flete's De Remediis Contra

Temptationes and Pseudo-Hugh of St Victor's De Pusillanimitate in London BL MS Royal 18.A.X.," *English Studies* 4 (1995): 307–54.

34 Margaret Connolly, "Public Revisions or Private Responses? The Oddities of Arundel 197, with special reference to *Contemplations of the Dread and Love of God*," *British Library Journal* 20 (1994): 57.

35 Connolly, Public Revisions or Private Responses?," 63.

36 John Considine, "Philemon Holland," *Oxford Dictionary of National Biography.* www.oxforddnb.com, accessed 9 June 2016.

37 See M. Teresa Brady, "Lollard Interpolations and Omissions in Manuscripts of the *Pore Caitif*," in *De Cella in Seculum: Religious and Secular Life and Devotion in Late Medieval England*, Michael Sargent, ed. (Cambridge: D.S. Brewer, 1989), 185–6. For more on *Pore Caitif* and lollardy, see M. Teresa Brady, "Lollard Sources of 'The Pore Caitif,'" *Traditio* 44 (1988): 389–418, and Nicole R. Rice, "Reformist Devotional Reading: The *Pore Caitif* in British Library, MS Harley 2322," *The Medieval Mystical Tradition in England: Papers Read at Charney Manor, July 2011 (Exeter Symposium 8)*, E.A. Jones, ed. (Cambridge: D.S. Brewer, 2013), 177–93. Kalpen Trivedi acknowledges that the term "lollard" is a loaded one and that it's better to think of it as proto-lollard, compiled and written by people influenced by Wycliffe's views. See Kalpen Trivedi, "'Trewe techyng and false heritikys': some 'Lollard' manuscripts of the *Pore Caitif*," in *Strange Countries: Middle English Literature and Its Afterlife*, David Matthews, ed. (Manchester: Manchester University Press, 2010), 132–56.

38 Ralph Hanna, *Introducing English Medieval Book History: Manuscripts, Their Producers and Their Readers* (Liverpool: Liverpool University Press, 2013), 81. Hanna has an entire chapter devoted to MS Rawlinson C.285.

39 Transcribed in Carl Horstmann, ed., *Yorkshire Writers: Richard Rolle of Hampole, an English Father of the Church and His Followers* (London: S. Sonnenschein & Co., 1895), 108. Also available online at http://name.umdl.umich.edu/rollewks.

40 Suzanne Noffke and Giuliana Cavallini, *Catherine of Siena: The Dialogue* (Mahwah, NJ: Paulist Press, 1980), 191–2; "'E però t'è di necessità, a volere venire alla purità che tu mi dimandi, di fare queste tre cose principali, cioè di unirti in me per affetto d'amore, portando nella memoria tua i benifici ricevuti da me; e con l'occhio de l'intelletto vedere l'affetto della mia carità che v'amo inestimabilemente; e nella volontà mia e non la mala volontà sua, però ch"io ne so' giudice: Io e non voi. E da questo ti verrà ogni perfezione.' Questa fu la dottrina data a te dalla mia Verità, se bene ti ricorda" (Giuliana Cavallini, ed., *Il Dialogo della Divina Provvidenza: ovvero Libro della divina dottrina*, Testi Cateriniani 1, 2nd ed. [Siena: Edizioni Cateriniane, 1995], 243).

41 Phyllis Hodgson and Gabriel Michael Liegey, eds., *The Orcherd of Syon*,
Early English Text Society, 258 (Oxford: Oxford University Press,
1966), 224.

42 Hodgson and Liegey, *The Orcherd of Syon*, 228–9; corresponds with
Edinburgh, MS 87 (D b IV 18), fol. 172v.

43 Margaret Connolly discusses this manuscript in relation to the copy of the
devotional text *Contemplations of the Dread and Love of God* contained therein
in "Mapping Manuscripts and Readers of *Contemplations of the Dread and
Love of God*," *Design and Distribution of Late Medieval Manuscripts in England*,
Margaret Connolly and Linne R. Moooney, ed. (Woodbridge: Boydell
and Brewer, 2008), 266. Vincent Gillespie also looks at the manuscript in
relation to *Contemplations of the Dread and Love of God* in "Vernacular Books
of Religion," *Book Production and Publishing in Britain 1375–1475*, Jeremy
Griffiths and Derek Pearsall, eds. (Cambridge: Cambridge University
Press, 1989), 331.

44 Other scholars have looked at "The Cleannesse of Sowle" in Harley 2409;
for example, see C. Annette Grisé, "Catherine of Siena in Middle English
Manuscripts: Transmission, Translation, and Transformation," in *The
Medieval Translator/Traduire au Moyen Age*, vol. 8, Rosalynn Voaden, René
Tixier, Teresa Sanchez Roura, and Jenny Rebecca Rytting, eds. (Turnhout:
Brepols, 2003), 152. Because "The Cleannesse" was thought to be part
of the *Dialogo* or the *Vita*, the speculation as to how it circulated in its
form were incorrect (that is, it is an expansion of "The Cleannesse" and a
conflation with another text).

45 See Barry Windeatt, "1412–1534: Texts," in *The Cambridge Companion to
Medieval English Mysticism*, Samuel Fanous and Vincent Gillespie, eds.
(Cambridge: Cambridge University Press, 2011), 201.

46 Since Catherine died in 1380, the 1386 date is clearly erroneous.

47 It reads "Incipit quaedam narratio eujusdam spiritualis doctrinae sive
documenti facta anno Domini M°CCC°LXXVI°, die VIIᵃ Januarii per
supradictum fratrem Guilielmum Anglicum, magistrum scientiae et
sanctitatis virum, quam doctrinam et documentum ipse tunc habuit a
beata matre beata virgine Katherina de Senis, oraculo vivae vocis et in
scriptis reduxit ut sequitur" (Fawtier, "Catheriniana," 88).

48 The other is Manchester, Chetham's Hospital Library, MS Mun.
A.7.1 (was acc. 6690). Both of these versions are "Version C" of "The
Cleannesse."

49 "Dixit sancta mater narrans de sicut de alia quod in principio
illuminationis suae posuit contra amorem proprium pro fondamento
totius vitae suae lapidem cogitionis sui ipsius, quem lapidem distinxit
in tres lapillos infrascriptos: Primus est considerato creationis quomodo

est nullum esse habebat a se sed solum a creatore dependens tam in productione quam in conservatione et hoc totum fecit Creator et fecit ex gratia. Secundus lapillus est consideratio Redemptionis quam prius destructum esse gratiae sanguine suo illud reparavit ex puro et ferventi amore, quem amorem non meruerat homo. Tertius lapillus est consideratio peccatorum factorum post baptismum et receptam gratiam quibus meruerat eternam damnationem pro quibus mirabatur de eterna bonitae Dei, quod non mandaverat terrae quam deglutiret. Ex hiis tribus resultabat tantum odium sui quod nihil appetebat juxta suum volitum sed tantum secundum voluntatetm Dei quam videbat velle solum bonum suum" (Fawtier, "Catheriniana," 88–9).

50 "Nam blanditias matris suae in quibus prius delectabatur fugiebat sicut gladium vel sicut venenum et injurias amplexabatur cum delectatione, et temptationes diaboli simul et amplectabatur et aspernabatur, amplectabatur in quantum vexabant eam, aspernabatur in quantum offerebant delectationes festivas" (Fawtier, "Catheriniana," 90).

51 "Post haec omnia venit ad maximum desiderium puritatis et orans per plures menses assidue Dominum ut daret sibi perfectam puritatem" (Fawtier, "Catheriniana," 90).

52 "Primus amor est causa omnium peccatorum tam carnalium quam aliorum manifestoru quae committuntur ex amore terrenorum seu creaturarum quando est propter illarum amorem contemnitur preceptum Creatoris. Secundus amor qui vocatur spiritualis est ille qui post contemptum terrenorum et omnium creaturarum ac etiam propriorum sensuum facit hominem ita inhabere proprio appetitu spirituali et propriae sentetiae quod non vult servire Deo aut per viam Dei incedere nisi vixit proprium appetitum seu proprium sensum" (Fawtier, "Catheriniana," 92).

53 "Et quia Deus vult hominem sine propria voluntate, omnino talis non potest stare in via Dei, imo necesse est eum cadere quia plus adhaeret propriae voluntati quam divinae" (Fawtier, "Catheriniana," 93).

54 Suzanne Noffke, ed. and trans., *The Letters of Catherine of Siena*, vol. 4 (Tempe: Medieval and Renaissance Texts & Studies, 2000–8), 80. (This is letter T328/G130 to Fra Antonio da Nizza, at Lecceto.)

55 This word is not "unbithinken" which means to forget, but rather "umbithinken," whose definitions include to reflect, to ponder, and to plan (MED); "Et ista cogitando amara fient dulcia haec illa" (Fawtier, "Catheriniana," 93).

56 Grazia Mangano Ragazzi has written on the subject of discretion through many of Catherine's writings in *Obeying the Truth: Discretion in the Spiritual Writings of Saint Catherine of Siena* (Oxford: Oxford University Press, 2014).

57 The passage from *The Orcherd* that corresponds very closely to "The Cleannesse" is part 5, chapter 2. The selection from *The Orcherd* that has its own circulation is as follows: "Aftir tyme siche han consceyued a greet loue in receyuynge of goostly cumfortis or visyouns, in what wise þat euere þei come, þei feeled a ioye, for þei haue þat þing which þei loueden and desireden. And þis may oftentymes come of þe feend. For þouȝ it come with gladnes, ȝit it eendiþ with peyne and prickynge of conscience and voyde fro þe desier of vertu. For, if sich gladnesse be founde wiþoute feruent desier of vertu & verry mekenes, brennyd in þe oven of my dyuyn charite, þat visitacioun, cumfort, and visyoun þat sich a soule resseyueþ is of þe feend, and not of me, þouȝ sche feele a tokene of gladnes" (Hodgson and Liegey, *The Orcherd of Syon*, 238); "Se questa allegrezza si truova senza l'affocato desiderio della virtú, unta d'umilità e arsa nella fornace della divina mia carità, quella visitazione e consolazione e visione che ella à ricevuta è dal dimonio e non da me, non obstante che si senta il segno de l'allegrezza" (Cavallini, *Il Dialogo della Divina Provvidenza*); corresponds with Edinburgh, MS 87 (D b IV 18), fols. 179r and 179v.

58 For more on this history, see Rosalynn Voaden, *God's Words, Women's Voices: The Discernment of Spirits in the Writing of Late-Medieval Women Visionaries* (York: York Medieval Press, 1999).

59 Henry of Langenstein, translated and quoted by Barbara Newman, in "What Did It Mean to Say 'I Saw'? The Clash between Theory and Practice in Medieval Visionary Culture," *Speculum* 80 (2005): 40.

60 Voaden, *God's Words, Women's Voices*, 55. See also, Wendy Love Anderson, "Gerson's Stance on Women," in *A Companion to Jean Gerson*, ed. Brian Patrick McGuire (Leiden: Brill, 2006), 293–316.

61 See Brian Patrick McGuire, *Jean Gerson and the Last Medieval Reformation*, (University Park: Pennsylvania State University Press, 2005), 250; and Euan K. Cameron, "Ways of Knowing in the Pre-and Post-Reformation Worlds," *Mysticism and Reform, 1400–1750*, Sara S. Poor and Nigel Smith, eds. (Notre Dame: University of Notre Dame Press, 2015), 29–48.

62 Windeatt, "1412–1534: Texts," 204. See also Paul Patterson, ed., *A Mirror to Devout People (Speculum Devotorum)*, Early English Text Society, 346 (Oxford: Oxford University Press, 2016), 20–1. I would also like to thank Paul Patterson for initially drawing my attention to this passage and to the mention of Catherine in the *Speculum Devotorum*.

63 Newman, "What Did It Mean to Say 'I Saw'?" 28.

64 The entire Wynkyn de Worde passage and Latin translation are footnoted at the end of these excerpts.

65 "[¶]Doctours of holy chyrche, whome I haue taught the trouthe, seyn, and soothe it is, that myn vysyon begynneth wyth a drede, but euer in

the passyng it setteth a sowle in greate reste and sekernes; It begynneth
wyth a maner of bytternes, but euermore more and more it wexith swete.
And the contrarye herto dothe the vysyon of the fende: It gyueth in
the begynnyng as it semeth a maner of gladdenes or sykernes or ellys
swetenesse, but whan it passeth awaye, euer it encreseth in the sowle
drede and bytternesse. This is the trewest knowleche for to knowe myn
wayes from the fendes wayes: [¶] The waye of penaunce and the kepynge
of myn preceptys and commaundementes in the begynnyng it semeth
harde and sharpe, but the more a sowle prouffyteth in kepyng of theym
the more esely it waxith; [¶] the waye of synne in the begynnyng semeth
full delectable but euer in encres therof a sowle is made more and more
dampnable. [¶] But yet shall I gyue the another token for to knowe myn
vysyon from the vysyon of the fende: Vnderstonde this for a sothe that
sythe it soo is that I am trouthe, euer of myn vysyons the sowle of man
receyueth a greater knowleche of trouthe; and by-cause that the knowleche
of trouthe is full necessarye to the soule as well to her-self as to me that
she may knowe me and her-self, of the whiche knowleche she passeth out
fro her-self in settinge lytyll by her-selfe and honoureth and worshyppeth
me, the whiche condycion properly is called the condycion of mekenes:
therfore it were full nedefull that a sowle sholde thus knowe her-self and
soo be made meke by (myn) vysyon. [¶] The contrarye is of the vysyon
of the fende: sythe it so is that the fende is fader of lesynge and kynge of
all the chyldren of pryde, and he may not gyue but that that he hathe,
as his lesyng and pryde, therfore as of his visyon a soule semeth moche
by her-self and is made glad and full of Ioye, the whiche is properly the
condycion of pryde, and so she is by-lefte swellyng and bolnyng in pryde:
Thenne therfore, yf thou examyne and dyscusse dylygently in thy-self,
mayste knowe whether (a) vysyon come to the of trouthe or ellys of
falsenesse; yf it come of trouthe, it maketh thyn sowle meke; yf it come
of falsenes and by desceyte, it maketh thyn sowle proude"] (Horstmann,
"The Lyf of Saint Katherin of Senis," 68. The Horstmann edition does
not use the paragraph signs, but they are in the de Worde text, so I
have inserted them here, especially because they correspond with the
paragraph signs in Harley 2409). "Illaque instantissime hoc supplicante,
respondit: 'Agile foret per inspirationem anumam tuam informare, quod
statim discerneret inter unam et aliam, set ut prosit tam aliis quam tibi
volo te verbo docere; et quidam doctores, quos ego docui, dicunt, et
verum est quod visio mea incipit cum terrore, sed semper in processu
dat maiorem securitatem, incipit cum aliquali amaritudine, sed semper
magis dulcescit, cuius oppositum habet pro sua conditione visio inimici.
Dat enim in principio, ut videtur, aliqualem letitiam, securitatem sive

dulcedinem, sed semper in processu timor et amaritudo in mente videntis continue crescunt; hoc est verissimum, quia etiam vie mee a viis suis eadem differentia differunt, via enim penitentie et mandatorum meorum in principio apparet aspera et difficilis, sed quanto plus proceditur in ea, plus dulcescit et magis est agilis, via autem vitiorum in principio apparet valde delectabilis, sed semper in processu amarior fit et dampnosior. Sed ego volo tibi dare unum aliud signum infallibilius et certius: habeas pro certo quod, cum ego sim veritas semper ex viosnibus meis resultat in anima maior cognito veritatis et quia veritatis cognitio magis necessaria ei est circa me et circa se, ut scilicet cognosocat se et cognoscat me, de qua cognitione semper egreditur quod se contempnit et me honorat, quod est proprium officicium humilitatis, necessarium est quod ex visionibus meis anima efficatur magis humilis magisque se ipsam se vilitatem suam cognoscens pariter et contempnens. Oppositum autem accidit de visionibus inimici, cum enim sit pater mendacii et rex super omnes filios superbie, nec possit dare nisi quod habet, semper ex viosnibus suis resultat in anima quedam propria reputop seu presumptio de se ipsa, quod est proprium officium superbie remanetque turgida et vento inflata. Tu igitur in te ipsa semper diligenter examinando perpendere poteris unde processit visio, a veritate scilicet an a mendacio, quia veritas semper facit animam humilem, mendacium autem facit eam superbam" (Raimondo da Capua, *Legenda maior*, 174–5).

66 Voaden, *God's Words, Women's Voices*, 57.

67 Nancy Caciola, *Discerning Spirits: Divine and Demonic Possession in the Middle Ages* (Ithaca: Cornell University Press, 2003), 280.

68 Dyan Elliot, *Proving Women: Female Spirituality and Inquisitional Culture in the Later Middle Ages* (Princeton: Princeton University Press, 2004), 284.

69 For a history of *discretio spirituum*, see Voaden, *God's Words, Women's Voices*, chap. 2. See also Elliot, *Proving Women*, part 3: "The Discernment of Spirits," and Caciola, *Discerning Spirits*.

70 Voaden, *God's Words, Women's Voices*, 47.

71 Phyllis Hodgson, ed., *The Cloud of Unknowing and the Book of Privy Counselling*, ed. Phyllis Hodgson, Early English Text Society, 218 (Oxford: Oxford University Press, 1944), 86.

72 Roger Ellis, ed., *The Liber Celestis of St. Bridget of Sweden*, Early English Text Society, 291 (Oxford: Oxford University Press, 1987), 349.

73 The de Worde version of the text reads as follows: "Knowest thou not, doughter, who thou arte and who I am? Yf thou knowe well these two wordes, thou art and shalt be blessyd. Thou art she that art not and I am he that am. Yf thou haue the veray knowleche of these two thynges in thy soule, thy ghostly enemye shall neuer dyseue the, but thou shalt escape gracyously

all his snares, ne thou shalte neuer consente to ony thyng that is ayenst my commaundementes and preceptes, but alle grace, alle treuthe, all charyte thou wylte wynne wythout ony hardenesse" (Horstmann, "The Lyf of Saint Katherin of Senis," 72). "Scisne filia que tu est et quis ego sum? Si hoc duo noveras beata eris. Tu enim es illa que non es, ego autem sum ille qui sum. Si hanc notitiam habueris in anima tua, numquam te decipere poterit inimicus omnesque laqueos eius evades. Nusquam consenties alicui rei contra mandata mea, omnem gratiam, omnem caritatem omnemque virtutem absque difficultate acquires" (Raimondo da Capua, *Legenda maior*, 180).

74 For more on the Pepwell excerpts, see chapter 5.

75 "Cui Dominus in sententia sic respondit: 'Desponsabo te mihi in fide'. Cumque virgo sepe ac diu orationem eandem repeteret et Dominus semper idem responsum reiteraret, accidit semel, tempore quo quadragesimalia ieiunia propinquabant et fideles cibariis carnium et de carnibus egredientium finem ponunt, ideo comedunt lautius solito et vanum festum quodammodo ventri celebrant, quod virgo sacra, in suo se reclusorio colligens vultumque sponsi eterni orationibus et ieiuniis queritans, prefatam orationem cum ingenti fervore instantissime replicabat. Cui Dominius … 'sicut promisi, mihi te desponsare in fide.' Adhuc eo loquente apparuere Virgo gloriosissima mater eius, beatissimus Iohannes evangelista, gloriosus Paulus sanctissimusque Dominicus, pater sue religionis" (Raimondo da Capua, *Legenda maior*, 198). This corresponds with the de Worde in Horstmann, "The Lyf of Saint Katherin of Senis," 83–4.

76 This corresponds to the *vita* in de Worde in Horstmann, "The Lyf of Saint Katherin of Senis," 83–4. "Ac cum hiis omnibus David propheta, psalterium musicum habens in manu sua, quo supersuavissime ac sonore pulsante, Virgo Dei genitrix virginis dexteram sua sacratissima cepit manu, digitosque illius extendens ad filium postulabat, ut ea sibi desponsare dignaretur in fide…Quem anulari digito dextere virginis dextera sua supersacra imponens: 'Ecce' inquit 'desponso te michi, creatori et salvatori tuo, in fide que, usque quo in celis tuas mecum nuptias perpetuas celebrabis, semper conservabit illibata. Age igitur filia viriliter amodo absque cunctatione quacumque illa, que ordinante mea providentia tuas deducentur ad manus, quia fortitudine fidei iam armata cunctos tibi adversantes feliciter superabis.' Hiis dictis disparuit visio, sed semper remansit anulus ille in digito non quidem secundum visionem aliorum, sed tantum secundum ipsius virginis visionem" (Raimondo da Capua, *Legenda maior*, 198–9).

77 See Robert P. Palazzo, "The Veneration of the Sacred Foreskin(s) of Baby Jesus – A Documented Analysis," in *Multicultural Europe and Cultural*

Exchange: In the Middle Ages and Renaissance, James Helfers, ed. (Turnhout: Brepols, 2005), 169–70.

78 Dyan Elliott, *The Bride of Christ Goes to Hell: Metaphor and Embodiment in the Lives of Pious Women, 200–1500* (Philadelphia: University of Pennsylvania Press, 2012), 216.

79 Lynn Staley, ed., *The Book of Margery Kempe* (Kalamazoo: TEAMS, in association with the University of Rochester by Medieval Institute Publications, Western Michigan University Press, 1996), 92.

4. *The Orcherd of Syon*: How to Read in the Convent

 1 See for a comparison of their epistolary political output, Joan Isobel Friedman, "Politics and the Rhetoric of Reform in the Letters of Saint Bridget of Sweden and Catherine of Siena," *Livres et Lectures de Femmes en Europe entre Moyen Âge et Renaissance,* Anne-Marie Legaré, ed. (Turnhout: Brepols, 2007), 279–94.

 2 See, in this volume, chapter 3's discussion of Catherine of Siena's "Discernment of Spirits" for more on this topic.

 3 For an excellent overview of Bridget of Sweden's cult in England, see Laura Saetveit Miles, "Bridget of Sweden," in *The History of British Women's Writing 700–1500,* Liz Herbert McAvoy and Diane Watt, eds. (New York: Palgrave, 2012), 207–15. For a history of Syon Abbey, see E.A. Jones, *England's Last Medieval Monastery: Syon Abbey 1415–2015* (Leominster: Gracewing, 2015). For more in-depth studies on the spirituality at Syon Abbey (both for the sisters and the brethren), see Roger Ellis, *Viderunt Eam Filie Syon: The Spirituality of the English House of a Medieval Contemplative Order from Its Beginnings to the Present Day* (Salzburg: Institut für Anglistik und Amerikanistik Universität Salzburg, 1984); Roger Ellis, "Further Thoughts on the Spirituality of Syon Abbey," in *Mysticism and Spirituality in England,* William Pollard and Robert Boenig, eds. (Woodbridge: D.S. Brewer, 1997), 219–43; Vincent Gillespie, "'Hid Diuinite': The Spirituality of the English Syon Brethren," in *The Medieval Mystical Tradition in England; Exeter Symposium VII: Papers Read at Charney Manor,* ed. E.A. Jones (Woodbridge: D.S. Brewer, 2004), 189–206; the introduction to *Syon Abbey with the Libaries of the Carthusians,* Vincent Gillespie and A.I. Doyle, eds. (London: The British Library, 2011), xxix–lxv; and *Syon Abbey and Its Books: Reading, Writing and Religion c. 1400–1700,* E.A. Jones and Alexandra Walsham, eds. (Woodbridge: Boydell and Brewer, 2010).

 4 Vincent Gillespie, "The Mole in the Vineyard: Wyclif at Syon in the Fifteenth Century," in *Text and Controversy from Wyclif to Bale: Essays in*

Honour of Anne Hudson, eds. Helen Barr and Ann M. Hutchison (Turnhout: Brepols, 2005), 134–5.

5 Gillespie, "The Mole in the Vineyard," 137.

6 Bridget also had a revelation that supported England's position against France in that war. Roger Ellis writes, "St. Bridget had early taken up a position supporting the English claim, and revelations including this material (IV, iii, ciii–cv, and …VI, lxiiii) were liable to be excerpted and used in writings against the French," in "'Flores ad Fabricandam … Coronam': An Investigation into the Uses of the Revelations of St. Bridget of Sweden in the Fifteenth-Century England," *Medium Aevum* 1 (1982): 172–3.

7 Gabriella Zarri, "Catherine of Siena and the Italian Public," in *Catherine of Siena: The Creation of a Cult,* Jeffrey F. Hamburger and Gabriela Signori, eds. (Turnhout: Brepols, 2013), 72.

8 Zarri, "Catherine of Siena and the Italian Public," 76. For more on the library at Paradiso, see Renato Piattoli, "Un capitol di storia dell'arte libraria ai primi del Quattrocento: rapporti tra il Monastero fiorentino del Paradiso e l'Ordine Francescano," *Studi Francescani* 29 (1932): 1–21. Eliana Corbari notes that Firenze, Biblioteca Riccardiana, MS 1345 was a MS owned by Paradiso that contains both Bridget's and Catherine's writings: "The second part of this manuscript contains vernacular *reportationes* of sermons given by Giordano alongside other important vernacular texts such as *vitae* of female saints; letters of Catherine of Siena; and the '*Sermone angielicho*' written by Bridget of Sweden for the Bridgettine sisters" (Corbari, *Vernacular Theology: Dominican Sermons and Audience in Late Medieval Italy* [Berlin: De Gruyter, 2013], 83).

9 See Eliana Corbari, "Laude for Catherine of Siena," in *A Companion to Catherine of Siena,* Carolyn Muessig, George Ferzoco, and Berverly Mayne Kienzle, eds. (Leiden: Brill, 2012), 243–6.

10 See Hans Cnattingius, *Studies in The Order of St. Bridget of Sweden I: The Crisis in the 1420's* (Stockholm: Almqvist and Wiksell, 1963), 108–10. Also, thank you to Vincent Gillespie for sharing with me his paper "The Third Policeman: Syon, Vadstena, and St Alban's," presented at the New Chaucer Society Conference in Reykjavik, Iceland, 2014, which contains the background to this.

11 Cnattingius notes that he definitely had a copy taken of St Bridget's canonization process, and that "further material was afterwards placed at Simon's disposal." See Cnattingius, *Studies in The Order of St. Bridget of Sweden I,* 132. Many of Syon's texts have been attributed to Simon Wynter or were clearly owned by him. See Vincent Gillespie, "Syon and the New

Learning," in *The Religious Orders in Pre-Reformation England*, James G. Clark, ed. (Woodbridge: Boydell, 2002), 75–95.

12 "The Will of Mary I," *Tudor History*, http://tudorhistory.org/primary/will.html, accessed 8 January 2016. Original source: J.M. Stone, *Mary I Queen of England* (1901), 507–20, from transcript in the Harleian MS 6949. Original no longer extant.

13 "The Will of Mary I," *Tudor History*.

14 Marguerite Tjader Harris, ed., and Albert Ryle Kezel, trans., *Birgitta of Sweden: Life and Selected Writings* (Mahwah, NJ: Paulist Press, 1989), 75.

15 John Henry Blunt, ed., *Myroure of Oure Ladye*, Early English Text Society, 19 (Oxford: Oxford University Press, 1873), 68. For more on the *Myroure* and reading practices, see Ann Hutchison, "Devotional Reading in the Monastery and in the Late Medieval Household," in *De cella in seculum: Religious and Secular Life and Devotion in Late Medieval England*, Michael Sargent., ed. (Cambridge: D.S. Brewer, 1989), 215–28; Ann Hutchison, "What the Nuns Read: Literary Evidence from the English Bridgettine House, Syon Abbey," *Mediaeval Studies* 57 (1995): 205–22; Elizabeth Schirmer, "Reading Lessons at Syon Abbey: *The Myroure of Oure Lady* and the Mandates of Vernacular Theology," in *Voices in Dialogue: Reading Women in the Middle Ages*, Linda Olson and Kathryn Kerby-Fulton, eds. (Notre Dame: University of Notre Dame Press, 2005), 345–76; and C. Annette Grisé, "Proliferation and Purification: The Use of Books for Nuns After Arundel," in *After Arundel: Religious Writing in Fifteenth-Century England*, Vincent Gillespie and Kantik Ghosh, eds. (Turnhout: Brepols, 2012), 503–19.

16 James Hogg, ed., *The Rewyll of Seynt Sauiour* (Salzburg: Institut fur Angelistik und Amerikanistik, 1980), 83.

17 For more on the literary culture of Barking Abbey, see Jennifer N. Brown and Donna Alfano Bussell, eds., *Barking Abbey and Medieval Literary Culture: Authorship and Authority in a Female Community* (York: York Medieval Press, 2012).

18 Rebecca Krug, *Reading Families: Women's Literature Practice in Late Medieval England* (Ithaca: Cornell University Press, 2002), 165.

19 Virginia R. Bainbridge, "Syon Abbey: Women and Learning c. 1415–1600," in *Syon Abbey and Its Books*, Jones and Walsham, 86. Also, for a thorough look at what the nuns read at Syon and surviving evidence of such, see Hutchison, "What the Nuns Read." See, too, for non-literary forms of reading done by Syon nuns, Marilyn Oliva, "Rendering Accounts: The Pragmatic Literacy of Nuns in Late Medieval England," in *Nuns' Literacies in Medieval Europe: The Hull Dialogue*, Virginia Blanton, Veronica O'Mara, and Patricia Stoop, eds. (Turnhout: Brepols, 2013), 51–68.

20 See Veronica O'Mara, "The Late Medieval English Nun and Her Scribal Activity: A Complicated Quest," in *Nuns' Literacies in Medieval Europe*, Blanton, O'Mara, and Stoop, 78.

21 See chapter 1 in this volume for more on Stephen Maconi and his letter.

22 See Nancy Warren, *The Embodied Word: Female Spiritualities, Contested Orthodoxies, and English Religious Cultures, 1350–1700* (Notre Dame: University of Notre Dame Press, 2010), esp. chap. 1, "The Incarnational and the International: St Birgitta of Sweden, St Catherine of Siena, Julian of Norwich and Aemelia Lanyer."

23 Vincent Gillespie, "1412–1534: Culture and History," in *The Cambridge Companion to Medieval English Mysticism*, Samuel Fanous and Vincent Gillespie, eds. (Cambridge: Cambridge University Press, 2011), 173.

24 Paul Patterson, ed., *A Mirror to Devout People (Speculum Devotorum)*, Early English Text Society, 346 (Oxford: Oxford University Press, 2016), xxiv–xxv. See also Paul Patterson, "Female Readers and the Sources of the Mirror to Devout People," *Journal of Medieval Religious Cultures* 42 (2016): 181–200.

25 Patterson, *A Mirror to Devout People*, 6.

26 Although Elizabeth of Hungary is likely Elizabeth of Töss. See Alexandra Barratt, "The Revelations of St. Elizabeth of Hungary: Problems of Attribution," *The Library*, 6th series, 14 (1992): 1–11, and the introduction to Sarah McNamer, ed., *The Two Middle English Translations of the Revelations of St. Elizabeth of Hungary* (Heidelberg: Universitätsverlag Winter, 1996).

27 Patterson, *A Mirror to Devout People*, 20.

28 See chapter 3 in this volume.

29 Ann Hutchinson, "St. Birgitta, the *Revelations*, and the Bridgettine Order," *The Medieval Mystical Tradition VII: Papers Read at Charney Manor 2004*, E.A. Jones, ed. (Cambridge: D.S. Brewer, 2004), 80–1.

30 Rosalynn Voaden, "The Company She Keeps: Mechthild of Hackeborn in Late Medieval Compilations," in *Prophets Abroad: The Reception of Continental Holy Women in Late-Medieval England*, Rosalynn Voaden, ed. (Cambridge: D.S. Brewer, 1996), 60. See also the introduction to Theresa A. Halligan, ed., *The Book of Gostlye Grace of Mechtild of Hackeborn* (Toronto: Pontifical Institute of Mediaeval Studies, 1979).

31 Roger, "'Flores ad Fabricandam … Coronam,'" 167.

32 Courtney E. Rydel, "Inventing a Male Writer in Mechtild of Hackeborn's *Booke of Gostlye Grace*," *The Journal of Medieval Religous Cultures* 40 (2014): 194.

33 Bainbridge, "Syon Abbey: Women and Learning c. 1415–1600," 86.

34 See Phyllis Hodgson, "The Orcherd of Syon and the English Mystical Tradition: The Sir Israel Gollancz Memorial Lecture," *Proceedings of the British Academy* 50 (1964): 230. For more on Stephen Maconi, see chapter 1. There

are no editions of any of the Latin redactions of Catherine's book. There are several editions of the Italian versions, with the most recent being P. Angiolo Puccetti, O.P. and P. Tito S. Centi, O.P., eds., *Il Dialogo della Divina Provvidenzia,* (Siena: Ediziono Cantagalli, 2011). I have opted to use Giuliana Cavallini, ed., *Il Dialogo della Divina Provvidenza* (Rome: Edizioni Cateriniane, 1968), as the basis for my comparisons, as most Catherine scholars agree that it is probably the most authoritative critical edition of *Il Dialogo* to date.

35 The convent of Catherine of Siena was short lived, as it was founded in 1517 and then dissolved with the dissolution of the monasteries. Some information on it can be found in George Seton, "The Convent of Saint Catherine of Sienna near Edinburgh: A Paper Read before the Architectural Institute of Scotland 11th April 1867" (Edinburgh: Printed for Private Circulation, 1871), https://play.google.com/books/reader?id=rswUAAAAQAAJ&printsec=frontcover&output=reader&hl=en&pg=GBS.PP4, accessed 19 July 2016. Edinburgh MS 87 (D b IV 18) is the version by Cristofano di Galgano Guidini, which is definitely the basis for *The Orcherd.* See Hodgson and Liegey, *The Orcherd of Syon,* vii, and Jane Chance, "St. Catherine of Siena in Late Medieval Britain," *Annali D'Italianistica* 13 (1995): 175. It also contains some insertions that do not exist in the Italian.

36 Guidini appears to have been a minor member of Catherine's *famiglia* during her life, but played an important role in the dissemination of her *Dialogo* and many of her letters after her death. See http://www.treccani.it/enciclopedia/cristoforo-guidini (Dizionario-Biografico)/, accessed 13 June 2016. Luisa Aurigemma suggests that Guidini's translation was done at the behest of Stephen Maconi. See "La tradizione manoscritta del 'Dialogo della Divina Provvidenza' di Santa Caterina da Siena," *Critica Letteraria* 16 (1988): 237–58.

37 Edinburgh MS 87 (D b IV 18). See Catherine Borland, *A Descriptive Catalogue of the Western Mediæval Manuscripts in Edinburgh University Library* (Edinburgh: University of Edinburgh Press, 1916), 142. For more on this manuscript, see Chance, "St. Catherine of Siena in Late Medieval Britain," which focuses on this text.

38 Blacman also bequeaths texts by Elizabeth of Schönau, Mechthild, and St Bridget. See E. Margaret Thompson, *The Carthusian Order in England* (London: Society for Promoting Christian Knowledge, 1930), 320–1.

39 There are three: British Library, Harley 3432, Cambridge, St John's College, MS C.25 (both dating from the first half of the fifteenth century), and Pierpont Morgan, MS 162 (dating from the second half). Edinburgh MS 87 (D b IV 18) is the only surviving exception.

40 Lambeth Palace, MS 436, fol. 52. See Halligan, *The Book of Gostlye Grace of Mechtild of Hackeborn*, 50.

41 Vincent Gillespie and A.I. Doyle, eds., *Syon Abbey with the Libraries of the Carthusians* (London: The British Library, 2001), 243, entry 804, and 330, entry 1012. Also, for more on the library and what is lost, see Vincent Gillespie, "The Book and the Brotherhood: Reflections on the Lost Library of Syon Abbey," in *The English Medieval Book: Studies in Memory of Jeremy Griffiths*, A.S.G. Edwards, Vincent Gillespie, and Ralph Hanna, eds. (London: The British Library, 2000), 185–208.

42 Hodgson and Liegey note that there are twenty-five extant manuscripts of the Italian and sixteen in Latin. See also, Cavallini, "Introduczione," in *Il Dialogo della Divina Provvidenza*, ix–xliii. An incomplete list of manuscripts (although with greater description for the ones it names) can be found in P. Innocenzo Taurisano, O.P., ed., *Dialogo della Divina Provvidenza* (Rome: Libreria Editrice F. Ferrari, 1947), liii–lxiv. In addition, of the three Italian fifteenth-century books printed of *Il Dialogo*, two are in Italian and only one in Latin. Hodgson and Liegey, *The Orcherd of Syon*, vi n7. Suzanne Noffke lists what she considers the most significant manuscripts in "The Writings of Catherine of Siena: The Manuscript Tradition," in *A Companion to Catherine of Siena*, Carolyn Muessig, George Ferzoco, and Berverly Mayne Kienzle, eds. (Leiden: Brill, 2012), 337.

43 Suzanne Noffke, ed. and trans., *The Dialogue of Catherine of Siena* (Mahwah, NJ: Paulist Press, 1980), 21.

44 Hodgson and Liegey, *The Orcherd of Syon*, xi.

45 A "Dane James" is named as the translator in the epilogue to the de Worde volume, and in MS Harley 3432, but it is a misreading of the text where the translator asks prayers of his helper, a brother James, who also laboured on *The Orcherd*. Although this was first pointed out by Sister Mary Denise in her 1958 article "The Orcherd of Syon: An Introduction," *Traditio* 14 (1958): 292, scholars still make the mistake of referring to the translator as James. The translator himself is unnamed. Denise suggests that the title "Dane" (or Don) may indicate a Carthusian (perhaps at Sheen) as the translator. Tamsin Woodward Smith suggests that Simon Wynter, a Bridgettine who translated other texts for the Syon nuns, is probably the translator in "A Critical Study of the Middle English *Orchard of Syon* in Both Manuscript and Print Form, with Particular Attention to Its Context and Audience" (PhD diss., Oxford University, 2006), 37–40; Dirk Schultze posits that the translator may be the same as the Carthusian translator of Suso's *Seven Points of True Love and Everlasting Wisdom*. See Dirk Schultze, "Translating

St. Catherine of Siena in Fifteenth-Century England," in *Catherine of Siena: The Creation of a Cult*, Hamburger and Signori, 202–3.

46 Hodgson and Liegey, eds., *The Orcherd of Syon*, 18.

47 Edinburgh MS 87 (D b IV 18) has the identical prologue on fol. 1R, demonstrating a close relationship between the two texts.

48 There is no edition of any Latin version of *Il Dialogo*, so I have no basis for comparison other than Giuliana Cavallini's 1995 Italian edition, which she bases on Rome, Biblioteca Casanatense, MS 292, a late fourteenth-century manuscript which she judges to be the closest to the original. Cavallini's first edition (1965) is the basis for Suzanne Noffke's edition, *The Dialogue of Catherine of Siena*.

49 Some sources indicate that Catherine dictated the entire *Dialogo* in the course of a few days, but this is contradicted in most of the writings by Catherine and her contemporaries, which show it took the better part of a year.

50 Nicky Hallett, *The Senses in Religious Communities, 1600–1800: Early Modern "Convents of Pleasure"* (New York: Routledge, 2013), 8.

51 Hodgson, "The Orcherd of Syon and the English Mystical Tradition," 240.

52 For more on how this manifests itself in Catherine's use of the image and metaphor of her heart, especially in her letters, see Heather Webb, "Catherine of Siena's Heart," *Speculum* 80 (2005): 802–17, as well as her book, *The Medieval Heart* (New Haven: Yale University Press, 2010).

53 Hodgson and Liegey, *The Orcherd of Syon*, 1.

54 Krug, *Reading Families*, 185.

55 Hodgson, "*The Orcherd of Syon* and the English Mystical Tradition," 236.

56 For more on trees and medieval devotion, see Sara Ritchey, "Spiritual Arborescence: Trees in the Medieval Christian Imagination," *Spiritus* 8.1 (2008): 64–82.

57 Raymond of Capua, *The Life of Catherine of Siena*, ed. and trans. Conleth Kearns, O.P. (Washington, DC: Dominicana Publications, 1994), 54. "Ut, priusquam sancte vita sue viridarium totum circumeundo perlustres, aliquos de fructibus eius primis et ultimis valeas prelibare, nec propter hoc dimictetur quin loco in suo iterum tibi eorundem fructuum species presentetur, cum ordo ipse requiret, concedente Altissimo, sed tamen hoc fit ut ad considerandum fructus virtutem eius exercitatior reddaris et aptior" (Raimondo da Capua, *Legenda maior Sive Legenda Admirabilis Virginis Catherine de Senis*, Silvia Nocentini, ed. [(Firenze: Sismel, 2013]), 156.

58 The Middle English only has the following sentence, without the section which precedes it setting up the metaphoric image: "I haue rehersed

somwhat in generall of her grete penaunce, and now I purpose to telle you, maydens, in speciall vnder fewe wordes the hardnesses of her penaunce, soo that ye of the grete vertuous herber of her holy lyvyng maye taste somewhat of the fruyte that growen aboute the herber, bothe of the fyrst and of the laste; and for the condycions and the kyndis of the fruyt, it shall be declared by the helpe of god afterward," Carl Horstmann, ed. "The Lyf of Saint Katherin of Senis: nach dem Drucke W. Caxtons (c. 1493)," *Archiv für das Studium der Neueren Sprachen und Litteraturen* 76 (1886), 55.

59 Hodgson and Liegey, *The Orcherd of Syon*, 1.

60 See E.A. Jones and Alexandra Walsham, "Introduction: Syon Abbey and its Books: Origin, Influences and Transitions," in *Syon Abbey and Its Books*, Jones and Walsham, 23.

61 Hodgson and Liegey, *The Orcherd of Syon*, 165; "Sí che vedi che questo battesmo è continuo, dove l'anima si debba battezzare infino all'ultimo, per lo modo detto. In questo battesmo cognosci che l'operazione mia, cioè della pena della croce, fu finita, ma il frutto della pena, il quale avete ricevuto per me, è infinito" (Cavallini, *Il Dialogo della Divina Provvidenza*, 166); corresponds with Edinburgh MS 87 (D b IV 18), fol. 127r.

62 Mechthild's book, known in Latin as *Liber spiritualis gratiae*, has two extant Middle English copies from the fifteenth century, as well as excerpts ad library entries pointing to a somewhat widespread circulation.

63 Alexandra Barratt, "Continental Women Mystics and English Readers," in *The Cambridge Companion to Medieval Women's Writing*, Carolyn Dinshaw and David Wallace, eds. (Cambridge: Cambridge University Press, 2003), 240–1.

64 Several scholars have drawn comparisons between Margery Kempe and Catherine of Siena. See chapter 5 for a more thorough analysis of this comparison.

65 Roger Ellis, ed., *The Liber Celestis of St. Bridget of Sweden* EETS (Oxford: Oxford University Press, 1987), 381.

66 Hodgson and Liegey, *The Orcherd of Syon* 177–8; "Congregate e unite tutte insieme queste potenzie, ed ammerse e affocate in me, il corpo perde il sentimento; chè l'occhio vedendo non vede, l'orecchio udendo non ode, la lingua parlando non parla – se non come alcuna volta per l'abbondanzia del cuore, permettarò ch'l membro della lingua parli per isfogamento del cuore e per gloria e loda del nome mio, sí che parlando non parla – la mano toccando non tocca, i piei andano non vanno: tuttte le membra sono legate e occupate dal legame e sentimento dell'amore. Per lo quale legame sonosi sottoposti alla ragione e uniti con l'affetto dell'anima; chè, quasi contra sua natura, a una voce tutte gridano a me, Padre eterno, di volere

essere separate dall'anima, e l'anima dal corpo" (Giuliana, *Il Dialogo della Divina Provvidenza: ovvero Libro della divina dottrina* Testi Cateriniani 1. 2nd ed. (Siena: Edizioni Cateriniane, 1995), 181; corresponds with fol. 135r in Edinburgh MS 87 (D b IV 18).

67 Karma Lochrie, *Margery Kempe and Translations of the Flesh* (Philadelphia: University of Pennsylvania Press, 1991), 85.

68 Hodgson argues that *The Orcherd*'s comparisons with Walter Hilton's mystical texts are so many and so close that the former's influence on the latter is highly probable. She also draws some clear comparisons between Julian's text and *The Orcherd*. See "The Orcherd of Syon and the English Mystical Tradition," esp. 243–8.

69 See Hodgson, "The Orcherd of Syon and the English Mystical Tradition," 249.

70 Patricia Dailey, *Promised Bodies: Time, Language, & Corporeality in Medieval Women's Mystical Texts* (New York: Columbia University Press, 2013), 73.

71 See Hodgson, "The Orcherd of Syon and the English Mystical Tradition," 233n2.

72 Hogdson, "The Orcherd of Syon and the English Mystical Tradition," 233n2.

73 There was a London rector of this name who founded a school in 1515 and who may be a candidate for the owner. See Arthur Francis Leach, *The Schools of Medieval England* (London: Methuen, 1915), 298. However, the name is common and shows up in various contexts.

74 Probably the printer and antiquarian Joseph Ames of London (1689–1759), author of *Typographical Antiquities* (1749).

75 Likely Richard How of Aspley in Bedfordshire (c. 1783–1812).

76 See my discussion in chapter 3 of this volume and my article, "The Many Misattributions of Catherine of Siena: Beyond *The Orcherd* in England," *The Journal of Medieval Religious Cultures* 41 (2015): 67–84.

77 Hodgson and Liegey, *The Orcherd of Syon*, 227; "Or fa che tu sempre ti unisca in me per affetto d'amore, però che Io so' somma ed terna purità e so' quel fuoco che purifico l'anima; e però quanto piú s'accosta a me tanto diventa piú pura, e quanto piú se ne parte tanto piú è immonda. E però caggiono in tante nequizie gli uomini del mondo perchè sono separati da me, ma l'anima che senza mezzo si unizce in me particpa della purità mia" (Cavallini, *Il Dialogo della Divina Provvidenza*, 242).

78 See chapter 2 in this volume for more on this.

79 See chapter 3 in this volume on the "Discernment of Spirits" for more on this section of the *Dialogo*.

80 This has been misidentified as part 1, chapter 12, in a few places, but this must be due to an original typo, as there is no chapter 12. "And þere I

shewide þee þat no penaunce which a deedly body may suffre, þat is
to seye, þat þat peyne oonly, so not sufficient to make satisfaccioun for
synne and for peyne for synne, but it be oonyd or ioyned wiþ desier or
wiþ affeccioun of charite and wiþ erry contricioun and displesaunce of
synnes. While þe penaunce is knyt to charite þanne þat penaunce makeþ
satisfaccioun, not by þe vertu oonli of actual peyne which a man suffreþ
but for sorrow þat a man haþ for sunne and for þe meryte of his charyte.
Which charyte a soule haþ purchasid wiþ a riȝt herte and wiþ a liberal and
fre liȝt of intellecte, biholdynge in me, which am þat charyte" (Hodgson
and Liegey, *The Orcherd of Syon*, 44); "T'ò dichiarato in che modo sí sodisfa
la colpa e la pena in te e nel prossimo tuo, dicendoti che – le pene che
sostiene la creatura mentre che è nel corpo mortale – non è sofficiente la
pena in sè sola a satsifare la colpa e la pena, se già ella non fosse unita con
l'affetto della carità e con la vera contrizione e dispiacimento del peccato,
come detto t'ò. Ma la pena allora satisfa quando è unita con la carità;
non per virtú di veruna pena attuale che si sostenga, ma per virtú della
carità e dolore della colpa commessa. La quale carità è acquistata col lume
dell'intelletto, con cuoure schietto e liberale, raguardando in me, obieto,
che so' essa carità" (Cavallini, *Il Dialogo della Divina Provvidenza*, 31);
corresponds with Edinburgh MS 87 (D b IV 18), fol. 29r.
81 Manchester, Rylands MS Latin 395, fol. 70v.
82 Several copies of the book survive, and it is available in PDF on the
Early English Books Online database (STC 4815–30). See Hodgson, "*The
Orcherd of Syon* and the English Mystical Tradition," 231, for more on the
comparison between Harley 3432 and de Worde's edition.
83 C. Annette Grisé, "'Moche profitable unto religious persones, gathered by
a brother of Syon': Syon Abbey and English Books," in *Syon Abbey and Its
Books*, Jones and Walsham, 131.
84 Wynkyn de Worde's *The Orcherd of Syon*, fol. 1r, British Museum copy, as
accessed through EEBO.
85 See Martha W. Driver, "Bridgettine Woodcuts in Printed Books Produced
for the English Market," in *Art into Life: Collected Papers from the Kresge
Art Museum Medieval Symposia*, Carol Garrett Fisher and Kathleen L.
Scott, eds. (East Lansing: Michigan State University Press, 1995), 249. See
also Schultze, "Translating St. Catherine of Siena in Fifteenth-Century
England."
86 Alexandra da Costa, *Reforming Printing: Syon Abbey's Defence of Orthodoxy
1525–1534* (Oxford: Oxford University Press, 2012), 143.
87 Martha Driver, "Pictures in Print: Late Fifteenth- and Early Sixteenth-
Century English Religious Books for Lay Readers," in *De Cella in Seculum:*

Religious and Secular Life and Devotion in Late Medieval England, Michael Sargent, ed. (Cambridge: D.S. Brewer, 1989), 242. See also David Griffith, "The Reception of Continental Women Mystics in Fifteenth- and Sixteenth-Century England: Some Artistic Evidence," in *The Medieval Mystical Tradition in England: Exeter Symposium VII*, E.A. Jones, ed. (Cambridge: D.S. Brewer, 2004), 97–118.

88 Driver, "Pictures in Print,"241. She also writes about this image in "Bridgettine Woodcuts in Printed Books Produced for the English Market," as well as in her book *The Image in Print: Book Illustration in Late Medieval England and Its Sources* (London: The British Library, 2004), esp. 140–50.

89 David Wallace discusses another woodcut from *The Orcherd* in "Nuns," in *Cultural Reformations: Medieval and Renaissance Literary History*, Brian Cummings and James Simpson, eds. (Oxford: Oxford University Press, 2010), 502–26. At least one copy of *The Orcherd* had the woodcuts painted over with watercolours, perhaps meant as a presentation copy for Syon Abbey. See Martha W. Driver, "Woodcuts and Decorative Techniques," in *A Companion to the Early Printed Book in Britain 1476–1558*, Vincent Gillespie and Susan Powell, eds. (Cambridge: D.S. Brewer, 2014), 96n5.

90 Wynkyn de Worde's *The Orcherd of Syon*, fol. 176.

91 Hodgson and Liegey, *The Orcherd of Syon*, 1.

92 Krug, *Reading Families*, 199–200.

93 Mary Erler, *Women, Reading, and Piety in Late Medieval England* (Cambridge: University of Cambridge Press, 2002), 46–7.

94 da Costa, *Reforming Printing*, 78–9.

95 de Worde, *The Orcherd of Syon*, fol. 2r.

96 de Worde, *The Orcherd of Syon*, fol. 3r.

97 C. Annette Grisé, "'In the Blessid Vyneȝard of Oure Holy Saueour': Female Religious Readers and Textual Reception in *The Myroure of Oure Ladye* and *The Orcherd of Syon*," in *The Medieval Mystical Tradition: Exeter Symposium VI*, Marion Glasscoe, ed. (Cambridge: D.S. Brewer, 1999), 208.

98 Eamon Duffy writes that both images of Catherine and Bridget appear to be taken from woodcuts used in Wynkyn de Worde publications, in Eamon Duffy, *The Stripping of the Altars: Traditional Religion in England 1400–1580* (New Haven: Yale University Press, 1992), 86. However, this is more clearly the case in Bridget's image than Catherine's, where the image has been badly defaced, and it is not altogether clear that the image is of her as it lacks a name and her traditional iconography.

99 Duffy, *The Stripping of the Altars*, 168.

100 Duffy, *The Stripping of the Altars*, 86.
101 Denise L. Despres, "Ecstatic Reading and Missionary Mysticism: *The Orcherd of Syon*," in *Prophets Abroad: The Reception of Continental Holy Women in Late-Medieval England*, Rosalynn Voaden, ed. (Woodbridge: D.S. Brewer, 1996), 155.
102 Grisé, "'In the Blessid Vyneȝard of Oure Holy Saueour,'" 199.
103 Grisé, "'In the Blessid Vyneȝard of Oure Holy Saueour,'" 204.
104 Gillespie, "1412–1534: Culture and History," 171. Elizabeth Barton is discussed in more detail in the conclusion.
105 Hogg, *The Rewyll of Seynt Sauiour*, 11.
106 Hodgson and Liegey, *The Orcherd of Syon*, 189; "Questo t'ò detto, dolcissima figliuola mia, per farti cognoscere la perfezione di questo stato unitivo dove, l'occhio de l'intelleto rapito dal fuoco della mia carità, nella quale carità ricevono il lume sopranturale, con esso lume amano me, perchè l'amore va dietro all'intelletto, e quanto piú ama, piú cognosce. Così l'uno nutrica l'altro" (Cavallini, *Il Dialogo della Divina Provvidenza*, 195); corresponds with Edinburgh, MS 87 (D b IV 18), fols 142v–143r.
107 Hodgson and Liegey, *The Orcherd of Syon*, 271. The full passage reads: "Hora t'ò mostrato, carissima figliuola, una sprizza de l'eccellenzia loro – una sprizza dico, per rispectto di quello che ella è – e narra'ti della dignità nella quale Io gli ò posti, perchè gli ò eletti e fatti miei ministri. E per quest dignità e autorità che Io ò data a loro, Io non voleva nè voglio che sieno toccati per veruno loro difetto per mano de'secolari, e toccandogli offendono me miserabilemente. Ma voglio che gli abbino in debita reverenzia: non loro per loro, come detto t'ò, ma per me, cioè per l'autorità che Io l'ò mai, perché in loro diminuisca la virtú, ne' virtuosi. De' quali Io t'ò narrato delle virtú loro, e postoteli ministratori del sole cioè del corpo e del sangue del mio Figliuolo, e degli altri sacramenti. Questa dignità tocca a' buoni e a' gattivi, ogni uno l'à a ministrare, come detto è" (Cavallini, *Il Dialogo della Divina Provvidenza*, 298–9); corresponds with Edingburgh MS 87 (D b IV 18), fol. 197r.
108 The word "menusid" here is from the verb "minishen," which means to be reduced or diminished (see MED "minishen"), https://quod.lib.umich.edu/cgi/m/mec/med-idx?size=First+100&type=headword&q1=minishen&rgxp=constrained, accessed 14 February 2018.

5. Catherine in Print: Lay Audiences and Reading Hagiography

1 Raymond of Capua, *The Life of Catherine of Siena*, Conleth Kearns, O.P., ed. and trans. (Washington, DC: Dominicana Publications, 1994), 7. The

Latin is available through the Acta Sanctorum, BHL Number 1702, and more recently through Raimondo da Capua, *Legenda maior sive Legenda Admirabilis Virginis Catherine de Senis*, Silvia Nocentini, ed. (Firenze: Sismel, 2013). As the latter is a critical edition, I will be using it rather than the AASS. The Latin reads, "quod in corpore muliebri, tam macerato vigiliis et inedia potius dat michi signum miraculi et infusionis supercelestis, quam cuiuscumque naturalis virtutis" (Raimondo da Capua, *Legenda maior*, 120).

2 Raymond of Capua, *The Life of Catherine of Siena*, 7; "Insuper, si quis respiciat librum, quem Spiritu sancto manifeste dictante composuit in idiomate proprio, quis possit imaginari aut credere illum factum per feminam?" (Raimondo da Capua, *Legenda maior*, 120).

3 The early modern translation done by John Fenn (1609) examined more closely in the next chapter is based on Lancellotto Politi's version, which also does not include it, but for de Worde, it appears to have been a deliberate choice.

4 The Wykyn de Worde edition has been edited by Carl Horstmann: see Carl Horstmann, ed., "The Lyf of Saint Katherin of Senis: nach dem Drucke W. Caxtons (c. 1493)," *Archiv für das Studium der Neueren Sprachen und Litteraturen* 76 (1886), 33–112, 265–314, 353–91. A PDF of the de Worde may also be accessed through EEBO STC (2nd ed.) 24766 for the 1492 edition, STC (2nd ed.) 24766.3 for the 1500 edition.

5 Silvia Nocentini, "La Tradizione Della 'Legenda maior,'" in Raimondo da Capua, *Legenda maior*, 4.

6 F. Thomas Luongo, "The Historical Reception of Catherine of Siena," in *A Companion to Catherine of Siena*, Carolyn Muessig, George Ferzoco, and Berverly Mayne Kienzle, eds. (Leiden: Brill, 2012), 27.

7 Excerpts of the Caffarini *Legenda minor* in Latin are in Bodleian Library, MS Digby 180 (fifteenth century), taking up the first thirty folios. The hand is Italian, although there is also an Anglican hand in the manuscript, so its provenance is unclear. See A.G. Watson, ed., *Bodleian Library Quarto Catalogues IX: Digby Manuscripts* (Oxford: Bodleian Library, 1999), 192–3. For Raymond's own strategies to promote Catherine's canonization in his *Legenda major*, see Beverly Mayne Kienzle, "Catherine of Siena, Preaching, and Hagiography in Renaissance Tuscany," in *A Companion to Catherine of Siena*, Muessig, Ferzoco, and Mayne Kienzle, 127–54.

8 Chiara Frugoni, "Female Mystics, Visions, and Iconography," *Women and Religion in Medieval and Renaissance Italy*, Daniel Bornstein and Roberto Rusconi, eds., and Margery J. Schneider, trans. (Chicago: University of Chicago Press, 1996), 152.

9 See Silvia Nocentini, "'Pro Solatio Illicteratorum': The Earliest Italian Translations of the *Legenda maior*," in *Catherine of Siena: The Creation of a*

Cult, Jeffrey Hamburger and Gabriel Signori, eds. (Turnhout: Brepols, 2013), 169–83, for a description of the Italian circulation; Thomas Brakmann, "The Transmission of the Upper German Life of Catherine of Siena," in *Catherine of Siena: The Creation of a Cult*, Hamburger and Signori, 83–108, for the German; and Jeffrey F. Hamburger and Gabriela Signori, "The Making of a Saint: Catherine of Siena, Tomaso Caffarini, and the Others – Introduction," In *Catherine of Siena: The Creation of a Cult*, Hamburger and Signori, 1–23, for a description of the French circulation. Also, Nocentini, "La Tradizione della 'Legenda maior,'" 1–114, which lays out the surviving manuscripts of the *Legenda major.*

10 There are excerpts of Raymond's *vita* in Oxford, Bodleian Library, Canon Misc. 205, which is a fifteenth-century manuscript of Italian provenance. Some seventy folios of the codex are parts of the *vita*, and it also contains some sections from Catherine's *Dialogo* and William Flete's sermon on Catherine. See Nocentini, "La Tradizione della 'Legenda maior,'" 54.

11 Although there is no clear picture of how many copies would have been in a print run, the estimated numbers run anywhere from 100 to 500; the labour involved in setting up the type and reprinting a previous text would not have been undertaken without sufficient demand. See Eric White's data on fifteenth-century printers in "Researching Print Runs," *Consortium of European Libraries*, https://www.cerl.org/resources/ links_to_other_resources/bibliographical_data#researching_print_runs, accessed 29 December 2015.

12 For more on this, see Thomas Luongo, "Catherine of Siena: Rewriting Female Holy Authority," in *Women, the Book and the Godly: Selected Proceedings of the St. Hilda's Conference, 1993*, vol. 1, Lesley Smith and Jane J.M. Taylor, eds. (Woodbridge: D.S. Brewer, 1995), 92.

13 The other books printed in these first two years are *The Book of Courtesy* (a reprint of Caxton's edition); *The Treatise of Love, The Chastising of God's Children*, a reprint of *The Golden Legend*; and John Mirk's *Liber Festivalis*. For more on the early English printing tradition, see William Kuskin, ed., *Caxton's Trace: Studies in the History of English Printing* (Notre Dame: University of Notre Dame Press, 2006); Vincent Gillespie and Susan Powell, eds., *A Companion to the Early Printed Book in Britain 1476–1558* (Woodbridge: D.S. Brewer, 2014); Alexandra Gillespie and Daniel Wakelin, eds., *The Production of Books in England 1350–1500* (Cambridge: Cambridge University Press, 2011); and Alexandra Gillespie, *Print Culture and the Medieval Author: Chaucer, Lydgate, and Their Books 1473–1557* (Oxford: Oxford University Press, 2006). Biographical information on Wynkyn de Worde is taken from Oxford Dictionary of National Biography, http://www.oxforddnb.com/, accessed 2 April 2014. This site requires opening an account for access.

14 See Lotte Hellinga, *William Caxton and Early Printing in England* (London: The British Library, 2010), 132. See also William N. West, "Old News: Caxton, de Worde, and the Invention of the Edition," in *Caxton's Trace: Studies in the History of English Printing,* William Kuskin, ed. (Notre Dame: University of Notre Dame Press, 2006), 241–74.

15 George R. Keiser, "The Mystics and the Early English Printers: The Economics of Devotionalism," in *The Medieval Mystical Tradition in England: Exeter Symposium IV, Papers Read at Dartington Hall, July 1987,* Marion Glasscoe, ed. (Cambridge: D.S. Brewer, 1987), 23.

16 See chapter 2 for more on William Flete. For more on de Worde's *Chastising,* see Steven Rozenski, "The Chastising of God's Children from Manuscript to Print," *Études Anglaises* 66 (2013): 369–78.

17 See Hellinga, *William Caxton and Early Printing in England,* esp. 158–62.

18 See chapter 1 for more on Arundel's Lambeth Constitutions.

19 For more information on de Worde's version of Margery Kempe's book, see Sue Ellen Holbrook, "Margery Kempe and Wynkyn de Worde," in *The Medieval Mystical Tradition in England: Exeter Symposium IV, Papers Read at Dartington Hall, July 1987,* Glasscoe, 27–46.

20 See Brenda M. Hosington, "Women Translators and the Early Printed Book," in *A Companion to the Early Printed Book in Britain 1476–1558,* Gillespie and Powell, 248–71; Rebecca Krug, *Reading Families: Women's Literature Practice in Late Medieval England* (Ithaca: Cornell University Press, 2002), esp. chap. 2, "Margaret Beaufort's Literate Practice: Service and Self-Inscription"; Susan Powell, "Margaret Beaufort and Her Books," *The Library,* 6th series, 20 (1998): 197–240; and C. Annette Grisé, "Holy Women in Print: Continental Female Mystics and the English Mystical Tradition," in *The Medieval Mystical Tradition: Exeter Symposium VII,* E.A. Jones, ed. (Woodbridge: D.S. Brewer, 2004), 83–95.

21 For more on Syon Abbey, see chapter 4.

22 See Vincent Gillespie and A.I. Doyle, eds., *Syon Abbey with the Libraries of the Carthusians* (London: The British Library, 2001), 246.

23 See Alexandra Barratt, "The Revelations of St. Elizabeth of Hungary: Problems of Attribution," *The Library,* 6th series, 14 (1992): 1–11, and the introduction to Sarah McNamer, ed., *The Two Middle English Translations of the Revelations of St. Elizabeth of Hungary* (Heidelberg: Universitätsverlag Winter, 1996).

24 Alexandra Barratt, "Continental Women Mystics and English Readers," in *The Cambridge Companion to Medieval Women's Writings,* Carolyn Dinshaw and David Wallace, eds. (Cambridge: Cambridge University Press, 2003), 248.

25 See the introduction to this volume for more on this. See also C.A.J. Armstrong, *England, France and Burgundy in the Fifteenth Century* (London: The Hambledon Press, 1983), 151.

26 For more on this, see Shannon McSheffrey, "Heresy, Orthodoxy and English Vernacular," *Past & Present* 186 (2005): 47–80, esp. 57.

27 See Andrew Hope, "The Printed Book Trade in Response to Luther," in *A Companion to the Early Printed Book in Britain 1476–1558*, Gillespie and Powell, 274.

28 For an overview of print censorship in England from Arundel's Lambeth Constitutions to the Reformation, see Thomas Betteridge, "Thomas More, Print and the Idea of Censorship," in *A Companion to the Early Printed Book in Britain 1476–1558*, Gillespie and Powell, 290–306. See also the conclusion of this volume for more on this subject and how it relates specifically to Catherine's texts printed during and post-Reformation.

29 See, for example, Roger Lovatt, "The 'Imitation of Christ' in Late Medieval England: The Alexander Prize Essay," in *Transactions of the Royal Historical Society*, 5th series, 18 (1968): 97–121.

30 The *Speculum Devotorum* can be found in Cambridge University Library, MS Gg 1.6, and Notre Dame University, MS 67.

31 Grisé, "Holy Women in Print," 85.

32 Jane Chance, *The Literary Subversions of Medieval Women* (New York: Palgrave, 2007), 106; Nancy Bradley Warren, *The Embodied Word: Female Spiritualities, Contested Orthodoxies, and English Religious Cultures, 1350–1700* (Notre Dame: University of Notre Dame Press, 2010), 22.

33 Gillespie, and Doyle, *Syon Abbey with the Libraries of the Carthusians*, 246.

34 Horstmann, "The Lyf of Saint Katherin of Senis," 33.

35 Horstmann, "The Lyf of Saint Katherin of Senis," 33.

36 Horstmann, "The Lyf of Saint Katherin of Senis," 34.

37 Alexandra Barratt, "English Translations of Didactic Literature for Women to 1550," *What Nature Does Not Teach: Didactic Literature in the Medieval and Early-Modern Periods*, J.F. Ruys, ed. (Turnhout: Brepols, 2008), 299–300.

38 See Mary C. Erler, *Women, Reading, and Piety in Late Medieval England* (Cambridge: University of Cambridge Press, 2002).

39 See, for example, Anne F. Sutton, "The Acquisition and Disposal of Books for Worship and Pleasure by Mercers of London in the Later Middle Ages" in *Manuscripts and Printed Books in Europe 1350–1550: Packaging, Presentation and Consumption*, Emma Cayley and Susan Powell, eds. (Liverpool: Liverpool University Press, 2013), 95–114.

40 Horstmann, "The Lyf of Saint Katherin of Senis," 34.

41 For more on this, see Constant J. Mews, "Thomas Aquinas and Catherine of Siena: Emotion, Devotion and Mendicant Spiritualities in the Late Fourteenth Century," *Digital Philology* 1.2 (2012): 235–52.

42 Maiju Lehmijoki-Gardner, "Denial as Action – Penance and its Place in the Life of Catherine of Siena," *A Companion to Catherine of Siena*, Muessig, Ferzoco, and Mayne Kienzle, 118.

43 Phyllis Hodgson and Gabriel M. Liegey, eds., *The Orcherd of Syon*, Early English Text Society, 258 (Oxford: Oxford University Press, 1966), 18, is one of many examples of this change.

44 Horstmann, "The Lyf of Saint Katherin of Senis," 40; "Quod cum illa stupens intueretur, fixit pedem et in reverberatis obtutibus Salvatorem suum aspicebat utriusque hominis oculis amorose" (Raimondo da Capua, *Legenda maior*, 137).

45 Horstmann, "The Lyf of Saint Katherin of Senis," 40; "Illa vero quasi de gravi sompno evigilans, demissis parumper oculis, inquit: 'O si videres quod video, ab hac tam dulci visione me nullatenus impedires!'" (Raimondo da Capua, *Legenda maior*, 137).

46 Horstmann, "The Lyf of Saint Katherin of Senis," 40–1; "accensus siquidem iam erat in corde ipsius ignis divini amoris, cuius virtute intellectus illustrabatur, voluntas fervebat, confortabatur memoria et exteriores actus legis divine regulam in omnibus pretendebant, prout enum mihi, nimis indigno, ipsa humiliter confessa est in secreto" (Raimondo da Capua, *Legenda maior*, 137–8). Note that the Middle English attaches the last clause to the following sentence – the confessed moment is about the next episode, not this previous one.

47 Horstmann, "The Lyf of Saint Katherin of Senis," 41; "et potissime beati Dominici" (Raimondo da Capua, *Legenda maior*, 138).

48 Horstmann, "The Lyf of Saint Katherin of Senis," 41; "Querebat enim latibula et secrete quadam cordula suum corpusculum flagellabat, orationibus et meditationibus, iocis ex toto relictis, assidue intendebat" (Raimondo da Capua, *Legenda maior*, 138).

49 Horstmann, "The Lyf of Saint Katherin of Senis," 41; "et secum se pariter flagellabant ac" (Raimondo da Capua, *Legenda maior*, 138).

50 See Jeffrey Hamburger, *The Visual and the Visionary: Art and Female Spirituality in Late Medieval Germany* (New York: Zone Books, 1998), 464.

51 The following passage is missing entirely: "Primus numerus in perfectione precedit ceteros numeros, secundus vero universitatis numerus ab omnibus theologis appellatur. Quid igitur per hec datur intelligi, nisi quod virtutum omnium perfectionem universalem hec virgo erat a Domino receptura et per consequens perfectum culmen glorie possessura? Primus etenim dicit perfectionem, secundus universitatem, quid ergo ambo

simul dicere possunt, nisi perfectionem universalem? Propter quod recte vocatum est nomen eius Caterina, quod proprie universitatem significat, prout in prologo primo plenius tactum est" (Raimondo da Capua, *Legenda maior,* 141).

52 Horstmann, "The Lyf of Saint Katherin of Senis," 43; "Perpendisne lector quam ordinate disponebantur per illam sapientiam, que cuncta fortiter suaviterque disponit, huius virginis sacre dona et opera virtuousa?" (Raimondo da Capua, *Legenda maior,* 141).

53 For example, "Ex uno potes lector perpendere" (Raimondo da Capua, *Legenda maior,* 144) becomes "Loo ye, maydenis" (Horstmann, "The Lyf of Saint Katherin of Senis," 46). Although the word "maiden" can mean simply "virgin" in Middle English, its overwhelming usage was to define unmarried, virginal women. See the Middle English Dictionary, https://quod.lib.umich.edu/cgi/m/mec/med-idx?type=id&id=MED26501, accessed 19 January 2017.

54 Horstmann, "The Lyf of Saint Katherin of Senis," 44; "Nunc autem, hoc sacro voto peracto, noveris sanctam puellulam effici cotidie sanctiorem cepitque Christi tyruncula iam bellare cum carne, que tamen adhuc rebellare non ceperat, auferreque proposuit carnes carni saltem, quantum erat sibi possibile" (Raimondo da Capua, *Legenda maior,* 143).

55 Horstmann, ""The Lyf of Saint Katherin of Senis," 45; "Hic crevit in mente sua desiderium maximum intrandi ordinem illum, ut posset cum aliis fratribus animarum saluti prodesse, sed cum videret in hoc repugnantiam sexus, cogitavit frequentius, ut ipsa michi confessa est, beatam Eufrosinam, cuius nomen a casu fuerat sibi olim impositum, in hoc imitari; ut scilicet illa, fingens se masculum, intravit monasterium monacorum, sic ista, remotas partes accedens ubi esset ignota, fingendo se masculum ordinem predicatorum intraret, ubi posset subvenire pereuntibus animabus" (Raimondo da Capua, *Legenda maior,* 143).

56 See Raymond of Capua, *The Life of Catherine of Siena,* 38n13.

57 The Middle English is available in Carl Horstmann, ed., *Sammlung altenglischer Legenden* (Heilbronn: Henninger, 1878), 174–82. For more on the Anglo-Saxon version, see Steven Stallcup, "The Old English *Life of Saint Euphrosyne* and the Economics of Sanctity," in *Anonymous Interpolations in Aelfric's* Life of Saints, Robin Norris, ed., Old English Newsletter Subsidia 35 (Kalamazoo: Western Michigan University Press, 2011), 13–28.

58 Allison Clark Thurber estimates 80 per cent of the 230 hermits in and around Siena were women. See "Female Urban Reclusion in Siena at the Time of Catherine of Siena," in *A Companion to Catherine of Siena,* Muessig, Ferzoco, and Mayne Kienzle, 47.

59 Suzanne Noffke, ed. and trans., *The Letters of Catherine of Siena*, vol. 1 (Tempe: Medieval and Renaissance Texts & Studies, 2000–8), 79. For more on Catherine and William Flete, see chapter 2 of this volume.

60 Noffke, *The Letters of Catherine of Siena*, vol. 1, 79.

61 For more about Raymond's balancing of Catherine's two roles throughout the *Legenda major*, see John Coakley, "Managing Holiness: Raymond of Capua and Catherine of Siena," in *Women, Men, & Spiritual Power: Female Saints & Their Male Collaborators* (New York: Columbia University Press, 2006).

62 See, for more on this, Sara Poor, "Women Teaching Men in the Medieval Devotional Imagination," in *Partners in Spirit: Women, Men, and Religious Life in Germany, 1100–1550*, Fiona J. Griffiths and Julie Hotchin, eds. (Turnhout: Brepols, 2014) 339–65, where she explores the "Sister Catherine Treatise," which, while not explicitly about Catherine of Siena, gestures to her with the use of her name. See also Coakley, *Women, Men, & Spiritual Power*, as well as the collected essays in Catherine M. Mooney, ed., *Gendered Voices: Medieval Saints and Their Interpreters* (Philadelphia: University of Pennsylvania Press, 1999).

63 This is a relationship dynamic I have explored between Marie of Oignies and her confessor, James of Vitry in Jennifer N. Brown, "The Chaste Erotics of Marie of Oignies and Jacques de Vitry," *Journal of the History of Sexuality* 19 (2010): 74–93.

64 See Dyan Elliot, *The Bride of Christ Goes to Hell: Metaphor and Embodiment in the Lives of Pious Women, 200–1500* (Philadelphia: University of Pennsylvania Press, 2012), 215.

65 "Et quia scio quod licet mihi, postquam evolavit ad celum, ea, potissime que in laudem eius cedunt, quamvis tunc secreta fuerint, revelare, disputationem, que circa hoc erat inter eam et me, interserere hic decrevi" (Raimondo da Capua, *Legenda maior*, 146).

66 Horstmann, "The Lyf of Saint Katherin of Senis," 47; "Que respondit quod nec umquam hoc in cor suum ascendit. Iterum petivi utrum preter virginitatis propositum hoc fecerit ad complacendum alicui homini in speciali vel in generali hominibus omnibus. Que respondit quod nulla sibi tanta pena erat quam homines intueri aut ab ipsis videri, vel etiam ubi essent se invenire, unde quando discipuli patris in arte tyncture, qui cum ipso habitabant, venissent ad locum ubi fuisset ipsa, mox ita celeriter fugiebat sicut serpentes supervenissent, ita quod omnes admirabantur" (Raimondo da Capua, *Legenda maior*, 146).

67 Horstmann, "The Lyf of Saint Katherin of Senis," 57; Raimondo da Capua, *Legenda maior*, 158.

68 Horstmann, "The Lyf of Saint Katherin of Senis," 57; "Habebat etenim catenam quandam ferream sua latera sine medio circumdantem sive cingentem tam fortiter, quod fere intrinsecata carni cutem reddiderat circum, circa exustam …" (Raimondo da Capua, *Legenda maior,* 158).

69 Horstmann, "The Lyf of Saint Katherin of Senis," 61; "Invenit siquidem modum novum corpus proprium etiam inter delicias affligendum, nam, simulans se velle balneari perfectius, ad canale conductus unde aque sulfuree procedebant se conferebat et ferventes aquas super nudam et teneram carnem sufferens patienter, diu fortius corpusculum affligebat, quam quando ipsum cum catena ferrea verberabat" (Raimondo da Capua, *Legenda maior,* 164).

70 Horstmann, "The Lyf of Saint Katherin of Senis," 61; "Occurit nunc memorie quod dum semel mater sua michi coram ea de dicto balneo verba movisset, ipsa silenter ea que supra nunc scripta sunt retulit et addebat quod, ut posset hoc liberius agere, suggesserat matri quod volebat se postquam omnes recesserant balneare, sicut et faciebat. Sciebat enim quod presente matre hoc facere nullatenus potuisset. Cumque petissem ab ea quomodo potuisset tantos sutinere fervores absque mortis periculo, in sua columbina simplicitate respondit: 'Ego dum eram ibi cogitabam assidue de penis inferni et purgatorii orabamque Creatorem meum, quem tantum offenderam, quod dignaretur penas illas, quas me noveram meruisse, in istas quas libenter sustinebam misericorditer commmutare'" (Raimondo da Capua, *Legenda maior,* 164).

71 The de Worde volume begins part 2 after the excised preface from the *Legenda major*. Horstmann, "The Lyf of Saint Katherin of Senis," 85. The excised Latin can be seen in Raimondo da Capua, *Legenda maior,* 201–2.

72 Horstmann, "The Lyf of Saint Katherin of Senis," 33.

73 See Barry Windeatt, "1412–1534: Texts," in *The Cambridge Companion to Medieval English Mysticism*, Samuel Fanous and Vincent Gillespie, eds. (Cambridge: Cambridge University Press, 2011), 201.

74 Much work has been done on Margery Kempe and the parallels between her model saints, including Catherine of Siena. See, for example, David Wallace, "Mystics and Followers in Siena and East Anglia: A Study in Taxonomy, Class and Cultural Mediation," in *The Medieval Mystical Tradition in England: VII*, Marion Glasscoe, ed. (Cambridge: D.S. Brewer, 1984), 169–91; Chance, *The Literary Subversions of Medieval Women*, chap. 5, "Unhomely Margery Kempe and St. Catherine of Siena: 'Communycacyon' and 'Conuersacion' as Homily," 99–126; and David Russell, "Religious Mystical Mothers: Margery Kempe and Caterina Benincasa," in *The Medieval Mystical Tradition in England: Exeter Symposium VIII*, E.A. Jones,

ed. (Woodbridge: D.S. Brewer, 2013), 75–92; Diane Watt, *Secretaries of God: Women Prophets in Late Medieval and Early Modern England* (Cambridge: D.S. Brewer, 1997), esp. chap. 2, "A Prophet in Her Own Country: Margery Kempe and the Medieval Tradition"; John H. Arnold and Katherine J. Lewis, eds., *A Companion to the Book of Margery Kempe* (Cambridge: D.S. Brewer, 2004); and Karma Lochrie, *Margery Kempe and Translations of the Flesh* (Philadelphia: University of Pennsylvania Press, 1991).

75 Roger Ellis, "Text and Controversy: In Defence of St. Birgitta of Sweden," in *Text and Controversy from Wyclif to Bale: Essays in Honour of Anne Hudson*, Helen Barr and Ann M. Hutchison, eds. (Turnhout: Brepols, 2005), 321.

76 Lynn Staley, ed., *The Book of Margery Kempe* (Kalamazoo: TEAMS, in association with the University of Rochester by Medieval Institute Publications, Western Michigan University Press, 1996), 148–9, lines 3608–15.

77 Many people have written about Margery Kempe's tears and relationship to her body. For a nice overview of these debates, see the introduction to Liz Herbert McAvoy, *Authority and the Female Body in the Writings of Julian of Norwich and Margery Kempe* (Cambridge: D.S. Brewer, 2004).

78 See Heather Webb, "Lacrime Cordiali: Catherine of Siena on the Value of Tears," in *A Companion to Catherine of Siena*, Muessig, Ferzoco, and Mayne Kienzle, 99–112.

79 Horstmann, "The Lyf of Saint Katherin of Senis," 84; "Quod Dei unigenitus gratantissime annuens, anulum protulit aureum habentem in suo circulo quattuor margaritas ac adamantinam gemmam superpulcram in summitate inclusam" (Raimondo da Capua, *Legenda maior*, 198).

80 In Catherine's letters and subsequent depictions of this moment, the ring is described as being made of Jesus' foreskin, but this detail is in none of the extant English records. For more on this, see Robert P. Palazzo, "The Veneration of the Sacred Foreskin(s) of Baby Jesus – A Documented Analysis," in *Multicultural Europe and Cultural Exchange: In the Middle Ages and Renaissance*, James Helfers, ed. (Turnhout: Brepols, 2005), 169–70.

81 Horstmann, "The Lyf of Saint Katherin of Senis," 68; "Occurebat enim, quod nunc tempus est illius tertie bestie pellis leopardine, per quam ipocrite designantur, et quod diebus meis aliquas deceptiones inveneram et potissime in feminis, que agiliter vacillant in capite agiliusque seducuntur ab hoste, sicut patuit in prima omnium matre, pluraque similia menti tunc mee porrigebantur que ipsam fluctuare cogebant circa istam materiam" (Raimondo da Capua, *Legenda maior*, 176).

82 Horstmann, "The Lyf of Saint Katherin of Senis," 103; "Et hiis dictis mox spineum diadema cum utraque manu de Salvatoris manibus ferventer arripuit capitique suo violentia cum tanta imposuit, quod

spine violenter caput undique perforabant, adeo ut post hanc visionem pluribus diebus actualem dolorem capitis ex spinarum illarum punctura sentiret, ut ipsa testata est oraculo vive vocis" (Raimondo da Capua, *Legenda maior,* 232).

83 Horstmann, "The Lyf of Saint Katherin of Senis," 105; "… applicansque dexteram ad collum virgineum et ipsam ad lateris proprii vulnus appropians: 'Bibe' inquit 'filia de latere meo potum quo anima tua tanta suavitate replebitur, quod etiam in corpus, quod propter me contempsisti, mirabiliter redundabit'" (Raimondo da Capua, *Legenda maior,* 236).

84 Horstmann, "The Lyf of Saint Katherin of Senis," 270; "'Scitis pater qualiter Dominus illa die fecit anime mee, sicut facit mater filio parvulo, quem tenere diligit, ostendit sibi ubera et permictit stare a remotis ut ploret, dumque de fletu filii paulisper ridit, amplexatur eum et deosculans prebet sibi ubera letanter et abundanter. Sic' inquiebat 'fecit michi Dominus ille die, ostendebat enim mihi latus sacratissimum suum, sed a remotis" (Raimondo da Capua, *Legenda maior,* 256).

85 Hamburger, *The Visual and the Visionary,* 460.

86 Nicholas Watson and Jacqueline Jenkins, eds., *The Writings of Julian of Norwich: A Vision Showed to a Devout Woman and a Revelation of Love* (University Park: The Pennsylvania University State Press, 2006), 313.

87 This metaphor of Jesus-as-Mother is not without a theological history. See Caroline Walker Bynum, *Jesus as Mother: Studies in the Spirituality of the High Middle Ages* (Berkeley: University of California Press, 1982), esp. chap. 4.

88 Chance, *The Literary Subversions of Medieval Women,* 104–5.

89 Horstmann, "The Lyf of Saint Katherin of Senis," 86; "Scilicet quod possim ego misella et omni ex parte fragilis esse utilis animabus? Sexus enim contradicit ut nosti ex puribus causis, tum quia docere alios ad eum non pertinet, tum quia contemptibilis est coram hominibus, tum etiam quia honestate cogente non decet talem sexum cum sexu alio conversari" (Raimondo da Capua, *Legenda maior,* 204).

90 Horstmann, "The Lyf of Saint Katherin of Senis," 86; "Nonne sum ego ille qui humanum creavi genus sexusque formavi ac gratiam Spiritus mei ubi volo effundo? Non est apud me masculus et femina … Verum, quia scio quod non ex infidelitate sed ex humilitate sic loqueris, scire te volo quod isto in tempore tantum abundavit humana superbia et potissime illorum qui literatos et sapientes se reputant, quod iustitia mea non potest amplius substinere quin eos iudicio iusto suo confundat. Sed, quia misericordia mea est super omnia opera mea, primo dabo eis confusionem salubrem et utilem, si voluerint se recognoscendo humiliare" (Raimondo da Capua, *Legenda maior* 204–5).

91   Horstmann, "The Lyf of Saint Katherin of Senis," 86; "vasa fragilia"
     (Raimondo da Capua, *Legenda maior*, 205).
92   Raymond of Capua, *The Life of Catherine of Siena*, 117; "Non est apud
     me masculus et femina, nec plebeius et nobilis, sed cuncta equalia sunt
     coram me, quia cuncta equaliter possum. Sic enim mihi agile est creare
     angelum ut formicam et celos omnes sicut unum vermiculum facere;
     scriptumque est de me quod omnia quecumque volui feci, quia nullum
     intelligibile impossibile apud me potest esse" (Raimondo da Capua,
     Legenda maior, 204).
93   Watson and Jenkins, *The Writings of Julian of Norwich*, 75.
94   de Worde's four executers were all printers: Henry Watson, Henry
     Pepwell, John Gough, and John Gaver. See Lotte Hellinga, *William
     Caxton and Early Printing in England* (London: The British Library, 2010),
     179.
95   To see in what ways the de Worde edition (and by extension the Pepwell
     edition) takes excerpts from *The Book of Margery Kempe* to create a new
     text of hers, see Holbrook, "Margery Kempe and Wynkyn de Worde."
96   Alexandra Gillespie, "Henry Pepwell," *Oxford Dictionary of National
     Biography*, http://www.oxforddnb.com/view/article/21901, accessed 2
     April 2014. This site requires opening an account for access.
97   Hanna bases this on the observation that "the volume is equipped with
     seven separate title pages, but five of these appear inside the constituent
     quires in which Pepwell's compositor's set the book; one even occurs
     on the verso of a leaf." See Ralph Hanna, *English Medieval Book History:
     Manuscripts, Their Producers and Their Readers* (Liverpool: Liverpool
     University Press, 2013), 39.
98   Hanna, *English Medieval Book History*, 40.
99   Margaret Connolly and Raluca Radulescu, introduction to *Insular Books:
     Vernacular Manuscript Miscellanies in Late Medieval Britain, Proceedings of
     the British Academy*, vol. 201, Margaret Connolly and Raluca Radulescu,
     eds. (Oxford: Oxford University Press, 2015), 29.
100 Edmund G. Gardner, *The Cell of Self-Knowledge: Seven Early English
     Mystical Treatises Printed by Henry Pepwell in 1521* (London: Chatto and
     Windus, 1910).
101 Page 16r. EEBO edition "Richard of St. Victor" STC 20972. See Gardner,
     The Cell of Self-Knowledge, 37. I've taken the quotations here from
     Gardner, as the spelling is slightly modernized.
102 16v, EEBO edition. See Gardner, *The Cell of Self-Knowledge*, 37.
103 Grisé, "Holy Women in Print, 93.
104 17v–18r, EEBO. See Gardner, *The Cell of Self-Knowledge*, 40; "Porro ex hac
     coniunctione doctrix hec discipline Dei unam aliam inferebat, quam non

cessabat hiis quos in via Dei volebat instruere cotidie replicare, quod videlicet talis anima, sicut supra dicimus, Deo coniuncta quantum habet de amore Dei, tantum habet de odio sancto partis proprie sensitive, sive proprie sensualitatis, quia enim ex amore Dei naturaliter procedit odium culpe que contra Deum commictitur. Videns anima fomitem et originem omnis culpe in parte sensitiva regnare, in ipsaque sancto movetur odio contra eam conaturque totis viribus non occidere ipsam, sed fomitem illum radicatum in ea. Quod tanem fieri non potest absque sensualitatis afflictione non parva nec brevi. Verum quia fieri non potest quin semper remaneat aliqua radix saltem parvarum culparum, iuxta illud Iohannis *si dixerimus quod peccatum non habemus* etc., concipit quamdam displicentiam de se ipsa, ex qua oritur odium sanctum iam dictum et contemptus sui ipsius et hominum. Nichil est enim quod tantum teneat animan securam et fortem quantum odium illud sanctum, quod volebat exprimere apostolus cum dicebat: '*cum infirmor tunc fortior sum*'" (Raimondo da Capua, *Legenda maior*, 187). This passage is also discussed in relation to "The Cleannesse of Sowle" in chapter 3 of this volume.

105   Horstmann, "The Lyf of Saint Katherin of Senis," 79; "Primoque inchoant a temptatione carnali, quam non tantum per cogitationes immictunt interius, non solum per illusiones et fantasias in somnis, sed per apertas visiones quas, assumptis corporibus aereis, suis oculis et auribus ingerebant modis sibi multimodis ministrabant. Horror est prelia illa redicere, sed victoriam audire pyris mentibus nimis delectabile invenitur" (Raimondo da Capua, *Legenda maior*, 190). This passage is also discussed in relation to William Flete in chapter 2 of this volume.

106   20r–v, EEBO. See Gardner, *The Cell of Self-Knowledge*, 45–6.

107   21v, EEBO. See Gardner, *The Cell of Self-Knowledge*, 46–7.

108   For Wynkyn de Worde, see EEBO "Kempe, Margery," STC 14924; for Pepwell, see "Richard of St. Victor," STC 20972.

109   Lochrie, *Margery Kempe and Translations of the Flesh*, 224.

110   To see other ways in which Margery Kempe and Catherine of Siena can intersect, see Russell, "Religious Mystical Mothers."

111   Grisé, "Holy Women in Print, 93.

112   Gardner, *The Cell of Self-Knowledge*, xxi. Grisé writes that this excerpted version of Margery is in fact exactly what Pepwell and others have done to Catherine and other mystical writers, distilling long and unwieldy texts to an essential bit that inspires prayer and devotion. See Grisé, "Holy Women in Print," 94.

113   Jennifer Summit, *Lost Property: The Woman Writer and English Literary History, 1380–1589* (Chicago: University of Chicago Press, 200), 133.

114   Summit does reference the Catherine texts in her book, but misattributes the Pepwell excerpts to *Il Dialogo* (or actually *The Orcherd of Syon*) rather than the *vita*. Summit, *Lost Property*, 128–9.
115   Summit, *Lost Property*, 137–8.
116   I will explore the post-Reformation role of Catherine in more detail in chapter 5 of this volume.
117   See chapter 3 of this volume for a discussion of Catherine's "Discernment of Spirits."

Conclusion – Reforming Reading: Catherine of Siena in an Age of Reform

1   See James Simpson, "1534–1550s: Texts," in *The Cambridge Companion to Medieval English Mysticism*, Samuel Fanous and Vincent Gillespie, eds. (Cambridge: Cambridge University Press, 2011), 250–1.
2   For more on both sides of the book trade pre- and post-Reformation, see *A Companion to the Early Printed Book in Britain 1476–1558*, Vincent Gillespie and Susan Powell, eds. (Woodbridge: D.S. Brewer, 2014), including Andrew Hope, "The Printed Book Trade in Response to Luther," 272–89; Thomas Betteridge, "Thomas More, Print and the Idea of Censorship," 290–306; and Lucy Wooding, "Catholicism, the Printed Book and the Marian Restoration," 307–24.
3   Euan K. Cameron, "Ways of Knowing in the Pre-and Post-Reformation Worlds," *Mysticism and Reform, 1400–1750*, Sara S. Poor and Nigel Smith, eds. (Notre Dame: University of Notre Dame Press, 2015), 30.
4   Genelle C. Gertz, "Quaker Mysticism as the Return of the Medieval Repressed: English Women Prophets before and after the Reformation," in *Mysticism and Reform, 1400–1750*, Poor and Smith, 185.
5   Tyndale, as quoted in Alexandra da Costa, *Reforming Printing: Syon Abbey's Defence of Orthodoxy 1525–1534* (Oxford: Oxford University Press, 2012), 80.
6   See Vincent Gillespie, "'Hid Diuinite': The Spirituality of the English Syon Brethren," in *The Medieval Mystical Tradition in England; Exeter Symposium VII: Papers Read at Charney Manor*, E.A. Jones, ed. (Woodbridge: D.S. Brewer, 2004), 189–206. Alexandra da Costa writes, "In the strictly enclosed environment at Syon, the work of Betson and his successors could only come to the printers with the sanction, if not the instruction, of the Abbess and General Confessor," in *Reforming Printing*, 41.
7   See da Costa, *Reforming Printing*, 42.
8   See chapter 4 of this volume. See also da Costa, *Reforming Printing*, and Martha W. Driver, "Bridgettine Woodcuts in Printed Books Produced for

the English Market," in *Art into Life: Collected Papers from the Kresge Art Museum Medieval Symposia*, Carol Garrett Fisher and Kathleen L. Scott, eds. (East Lansing: Michigan State University Press, 1995), 249. See also Dirk Schultze, "Translating St. Catherine of Siena in Fifteenth-Century England," In *Catherine of Siena: The Creation of a Cult*, Jeffrey Hamburger and Gabriel Signori, eds. (Turnhout: Brepols, 2013), 185–212.

9 *The Dyetary of Ghostly Helthe*, EEBO, STC 6836.881, fol. 8r.

10 Thomas Godfray was a London printer who is known to have printed only about thirty works, including a copy of *Chaucer's Works* in 1531. Generally, he does not seem to have had the interest in devotional texts that de Worde had. See also C.A. Grisé, "Richard Whytford, *The Golden Epistle*, and the Mixed Life Audience," *The Medieval Mystical Tradition in England: Papers Read at Charney Manor, July 2011 (Exeter Symposium 8)*, E.A. Jones, ed. (Woodbridge: Boydell and Brewer, 2013), 195–208.

11 Brandon Alakas "'Closed and kept most surely in religion': Piety and Politics in Richard Whitford's *The Pype, or Tonne, of the Lyfe of Perfection*," *Renaissance and Reformation / Renaiassance et Réforme* 36 (2013): 99.

12 James Hogg, ed., *Richard Whytford*, vol. 5, *A Werke for Housholders, A Dayly Exercyse and Experyence of Dethe* (Salzburg: Institut Für Anglistik und Amerikanistik Universität Salzburg, 1979), 64.

13 Hogg, *Richard Whytford*, vol. 5, 97–8.

14 For more on this text, see Alakas, "'Closed and kept most surely in religion."

15 STC 14533.

16 See Jennifer N. Brown, *Three Women of Liège: A Critical Edition of and Commentary on the Middle English Lives of Elizabeth of Spalbeek, Christina Mirabilis, and Marie d'Oignies* (Turnhout: Brepols, 2008).

17 da Costa, *Reforming Printing*, 138.

18 See E.J. Devereux, "Elizabeth Barton and Tudor Censorship," *Bulletin of the John Rylands Library* 49 (1966–7): 91–106.

19 An edition of the sermon can be found in L.E. Whatmore, "The Sermon against the Holy Maid of Kent and Her Adherents, Delivered at Paul's Cross November the 23rd, 1533, and at Canterbury, December the 7th," *The English Historical Review* 58 (1943): 463–75.

20 Whatmore, "The Sermon against the Holy Maid of Kent and Her Adherents,"469.

21 Whatmore, "The Sermon against the Holy Maid of Kent and Her Adherents," 469.

22 Barry Windeatt, "1412–1534: Texts," in *The Cambridge Companion to Medieval English Mysticism*, Fanous and Gillespie, 218.

23 Rev. Henry Jenkins, ed., *The Remains of Thomas Cranmer, D.D. Archbishop of Canterbury* (Oxford, Oxford University Press, 1833), 118, Letter 119.

24 E.A. Jones, *England's Last Medieval Monastery: Syon Abbey 1415–2015* (Leominster: Gracewing, 2015), 45–7.

25 Diane Watt, "Reconstructing the Word: The Political Prophecies of Elizabeth Barton (1506–1534)," *Renaissance Quarterly* 50.1 (1997): 157.

26 See Diane Watt, *Secretaries of God: Women Prophets in Late Medieval and Early Modern England* (Cambridge: D.S. Brewer, 1997), 69–70. See also, Diane Watt, "The Prophet at Home: Elizabeth Barton and the Influence of Bridget of Sweden and Catherine of Siena," in *Prophets Abroad: The Reception of Continental Holy Women in Late-Medieval England*, Rosalynn Voaden, ed. (Cambridge: D.S. Brewer, 1996), 161–76; Nancy Bradley Warren, *Women of God and Arms: Female Spirituality and Political Conflict, 1380–1600* (Philadelphia: University of Pennsylvania Press, 2005), esp. chap. 5, "The Mystic, the Monarch, and the Persistence of 'The Medieval': Elizabeth Barton and Henry VIII," for further analysis on this event.

27 Elizabeth Frances Rogers, ed., *The Correspondence of Sir Thomas More* (Princeton: Princeton University Press, 1947), 483–4, Letter 197.

28 Rogers, *The Correspondence of Sir Thomas More*, 466, Letter 192.

29 This text shows the influence of St Bridget's *Revelations*, as described by Mary Erler in "'A Revelation of Purgatory' (1422): Reform and the Politics of Female Visions," *Viator* 38.1 (2007): 321–47.

30 For more information on English nuns exiled during and after the Reformation, see Caroline Bowden, ed., *English Convents in Exile, 1600–1800*, vols. 1–3 (London: Pickering and Chatto, 2012).

31 See Jenna Lay, *Beyond the Cloister: Catholic Englishwomen and Early Modern Literary Culture* (Philadelphia: University of Pennsylvania Press, 2016).

32 Ann Hutchinson, "Beyond the Margins: The Recusant Bridgettines," *Studies in St. Birgitta and the Brigittine Order, Analecta Cartusiana* 35.19 (1993): 275, and "Mary Champney: A Bridgettine Nun under the Rule of Queen Elizabeth I," *Birgittiania* 13 (2002): 3–89, for an introduction to an edition of the text.

33 Frances E. Dolan, *Whores of Babylon: Catholicism, Gender, and Seventeenth-Century Print Culture* (Ithaca: Cornell University Press, 1999), 27.

34 Lay, *Beyond the Cloister*, 17.

35 Thomas Robinson, *The Anatomy of the English Nunnery at Lisbon in Portugall* (London: Printed by George Purslowe, for Robert Mylbourne and Philemon Stephens, 1622), reprinted in 1623, 1630, 1637, and 1662, accessed via EEBO, 28 August 2017. See also Lay, *Beyond the Cloister*, chap. 2.

36 Mary Erler, *Reading and Writing during the Dissolution: Monks, Friars, and Nuns 1530–1558* (Cambridge: Cambridge University Press, 2013), 11.

37 See Arthur F. Marotti, "Saintly Idiocy and Contemplative Empowerment: The Example of Dame Gertrude More," in *Mysticism and Reform, 1400–1750,* Poor and Smith, 151–76. For More's own book, see *The holy practises of a devine lover,* EEBO Wing / M2631A, accessed 15 February 2017.

38 Augustine Baker, *Sancta Sophia, or, Directions for the prayer of contemplation &c. extracted out of more then (sic) XL treatises / written by the late Ven. Father F. Augustin Baker, a monke of the English congregation of the Holy Order of S. Benedict, and methodically digested by the R.F. Serenvs Cressy of the same order and congregatiom* (1657) Wing / B480. EEBO. fols. 34 and 75, accessed 16 September 2017.

39 Ceri Sullivan, *Dismembered Rhetoric: English Recusant Writing, 1580 to 1603* (Madison, NJ: Fairleigh Dickinson University Press, 1995), 36.

40 A.C. Southern, *Elizabethan Recusant Prose 1559–1582* (London: Sands & Co., 1950), 34.

41 Biographical information taken from Dom Adam Hamilton, OSB, ed., *The Chronicle of the English Augustinian Canonesses Regular of the Lateran, at St. Monica's in Louvain (Now at St. Augustine's Priory, Newton Abbot, Devon) 1548 to 1625* (Edinburgh: Sands & Co., 1904), and the Oxford Dictionary of National Biography entry for John Fenn written by Peter E.B. Harri, http://www.oxforddnb.com/view/10.1093/ref:odnb/9780198614128.001.0001/odnb-9780198614128-e-9282?docPos=2, accessed 8 January 2016. This site requires opening an account for access.

42 John Fenn, trans., *The Life of the Blessed Virgin, Sainct Catharine of Siena* (Leuven, 1609), 1; EEBO, STC (2nd ed. 4830), accessed 14 February 2018.

43 Lancellotto de' Politi was also known as Ambrosisu Catharinus Politus, a name he took in homage to Catherine of Siena. See Carolyn Muessig, Introduction to *A Companion to Catherine of Siena*, 11. n.53. This is the "Doctor Caterinus Senensis" referred to in the preface here, not Catherine herself.

44 John is also known in some documents as Roger Heigham.

45 Information about John Heigham taken from Paul Arblaster, "John Heigham," *Oxford Dictionary of National Biography*, http://www.oxforddnb.com.w.ezproxy.nypl.org/view/article/12868?docPos=3, accessed 13 November 2015.

46 Fenn, *The Life of the Blessed Virgin, Sainct Catharine of Siena*, 1.

47 Fenn, *The Life of the Blessed Virgin, Sainct Catharine of Siena*, 4.

48 Fenn, *The Life of the Blessed Virgin, Sainct Catharine of Siena*, 41–2.

49 Although "The Life and Good End of Sister Marie" shows that the nuns at Syon abroad were threatened by starvation and other mistreatment, which prompts the community to send its youngest nuns back to England. See Hutchinson, "Beyond the Margins, 268.

50 Fenn, *The Life of the Blessed Virgin, Sainct Catharine of Siena*, 57.

51 Fenn, *The Life of the Blessed Virgin, Sainct Catharine of Siena*, 57.

52 Fenn, *The Life of the Blessed Virgin, Sainct Catharine of Siena*, 275.

53 Fenn, *The Life of the Blessed Virgin, Sainct Catharine of Siena*, 276–7.

54 The use of the term to mean specifically the Protestant changes to the Church were documented as early as 1531. See OED, "Reformation," n1, b, accessed 15 January 2018.

55 Fenn, *The Life of the Blessed Virgin, Sainct Catharine of Siena*, 279.

56 For example, Nancy Warren writes about Mary Birbeck, the early eighteenth-century prioress of a community of English Carmelite nuns in Antwerp who collected and wrote a collection of spiritual autobiographies of the nuns in her community, inspired by St Theresa of Avila, whom they understood to be inspired by Catherine. See Nancy Bradley Warren, *The Embodied Word: Female Spiritualities, Contested Orthodoxies, and English Religious Cultures, 1350–1700* (Notre Dame: University of Notre Dame Press, 2010), 2–3.

57 Fulvio Androzzi, *Meditations vppon the passion of our Lord Iesus Christ made by the reuerend father Fulvius Androtius … ; newlie translated out of Italian into English*. (1606) STC (2nd ed.) 632.7. EEBO, fol. 82, accessed 16 September 2017.

58 Étienne Binet, *Purgatory surveyed, or, A particular accompt of the happy and yet thrice unhappy state of the souls there also of the singular charity and wayes we have to relieve them: and of the devotion of all ages for the souls departed: with twelve excellent means to prevent purgatory and the resolution of many curious and important points* (1663) Wing / B2915, EEBO, fol. 225, accessed 16 September 2017.

59 Girolamo Piatti, *The happines of a religious state diuided into three bookes. Written in Latin by Fa. Hierome Platus of the Societie of Iesus. And now translated into English*. (1632) STC (2nd ed.) 20001. EEBO, fol. 86, accessed 16 September 2017.

60 Thomas M. McCoog, "John Sweetnam [Swetnam]," *Oxford Dictionary of National Biography*, http://www.oxforddnb.com/, accessed 14 September 2017.

61 John Sweetnam, *S. Mary Magdalens pilgrimage to paradise. Wherein are liuely imprinted the foote-steps of her excellent vertues, for sinners to follow, who*

desire to accompany her thither. (1617) STC (2nd ed.) 23532. EEBO, fol. 136, accessed 16 September 2017.

62 John Foxe, *The Unabridged Acts and Monuments Online at TAMO* (Second Edition) (Sheffield: HRI Online Publications, 2011), https://www.johnfoxe. org, accessed 2 December 2015.

63 Foxe, *The Unabridged Acts and Monuments,* 544, accessed 2 December 2015.

64 Foxe, *The Unabridged Acts and Monuments,* 538, accessed 2 December 2015.

65 Foxe, *The Unabridged Acts and Monuments,* 538, accessed 4 December 2015.

66 Foxe, *The Unabridged Acts and Monuments,* 538, accessed 30 July 2015.

67 Warren, *The Embodied Word,* 213.

68 Foxe, *The Unabridged Acts and Monuments,* 538, accessed 4 December 2015.

69 An "ouche" is a gem or ornament (see OED, "ouche, n." Accessed 11 December 2015).

70 Foxe, *The Unabridged Acts and Monuments,* 538, accessed 30 July 2015.

71 For more on the post-Reformation response to visions and visionaries, both by Protestants and Catholics, see Stuart Clark, *Vanities of the Eye: Vision in Early Modern European Culture* (Oxford: Oxford University Press, 2007). See also Euan Cameron, *Enchanted Europe: Superstition, Reason, and Religion, 1250-1750* (Oxford: Oxford University Press, 2007).

72 Foxe, *The Unabridged Acts and Monuments,* 1007, accessed 30 July 2015.

73 Claire Falck, "'Heavenly Lineaments' and the Invisible Church in Foxe and Spenser," *Studies in English Literature 1500–1900* 53 (2013): 6.

74 Nicholas W.S. Cranfield, "Matthew Sutcliffe," *Oxford Dictionary of National Biography,* www.oxforddnb.com, accessed 15 September 2017.

75 Matthew Sutcliffe, *An abridgement of suruey of poperie conteining a compendious declaration of the grounds, doctrines, beginnings, proceedings, impieties, falsities, contradictions, absurdities, fooleries, and other manifold abuses of that religion, which the Pope and his complices doe now manteine, and wherewith they haue corrupted and deformed the true Christian faith.* (1606) STC (2nd ed.) 23448. EEBO, fol. 293, accessed 16 September 2017.

76 Matthew Sutcliffe, *A Challenge Concerning the Romish Church, Her Doctrine and Practices.* (1602) STC (2nd ed.) 23454. EEBO, fol. 9, emphasis in original, accessed 16 September 2017.

77 See Eamon Duffy, *The Stripping of the Altars: Traditional Religion in England 1400–1580* (New Haven: Yale University Press, 1992), 166, for more on this image.

78 Mary C. Erler, *Women, Reading, and Piety in Late Medieval England* (Cambridge: University of Cambridge Press, 2002), 47.

79 While people are petitioning for her canonization, Ward has not yet been named a saint.
80 See David Wallace, "Periodizing Women: Mary Ward (1586–1645) and the Premodern Canon," *Journal of Medieval and Early Modern Studies* 36.2 (2006): 404. See also David Wallace, *Strong Women: Life, Text, and Territory 1347–1645* (Oxford: Oxford University Press, 2011).

Bibliography

All references from early modern editions correspond to copies held at the libraries listed here. In the case of English titles, the Short Title Catalogue (STC) reference is provided as well as the Early English Books Online (EEBO, https://eebo.chadwyck.com/home).

Manuscripts

Beeleigh Abbey, Miss C. Foyle s.xv
Bodleian Library, MS Bodley 131 (a.k.a. Bodl 1999)
Bodleian Library, MS Bodley 630
Bodleian Library, MS Canon ital. 283
Bodleian Library, MS Canon. Misc. 205
Bodleian Library, MS Digby 180
Bodleian Library, MS Douce 114
Bodleian Library, MS Holkham misc. 41
Bodleian Library, MS Laud Misc. 108
Bodleian Library, MS Rawlinson C.285 (a.k.a. Bodl 12143)
British Library, MS Arundel 197
British Library, C.37.f.19
British Library, MS Harley 612
British Library, MS Harley 1706
British Library, MS Harley 2409
British Library, MS Harley 3432
British Library, MS Harley 3480
British Library, MS Royal 18.A.X.
British Library, MS Sloane 982
British Library, MS Sloane 3548
Brotherton Collection, MS 501

Cambridge, Corpus Christi College, MS 141
Cambridge, Fitzwilliam Museum, MS 48
Cambridge, St John's College, MS 75
Cambridge, St John's College, MS C.25
Cambridge, Trinity College, MS 336 (B.14.53)
Cambridge University Library, Ff.5.40
Cambridge University Library, Ii.vi.3
Cambridge University Library, MS Gg 1 6
Edinburgh, MS 87 (D b IV 18)
Firenze, Biblioteca Riccardiana, MS 1345
Lambeth Palace, MS 436
Manchester, Chetham's Hospital Library, MS Mun.A.7.1. (was acc. 6690)
Manchester, Rylands MS Latin 395
Milano, Biblioteca Nacionale Braidense AD.IX.11
New York Public Library Spencer MS 1519
Notre Dame University, MS 67
Oxford University College, MS 14
Pierpont Morgan, MS 162
Siena, Biblioteca comunale degli Intronati, C.v.24
Siena, Biblioteca comunale degli Intronati, T.II.7

Primary sources

Acta Sanctorum, BHL Number 1702.
Acta Sanctorum, "EPISTOLA DOMNI STEPHANI de gestis & virtutibus S. Catharinæ," *BHL* 1703, Col. 0961C.
Allen, Hope Emily, ed. *Writings Ascribed to Richard Rolle Hermit of Hampole and Materials for His Biography.* London: Oxford University Press, 1927.
Androzzi, Fulvio. *Meditations vppon the passion of our Lord Iesus Christ made by the reuerend father Fulvius Androtius ... ; newlie translated out of Italian into English.* (1609) STC (2nd ed.) 632.7. EEBO. Accessed 16 September 2017.
Baker, Augustine. *Sancta Sophia, or, Directions for the prayer of contemplation &c. extracted out of more then (sic) XL treatises / written by the late Ven. Father F. Augustin Baker, a monke of the English congregation of the Holy Order of S. Benedict, and methodically digested by the R.F. Serenvs Cressy of the same order and congregation.* (1657) Wing / B480. EEBO. Accessed 16 September 2017.
Binet, Étienne. *Purgatory surveyed, or, A particular accompt of the happy and yet thrice unhappy state of the souls there also of the singular charity and wayes we have to relieve them: and of the devotion of all ages for the souls departed: with twelve excellent means to prevent purgatory and the resolution of many curious and important points.* (1663) Wing / B2915, EEBO. Accessed 16 September 2017.

Brown, Jennifer N. *Three Women of Liège: A Critical Edition of and Commentary on the Middle English Lives of Elizabeth of Spalbeek, Christina Mirabilis, and Marie d'Oignies.* Turnhout: Brepols, 2008.

Blunt, John Henry, ed. *Myroure of Oure Ladye,* Eearly English Text Society, 19. Oxford: Oxford University Press, 1873.

Caffarini, Tomaso. *Sancta Catherinae Senensis Legenda minor.* Edited by Ezio Franceschini. Fontes vitae S. Catherinae Senensis Historici, 10. Milano: Bocca, 1942.

– *Libellus de supplemento: Legende prolixe virginis beate Catherine de Senis.* Edited by Giuliana Cavallini and Imelda Foralosso. Testi catariniani 3. Rome: Cateriniane, 1974.

Cavallini, Giuliana, ed. *Il Dialogo della Divina Provvidenza.* Rome: Edizioni Cateriniane, 1968.

– ed. *Le Orazioni di S. Caterina da Siena.* I classici cristiaini, 287. Siena: Cantagalli, 1993.

– ed. *Il Dialogo della Divina Provvidenza: ovvero Libro della divina dottrina.* Testi Cateriniani 1, 2nd ed. Siena: Edizioni Cateriniane, 1995.

Colledge, Eric, and Noel Chadwick, eds. "'Remedies against Temptactions': The Third English Version of William Flete." *Archivo Italiano per la storia della pietà* 5 (1968): 201–40.

Diekstra, F.N.M. "*A Good Remedie aȝens Spirituel Temptacions*: A Conflated Middle English Version of William Flete's *De Remediis Contra Temptationes* and Pseudo-Hugh of St. Victor's *De Pusillanimitate* in London BL MS Royal 18.A.X." *English Studies* 4 (1995): 307–54.

Ellis, Roger, ed. *The Liber Celestis of St. Bridget of Sweden.* Early English Text Society, 291. Oxford: Oxford University Press, 1987.

Fawtier, Robert, ed. "Catheriniana." *Mélanges d'archéologie et d'histoire* 34.1 (1914): 3–96.

Fenn, John, trans. *The Life of the Blessed Virgin, Sainct Catharine of Siena.* Leuven, 1609. EEBO. Accessed 14 February 2018.

Foxe, John. *The Unabridged Acts and Monuments Online at TAMO (Second Edition).* Sheffield: HRI Online Publications, 2011. https://www.johnfoxe.org. Accessed 2 December 2015.

Gardner, Edmund, ed. *The Cell of Self-Knowledge: Seven Early English Mystical Treatises Printed by Henry Pepwell in 1521.* London: Chatto and Windus, 1910.

Gigli. Girolamo, ed. *Opere della serafica Santa Caterina da Siena.* 4 vols. Lucca, 1707–21.

Gillespie, Vincent, and A.I. Doyle, eds. *Syon Abbey with the Libraries of the Carthusians.* London: The British Library, 2001.

Halligan, Theresa A., ed. *The Book of Gostlye Grace of Mechtild of Hackeborn.* Toronto: Pontifical Institute of Mediaeval Studies, 1979.

Harris, Marguerite Tjader, ed., and Albert Ryle Kezel, trans. *Birgitta of Sweden: Life and Selected Writings*. Mahwah, NJ: Paulist Press, 1989.

Hodgson, Phyllis, ed. *The Cloud of Unknowing and the Book of Privy Counselling*. Early English Text Society, 218. Oxford: Oxford University Press, 1944.

Hodgson, Phyllis, and Gabriel Michael Liegey, eds. *The Orcherd of Syon*. Early English Text Society, 258. Oxford: Oxford University Press, 1966.

Hogg, James, ed. *Whytford, Richard*. Volume 5: *A Werke for Housholders, A Dayly Exercyse and Experyence of Dethe*. Salzburg: Institut Für Anglistik und Amerikanistik Universität Salzburg, 1979.

– ed. *The Rewyll of Seynt Sauiour*. Salzburg: Institut fur Angelistik und Amerikanistik, 1980.

Horstmann, Carl, ed. *Sammlung altenglischer Legenden*. Heilbronn: Henninger, 1878. https://quod.lib.umich.edu/cgi/t/text/text-idx?c=cme;cc=cme;view=toc;idno=AJD8171.0001.001. Accessed 14 September 2017.

– ed. "The Lyf of Saint Katherin of Senis: nach dem Drucke W. Caxtons (c. 1493)." *Archiv für das Studium der Neueren Sprachen und Litteraturen* 76 (1886), 33–112, 265–314, 353–91.

– ed. *Yorkshire Writers: Richard Rolle of Hampole, an English Father of the Church and His Followers*. London: S. Sonnenschein & Co., 1895.

I Miracoli di Caterina di Iacopo da Siena di anonimo fiorentino. Fontes Vitae S. Caterinae Senensi Historici 4. Florence: Sansoni, 1936.

Jenkins, Rev. Henry, ed. *The Remains of Thomas Cranmer, D.D. Archbishop of Canterbury*. Oxford: Oxford University Press, 1833.

Laurent, Marie-Hyacinthe, ed. *Il Processo Castellano. Con appendice di documenti sul culto e la canonizzazione di S. Caterina*. Fontes Vitae S. Catherinae Senenis Historici 9. Milan: Bocca, 1942.

Lehmijoki-Garner, Maiju, ed. and trans. *Dominican Penitent Women*. New York: Paulist Press, 2005.

Love, Nicholas. *The Mirror of the Blessed Life of Jesus Christ: A Full Critical Edition, based on Cambridge University Library MSS 6578 and 6686, with Introduction, Notes and Glossary*. Edited by Michael Sargent. Exeter: Exeter University Press, 2005.

McNamer, Sarah ed. *The Two Middle English Translations of the Revelations of St. Elizabeth of Hungary*. Heidelberg: Universitätsverlag Winter, 1996.

More, Gertrude. *The Holy Practises of a Devine Lover, or, The Sainctly Ideots Deuotions*. (1657) EEBO. Wing / M2631A. Accessed 15 February 2018.

Nichols, John Gough, and John BruceWills, eds. *Doctors' Commons: A Selection from the Wills of Emininent Persons Proved in the Prerogative Court of Canterbury. 1495–1695*. London: The Camden Society, 1863.

Noffke, Suzanne, ed. and trans. *The Dialogue of Catherine of Siena*. Mahwah, NJ: Paulist Press, 1980.

– ed. and trans. *The Letters of Catherine of Siena*, 4 vols. Tempe: Medieval and Renaissance Texts & Studies, 2000–8.

– ed. and trans. *The Prayers of Catherine of Siena*. Mahwah, NJ: Paulist Press, 2001.

"Orders and Rules of the Princess Cecill." *A Collection of Ordinances and Regulations for the Government of the Royal Household Made in Divers Reigns*, 37–9. London: Society of Antiquaries, 1790.

Patterson, Paul, ed. *A Mirror to Devout People (Speculum Devotorum)*, Early English Text Society, 346. Oxford: Oxford University Press, 2016.

Piatti, Girolamo. *The happines of a religious state diuided into three bookes. Written in Latin by Fa. Hierome Platus of the Societie of Iesus.* And now translated into English. (1632) STC (2nd ed.) 20001. EEBO. Accessed 16 September 2017.

Puccetti, P. Angiolo, O.P., and P. Tito S. Centi, O.P., eds. *Il Dialogo della Divina Provvidenzia*. Siena: Ediziono Cantagalli, 2011.

Raimondo da Capua. *Legenda maior Sive Legenda Admirabilis Virginis Catherine de Senis.* Edited by Silvia Nocentini. Firenze: Sismel, 2013.

Raymond of Capua. *The Life of Catherine of Siena.* Edited and translated by Conleth Kearns, O.P. Washington, DC: Dominicana Publications, 1994.

Robinson, Thomas. *The Anatomy of the English Nunnery at Lisbon in Portugall.* London: Printed by George Purslowe, for Robert Mylbourne and Philemon Stephens, 1622. Reprinted in 1623, 1630, 1637, and 1662.

Rogers, Elizabeth Frances, ed. *The Correspondence of Sir Thomas More.* Princeton: Princeton University Press, 1947.

Sbaffoni, Fausto, ed. *Santa Caterina da Siena: Opera Omnia. Testi e concordanze.* Pistoia: Provincia romana dei Frati Predicatori Centro riviste, 2002. CD-ROM.

Staley, Lynn, ed. *The Book of Margery Kempe.* Kalamazoo: TEAMS, in association with the University of Rochester by Medieval Institute Publications, Western Michigan University Press, 1996.

Sutcliffe, Matthew. *A Challenge Concerning the Romish Church, Her Doctrine and Practices.* (1602) STC (2nd ed.) 23454. EEBO. Accessed 16 September 2017.

– *An abridgement of suruey of poperie conteining a compendious declaration of the grounds, doctrines, beginnings, proceedings, impieties, falsities, contradictions, absurdities, fooleries, and other manifold abuses of that religion, which the Pope and his complices doe now manteine, and wherewith they haue corrupted and deformed the true Christian faith.* (1606) STC (2nd ed.) 23448. EEBO. Accessed 16 September 2017.

Sweetnam, John. *S. Mary Magdalens pilgrimage to paradise. Wherein are liuely imprinted the foote-steps of her excellent vertues, for sinners to follow, who desire to accompany her thither.* (1617) STC (2nd ed.) 23532. EEBO. Accessed 16 September 2017.

Taurisano, P. Innocenzo O.P., ed. *Dialogo della Divina Provvidenza.* Rome: Libreria Editrice F. Ferrari, 1947.

Watson, Nicholas, and Jacqueline Jenkins, eds. *The Writings of Julian of Norwich: A Vision Showed to a Devout Woman and a Revelation of Love*. University Park: The Pennsylvania University State Press, 2006.

Webber, T., and A.G. Watson, eds. *The Libraries of the Augustinian Canons*. London: The British Library, 1998.

Secondary sources

Adams, Gwenfair Walters. *Visions in Late Medieval England: Lay Spirituality and Sacred Glimpses of the Hidden Worlds of Faith*. Leiden: Brill, 2007.

Alakas, Brandon. "'Closed and kept most surely in religion': Piety and Politics in Richard Whitford's *The Pype, or Tonne, of the Lyfe of Perfection*." *Renaissance and Reformation / Renaiassance et Réforme* 36 (2013): 93–128.

Anderson, Wendy Love. "Gerson's Stance on Women." In *A Companion to Jean Gerson*, edited by Brian Patrick McGuire, 293–316. Leiden: Brill, 2006.

Arblaster, Paul. "John Heigham," *Oxford Dictionary of National Biography*. www.oxforddnb.com. Accessed 13 November 2015.

Armstrong, C.A.J. *England, France and Burgundy in the Fifteenth Century*. London: The Hambledon Press, 1983.

– "The Piety of Cecily Duchess of York: A Study in Late Medieval Culture." In *For Hilaire Belloc: Essays in Honor of His 71st Birthday*, edited by Douglas Woodruff, 68–91. New York: Greenwood Press, 1969.

Aurigemma, Luisa. "La tradizione manoscritta del 'Dialogo della Divina Provvidenza' di Santa Caterina da Siena." *Critica Letteraria* 16 (1988): 237–58.

Bainbridge, Virginia R. "Syon Abbey: Women and Learning c. 1415–1600." In *Syon Abbey and Its Books: Reading, Writing and Religion c. 1400–1700*, edited by E.A. Jones and Alexandra Walsham, 82–103. Woodbridge: Boydell and Brewer, 2010.

Bartlett, Anne Clark. *Male Authors, Female Readers: Representation and Subjectivity in Middle English Devotional Literature*. Ithaca: Cornell University Press, 1995.

Barratt, Alexandra. "The Revelations of St. Elizabeth of Hungary: Problems of Attribution." *The Library*, 6th series, 14 (1992): 1–11.

– "Continental Women Mystics and English Readers." In *The Cambridge Companion to Medieval Women's Writing*, edited by Carolyn Dinshaw and David Wallace, 140–255. Cambridge: Cambridge University Press, 2003.

– "English Translations of Didactic Literature for Women to 1550." In *What Nature Does Not Teach: Didactic Literature in the Medieval and Early-Modern Periods*, edited by J.F. Ruys, 287–304. Turnhout: Brepols, 2008.

Beattie, Blake. "Catherine of Siena and the Papacy." In *A Companion to Catherine of Siena*, edited by Carolyn Muessig, George Ferzoco, and Berverly Mayne Kienzle, 73–98. Leiden: Brill, 2012.

Bell, David. *What Nuns Read: Books and Libraries in Medieval English Nunneries.* Kalamazoo: Cistercian Publications, 1995.

Bell, Kimberly K., and Julie Nelson Crouch. "Introduction: Reading Oxford, Bodleian Library, MS Laud Misc. 108 as a 'Whole Book.'" In *The Texts and Contexts of Oxford, Bodleian Library, MS Laud Misc. 108: The Shaping of English Vernacular Narrative*, edited by Kimberly K. Bell and Julie Nelson Crouch, 1–20. Leiden: Brill, 2011.

Benedict, Kimberly M. *Empowering Collaborations: Writing Partnerships Between Religious Women and Scribes in the Middle Ages.* New York: Routledge, 2004.

Benskin, Michael, Margaret Laing, Vasilis Kariaskos, and Keith Williamson. *An Electronic Version of a Linguistic Atlas of Late Mediaeval English.* Edinburgh: University of Edinburgh, 2013. http://www.lel.ed.ac.uk/ihd/elalme/elalme_frames.html.

Betteridge, Thomas. "Thomas More, Print and the Idea of Censorship." In *A Companion to the Early Printed Book in Britain 1476–1558*, edited by Vincent Gillespie and Susan Powell, 290–306. Woodbridge: D.S. Brewer, 2014.

Boffey, Julia. "Some Women Readers and a Text of *The Three Kings of Cologne.*" *The Ricardian* 10 (1996): 387–96.

Boffey, Julia, and A.S.G. Edwards. "Towards a Taxonomy of Middle English Manuscript Assemblages." In *Insular Books: Vernacular Miscellanies in Late Medieval Britain, Proceedings of the British Academy.* Volume 201, edited by Margaret Connolly and Raluca Radulescu, 263–79. Oxford: Oxford University Press, 2015.

Borland, Catherine. *A Descriptive Catalogue of the Western Mediæval Manuscripts in Edinburgh University Library.* Edinburgh: University of Edinburgh Press, 1916.

Bornstein, Daniel. "Spiritual Kinship and Domestic Devotions." In *Gender and Society in Renaissance Italy*, edited by Judith C. Brown and Robert C. Davis, 173–92. Essex: Longman, 1998.

Bowden, Caroline, ed. *English Convents in Exile, 1600–1800.* Vols. 1–3. London: Pickering and Chatto, 2012.

Brady, M. Teresa. "Lollard Sources of 'The Pore Caitif.'" *Traditio* 44 (1988): 389–418.

– "Lollard Interpolations and Omissions in Manuscripts of the *Pore Caitif.*" In *De Cella in Seculum: Religious and Secular Life and Devotion in Late Medieval England*, edited by Michael G. Sargent, 183–203. Cambridge: D.S. Brewer, 1989.

Brakmann, Thomas. "The Transmission of the Upper German Life of Catherine of Siena." In *Catherine of Siena: The Creation of a Cult*, edited by Jeffrey Hamburger and Gabriel Signori, 83–107. Turnhout: Brepols, 2013.

Brantley, Jessica. *Reading in the Wilderness: Private Devotion and Public Performance in Late Medieval England*. Chicago: University of Chicago Press, 2007.

Brown, Jennifer N. *Three Women of Liège: A Critical Edition of and Commentary on the Middle English Lives of Elizabeth of Spalbeek, Christina Mirabilis, and Marie d'Oignies*. Turnhout: Brepols, 2008.

– "The Chaste Erotics of Marie of Oignies and Jacques de Vitry." *Journal of the History of Sexuality* 19 (2010): 74–93.

– "From the Charterhouse to the Printing House: Catherine of Siena in Medieval England." In *Middle English Religious Writing in Practice: Texts, Readers, and Transformations*, edited by Nicole Rice, 17–45. Turnhout: Brepols, 2013.

– "The Many Misattributions of Catherine of Siena: Beyond *The Orcherd* in England." *The Journal of Medieval Religious Cultures* 41 (2015): 67–84.

Brown, Jennifer N., and Donna Bussell, eds. *Barking Abbey and Medieval Literary Culture*. York: York Medieval Press, 2012.

Bryan, Jennifer. *Looking Inward: Devotional Reading and the Private Self in Late Medieval England*. Philadelphia: University of Pennsylvania Press, 2008.

Caciola, Nancy. *Discerning Spirits: Divine and Demonic Possession in the Middle Ages*. Ithaca: Cornell University Press, 2003.

Cameron, Euan K. *Enchanted Europe: Superstition, Reason, and Religion, 1250–1750*. Oxford: Oxford University Press, 2007.

– "Ways of Knowing in the Pre-and Post-Reformation Worlds." In *Mysticism and Reform, 1400–1750*, edited by Sara S. Poor and Nigel Smith, 29–48. Notre Dame: University of Notre Dame Press, 2015.

Catto, Jeremy. "1349–1412: Culture and History." In *The Cambridge Companion to Medieval English Mysticism*, edited by Samuel Fanous and Vincent Gillespie, 113–32. Cambridge: Cambridge University Press, 2011.

Cavallini, Giuliana. "Introduczione." In *Il Dialogo della Divina Provvidenza*, edited by Giuliana Cavallini, ix–xliii. Rome: Edizioni Cateriniane, 1968.

Chance, Jane. "St. Catherine of Siena in Late Medieval Britain." *Annali D'Italianistica* 13 (1995): 163–203.

– *The Literary Subversions of Medieval Women*. New York: Palgrave, 2007.

Clark, Stuart. *Vanities of the Eye: Vision in Early Modern European Culture*. Oxford: Oxford University Press, 2007.

Cnattingius, Hans. *Studies in The Order of St. Bridget of Sweden I: The Crisis in the 1420's*. Stokholm: Almqvist and Wiksell, 1963.

Coakley, John. *Women, Men, & Spiritual Power: Female Saints & Their Male Collaborators*. New York: Columbia University Press, 2006.

Connolly, Margaret. "Public Revisions or Private Responses? The Oddities of Arundel 197, with special reference to Contemplations of the Dread and Love of God.'" *British Library Journal* 20 (1994): 55–64.

– "Mapping Manuscripts and Readers of Contemplations of the Dread and Love of God." In *Design and Distribution of Late Medieval Manuscripts in England*, edited by Margaret Connolly and Linne R. Moooney, 261–78. Woodbridge: Boydell and Brewer, 2008.

Connolly, Margaret, and Raluca Radulescu. Introduction to *Insular Books: Vernacular Miscellanies in Late Medieval Britain, Proceedings of the British Academy*. Volume 201, edited by Margaret Connolly and Raluca Radulescu, 1–29. Oxford: Oxford University Press, 2015.

Considine, John. "Philemon Holland." *Oxford Dictionary of National Biography.* www.oxforddnb.comhttp://www.oxforddnb.com.i.ezproxy.nypl.org/view/article/13535. Accessed 9 June 2016.

Corbari, Eliana. "Laude for Catherine of Siena." In *A Companion to Catherine of Siena*, edited by Carolyn Muessig, George Ferzoco, and Berverly Mayne Kienzle, 227–58. Leiden: Brill, 2012.

– *Vernacular Theology: Dominican Sermons and Audience in Late Medieval Italy*. Berlin: De Gruyter, 2013.

Cranfield, Nicholas W.S. "Matthew Sutcliffe." *Oxford Dictionary of National Biography.* www.oxforddnb.com. Accessed 15 September 2017.

Cré, Marleen. "Women in the Charterhouse? Julian of Norwich's *Revelations of Divine Love* and Marguerite Porete's *Mirror of Simple Souls* in British Library, MS Additional 37790." In *Writing Religious Women: Female Spiritual and Textual Practices in Late Medieval England*, edited by Denis Renevey and Christiania Whitehead, 43–62. Toronto: University of Toronto Press, 2000.

da Costa, Alexandra. *Reforming Printing: Syon Abbey's Defence of Orthodoxy 1525–1534*. Oxford: Oxford University Press, 2012.

Dailey, Patricia. *Promised Bodies: Time, Language, & Corporeality in Medieval Women's Mystical Texts*. New York: Columbia University Press, 2013.

Davies, Richard. "Richard II and the Church." In *Richard II: The Art of Kingship*, edited by Anthony Goodman and James Gillespie, 83–106. Oxford: Clarendon Press, 1999.

Denise, Sr. Mary. "The Orcherd of Syon: An Introduction." *Traditio* 14 (1958): 269–93.

Despres, Denise L. "Ecstatic Reading and Missionary Mysticism." In *Prophets Abroad: The Reception of Continental Holy Women in Late-Medieval England*, edited by Rosalynn Voaden, 141–60. Cambridge: D.S. Brewer, 1996.

Devereux, E.J. "Elizabeth Barton and Tudor Censorship." *Bulletin of the John Rylands Library* 49 (1966–7): 91–106.

Dolan, Frances E. *Whores of Babylon: Catholicism, Gender, and Seventeenth-Century Print Culture*. Ithaca: Cornell University Press, 1999.

Driver, Martha W. "Pictures in Print: Late Fifteenth- and Early Sixteenth-Century English Religious Books for Lay Readers." In *De Cella in Seculum: Religious and Secular Life and Devotion in Late Medieval England*, edited by Michael Sargent, 229–44. Cambridge: D.S. Brewer, 1989.

– "Bridgettine Woodcuts in Printed Books Produced for the English Market." In *Art into Life: Collected Papers from the Kresge Art Museum Medieval Symposia*, edited by Carol Garrett Fisher and Kathleen L. Scott, 237–67. East Lansing: Michigan State University Press, 1995.

– *The Image in Print: Book Illustration in Late Medieval England and Its Sources*. London: The British Library, 2004.

– "Woodcuts and Decorative Techniques." In *A Companion to the Early Printed Book in Britain 1476–1558*, edited by Vincent Gillespie and Susan Powell, 95–123. Cambridge: D.S. Brewer, 2014.

Duffy, Eamon. *The Stripping of the Altars: Traditional Religion in England 1400–1580*. New Haven: Yale University Press, 1992.

Dutton, Anne M. "Passing the Book: Testamentary Transmission of Religious Literature to and by Women in England 1350–1500." In *Women, the Book and the Godly*, edited by Lesley Smith and Jane H.M. Taylor, 41–54. Cambrdge: D.S. Brewer, 1995.

Edinburgh Southside Heritage Group. https://sites.google.com/site/southsideheritagegroup/the-south-side-story/convent-of-st-catherine-of-siena. Accessed 31 July 2015.

Ellis, Roger. "Flores and Fabricandam ... Coranam: An Investigation into the Uses of the Revelations of St. Bridget of Sweden in Fifteenth-Century England." *Medium Aevum* 51 (1982): 163–86.

– *Viderunt Eam Filie Syon: The Spirituality of the English House of a Medieval Contemplative Order from Its Beginnings to the Present Day*. Salzburg: Institut für Anglistik und Amerikanistik Universität Salzburg, 1984.

– ed. *The Liber Celestis of St. Bridget of Sweden*. Early English Text Society, 291. Oxford: Oxford University Press, 1987.

– "Further Thoughts on the Spirituality of Syon Abbey." In *Mysticism and Spirituality in England*, edited by William Pollard and Robert Boenig, 219–43. Woodbridge: D.S. Brewer, 1997.

– "Text and Controversy: In Defence of St. Birgitta of Sweden." In *Text and Controversy from Wyclif to Bale: Essays in Honour of Anne Hudson*, edited by Helen Barr and Ann M. Hutchison, 303–21. Turnhout: Brepols, 2005.

Elliot, Dyan. *Proving Women: Female Spirituality and Inquisitional Culture in the Later Middle Ages.* Princeton: Princeton University Press, 2004.

– *The Bride of Christ Goes to Hell: Metaphor and Embodiment in the Lives of Pious Women, 200–1500.* Philadelphia: University of Pennsylvania Press, 2012.

Erler, Mary. *Women, Reading, and Piety in Late Medieval England.* Cambridge: University of Cambridge Press, 2002.

– "'A Revelation of Purgatory' (1422): Reform and the Politics of Female Visions." *Viator* 38.1 (2007): 321–47.

– *Reading and Writing during the Dissolution: Monks, Friars, and Nuns 1530–1558.* Cambridge: Cambridge University Press, 2013.

Falck, Claire. "'Heavenly Lineaments' and the Invisible Church in Foxe and Spenser." *Studies in English Literature 1500–1900* 53 (2013): 1–28.

Fanning, Steven. *Mystics of the Christian Tradition.* London: Routledge, 2001.

Fawtier, Robert. *Sainte Catherine de Sienne : Essai de critique des sources. Sources hagiographiques.* Paris: Boccard, 1921.

Ferzoco, George. "The Processo Castellano and the Canonization of Catherine of Siena." In *A Companion to Catherine of Siena*, edited by Carolyn Muessig, George Ferzoco, and Berverly Mayne Kienzle, 185–201. Leiden: Brill, 2012.

Friedman, Joan Isobel. "Politics and the Rhetoric of Reform in the Letters of Saint Bridget of Sweden and Catherine of Siena." *Livres et Lectures de Femmes en Europe entre Moyen Âge et Renaissance*, edited by Anne-Marie Legaré, 279–94. Turnhout: Brepols, 2007.

Friedman, John B. *Northern English Books, Owners, and Makers in the Late Middle Ages.* Syracuse: Syracuse University Press, 1995.

Frugoni, Chiara. "Female Mystics, Visions, and Iconography." In *Women and Religion in Medieval and Renaissance Italy*, edited by Daniel Bornstein and Roberto Rusconi and translated by Margery J. Schneider, 130–64. Chicago: University of Chicago Press, 1996.

Gertz, Genelle C. "Quaker Mysticism as the Return of the Medieval Repressed: English Women Prophets before and after the Reformation." In *Mysticism and Reform, 1400–1750*, edited by Sara S. Poor and Nigel Smith, 177–97. Notre Dame: University of Notre Dame Press, 2015.

Gillespie, Alexandra. *Print Culture and the Medieval Author: Chaucer, Lydgate, and Their Books 1473–1557.* Oxford: Oxford University Press, 2006.

Gillespie, Vincent. "Vernacular Books of Religion." In *Book Production and Publishing in Britain 1375–1475*, edited by Jeremy Griffiths and Derek Pearsall, 317–44. Cambridge: Cambridge University Press, 1989.

– "The Book and the Brotherhood: Reflections on the Lost Library of Syon Abbey." In *The English Medieval Book: Studies in Memory of Jeremy Griffiths,* edited by A.S.G. Edwards, Vincent Gillespie and Ralph Hanna, 185–208. London: The British Library, 2000.

– "Syon and the New Learning." In *The Religious Orders in Pre-Reformation England*, edited by James G. Clark, 75–95. Woodbridge: Boydell, 2002.

– "'Hid Diuinite': The Spirituality of the English Syon Brethren." In *The Medieval Mystical Tradition in England; Exeter Symposium VII: Papers Read at Charney Manor*, edited by E.A. Jones, 189–206. Woodbridge: D.S. Brewer, 2004.

– "The Mole in the Vineyard: Wyclif at Syon in the Fifteenth Century." In *Text and Controversy from Wyclif to Bale: Essays in Honour of Anne Hudson*, edited by Helen Barr and Ann M. Hutchison, 131–62. Turnhout: Brepols, 2005.

– "1412–1534: Culture and History." In *The Cambridge Companion to Medieval English Mysticism*, edited by Samuel Fanous and Vincent Gillespie, 163–93. Cambridge: Cambridge University Press, 2011.

Gillespie, Vincent, and Kantik Ghosh, eds. *After Arundel: Religious Writing in Fifteenth-Century England*. Turnhout: Brepols, 2012.

Giunta, Diego. "The Iconography of Catherine of Siena's Stigmata." In *A Companion to Catherine of Siena*, edited by Carolyn Muessig, George Ferzoco, and Berverly Mayne Kienzle, 259–94. Leiden: Brill, 2012.

Griffith, David. "The Reception of Continental Women Mystics in Fifteenth- and Sixteenth-Century England: Some Artistic Evidence." In *The Medieval Mystical Tradition in England: Exeter Symposium VII*, edited by E.A. Jones, 97–118. Cambridge: D.S. Brewer, 2004.

Grisé, C. Annette. "'In the Blessid Vyneʒard of Oure Holy Saueour': Female Religious Readers and Textual Reception in *The Myroure of Oure Ladye* and *The Orcherd of Syon*." In *The Medieval Mystical Tradition: Exeter Symposium VI*, edited by Marion Glasscoe, 193–213. Cambridge: D.S. Brewer, 1999.

– "Catherine of Siena in Middle English Manuscripts: Transmission, Translation, and Transformation." In *The Medieval Translator/Traduire au Moyen Age*. Volume 8, edited by Rosalynn Voaden, René Tixier, Teresa Sanchez Roura, and Jenny Rebecca Rytting, 149–59. Turnhout: Brepols, 2003.

– "Holy Women in Print: Continental Female Mystics and the English Mystical Tradition." In *The Medieval Mystical Tradition: Exeter Symposium VII*, edited by E.A. Jones, 83–95. Woodbridge: D.S. Brewer, 2004.

– "'Moche profitable unto religious persones, gathered by a brother of Syon': Syon Abbey and English Books." In *Syon Abbey and Its Books: Reading, Writing and Religion c. 1400–1700*, edited by E.A. Jones and Alexandra Walsham, 129–54. Woodbridge: Boydell and Brewer, 2010.

– "Catherine of Siena." In *The History of British Women's Writing, 700–1500*. Volume 1, edited by Liz Herbert McAvoy and Diane Watt, 216–22, New York: Palgrave, 2012.

– "Proliferation and Purification: The Use of Books for Nuns After Arundel."
  In *After Arundel: Religious Writing in Fifteenth-Century England*, edited by
  Vincent Gillespie and Kantik Ghosh, 503–19. Turnhout: Brepols, 2012.
– "Richard Whytford, *The Golden Epistle*, and the Mixed Life Audience." In
  *The Medieval Mystical Tradition in England: Papers Read at Charney Manor,
  July 2011 (Exeter Symposium 8)*, edited by E.A. Jones, 195–208. Woodbridge:
  Boydell and Brewer, 2013.
Gwynn, Aubrey, S.J. *The English Austin Friars in the Time of Wyclif.* Oxford:
  Oxford University Press, 1940.
Hackett, M.B. "The Spiritual Life of the English Austin Friars of the
  Fourteenth Century." In *Sanctus Augustinus Vitae Spritualis Magister:
  Settimana internazionale di spiritualità agostiniana: Roma, 22–27 Ottobre 1956*,
  421–92. Rome, 1956.
– "William Flete and the *De Remediis Contra Temptaciones*." In *Medieval Studies
  Presented to Aubrey Gwynn*, edited by F.X. Martin, 330–48. Dublin: Three
  Candles Press, 1961.
– "William Flete." In *Pre-Reformation English Spirituality*, edited by James
  Walsh, 158–69. New York: Fordham, 1965.
– "Catherine of Siena and William of England: A Curious Partnership."
  *Proceedings of the PMR Conference: Annual Publication of the International
  Patristic, Mediaeval and Renaissance Conference 5*, 29–47. Villanova, PA:
  Augustinian Historical Institute, 1980.
– *William Flete, OSA, and Catherine of Siena: Masters of Fourteenth Century
  Spirituality.* Villanova, PA: Augustinian Press, 1992.
Hackett, M.B., Eric Colledge, and Noel Chadwick. "William Flete's 'De
  Remedies contra Temptaciones' in its Latin and English Recensions: The
  Growth of a Text." *Mediaeval Studies* 26 (1964): 210–30.
Hallett, Nicky. *The Senses in Religious Communities, 1600–1800: Early Modern
  "Convents of Pleasure."* New York: Routledge, 2013.
Hamburger, Jeffrey. *The Visual and the Visionary: Art and Female Spirituality in
  Late Medieval Germany.* New York: Zone Books, 1998.
Hamburger, Jeffrey F., and Gabriela Sighnori. "The Making of a Saint:
  Catherine of Siena, Tomaso Caffarini, and the Others – Introduction." In
  Catherine of Siena: The Creation of a Cult, edited by Jeffrey Hamburger and
  Gabriel Signori, 1–22. Turnhout: Brepols, 2013.
Hamilton, Dom Adam, OSB, ed. *The Chronicle of the English Augustinian
  Canonesses Regular of the Lateran, at St. Monica's in Louvain (Now at St.
  Augustine's Priory, Newton Abbot, Devon) 1548 to 1625.* Edinburgh: Sands &
  Co., 1904.
Hanna, Ralph. *Pursuing History: Middle English Manuscripts and Their Texts.*
  Stanford: Stanford University Press, 1996.

– *Introducing English Medieval Book History: Manuscripts, Their Producers and Their Readers*. Liverpool: Liverpool University Press, 2013.

Harvey, Margaret. "Adam Easton and the Condemnation of John Wyclif, 1377." *English Historical Review* 118 (1998): 321–34.

Hellinga, Lotte. *William Caxton and Early Printing in England*. London: The British Library, 2010.

Hodgson, Phyllis. "*The Orcherd of Syon* and the English Mystical Tradition: The Sir Israel Gollancz Memorial Lecture." *Proceedings of the British Academy* 50 (1964): 229–50.

Hogg, James. "Adam Easton's Defensorum sanctae Birgittae." In *The Medieval Mystical Tradition England, Ireland, and Wales: Exeter Symposium VI*, edited by Marion Glasscoe, 213–40. Suffolk: D.S. Brewer, 1999.

– "Middle English Translations of the Birgittine Rule." In *The Translation of the Works of St. Birgitta of Sweden into the Medieval European Vernaculars: The Medieval Translator*. Volume 7, edited by Bridget Morris and Veronica O'Mara, 152–69. Turnhout: Brepols Press, 2000.

Holbrook, Sue Ellen. "Margery Kempe and Wynkyn de Worde." In *The Medieval Mystical Tradition in England: Exeter Symposium IV, Papers Read at Dartington Hall, July 1987*, edited by Marion Glasscoe, 27–46. Cambridge: D.S. Brewer, 1987.

Hollywood, Amy. *Sensible Ecstasy: Mysticism, Sexual Difference, and the Demands of History*. Chicago: University of Chicago Press, 2002.

Hope, Andrew. "The Printed Book Trade in Response to Luther." In *A Companion to the Early Printed Book in Britain 1476–1558*, edited by Vincent Gillespie and Susan Powell, 272–89. Woodbridge: D.S. Brewer, 2014.

Hosington, Brenda M. "Women Translators and the Early Printed Book." In *A Companion to the Early Printed Book in Britain 1476–1558*, edited by Vincent Gillespie and Susan Powell, 248–71. Woodbridge: D.S. Brewer, 2014.

Hutchinson, Ann. "Devotional Reading in the Monastery and in the Late Medieval Household." In *De cella in seculum: Religious and Secular Life and Devotion in Late Medieval England*, edited by Michael Sargent, 215–28. Cambridge: D.S. Brewer, 1989.

– "Beyond the Margins: The Recusant Bridgettines." In *Studies in St. Birgitta and the Brigittine Order, Analecta Cartusiana* 35.19 (1993): 267–84.

– "What the Nuns Read: Literary Evidence from the English Bridgettine House, Syon Abbey." *Mediaeval Studies* 57 (1995): 205–22.

– "Mary Champney: A Bridgettine Nun under the Rule of Queen Elizabeth I." *Birgittiania* 13 (2002): 3–89.

– "St. Birgitta, the Revelations, and the Bridgettine Order." In *The Medieval Mystical Tradition VII: Papers Read at Charney Manor 2004*, edited by E.A. Jones, 69–82. Cambridge: D.S. Brewer, 2004.

Johnston, F.R. "English Defenders of St. Bridget." In *Studies in St. Brirgitta and the Birgittine Order.* Volume 1, edited by James Hogg, 263–75. Salzburg: Institut für Anglistik und Americkanistik, Universität Salzburg, 1993.

Joliffe, P.S. *Checklist of Middle English Writings.* Toronto: Toronto University Press, 1974.

Jones, E.A. *England's Last Medieval Monastery: Syon Abbey 1415–2015.* Leominster: Gracewing, 2015.

Jones, E.A., and Alexandra Walsham. "Introduction: Syon Abbey and Its Books: Origin, Influences and Transitions." In *Syon Abbey and Its Books: Reading, Writing and Religion c. 1400–1700*, edited by E.A. Jones and Alexandra Walsham, 1–38. Woodbridge: Boydell and Brewer, 2010.

Jungmayr, Jörg. "Die Legenda maior (Vita Catherinae Senensis) des Raimund von Capua in Italien und Deutschland." In *"Der Buchstab tödt - der Geist macht lebendig": Festschrift zum 60. Geburtstag von Hans-Gert Roloff*, edited by James Hardin, 223–59. Bern: Peter Lang, 1992.

Keiser, George R. "The Mystics and the Early English Printers: The Economics of Devotionalism." In *The Medieval Mystical Tradition in England: Exeter Symposium IV, Papers Read at Dartington Hall, July 1987*, edited by Marion Glasscoe, 9–26. Cambridge: D.S. Brewer, 1987.

Kerby-Fulton, Kathryn. *Books Under Suspicion: Censorship and Tolerance of Revelatory Writing in Late Medieval England.* Notre Dame: University of Notre Dame, 2006.

Kienzle, Beverly Mayne. "Catherine of Siena, Preaching, and Hagiography in Renaissance Tuscany." In *A Companion to Catherine of Siena*, edited by Carolyn Muessig, George Ferzoco, and Berverly Mayne Kienzle, 127–54. Leiden: Brill, 2012.

Krafft, Otfried. "Many Strategies and One Goal: The Difficult Road to the Canonization of Catherine of Siena." In *Catherine of Siena: The Creation of a Cult*, edited by Jeffrey Hamburger and Gabriel Signori, 125–45. Turnhout: Brepols, 2013.

Krug, Rebecca. *Reading Families: Women's Literature Practice in Late Medieval England.* Ithaca: Cornell University Press, 2002.

Lay, Jenna. *Beyond the Cloister: Catholic Englishwomen and Early Modern Literary Culture.* Philadelphia: University of Pennsylvania Press, 2016.

Leach, Arthur Francis. *The Schools of Medieval England.* London: Methuen, 1915.

Lee, Paul. *Nunneries, Learning, and Spirituality in Late Medieval English Society: The Dominican Priory of Dartford.* York: York Medieval Press, 2001.

Le Goff, Jacques. *Saint Louis.* Notre Dame: University of Notre Dame Press, 2009.

Lehmijoki-Gardner, Maiju. "Denial as Action – Penance and Its Place in the Life of Catherine of Siena." In *A Companion to Catherine of Siena*, edited by

Carolyn Muessig, George Ferzoco, and Berverly Mayne Kienzle, 113–26. Leiden: Brill, 2012.

Lerer, Seth. "Medieval English Literature and the Idea of the Anthology" *PMLA* 118.5 (2003): 1251–67.

Lochrie, Karma. *Margery Kempe and Translations of the Flesh*. Philadelphia: University of Pennsylvania Press, 1991.

Lovatt, Roger. "The 'Imitation of Christ' in Late Medieval England." *Transactions of the Royal Historical Society*, 5th series, 18 (1968): 97–121.

Luongo, F. Thomas. "Catherine of Siena: Rewriting Female Holy Authority." In *Women, the Book and the Godly: Selected Proceedings of the St. Hilda's Conference, 1993*. Volume 1, edited by Lesley Smith and Jane J.M. Taylor, 89–103. Woodbridge: D.S. Brewer, 1995.

– "Cloistering Catherine: Religious Identity in Raymond of Capua's *Legenda maior* of Catherine of Siena." *Studies in Medieval and Renaissance History* 3 (2006): 25–69.

– *The Saintly Politics of Catherine of Siena*. Ithaca: Cornell University Press, 2006.

– "The Historical Reception of Catherine of Siena." In *A Companion to Catherine of Siena*, edited by Carolyn Muessig, George Ferzoco, and Berverly Mayne Kienzle, 23–46. Leiden: Brill, 2012.

Macmillan, Sarah. "Mortifying the Mind: Asceticism, Mysticism and Oxford, Bodleian Library MS Douce 114." In *The Medieval Mystical Tradition in England: Papers Read at Charney Manor, July 2011 (Exeter Symposium 8)*, edited by E.A. Jones, 109–24. Woodbridge: Boydell and Brewer, 2013.

Marotti, Arthur F. "Saintly Idiocy and Contemplative Empowerment: The Example of Dame Gertrude More." In *Mysticism and Reform, 1400–1750*, edited by Sara S. Poor and Nigel Smith, 151–76. Notre Dame: University of Notre Dame Press, 2015.

Martin, Dennis D. "Carthusians as Advocates of Women Visionary Reformers." In *Studies in Carthusian Monasticism in the Late Middle Ages*, edited by Julian Luxford, 127–53. Turnhout: Brepols, 2009.

McAvoy, Liz Herbert. *Authority and the Female Body in the Writings of Julian of Norwich and Margery Kempe*. Cambridge: D.S. Brewer, 2004.

– "'O der lady, be my help': Women's Visionary Writing and the Devotional Literary Canon." *The Chaucer Review* 51 (2016): 68–87.

McCoog, Thomas M. "John Sweetnam [Swetnam]." *Oxford Dictionary of National Biography*. www.oxforddnb.com. Accessed 14 September 2017.

McGinn, Bernard. "'Evil-sounding, rash, and suspect of heresy': Tensions between Mysticism and Magisterium in the History of the Church." *The Catholic Historical Review* 90 (2004): 193–212.

McGuire, Brian Patrick. *Jean Gerson and the Last Medieval Reformation*. University Park: The Pennsylvania State University Press, 2005.

McSheffrey, Shannon. "Heresy, Orthodoxy and English Vernacular." *Past &* *Present* 186 (2005): 47–80.

Meale, Carol M., ed. *Women and Literature in Britain 1150–1500*. Cambridge: Cambridge University Press, 1993.

Mews, Constant J. "Thomas Aquinas and Catherine of Siena: Emotion, Devotion and Mendicant Spiritualities in the Late Fourteenth Century." *Digital Philology* 1.2 (2012): 235–52.

Miles, Laura Saetveit. "Bridget of Sweden." In *The History of British Women's Writing 700–1500*, edited by Liz Herbert McAvoy and Diane Watt, 207–15. New York: Palgrave, 2012.

Minnis, Alastair. "1215–1349." In *The Cambridge Companion to Medieval English Mysticism*, edited by Samuel Fanous and Vincent Gillespie, 69–83. Cambridge: Cambridge University Press, 2011.

Mooney, Catherine. "Wondrous Words: Catherine of Siena's Miraculous Reading and Writing According to the Early Sources." In *Catherine of Siena: The Creation of a Cult*, edited by Jeffrey Hamburger and Gabriel Signori, 263–90. Turnhout: Brepols, 2013.

Muessig, Carolyn. "Catherine of Siena in Late Medieval Sermons." In *A Companion to Catherine of Siena*, edited by Carolyn Muessig, George Ferzoco, and Berverly Mayne Kienzle, 203–26. Leiden: Brill, 2012.

Newman, Barbara. "What Did It Mean to Say 'I Saw'? The Clash between Theory and Practice in Medieval Visionary Culture." *Speculum* 80 (2005): 1–43.

Noncentini, Silvia. "La Tradizione della 'Legenda maior'." In *Legenda maior sive Legenda Admirabilis Virginis Catherine de Senis*, edited by Silvia Noncentini, 1–114. Florence: Sismel, 2013.

– "'Pro Solatio Illicteratorum': The Earliest Italian Translations of the Legenda maior." In *Catherine of Siena: The Creation of a Cult*, edited by Jeffrey Hamburger and Gabriel Signori, 169–83. Turnhout: Brepols, 2013.

Noffke, Suzanne. "Catherine of Siena." In *Medieval Holy Women in the Christian Tradition c. 1100–c. 1500*, edited by Alastair Minnis and Rosalynn Voaden, 601–22. Turnhout: Brepols, 2010.

– "The Writings of Catherine of Siena: The Manuscript Tradition." In *A Companion to Catherine of Siena*, edited by Carolyn Muessig, George Ferzoco, and Berverly Mayne Kienzle, 295–337. Leiden: Brill, 2012.

Norton, Christopher, David Park, and Paul Binski. *Dominican Painting in East Anglia: The Thornham Parva Retable and the Musée de Cluny Frontal*. Woodbridge: Boydell and Brewer, 1987.

Oliva, Marilyn. "Rendering Accounts: The Pragmatic Literacy of Nuns in Late Medieval England." In *Nuns' Literacies in Medieval Europe: The Hull Dialogue*, edited by Virginia Blanton, Veronica O'Mara, and Patricia Stoop, 51–68. Turnhout: Brepols, 2013.

O'Mara, Veronica. "The Late Medieval English Nun and her Scribal Activity: A Complicated Quest." In *Nuns' Literacies in Medieval Europe: The Hull Dialogue*, edited by Virginia Blanton, Veronica O'Mara, and Patricia Stoop, 69–93. Turnhout: Brepols, 2013.

Palazzo, Robert P. "The Veneration of the Sacred Foreskin(s) of Baby Jesus – A Documented Analysis." In *Multicultural Europe and Cultural Exchange: In the Middle Ages and Renaissance*, edited by James Helfers, 155–76. Turnhout: Brepols, 2005.

Parsons, Gerald. *The Cult of Saint Catherine of Siena: A Study in Civil Religion.* Aldershot: Ashgate, 2008.

Patterson, Paul. "Female Readers and the Sources of the Mirror to Devout People." *Journal of Medieval Religious Cultures* 42 (2016): 181–200.

Perry, Ryan. *The Material Text: A Study of Middle English Manuscript Cultures, 1380–1440.* Turnhout: Brepols Press, 2017.

Peters, Christine. *Patterns of Piety: Women, Gender and Religion in Late Medieval and Reformation England.* Cambridge: Cambridge University Press, 2003.

Piattoli, Renato. "Un capitol di storia dell'arte libraria ai primi del Quattrocento: rapporti tra il Monastero fiorentino del Paradiso e l'Ordine Francescano," *Studi Francescani* 29 (1932): 1–21.

Pickering, O.S. "Brotherton Collection MS 501: a Middle English Anthology Reconsidered." *Leeds Studies in English* 21 (1990): 141–65.

Poor, Sara. *Mechthild of Magdeburg and Her Book: Gender and the Making of Textual Authority.* Philadelphia: University of Pennsylvania Press, 2004.

– "Women Teaching Men in the Medieval Devotional Imagination." In *Partners in Spirit: Women, Men, and Religious Life in Germany, 1100–1550*, edited by Fiona J. Griffiths and Julie Hotchin, 339–65. Turnhout: Brepols, 2014.

Powell, Susan. "Margaret Beaufort and Her Books." *The Library*, 6th series, 20 (1998): 197–240.

Ragazzi, Grazia Mangano. *Obeying the Truth: Discretion in the Spiritual Writings of Saint Catherine of Siena.* Oxford: Oxford University Press, 2014.

Renevey, Denis. "1215–1349." In *The Cambridge Companion to Medieval English Mysticism*, edited by Samuel Fanous and Vincent Gillespie, 91–112. Cambridge: Cambridge University Press, 2011.

Rice, Nicole R. *Lay Piety and Religious Discipline in Medieval English Literature.* Cambridge: Cambridge University Press, 2008.

– "Reformist Devotional Reading: The *Pore Caitif* in British Library, MS Harley 2322." In *The Medieval Mystical Tradition in England: Papers Read at Charney Manor, July 2011 (Exeter Symposium 8)*, edited by E.A. Jones, 177–93. Woodbridge: D.S. Brewer, 2013.

Ritchey, Sara. "Spiritual Arborescence: Trees in the Medieval Christian Imagination." *Spiritus* 8.1 (2008): 64–82.

Rozenski, Steven. "The Chastising of God's Children from Manuscript to Print." *Études Anglaises* 66 (2013): 369–78.

Russell, Alexander. *Conciliarism and Heresy in Fifteenth-Century England.* Cambridge: Cambridge University Press, 2017.

Russell, David. "Religious Mystical Mothers: Margery Kempe and Caterina Benincasa." In *The Medieval Mystical Tradition in England: Papers Read at Charney Manor, July 2011 (Exeter Symposium 8)*, edited by E.A. Jones, 75–92. Woodbridge: D.S. Brewer, 2013.

Rydel, Courtney E. "Inventing a Male Writer in Mechtild of Hackeborn's Booke of Gostlye Grace." *The Journal of Medieval Religous Cultures* 40 (2014): 192–216.

Salter, Elizabeth. *Popular Reading in English c. 1400–1600.* Manchester: Manchester University Press, 2012.

Sandler, Lucy Freeman. *A Survey of Manuscripts Illuminated in the British Isles.* Volume 5: *Gothic Manuscripts (II) 1285–1385.* Oxford: Harvey Miller Publishers, 1986.

Sargent, Michael G. "The Transmission by the English Carthusians of Some Late Medieval Spiritual Writings." *Journal of Ecclesiastical History* 27 (1976): 225–40.

– "Mystical Writings and Dramatic Texts in Late Medieval England." *Religion & Literature* 37 (2005): 77–98.

– "Medieval and Modern Readership of Marguerite Porete's *Mirouer des Simples Âmes Anienties*: The French and English Traditions." In *Middle English Religious Writing in Practice: Texts, Readers, and Transformations*, edited by Nicole Rice, 47–89. Turnhout: Brepols, 2013.

– "Nicholas Love's Mirror of the Blessed Life of Jesus Christ." In *The Wycliffite Bible: Origin, History and Interpretation*, edited by Elizabeth Solopova, 389–405. Leiden: Brill, 2017.

– "The Anxiety of Authority, the Fear of Translation: The Prologues to *The Myroure of Oure Ladye*." In *The Medieval Translator*. Volume 14: *Essays on the Theory and Practice of Translation in the Middle Ages in Honour of Roger Ellis*, edited by René Tixier and Catherine Batt. Forthcoming.

Scase, Wendy. "Reginald Pecock, John Carpenter and John Colop's 'Common Profit' Books: Aspects of Book Ownership and Circulation in Fifteenth-Century London." *Medium Aevum* 61 (1992): 261–75.

Schirmer, Elizabeth. "Reading Lessons at Syon Abbey: *The Myroure of Oure Lady* and the Mandates of Vernacular Theology." In *Voices in Dialogue: Reading Women in the Middle Ages*, edited by Linda Olson and Kathryn Kerby-Fulton, 345–76. Notre Dame: University of Notre Dame Press, 2005.

Schultze, Dirk. "Translating St. Catherine of Siena in Fifteenth-Century England." In *Catherine of Siena: The Creation of a Cult*, edited by Jeffrey Hamburger and Gabriel Signori, 185–212. Turnhout: Brepols, 2013.

Scott, Karen. "Catherine of Siena and Lay Sanctity in Fourteenth-Century Italy." In *Lay Sanctity, Medieval and Modern: A Search for Models*, edited by Ann W. Astell, 77–90. Notre Dame: University of Notre Dame Press, 2000.

Seton, George. "The Convent of Saint Catherine of Sienna near Edinburgh: A Paper Read before the Architectural Institute of Scotland 11th April 1867." Edinburgh: Printed for Private Circulation, 1871. https://play.google.com/books/reader?id=rswUAAAAQAAJ&printsec=frontcover&output=reader&hl=en&pg=GBS.PP4. Accessed 19 July 2016.

Simpson, James. "1534–1550s: Texts." In *The Cambridge Companion to Medieval English Mysticism*, edited by Samuel Fanous and Vincent Gillespie, 249–64. Cambridge: Cambridge University Press, 2011.

Southern, A.C. *Elizabethan Recusant Prose 1559–1582*. London: Sands & Co, 1950.

Stallcup, Steven. "The Old English Life of Saint Euphrosyne and the Economics of Sanctity." In *Anonymous Interpolations in Aelfric's Life of Saints*, edited by Robin Norris (Old English Newsletter Subsidia 35), 13–28. Kalamazoo: Western Michigan University Press, 2011.

Stock, Brian. *The Implications of Literacy: Written Language and Models of Interpretation in the Eleventh and Twelfth Centuries*. Princeton: Princeton University Press, 1983.

Sullivan, Ceri. *Dismembered Rhetoric: English Recusant Writing, 1580 to 1603*. Madison, NJ: Fairleigh Dickinson University Press, 1995.

Summit, Jennifer. *Lost Property: The Woman Writer and English Literary History, 1380–1589*. Chicago: University of Chicago Press, 2000.

Sutton, Anne F. "The Acquisition and Disposal of Books for Worship and Pleasure by Mercers of London in the Later Middle Ages." In *Manuscripts and Printed Books in Europe 1350–1550: Packaging, Presentation and Consumption*, edited by Emma Cayley and Susan Powell, 95–114. Liverpool: Liverpool University Press, 2013.

Taylor, Andrew. "Displaying Privacy: Margaret of York as Devotional Reader." In *Cultures of Religious Reading in the Late Middle Ages: Instructing the Soul, Feeding the Spirit, and Awakening the Passion*, edited by Sabrina Corbellini, 275–95. Turnhout: Brepols, 2013.

Thompson, E. Margaret. *The Carthusian Order in England*. London: Society for Promoting Christian Knowledge, 1930.

Thurber, Allison Clark. "Female Urban Reclusion in Siena at the Time of Catherine of Siena." In *A Companion to Catherine of Siena*, edited by Carolyn

Muessig, George Ferzoco, and Berverly Mayne Kienzle, 47–72. Leiden: Brill, 2012.

Trivedi, Kalpen. "'Trewe techyng and false heritikys': some 'Lollard' manuscripts of the *Pore Caitif.*" In *Strange Countries: Middle English Literature and its Afterlife*, edited by David Matthews, 132–56. Manchester: Manchester University Press, 2010.

Tylus, Jane. *Reclaiming Catherine of Siena: Literacy, Literature, and the Signs of Others.* Chicago: Chicago University Press, 2009.

– "Mystical Literacy: Writing and Religious Women in Late Medieval Italy." In *A Companion to Catherine of Siena*, edited by Carolyn Muessig, George Ferzoco, and Berverly Mayne Kienzle, 155–84. Leiden: Brill, 2012.

– "Writing versus Voice: Tommaso Caffarini and the Production of a Literate Catherine." In *Catherine of Siena: The Creation of a Cult*, edited by Jeffrey Hamburger and Gabriel Signori, 291–312. Turnhout: Brepols, 2013.

Vander Veen, Brian C. "The Vitae of Bodleian Library MS Douce 114." PhD diss., University of Nottingham, 2007.

Vauchez, André. *The Laity in the Middle Ages: Religious Beliefs and Devotional Practices.* Edited by Daniel Bornstein and translated by Margery J. Schneider. Notre Dame: University of Notre Dame Press, 1993.

Voaden, Rosalynn. "The Company She Keeps: Mechthild of Hackeborn in Late Medieval Compilations." In *Prophets Abroad: The Reception of Continental Holy Women in Late-Medieval England*, edited by Rosalynn Voaden, 51–69. Cambridge: D.S. Brewer, 1996.

– *God's Words, Women's Voices: The Discernment of Spirits in the Writing of Late-Medieval Women Visionaries.* York: York Medieval Press, 1999.

– "Rewriting the Letter: Variations in the Middle English Translation of the Epistola solitarii ad reges of Alfonso of Jaén." In *The Translation of the Works of St. Birgitta of Sweden into the Medieval European Vernaculars: The Medieval Translator.* Volume 7, edited by Bridget Morris and Veronica O'Mara, 170–85. Turnhout: Brepols Press, 2000.

Wallace, David. "Mystics and Followers in Siena and East Anglia: A Study in Taxonomy, Class and Cultural Mediation." In *The Medieval Mystical Tradition in England: VII*, edited by Marion Glasscoe, 169–91. Cambridge: D.S. Brewer, 1984.

– "Periodizing Women: Mary Ward (1586–1645) and the Premodern Canon." *Journal of Medieval and Early Modern Studies* 36.2 (2006): 397–453.

– "Nuns." In *Cultural Reformations: Medieval and Renaissance Literary History*, edited by Brian Cummings and James Simpson, 502–26. Oxford: Oxford University Press, 2010.

– *Strong Women: Life, Text, and Territory 1347–1645.* Oxford: Oxford University Press, 2011.

Warren, Nancy Bradley. *Women of God and Arms: Female Spirituality and Political Conflict, 1380–1600*. Philadelphia: University of Pennsylvania Press, 2005.

– *The Embodied Word: Female Spiritualities, Contested Orthodoxies, and English Religious Cultures, 1350–1700*. Notre Dame: University of Notre Dame Press, 2010.

Watson, A.G., ed. *Bodleian Library Quarto Catalogues IX: Digby Manuscripts*. Oxford: Bodleian Library, 1999.

Watson, Nicholas. *Richard Rolle and the Invention of Authority*. Cambridge: Cambridge University Press, 1991.

– "Censorship and Cultural Change in Late-Medieval England: Vernacular Theology, the Oxford Translation Debate, and Arundel's Constitutions of 1409." *Speculum* 70 (1995): 822–64.

– Introduction to *The Cambridge Companion to Medieval English Mysticism*, edited by Samuel Fanous and Vincent Gillespie, 1–28. Cambridge: Cambridge University Press, 2011.

Watt, Diane. "The Prophet at Home: Elizabeth Barton and the Influence of Bridget of Sweden and Catherine of Siena." In *Prophets Abroad: The Reception of Continental Holy Women in Late-Medieval England*, edited by Rosalynn Voaden, 161–76. Cambridge: D.S. Brewer, 1996.

– "Reconstructing the Word: The Political Prophecies of Elizabeth Barton (1506–1534)." *Renaissance Quarterly* 50.1 (1997): 136–63.

– *Secretaries of God: Women Prophets in Late Medieval and Early Modern England*. Cambridge: D.S. Brewer, 1997.

– *Medieval Women's Writing: Works by and for Women in England, 1100–1500*. Cambridge: Polity Press, 2007.

Webb, Heather. "Catherine of Siena's Heart." *Speculum* 80 (2005): 802–17.

– *The Medieval Heart*. New Haven: Yale University Press, 2010.

– "Lacrime Cordiali: Catherine of Siena on the Value of Tears." In *A Companion to Catherine of Siena*, edited by Carolyn Muessig, George Ferzoco, and Berverly Mayne Kienzle, 99–112. Leiden: Brill, 2012.

West, William N. "Old News: Caxton, de Worde, and the Invention of the Edition." In *Caxton's Trace: Studies in the History of English Printing*, edited by William Kuskin, 241–74. Notre Dame: University of Notre Dame Press, 2006.

Whatmore, L.E. "The Sermon against the Holy Maid of Kent and Her Adherents, Delivered at Paul's Cross November the 23rd, 1533, and at Canterbury, December the 7th." *The English Historical Review* 58 (1943): 463–75.

White, Eric. "Researching Print Runs." *Consortium of European Libraries*. https://www.cerl.org/resources/links_to_other_resources/ bibliographical_data#researching_print_runs. Accessed 29 December 2015.

Williams, Michael Aufrère. "Medieval English Roodscreens with Special Reference to Devon." PhD diss., University of Exeter, 2008. https://ore.exeter.ac.uk/repository/bitstream/handle/10036/89276/WilliamsM.pdf. Accessed 20 August 2015.

Windeatt, Barry. "1412–1534: Texts." In *The Cambridge Companion to Medieval English Mysticism*, edited by Samuel Fanous and Vincent Gillespie, 195–224. Cambridge: Cambridge University Press, 2011.

Wogan-Browne, Jocelyn. *Saints' Lives & Women's Literary Culture: Virginity and Its Authorizations*. Oxford: Oxford University Press, 2001.

Wooding, Lucy. "Catholicism, the Printed Book and the Marian Restoration." In *A Companion to the Early Printed Book in Britain 1476–1558*, edited by Vincent Gillespie and Susan Powell, 307–24. Woodbridge: D.S. Brewer, 2014.

Woodward Smith, Tamsin. "A Critical Study of the Middle English *Orcherd of Syon* in Both Manuscript and Print Form, with Particular Attention to Its Context and Audience." PhD diss., Oxford University, 2006.

Zarri, Gabriella. "Catherine of Siena and the Italian Public." In *Catherine of Siena: The Creation of a Cult*, edited by Jeffrey Hamburger and Gabriel Signori, 69–79. Turnhout: Brepols, 2013.

Index